On Building, Defending and Regulating the Self

On Building, Defending and Regulating the Self

A Psychological Perspective

161101

Edited by
Abraham Tesser
Joanne V. Wood
Diederik A. Stapel

Psychology Press
New York • Hove

Published in 2005 by
Psychology Press
Taylor & Francis Group
270 Madison Avenue
New York, NY 10016
www.psypress.com

Published in Great Britain by
Psychology Press
Taylor & Francis Group
27 Church Road
Hove, East Sussex BN3 2FA
www.psypress.co.uk

10 9 8 7 6 5 4 3 2 1

Library of Congress Cataloging-in-Publication Data

On building, defending, and regulating the self : a psychological perspective / edited by Abraham
Tesser, Joanne V. Wood, Diederik Stapel.
    p. cm.
  Includes bibliographical references and index.
  ISBN 1-84169-405-3 (hardback : alk. paper)
  1. Self. I. Tesser, Abraham. II. Wood, Joanne V. III. Stapel, Diederik A.

BF697.043 2005
155.2'5—dc22

2004009906

Contents

About the Editors

Abraham Tesser, research professor emeritus at the University of Georgia, is a former editor of the *Journal of Personality and Social Psychology* and a former president of the Society for Personality and Social Psychology. Recognition of his research on self-evaluation and on thought and ruminative processes includes the Donald T. Campbell Award from the Society for Personality and Social Psychology and the Career Award from the International Society for Self and Identity.

Joanne V. Wood, since completing her Ph.D. at the University of California, Los Angeles, has held faculty positions at the State University of New York at Stony Brook and at the University of Waterloo. She has served as an associate editor of *Personality and Social Psychology Bulletin* and on the editorial boards of the *Journal of Personality and Social Psychology*, *Journal of Experimental Social Psychology*, *Personality and Social Psychology Bulletin*, and *Self and Identity*. Wood's publications concern affect regulation, social comparison, and mechanisms underlying the maintenance of self-esteem.

Diederik A. Stapel, professor at the University of Groningen, is a former associate editor of the *British Journal of Social Psychology* and has served on the editorial boards of *Self and Identity*, *European Journal of Social Psychology*, and *Personality and Social Psychology Bulletin*. For his research on knowledge accessibility effects, he earned the Jos Jaspars Award of the European Association of Experimental Social Psychology. Stapel's publications concern person perception, unconscious emotional responses, and social comparison.

Contributors

Jennifer S. Beer, University of California, Berkeley

Kenneth G. DeMarree, Ohio State University

Naomi I. Eisenberger, University of California, Los Angeles

Andrew J. Elliot, University of Rochester

Brian M. Goldman, University of Georgia

Melanie C. Green, University of Pennsylvania

Christian H. Jordan, University of Waterloo

Nils B. Jostmann, Free University Amsterdam

Dacher Keltner, University of California, Berkeley

Michael H. Kernis, University of Georgia

Sander L. Koole, Free University Amsterdam

Julius Kuhl, University of Osnabrück

Madoka Kumashiro, University of North Carolina at Chapel Hill

Matthew D. Lieberman, University of California, Los Angeles

Christine E. R. Logel, University of Waterloo

Rachel R. Mapes, University of Rochester

Carolyn C. Morf, Universität Bern

Richard E. Petty, Ohio State University

Jesse Preston, Harvard University

Frederick Rhodewalt, University of Utah

Caryl E. Rusbult, University of North Carolina at Chapel Hill

Steven J. Spencer, University of Waterloo

Diederik A. Stapel, University of Groningen

Shevaun L. Stocker, University of North Carolina at Chapel Hill

Abraham Tesser, University of Georgia

Kathleen D. Vohs, University of British Columbia

Daniel M. Wegner, Harvard University

S. Christian Wheeler, Stanford University

Scott T. Wolf, University of North Carolina at Chapel Hill

Joanne V. Wood, University of Waterloo

Mark P. Zanna, University of Waterloo

Introduction: An Overview of Building, Defending, and Regulating the Self

ABRAHAM TESSER,
JOANNE V. WOOD,
AND DIEDERIK A. STAPEL

This is the third in a series of volumes sponsored by the International Society for Self and Identity (ISSI). Like those that came before (Tesser, Felson, & Suls, 2000; Tesser, Stapel, & Wood, 2002), this volume is intended to pull together and present in a single place some of the research that is currently leading scientific inquiry into aspects of self and identity.

Collecting a balanced set of such work is a difficult task—not because there is a paucity of research on the self but because productive and exciting investigations and research programs abound. They bubble up through numerous specialized and general journals and conferences. The task of picking from among these is daunting. We, the editors, sought suggestions from active researchers in the area and pooled our own expertise to boil down the list to a manageable number of programs of research that we all agreed were exciting and productive lines of inquiry.

Each chapter in this book provides a coherent point of view about an aspect of the self. Although the ratio of theory to data varies across chapters, each chapter is driven by a theoretical framework and each provides a review of at least some empirical work related to the theoretical ideas. In some cases the empirical work is new, not yet published elsewhere. Each chapter presents a story in progress—more remains to be done before the case is closed.

We are proud to present you with what we believe is a representative cross-section of cutting-edge research on the self. This collection should be useful to active researchers in the area and to students entering the field. The chapters are written in such a clear and engrossing way that the volume may even prove informative to readers with an interest in the area but with a less technical background.

THE CONTENTS OF THE BOOK

The particular chapters were invited because, in each case, we thought that the research perspective of the author(s) was interesting and pushed our understanding of the self and self processes in productive new directions. We had no particular point of view in mind, nor did we attempt to pursue a particular theoretical, substantive, or methodological theme. Nevertheless, like any intellectual product, research that is cast at a particular time and place is likely to share some features. Themes and organizing "issues" naturally emerge.

Our organizational schema is concerned with the nature of the self and self-change. There are at least three approaches to stasis and change in the literature on the self and in popular culture. A major theme for at least half a century in the psychological research literature (e.g., Rogers, 1951) and also in the more popular self-help books has concerned the social and psychological benefits of becoming open to who we truly are—for example, living our lives with authenticity, moving toward our ideal selves, and being open to what is around us. This is a kind of self-growth or self-building perspective. A second view of self and self-change has generated, perhaps, more research than any other in the last 30 or 40 years. This view characterizes the self as protective and defensive. It has documented the self as motivated toward maintaining illusions and a flattering self-image (e.g., Kunda, 1987) and it has detailed many of the mechanisms by which these illusions are maintained (e.g., Tesser, 2000). A third view of self, like the self-growth perspective, is reflected in popular self-help books. This view recognizes that we regulate everything from our food intake to our emotional responses. It sees the self as a self-regulating organism. Research on self-regulation has enjoyed a large spike in research popularity in the last 15 years or so. Each of these views of self-change is reflected in the work described in this volume.

Building the Self

Some research perspectives suggest that the self is highly malleable. Forces in the immediate situation shape who we are or who we think we are. In some instances we may know no more about our own self then we do about the self of others (e.g., em, 1972). Our first set of chapters takes a different perspective. This view of self suggests that who we are is not arbitrary; there are intrinsic, cross-situational aspects of the self that reflect who we are or who we might ideally become. The chapter by Caryl E. Rusbult, Madoka Kumashiro, Shevaun L. Stocker, and Scott T. Wolf analyzes how relationship partners might help change us to become a better reflection of our own personal ideals. The chapter by Michael H. Kernis and Brian M. Goldman suggests that there are costs to ignoring genuine aspects of self. The chapter by Melanie C. Green discusses how involvement in stories can move us toward cultural ideals as revealed in narrative materials. Finally, Matthew D. Leiberman and Naomi I. Eisenberger take on the fundamental question of how we come to define our selves.

Rusbult, Kumashiro, Stocker, and Wolf describe what they call the Michelangelo effect. Theirs is an interpersonal theory of self-change. The Michelangelo phenomenon "describes a congenial pattern of interdependence in which close partners sculpt one another in such a manner as to bring each person closer to his or her ideal self" (p. 24). The theory suggests that being affirmed by one's partner and moving toward one's ideals promotes (a) personal well-being and (b) relationship well-being. Multimethod research including laboratory studies, diary studies, and survey studies tend to yield support for the Michelangelo hypotheses.

The idea that a literary text might be consequential for a reader is certainly not new. However, to our knowledge, this has rarely been studied systematically by empirically based social scientists. Green's work is a welcome exception; she suggests that narrative worlds might provide identities toward which an individual might move. The extent to which individuals "get into" or are "transported" by a narrative world should determine the magnitude of the influence of the text. She notes, "Individuals who are immersed in story worlds may relax the boundaries of the self, identifying with characters and sympathizing with them. Reading narratives … can provide blueprints for possible selves" (p. 71). Although the empirical work on this thesis is still in the early stages, the ideas hold great promise for researchers on the self.

The work of Rusbult et al. and Green provide hints about the circumstances under which we expect productive changes in the self. Kernis and Goldman focus on the personal and interpersonal consequences of behaving in ways that are or are not consistent with one's authentic self. Their view of authenticity "involves an awareness of one's self; unbiased processing of self-relevant information; behaving in accord with one's core values, inclinations, needs, and so forth; and relating to close others in genuine, trustworthy, and honest ways" (p. 50). Kernis and Goldman have developed individual-differences measures for each of the four components. Their data suggest that each of the separate components as well as the sum of the components relate to self-reported individual differences in well-being, such as life satisfaction and noncontingent self-esteem.

All the chapters in this section (and almost all the chapters in the book) rely on individuals having a self-definition. By what process(es) does one's self-definition emerge? In their chapter, Lieberman and Eisenberger review two processes. Like other dual-process models, they suggest that there are controlled and automatic processes. The controlled-response system deals with conflict and emerges when habitual responses are not appropriate. This yields a rational, evidence-based system of self-knowledge. There is also an intuitive self-knowledge system that is built up slowly and based on habitual (automatic) responses to situations. One of the things that make this chapter particularly exciting and unique is its heavy reliance on neurological data and the identification of neural structures associated with each of the systems. "The subtext of this chapter," note the authors, "was meant to demonstrate the value of cognitive neuroscience research and neuroimaging tools in advancing social psychological theories of the self" (p. 95).

Defending the Self

Psychologists in great numbers have produced research in great volumes documenting defensive tendencies. When a new point of view in this domain emerges, then, it is most welcome. At least three of the present chapters put such a new spin on understanding defensive processes. Jesse Preston and Daniel M. Wegner's work on "ideal agency" describes how we protect the illusion of will. Frederick Rhodewalt and Carolyn C. Morf describe a dance between interpersonal and intrapersonal processes that engages narcissistic individuals. And Steven J. Spencer, Christian H. Jordan, Christine E. R. Logel, and Mark P. Zanna provide a window on their struggle to understand implicit self-esteem and how it functions along with explicit self–esteem to predispose persons toward defensiveness.

The notion that we tend to distort the world to see ourselves as more effective or influential than we might actually be is not new (e.g., Taylor & Brown, 1988). However, feelings of control or effectiveness have generally been treated as unitary constructs. In their chapter, Preston and Wegner reveal the anatomy of these constructs. According to the authors, to be an effective agent, three things are necessary. An effective agent thinks about options and possibilities, wills certain actions, and takes action to effect an outcome. If any of these components is missing from an episode, there is no evidence for agency. Thus, if we assume, as do Preston and Wegner, that people are motivated to see themselves as effective agents, then they will be motivated to see each of these components in themselves even when a component is absent. The authors note that "distortions take three forms: intention confabulation (when we have will and action but must infer thought), apparent mental causation (when we have thought and action and so infer will) and action misperception (when we have will and thought but must infer action)" (p. 121). A series of creative experiments demonstrate each of these motivated distortions.

According to Greek mythology, Narcissus is a boy who is in love with his own image. Sigmund Freud (1914/1953) and other psychoanalysts, particularly in the object-relations traditions (e.g., Kohut, 1971), elaborated on the characteristics of the narcissistic personality. Thus, the narcissism construct is not new. What is new is Rhodewalt and Morf's attempt to understand the construct in dynamic process terms rather than static "type" or "syndrome" terms. In their individual-differences model, persons identified as narcissists attempt to maintain an unrealistically high level of admiration from their social environment. The processes by which they attempt to accomplish this are spelled out. "Intrapersonal strategies," note the authors, "include distorted interpretations of outcomes and selective recall of past events. Interpersonal regulation covers a multitude of self-presentational gambits and social manipulations also in the service of engineering positive feedback or blunting negative feedback about the self" (p. 129). Tests of this sophisticated model, including psychometric and laboratory approaches, are encouraging. In addition, the theoretical and empirical approaches may serve as a template for understating other personality dimensions.

Self-esteem is probably the single most popular construct used in studying individual differences in defensiveness. Indeed, it is difficult to find research on defensiveness in which self-esteem is not measured. Perhaps the most popular measure of self-esteem is a self-report measure developed by Morris Rosenberg (1965). The chapter by Spencer, Jordan, Logel, and Zanna is about individual differences in defensiveness as a function of self-esteem, and it uses the Rosenberg measure of self-esteem. So, what's new about that? Recently introduced implicit measures of self-esteem (e.g., Greenwald & Farnham, 2000) seem to have caught the attention of a broad swath of researchers in personality and social psychology. Implicit measures appear to be less susceptible to impression management and may reveal things about the individual that the individual may be unaware of, but that, according to Spencer et al., may leak into consciousness.

Spencer et al.'s new twist in the self-esteem–defensiveness saga is the attempt to simultaneously harness conscious self-reports of self-esteem and implicit measures of self-esteem to the theoretical wagon. When faced with threatening feedback, individuals with high explicit self-esteem may be particularly defensive if they have low implicit self-esteem (a nagging doubt) rather than high implicit self-esteem. When faced with potential success, persons with low explicit self-esteem but high implicit self-esteem may experience a glimmer of hope and respond with increased vigor; those with both low explicit and implicit self-esteem may respond with defensiveness and withdrawal. In short, "it is the discrepancy between implicit and explicit self-views that will be particularly potent in determining behavior" (p. 152). A series of preliminary studies are encouraging for this dual, explicit–implicit self-esteem model of defensiveness.

Regulating the Self

Where there are goals there must be some form of regulation. Thus, growing and defending the self are, in a broad sense, forms of self-regulation. These forms of self-regulation have historically occupied a special place in the literature, at least in part because they were and are frequent concerns of researchers of the self and also because the motivational aspects of self-growth and self-defense are concerned with the self per se. In their chapter, Andrew J. Elliot and Rachel R. Mapes go beyond self-defense/enhancement and argue for the utility of drawing a distinction between approach and avoidance motivation in understanding how people evaluate multiple aspects of the self-concept. But all of us are concerned with goals and regulating behavior in a variety of other domains as well. The self figures prominently into the regulation of many of those other domains. In this section of the book we learn about recent thinking on aspects of the regulation of emotion in the chapters by Dacher Keltner and Jennifer S. Beer and by Sander L. Koole, Julius Kuhl, Nils Jostmann, and Kathleen D. Vohs and the regulation of automatic behavioral responses in the chapter by S. Chrsitian Wheeler, Kenneth G. DeMarree, and Richard E. Petty.

Sometimes being reminded of important distinctions and showing how they apply in new contexts is a particularly useful contribution. After discussing a variety of historical views of differences in approach and avoidance motivation, Elliot and Mapes provide their own generalized definition. The idea is that moving toward a positive is qualitatively different from moving away from a negative. This difference is detectable in the factor structure of individual differences, it is detectable in the physiological representation of motivation, and it is detectable in the emotions accompanying the playing out of these motives. In their chapter Elliot and Mapes remind us that enhancing (approach toward) or defending (avoidance of) the self may entail qualitatively different processes. We are also reminded that there is more to self-evaluation than self-enhancement/defense; that is, there are self-verification (constancy of the self-concept), self-assessment (certainty of the self-concept), and self-improvement (change in the self-concept). Elliot and Mapes argue persuasively that our understanding of each of these aspects of self-evaluation can be improved by separating the approach and avoidance components.

Any regulatory system involves a standard, a way of detecting discrepancies from the standard, and feedback that influences behavior so as to reduce the discrepancy. When the standard involves expectations regarding the self, discrepancies from those standards result in self-conscious emotions such as shame, embarrassment, and guilt. In their broad and particularly insightful chapter, Keltner and Beer argue that self-conscious emotions promote adaptive social behavior both inter- and intrapersonally. The experience of these emotions provides feedback to the self regarding social problems. The display of emotions such as embarrassment and shame may even appease or generate sympathy from others. The importance of these emotions in self-regulation is underlined by the observation that individuals less able to experience and display these emotions tend to be less well-adjusted than people who do experience and display these emotions.

All of us experience bouts of unpleasant, perhaps debilitating emotions such as anger and depression, and being unable to control or regulate these emotions would seem to be an unmitigated bad thing. Koole, Kuhl, Jostmann, and Vohs take a contrarian point of view in their chapter. They propose that "state orientation, defined as the inability to exert volitional control over one's feelings, has both psychological costs and benefits" (p. 216). The costs are obvious; the three benefits are less obvious. They are as follows: State-oriented individuals are better able to attract and be soothed by supportive social relationships. Uncontrolled affective reactions are likely to result in "regression," the movement from top–down processing to lower level processing. Lower level processing is more energy efficient, is particularly useful in unpredictable environments, and sets the stage for profound self-learning. The third benefit is to the social order rather than to the individual—state-oriented individuals are more likely to follow social dictums even at substantial personal cost; their "altruism" can be construed as a benefit to all. The case made in this chapter is, indeed, contrarian and thought provoking.

One of the most intriguing phenomena to come to light in the last decade is the effect of priming on behavior. Priming a stereotype often produces behavior consistent with the stereotype. For example, college students primed with information from a stereotype of old people walk slower than students not so primed (Bargh, Chen, & Burrows, 1996). This effect was surprising to many (although predicted by the researchers), reliable across labs, and general across other stereotypes. However, the explanation for the effect was not immediately intuitively obvious. In their chapter, Wheeler, DeMarree, and Petty review this phenomenon and the explanations that have appeared in the literature. Their new explanation suggests that self-representations play a crucial role in this phenomenon. They note, "Assimilative, contrastive, or relational components of the self could be activated after exposure to primes" (p. 262). For example, if the stereotype-relevant behavior is or becomes part of one's self-representation, then priming will result in behavior that is assimilated to the stereotype; if the stereotype-relevant behavior is rejected in the self-representation, then priming might result in behavior that contrasts with the stereotype. The chapter emphasizes flexibility in response to primes and is integrative across a variety of literatures. This integration is supported by laboratory studies specifically designed to test it.

THE SELF IS INTERPERSONAL

We have focused on processes of self-maintenance and change in our organization of the present chapters. Organizing research reduces complexity by bringing coherence to the research domain, and we hope that we are at least somewhat successful at doing that. However, any organization of chapters is arbitrary and tends to emphasize one theme over another. In the present case there is a theme that is so clearly manifest across the chapters that we believe it deserves a special note. This theme runs through most of the chapters and cross-cuts the themes of building the self, defending the self, and regulating the self. What we are referring to is the emphasis on interpersonal processes.

Although interpersonal processes play a starring role, even the plot line, in Rusbult et al.'s chapter, many other chapters emphasize how the self reacts to—and at times, is even defined by—other people or other people's imagined reactions. For example, Spencer et al. discussed how impression management processes could contribute to explicit self-esteem's discrepancy from implicit self-esteem. Wheeler et al. discussed how other people prime aspects of the self. Individuals' beliefs about how other people see them give rise to the self-conscious emotions discussed by Keltner and Beer, which, as they point out, promote adaptive social behavior. The self also exerts influence on other people. This theme is evident in Koole et al.'s discussion of how a state orientation can elicit close others' support, Kernis and Goldman's discussion of the effects of authenticity on interpersonal relationships, and Rhodewalt and Morf's discussion of how narcissists use self-presentational strategies and social manipulations.

This emerging interpersonal emphasis contrasts sharply with the earlier research on the self. Empirical research has tended to put more emphasis on intrapersonal processes; much of the focus of earlier work was stuck in the head and the heart of the individual. As these chapters make clear, however, research on the self has evolved to examine more richly how other people influence the self and how the self influences the social world.

If the work presented in this volume is representative of the research currently going on regarding the self, and we believe that it is, then the field is in very good shape. We are proud of the richness, thoughtfulness, depth, breadth, and creativity embodied in the work of our colleagues. We hope that you, too, will find these chapters informative and useful in your own work.

REFERENCES

Bargh, J. A., Chen, M., & Burrows, L. (1996). Automaticity of social behavior: Direct effects of trait construct and stereotype activation on action. *Journal of Personality and Social Psychology, 71*, 230–244.

Bem, D. J. (1972). Self-perception theory. In L. Berkowitz (Ed.), *Advances in experimental social psychology* (Vol. 6, pp. 2–62). New York: Academic Press.

Freud, S. (1953). On narcissism: An introduction. In J. Strachey (Ed. & Trans.), *The standard edition of the complete psychological works of Sigmund Freud* (Vol. 14, pp. 69–102). London: Hogarth Press. (Original work published 1914)

Greenwald, A. G., & Farnham, S. (2001). Using the Implicit Association Test to measure self-esteem and self-concept. *Journal of Personality and Social Psychology, 79,* 1022–1038.

Kohut, H. (1971). *The analysis of the self.* New York: International Universities Press.

Kunda, Z. (1987). Motivated inference: Self-serving generation and evaluation of causal theories. *Journal of Personality and Social Psychology, 53,* 636–647.

Rogers, C. R. (1951). *Client-centered therapy: Its current practice, implications, and theory.* Boston: Houghton Mifflin.

Rosenberg, M. (1965). *Society and the adolescent self-image.* Princeton, NJ: Princeton University Press.

Taylor, S. E., & Brown, J. D. (1988). Illusion and well-being: A social psychological perspective on mental health. *Psychological Bulletin, 103,* 193–210.

Tesser, A. (2000) On the confluence of self-esteem maintenance mechanisms. *Personality and Social Psychology Review, 4,* 290–299.

Tesser, A., Felson, R., & Suls, J. (Eds.). (2000). *Psychological perspectives on self and identity.* Washington, DC: American Psychological Association.

Tesser, A., Stapel, D. A., & Wood, J. V. (Eds.). (2002). *Self and motivation: Emerging psychological perspectives.* Washington, DC: American Psychological Association.

1

The Michelangelo Phenomenon in Close Relationships

CARYL E. RUSBULT, MADOKA KUMASHIRO, SHEVAUN L. STOCKER, AND SCOTT T. WOLF

The film *Jerry Maguire* (Brooks & Crowe, 1996) concerns possible selves—in particular, pursuit of the ideal self and dread of the feared self. The film's protagonist is disillusioned with his career in sports management. During the opening credits, Jerry notes, "In the quest for the big dollars, a lot of little things were going wrong." We see Jerry champion an athlete convicted of a sex crime; we watch him pressure an injured player to return to the game; we observe behavior driven by financial sponsors rather than love of the sport. He asks, "Who had I become—just another shark in a suit?" With increasing self-loathing, Jerry writes of his dream for a better life; what begins as a memo spills out of his PC as a protracted "mission statement." He exclaims, "Suddenly, I was my father's son again! I was remembering the simple pleasures of this job—the way a stadium sounds when one of my players performs well on the field, the way we are meant to protect them in health and in injury.... With so many clients, we had forgotten what was important. Suddenly, it was all pretty clear: The answer was fewer clients, less money ... more attention, caring for them, and the games, too.... I'll be the first to admit it was pretty touchy-feely. I didn't care; I'd lost the ability to bullshit. It was the 'me' I'd always wanted to be."

Unfortunately, being the "me" he'd "always wanted to be" is a fleeting experience. In the elation accompanying apprehension of his ideal, Jerry distributes copies of his mission statement, and his colleagues read of his dream for a better life. In a field as competitive and cynical as sports management, it comes as no surprise that Jerry gets precisely what he wished for—he is fired, and becomes a lone agent with a single client. The remaining 134 min of the film describe Jerry's striving for his ideal self, depicting a man's development from pupa to chrysalis to butterfly. The film illustrates two critical principles: First, the journey toward one's ideal self is an incremental and sometimes painful process. Second, such journeys frequently are not solo voyages. The film introduces three people who play a role in Jerry's journey (for good or ill): Avery, his coworker (and initially, his fiancée), a hard-nosed, competitive woman who "doesn't have the sensitivity thing"; Dorothy Boyd, his accountant (and later, his wife), who shares Jerry's dream, thinks that "optimism is revolutionary," and yearns to "be part of something [she] believes in"; and Rod Tidwell, his one remaining client (and later, his best friend), who has lost the "pure joy of the game" and become a "paycheck player." Jerry's journey with his loved ones serves as a suitable backdrop for theory and research regarding the Michelangelo phenomenon.

We begin this chapter by reviewing three theoretical traditions that form the basis for our work—the behavioral confirmation, interdependence, and self-discrepancy traditions. Then we describe the Michelangelo phenomenon and its consequences, beginning with the concept of partner affirmation, or the extent to which people think and behave in ways that are geared toward eliciting others' "best selves." Partner affirmation plays a central role in the Michelangelo phenomenon, a congenial pattern of interdependence in which partners sculpt one another in such a manner as to bring each person closer to his or her ideal self. We suggest that the Michelangelo phenomenon yields benefits for the self and dyad, promoting both personal well-being and couple well-being. After reviewing empirical findings in support of key model predictions, we discuss specific self and partner processes that are relevant to understanding the Michelangelo phenomenon. Finally, we explain how this phenomenon differs from other self-relevant processes, such as partner verification and self-expansion processes.

THEORETICAL BACKGROUND

Our work regarding the Michelangelo phenomenon is predicated on the assumption that the self does not spring full-blown from a vacuum: Human dispositions, values, and behavioral tendencies are fashioned at least in part by interpersonal experience. Among the many interpersonal forces that shape the self, few, if any, sculptors are likely to exert effects as powerful as those of our close partners. On the face of it, it seems clear that such effects can vary from exceedingly positive to exceedingly negative: Some partners bring out the very best in each other, whereas others either fail to do so or bring out the worst in each other.

Behavioral Confirmation Processes

Our analysis begins with the concept of *behavioral confirmation*, defined as the means by which an interaction partner's expectations about the self become reality by eliciting behaviors from the self that confirm the partner's expectations (Darley & Fazio, 1980; Harris & Rosenthal, 1985). How does this process unfold? Interaction partners develop beliefs about the self's strengths and limitations, preferences and disinclinations.[1] During interaction, partners tend to act in accord with their beliefs about the self. In so doing, partners create opportunities for the self to display some behaviors, constrain interaction in such a manner as to inhibit the display of other behaviors, and thereby elicit a subset of the self's full repertoire of possible behaviors (Rosenthal & Jacobson, 1968; Snyder, Tanke, & Berscheid, 1977). For example, at his nadir, Jerry's behavior reflects the expectations of his friends and coworkers, who regard him as superficial, cagey, and ruthless—as a guy who will say and do whatever is necessary to close a deal. Importantly, research regarding behavioral confirmation suggests that self-perceptions frequently become aligned with others' expectations (Fazio, Effrein, & Falender, 1981; Murray, Holmes, & Griffin, 1996)—Jerry has come to regard himself as the cynical and cutthroat person that others perceive him to be.

Interdependence Processes

Of course, some interaction partners yield stronger confirmation effects than others. Interdependence theory suggests that in ongoing close relationships the confirmation process is likely to be rather powerful, in that over the course of extended involvement, the behaviors that begin as interaction-specific adaptations become embodied in stable dispositions and habits (Kelley & Thibaut, 1978; Rusbult & Van Lange, 2003). How so? In interdependent relationships, the well-being of the self is influenced not only by the self's preferences and behavior but also by the preferences and behavior of the partner. Thus, strong interdependence creates diverse opportunities for a partner to modify the self. The self's adjustments to a partner are described in terms of *adaptation*, in recognition of the fact that a close partner may behave in ways that make it desirable for the self to enact some behaviors while inhibiting others, or may possess dispositions or motives, the display of which make it desirable for the self to cultivate some dispositions while extinguishing others.

For example, prior to apprehending his ideal self, Jerry Maguire had been powerfully shaped by Avery, to whom he was initially engaged to be married. As a consequence of repeated interaction—during which Jerry adapted to his fiancée by selectively developing some tendencies and eliminating others—Avery powerfully influenced Jerry's behavioral repertoire, long-term motives, and stable dispositions. Jerry's attempts to behave in a warm and caring manner repeatedly were met by derision and scorn on the part of Avery, and Jerry adopted a habitually sarcastic and disdainful demeanor. As a consequence of such day-to-day adaptations, Avery sculpted Jerry's self, chipping away his warm and caring qualities and revealing his most distrustful and cynical self. Over time, Jerry's self became a reflection of the interdependence reality created by Avery ("great at friendship, bad at intimacy").

Self-Discrepancy Processes

What is the Michelangelo phenomenon, and how does it relate to behavioral confirmation in ongoing relationships? In introducing this phenomenon it is useful to employ a metaphor, considering the manner in which sculpting was envisioned by its greatest practitioner. As Gombrich (1995) noted, "Michelangelo conceived his figures as lying hidden in the block of marble.... The task he set himself as a sculptor was merely to extract the ideal form ... to remove the stone that covered [the ideal]" (p. 313).

Thus, Michelangelo conceived of sculpting as a process whereby the artist released a figure from the block of stone in which it slumbered. The creative process and the artist's tools were aspects of salvation: By chipping away at the stone, the form slumbering in the block was allowed to emerge. In Michelangelo's vision, the figure hidden in the stone was something heroic, vibrant, and divine—the figure slumbering in the stone was the "ideal form."

Like blocks of stone, humans, too, possess ideal forms. The human equivalent of Michelangelo's slumbering form is a possible self to which the individual aspires (Higgins, 1987, 1996; Markus & Nurius, 1986). In particular, individuals possess an *ideal self*, defined in terms of the constellation of dispositions, motives, and behavioral tendencies each individual ideally wishes to acquire. For example, Jerry dreams that he might once again "become his father's son," loving his work and his life and himself—that he might take pleasure in the way a stadium sounds when his player performs well, that he might become complete by sharing his "project" with a loved one. Although the ideal self to some degree may slumber, this hidden, internal construct can powerfully influence personal well-being: Individuals experience distress to the extent that they perceive discrepancies between the ideal self and the *actual self*, defined in terms of the dispositions, motives, and behavioral tendencies an individual believes he or she actually possesses. Actual-self/ideal-self-discrepancies are motivating. For example, because Jerry's actual self is discrepant from his ideal self, he suffers sadness, dejection, and frustration. Therefore, he becomes motivated to bring his actual self into alignment with his ideal self.

THE MICHELANGELO PHENOMENON AND ITS CONSEQUENCES

She thought often about Michelangelo's statues that they had seen years ago in Florence ... figures hidden in the block of stone, uncovered only by the artist's chipping away the excess, the superficial blur, till smooth and spare, the ideal shape was revealed. She and Ivan were hammer and chisel to each other.

—Lynn Sharon Schwartz, *Rough Strife*

Partner Affirmation Versus Disaffirmation

The concept of partner affirmation describes the manner in which a partner sculpts the self, or the degree to which the partner is an ally (vs. foe) in the self's goal pursuits. *Partner perceptual affirmation* describes the degree to which a partner's perceptions of the self are congruent with the ideal self: Does Dorothy hold beliefs about Jerry that are close to what he ideally would like to be—does she "see the best in what Jerry might be?" As illustrated in Figure 1.1, we suggest that partner perceptual affirmation promotes *partner behavioral affirmation*, which describes the degree to which a partner's behavior toward the self is congruent with the self's ideal: Does Dorothy say or do things that are likely to elicit components of Jerry's ideal self—is her behavior geared toward "drawing out the best in Jerry"? In turn, behavioral affirmation yields *self-movement toward the ideal self*—Jerry becomes a reflection of that which he ideally wishes to be. This three-step process is the Michelangelo phenomenon (Drigotas, Rusbult, Wieselquist, & Whitton, 1999). Thus, the Michelangelo metaphor describes a beneficent unfolding of the confirmation process. When Dorothy's perceptions and behavior are congruent with Jerry's ideal, she "sculpts" toward that ideal, eliciting behaviors and dispositions that are consistent with his ideal self. For example, at a critical meeting with a client, Dorothy directs conversation in such a manner as to call forth Jerry's ideal self: When his client proposes a risky but potentially lucrative strategy, Dorothy helps Jerry control his impulse to "go for the money" and instead attend to the risks to his client of this course of action. Over the course of frequent interactions, during which Dorothy helps him display his best self, Jerry flourishes, moving closer to the genuinely caring and other-oriented person that he ideally would like to be.

Of course, the sculpting process may bring out the best in the self, or it may bring out the worst. The concept of affirmation is a continuum, ranging from

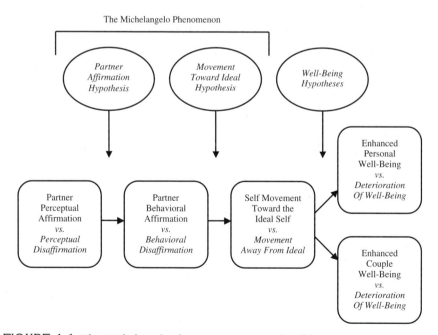

FIGURE 1.1 The Michelangelo phenomenon, personal well-being, and couple well-being.

affirmation at the upper end of the continuum, through failure to affirm, to disaffirmation at the lower end of the continuum. There are two ways in which a partner may fail to affirm (or disaffirm) the self's ideal. First, a partner's perceptions and behavior may be antithetical to the self's ideal. For example, Avery believes that Jerry is ruthless and competitive. On the basis of such beliefs, she inadvertently (or deliberately) creates situations in which Jerry is likely to appear ruthless. He finds that it is difficult to behave in a compassionate manner when Avery is present, and he becomes an increasingly insensitive and unsympathetic person. Moreover, Jerry eventually recognizes that he is not at his best when he is with Avery and feels disappointed that her opinion of him is antithetical to his ideal self.

Second, a partner's perceptions and behavior may be oriented toward goals that are irrelevant to the self's ideal. For example, Jerry is indifferent to rock climbing, yet Avery adores it. Seeking to encourage excellence in this domain, Avery may expend a good deal of energy promoting Jerry's rock-climbing abilities—she may point out poorly executed moves, suggest increasingly challenging goals, and encourage risk taking. At some level, Jerry may appreciate Avery's desire to broaden his horizons and enhance his skills; he may even develop improved rock-climbing abilities. At the same time, her behavior will do little to promote qualities that are central to his ideal self. He will increasingly recognize that Avery's goals are irrelevant to his aspirations, and feel disappointed that she has missed the point in her construal of his core values.

Empirical Support for the Partner Affirmation and Movement-Toward-Ideal Hypotheses

We have observed good support for the partner affirmation and movement-toward-ideal hypotheses (see Figure 1.1) using a variety of methods and measurement techniques. Table 1.1 summarizes empirical evidence regarding these hypotheses. In several studies we employed straightforward self-report measures of key model variables—self-reports of the extent to which the partner perceptually and behaviorally affirms the self (e.g., "My partner sees me as the person I ideally would like to be"; "My partner behaves in ways that allow me to become who I most want to be") and the self exhibits movement toward the ideal self (for each of the five most important qualities of the ideal self, participants indicate the degree to which—due to involvement with the partner—they have moved further from vs. closer to each attribute). Analyses examining data from longitudinal studies of dating and marital relationships reveal support for (a) the partner affirmation hypothesis—earlier partner perceptual affirmation predicts increases over time in partner behavioral affirmation—and (b) the movement-toward-ideal hypothesis—earlier partner behavioral affirmation predicts increases over time in self-movement toward ideal (see Table 1.1; Drigotas et al., 1999; Rusbult, Kumashiro, Finkel, et al., 2003).[2]

These findings do not appear to be attributable to socially desirable response tendencies. For example, in one study we asked each participant to bring a friend with him or her to the research session. Participants provided self-report data

TABLE 1.1. Empirical Evidence Regarding Key Hypotheses and Principles

Hypothesis or principle	Coolsen et al. (2003)	Drigotas et al. (1999)	Kirchner et al. (2003)	Kumashiro, Rusbult, et al. (2003)	Kumashiro, Wolf, et al. (2003)	Rusbult, Coolsen, et al. (2003)	Rusbult, Kumashiro, Coolsen, et al. (2003)	Rusbult, Kumashiro, Finkel et al. (2003)	Rusbult, Reis, et al. (2003)	Stocker et al. (2003)
Empirical evidence regarding basic hypotheses										
Partner affirmation hypothesis	✓	✓		✓		✓		✓		
Movement-toward-ideal hypothesis	✓	✓		✓	✓	✓		✓		
Personal well-being hypothesis										
Self-esteem (Rosenberg, 1965)	✓	✓		✓		✓		✓		
Self-respect (Kumashiro et al., 2002)								✓		
Autonomy, competence (Deci & Ryan, 2000)				✓		✓				
Subjective well-being (Diener et al., 1985)				✓		✓		✓		
Depression (Derogatis, 1994)						✓		✓		
Couple well-being hypothesis										
Dyadic adjustment (Spanier, 1976)	✓	✓		✓		✓		✓		
Persistence vs. breakup	✓	✓			✓					
Anticipated liking, enjoyable interaction										
Commitment, satisfaction (Rusbult et al., 1998)				✓		✓		✓		
Self–other merger (Aron et al., 1992)				✓		✓		✓		
Trust (Rempel et al., 1985)				✓		✓		✓		
Empirical evidence regarding temporal sequencing										
Presumed proximal causes mediate associations of presumed distal causes with criteria	✓						✓	✓		✓
Earlier predictors account for change over time in criteria	✓							✓		
Experimental evidence that predictors cause criteria					✓					

TABLE 1.1. Continued

Empirical evidence regarding possible confounds										
Model variables account for unique variance beyond…										
Self-deception; impression management (Paulhus, 1984)	✓			✓	✓					
Self-esteem (Rosenberg, 1965)	✓			✓	✓					
Depression (Derogatis, 1994)				✓	✓					
Satisfaction level (Rusbult et al., 1998)					✓					
Self-enhancement; self-verification	✓	✓		✓	✓					
Self–other merger			✓							
Pygmalion phenomenon				✓	✓					

Note. Check marks denote publications in which a given hypothesis or principle was tested and confirmed; there are no publications in which null or negative findings were observed.

regarding themselves and their partners, and friends provided friend-report data regarding the participant and the participant's partner. It is noteworthy that we observed good support for the partner affirmation and movement-toward-ideal hypotheses in analyses examining the association of participant reports of criteria with friend reports of predictors; support for predictions is also evident when we examine the association of self-reports with partner reports (see Table 1.1; Drigotas et al., 1999; Rusbult, Kumashiro, Coolsen, Kirchner, & Stocker, 2003; Rusbult, Kumashiro, Finkel, et al., 2003). These findings not only help rule out self-report bias as an explanation of our findings but also demonstrate that the Michelangelo phenomenon is evident to people other than the self, including romantic partners and friends.

Moreover, we have obtained support for our hypotheses in research employing quite indirect measurement techniques. For example, in one study participants responded to each of 25 attributes (e.g., *outgoing, ambitious*), rating the extent to which (a) they actually possessed each attribute, (b) they regarded each attribute as ideal, (c) the partner perceived that they possessed each attribute, and (d) the partner behaviorally elicited each attribute. We used these data to develop within-participant correlation-based measures of key variables, including partner percep-tual affirmation (the correlation of partner-perception ratings with ideal-self rat-ings), partner behavioral affirmation (the correlation of partner-behavior ratings with ideal-self ratings), and closeness to the ideal self (the correlation of actual-self ratings with ideal-self ratings). Analyses examining associations among these indirect, correlation-based measures revealed good support for predictions (see Table 1.1; Drigotas et al., 1999).

In addition, we have observed good support for the model using measures derived from couples' goal-relevant interactions. For example, in one study we asked married couples to discuss one partner's pursuit of an important personal goal. Participants later reviewed their videotapes and provided online ratings of both the spouse's behavior (e.g., "My partner said and did things that helped me move closer to my goal") and their own behavior (e.g., "I moved closer to attaining my goal"). We also developed a coding scheme to tap relevant variables and trained a team of research assistants to code partner behaviors (e.g., "Partner helped target clarify plan," "Partner criticized target's goal pursuits") and self behaviors during these interactions (e.g., "Target expressed determination about goal pursuits," "Target made insincere promises about change"). Analyses examining both online reports and behavioral coding data revealed good support for the affirmation and movement predictions (see Table 1.1; Rusbult, Kumashiro, Finkel, et al., 2003).

Finally, we have obtained good support for model predictions in research employing experimental methods: Participants reacted to potential dating partners on the basis of "information from the potential date" regarding attributes that person believed the participant possessed. This information centered on qualities the participant had previously identified as part of his or her ideal self, indifferent self, or feared self. In comparison to the feared-self and indifferent-self conditions, when partners perceived that participants possessed attributes participants regarded as ideal, participants anticipated that over the course of interaction with the partner, they would enjoy greater movement toward the ideal self (see Table 1.1; Rusbult, Kumashiro, Finkel, et al., 2003).

Personal Well-Being and Couple Well-Being

As illustrated in Figure 1.1, we suggest that the Michelangelo phenomenon is associated with enhanced personal well-being and couple well-being. Why might the Michelangelo phenomenon promote personal well-being? Many social scientists have proposed such an association, arguing that growth striving is a primary human motive. For example, Freud (1923) argued for such a motive in his discussion of ego ideal, Rogers (1961) and Maslow (1962) described such a motive in terms of self-actualization, and Bowlby (1969) addressed growth striving in his concept of exploration. Contemporary theories of motivation, too, emphasize the importance of self-determination and personal growth (Deci & Ryan, 2000; Emmons, 2003). To the extent that striving for personal growth is indeed a primary human motive, we should find that when individuals move closer to their ideal selves, this motive is gratified. Accordingly, movement toward the ideal self should be associated with a wide range of personal benefits, including enhanced life satisfaction and superior psychological adjustment (Higgins, 1987).

Why might the Michelangelo phenomenon promote couple well-being? First, a partner who perceptually affirms the self demonstrates empathic understanding (Ickes, Stinson, Bissonnette, & Garcia, 1990). Such understanding should enhance feelings of love ("You see me as I ideally want to be"). Also, behavioral affirmation promotes outcome correspondence and ease of coordination, in that the behaviors of self and partner are synchronized (rather than at odds) in their pursuit of the self's ideal (Rusbult & Van Lange, 2003). Relationships with greater correspondence should exhibit greater adjustment ("We act in harmony, toward shared goals"). And finally, movement toward the ideal self is gratifying in itself (Deci & Ryan, 2000; Emmons, 2003). Partners who play a role in producing such gratifications are likely to be highly valued ("I'm a better person when I'm with you").

Empirical Support for the Well-Being Hypothesis

We have observed good support for the well-being hypotheses (see Figure 1.1) using a variety of methods and measurement techniques. Table 1.1 summarizes relevant empirical evidence. We have only begun to examine associations with personal well-being, but to date we have found that in both dating and marital relationships, self-reported movement toward ideal is positively associated with self-esteem, autonomy, competence, and subjective well-being; movement away from the ideal is associated with depression; in addition, movement toward the ideal self yields increases over time in subjective well-being (Rusbult, Coolsen, et al., 2003; Rusbult, Kumashiro, Finkel, et al., 2003). Parallel associations are evident in research examining movement toward ideal in everyday life, using measures obtained in daily interaction records (Kumashiro, Rusbult, et al., 2003).

Evidence for an association of movement toward ideal with personal well-being is also evident in data obtained from dating and married couples' goal-relevant interactions. As noted earlier, in some studies we asked participants to review their videotaped interactions and provide online ratings of the extent to which they experienced movement toward the specific goal addressed in the interaction, as well as toward their generalized goals, or ideal selves. These online ratings are positively associated with self-esteem and subjective well-being and are negatively associated with depression. Moreover, coders' ratings of the self's goal-relevant positivity during interaction are positively associated with subjective well-being (see Table 1.1; Rusbult, Coolsen, et al., 2003; Rusbult, Kumashiro, Finkel, et al., 2003).

We have also observed good support for the prediction that the Michelangelo phenomenon promotes couple well-being. In both dating and marital relationships, self-reported movement toward ideal is positively associated with scores on the Dyadic Adjustment Scale (Spanier, 1976), a "gold standard" for assessing quality of couple functioning. Parallel associations have been observed (a) in research examining self-movement toward ideal in everyday life, using measures from daily interaction records; (b) in research examining goal-relevant interactions, using participants' online reports of self-movement toward ideal; and (c) in analyses employing data from longitudinal studies to predict change over time in adjustment (see Table 1.1; Drigotas et al., 1999; Rusbult, Coolsen, et al., 2003; Rusbult, Kumashiro, Finkel, et al., 2003). Finally, this prediction was supported in an earlier-noted experiment in which participants confronted potential dates who believed that they possessed specified attributes: In comparison to the feared-self and indifferent-self conditions, participants in the ideal-self condition anticipated that they would like the partner more and experience more enjoyable interaction with that person (in "potential relationships," anticipated liking is a stand-in for couple well-being; Kumashiro, Wolf, et al., 2003).

It is noteworthy that movement toward the ideal self is positively associated with indices of couple well-being other than dyadic adjustment. For example, dating relationships are more likely to persist to the extent that the self exhibits greater movement toward ideal, as reported not only by participants but also by participants' friends and romantic partners (see Table 1.1; Drigotas et al., 1999).

Also, in both dating and marital relationships, measures of self-movement toward ideal obtained using global self-report measures, daily interaction records, and online reports from goal-relevant interactions tend to be positively associated with indices of couple well-being such as commitment, perceived self–other merger, and trust (Kumashiro, Rusbult, et al., 2003; Rusbult, Coolsen, et al., 2003; Rusbult, Kumashiro, Finkel, et al., 2003).

Empirical Evidence Regarding Temporal Sequencing of Variables

Figure 1.1 displays a very specific model of the causal associations among model variables. Is this model plausible? Table 1.1 summarizes relevant empirical evidence. First—and as predicted—mediation analyses reveal that (a) partner behavioral affirmation significantly (and fully) mediates the association of partner perceptual affirmation with self-movement toward ideal, and (b) self-movement toward ideal significantly (yet partially) mediates the association of partner behavioral affirmation with both personal and couple well-being. Interestingly, in several studies we have found that (c) in predicting couple well-being, partner behavioral affirmation may be as important as (or more important than) self-movement toward ideal—that is, whether the self is "on the road to wellness" (partner affirmation) may be as important as the self's "actual wellness" (self-closeness to ideal; see Table 1.1). Second, analyses performed on data from longitudinal studies reveal that (a) earlier affirmation predicts increased movement over time toward the ideal self and (b) earlier affirmation and movement toward ideal predict increases over time in subjective well-being and couple adjustment. And third, the experimental research described earlier (wherein participants encounter affirming vs. disaffirming potential dates) demonstrates that partner affirmation causes enhanced personal well-being and attraction to a partner.

Empirical Evidence Regarding Potential Confounds

Is it possible that empirical support for the model is attributable to variables with which model variables might be associated? For example, people with high self-esteem might report greater closeness to their ideal selves and feel more confident of their partners' positive regard (Murray et al., 1996). Or, for example, individuals who are experiencing depression might more readily perceive actual-self/ideal-self disparities, and their relationships might exhibit poorer adjustment (Gotlib & Whiffen, 1991). Alternatively, emotional states such as mood or satisfaction level might yield "emotional convergence," such that one partner's negative mood induces negative mood in the other, which in turn might inhibit goal-directed behavior (Isen, 1999; Karney & Bradbury, 1995). Table 1.1 summarizes relevant evidence regarding these and other potential confounds.[3] To explore possible confounding, we replicated key analyses controlling for relevant self and partner variables. Michelangelo model variables consistently account for unique variance beyond a variety of potential confounds; moreover, associations with model variables typically are stronger than associations with potential confounds (see Table 1.1).

SELF PROCESSES AND THE MICHELANGELO PHENOMENON

I'm beginning to think that maybe it's not just how much you love someone; maybe what matters is who you are when you're with them.

—Ann Tyler, *The Accidental Tourist*

Self Ideals: The Block of Stone and the Slumbering Figure

Our model rests on the assumption that there actually is a slumbering form inside the block of stone. That is, we assume that people possess ideal selves, defined as the constellation of dispositions, motives, and behavioral tendencies that an individual ideally wishes to acquire. We assume that the ideal self serves to frame and guide cognition and behavior, and that people are motivated to reduce discrepancies between the actual self and ideal self (Higgins, 1987, 1996).

Both theoretically and operationally, we emphasize the internal character of such goals, examining the qualities that individuals genuinely wish to acquire, not the attributes that parents, colleagues, friends, or lovers believe they ought to acquire. In short, our work concerns the ideal self, not the ought self. Paralleling prior conceptualizations, we suggest that (a) pursuit of the ideal self centers on aspirations, whereas pursuit of the ought self centers on obligations; (b) movement toward the ideal self yields exhilaration, whereas movement toward the ought self yields comfort; and (c) disparities from the ideal self induce dejection, whereas disparities from the ought self induce anxiety. As such, pursuit of the ideal self is at the core of personal growth strivings. Because we seek to illuminate the relational character of personal growth, we examine the motivational properties of perceived disparities between the actual and ideal selves.

Origins and Evolution of the Ideal Self

We examine the ideal self in an idiographic, person-specific manner, and observe considerable diversity in the content of ideals. Among young adults, important components of the ideal self tend to involve career goals (education, professional excellence), social goals (relations with partners, friends, parents), personal traits (becoming more spontaneous, generous, spiritual), accomplishments (traveling in Europe, developing musical abilities), material goals (wealth, wardrobe, home improvements), and health goals (diet, exercise).

Where does the ideal self come from? We employ an incremental model, proposing that (a) ideals typically develop in a step-by-step manner (rather than emerging full-blown in a flash of insight), (b) the emergence and modification of ideals may entail systematic or automatic processes, and (c) the ideal self may change over time (Higgins, 1987; Markus & Nurius, 1986). When Jerry Maguire apprehends the character of his goals and notes that he "was his father's son again," he hints that some components of his ideal began to emerge during childhood. As a child, Jerry may have begun to discover that he valued personal achievement. Over time, his orientation may have become more focused, such that he became oriented toward fostering athletic excellence in others. Prior to the epiphany at the beginning of the film, Jerry may seldom (if ever) have dedicated systematic thought to the character of his ideals, and may seldom (if ever) have articulated the specifics of his ideal self. It is only when he begins to suffer dejection—recognizing the awesome disparity between his actual self and his (implicit and somewhat unfocused) ideal self—that he devotes time and effort to apprehending the character of his ideals.

Does the desire to realize one's ideals vary as a function of life stage? Lay construals of growth frequently rest on the assumption that such strivings are confined to young adulthood, during which time people are particularly oriented toward achievement. Although we have not examined this issue empirically, our theoretical analysis suggests that we will not observe significant moderation of key findings as a function of age or life stage. Granted, the character of the ideal self may vary over the course of development. Important components of ideals may center on industry or professional achievement at one life stage, may center on intimacy concerns at another stage, and may center on generativity or ego integrity at yet other stages (Erikson, 1950). At the same time, we assume that the desire to realize one's ideals—whatever their character—is a relatively abiding human concern.

Thus far, we have represented the emergence of ideals as a self-driven process. However, just as movement toward the ideal self is partially governed by interpersonal forces, the character of the ideal self may be at least partially interpersonal. Parents, colleagues, friends, and lovers may play a role in shaping our ideals. Again, we suggest that this process is incremental and may entail systematic or automatic processes. For example, during Jerry's childhood, his father may have dedicated extensive thought to the nature of Jerry's aspirations, actively contemplating what he ideally would like to become and deliberately encouraging certain sorts of goals. Alternatively, he may have fostered particular ideals in a relatively unthinking, unsystematic, and incidental manner. For example, Jerry's father may have unintentionally oriented Jerry toward athletic excellence by giving him a baseball for his fifth birthday. The father's selection of the gift may have had little or nothing to do with Jerry's ideal self—he may simply have purchased a gift that the two could enjoy together. The fact that the gift simultaneously shaped Jerry's ideal self may have been an incidental consequence of the father's actions.

Role of the Self in the Sculpting Process

What qualities of the self are relevant to understanding movement toward one's ideal? Many social scientists have explored self-regulation, goal pursuit, and growth processes (Bandura, 2000; Carver & Scheier, 1998; Emmons, 2003; Mischel, Cantor, & Feldman, 1996). We limit our discussion to three classes of variable that are relevant to understanding the Michelangelo phenomenon—to variables resting on the self's insight, ability, and motivation. We suggest that all three classes of variable are critical to understanding movement toward the ideal self: People with enormous insight cannot achieve their ideals in the absence of adequate ability and sustained motivation. People with exceptional ability cannot achieve their ideals in the absence of keen insight and strong motivation. And people with powerful motivation cannot achieve their ideals in the absence of good insight and plenty of ability. Table 1.2 summarizes empirical evidence regarding some of the "self variables" that we have examined to date.

First, movement toward the ideal self should be more probable to the extent that individuals possess greater insight, or greater clarity in their construal of their actual and ideal selves (Campbell, 1990; Swann, 1990). If Jerry lacks insight into his actual self, he cannot gauge the amount of effort that will be necessary to achieve his ideal and cannot develop effective strategies to realize the ideal. In like manner, Jerry is unlikely to dedicate concerted and appropriate effort to pursuit of an ideal on the basis of a poorly conceptualized ideal self. In short, it will be more difficult for Jerry to move closer to his ideal to the extent that he lacks insightful and accurate knowledge of "where he stands" and "where he wishes to go." We have only begun to explore insight-relevant variables, but consistent with this reasoning, self- and partner-reports of the self's movement toward ideal are positively associated with the self's level of self-clarity (see Table 1.2, self variables).

Second, movement toward the ideal self should be more probable to the extent that an individual possesses adequate ability, or to the extent that the potential for achieving a given ideal realistically is greater. To begin with, we state the obvious: If Jerry lacks the native ability or the specific skills that are needed to achieve his ideal, little movement toward that ideal is probable. An equally obvious point is that Jerry is more likely to achieve a given ideal to the extent that he is closer to the ideal—to the extent that there is a smaller disparity between his actual and ideal selves. However, beyond this, Jerry must perceive that the resources relevant to attaining his goals are under his control, he must experience efficacy with respect to his goals and ideals, and he must develop good strategies for goal attainment (Bandura, 2000; Deci & Ryan, 2000; Mischel et al., 1996). And in understanding moment-to-moment effort expenditure, it may be important to take into account his self-regulatory resources, including both dispositional self-control and situation-specific depletion of regulatory resources (Baumeister & Vohs, 2003). Indeed, self-reports and partner reports of self-movement toward ideal are positively associated with self attributes such as competence, mastery, self-control, and perceived likelihood of attaining a goal (see Table 1.2).

TABLE 1.2. Empirical Evidence Regarding Self Variables, Partner Variables, and the Michelangelo Phenomenon

Self or partner variable	Source of empirical evidence									
	Coolsen et al. (2003)	Drigotas et al. (1999)	Kirchner et al. (2003)	Kumashiro, Rusbult, et al. (2003)	Kumashiro, Wolf, et al. (2003)	Rusbult, Coolsen, et al. (2003)	Rusbult, Kumashiro, Coolsen, et al. (2003)	Rusbult, Kumashiro, Finkel, et al. (2003)	Rusbult, Reis, et al. (2003)	Stocker et al. (2003)
Self-insight variables										
Self-clarity (Campbell, 1990)				✓		✓		✓		
Self-ability variables										
Autonomy, competence (Deci & Ryan, 2000)				✓		✓				
Mastery (Pearlin et al. 1981)								✓		
Self-control (Tangney & Baumeister, 2001)				✓		✓		✓		
Perceived closeness to goal, likelihood of achieving goal				✓				✓		
Self-motivation variables										
Promotion orientation (Lockwood et al., 2002)	✓									
Self-esteem (Rosenberg, 1965)		✓		✓		✓		✓		
Self-respect (Kumashiro et al., 2002)								✓		
Costs–benefits of self goals to partner, relationship				✓		✓				
Self-elicitation of partner insight, ability, and motivation										
Perspective taking (Rusbult et al., 1991)										✓
Security of attachment (Fraley et al., 2000)			✓							
Receptiveness to affirmation; value placed on affirmation				✓		✓		✓		✓
Behavioral elicitation of partner affirmation						✓		✓		✓
Communication of gratitude for partner affirmation						✓		✓		
Self–partner discussion of self ideals						✓		✓		
Partner insight variables										
Empathy, perspective taking (Davis, 1983)										✓
Responsiveness: Understanding (Reis, 2003)									✓	
Perceptually, behaviorally attentive to self's actual self						✓		✓		✓

TABLE 1.2. Continued

Partner ability variables										
Competence (Deci & Ryan, 2000)				✓		✓				
Self-control (Tangey & Baumester, 2001)				✓		✓		✓		
Skill, assistance, participation				✓		✓		✓		
Partner possession of self's ideals							✓			
Partner motivation variables										
Promotion orientation (Lockwood et al., 2002)	✓									
Security of attachment (Fraley et al., 2000)			✓							
Responsiveness: Validation, caring (Reis, 2003)								✓		
Encouragement, challenge, unconditional support			✓							
Perception of self-goal pursuits as a "team effort"						✓		✓		✓

Note. Check marks denote publications in which a given hypothesis or principle was tested and confirmed; there are no publications in which null or negative findings were observed.

Third, movement toward the ideal self should be more probable to the extent that motivation is greater. On average, Jerry may be most likely to attain those components of his ideal self that are most important to him, in that he is more likely to assiduously dedicate himself to those goals. For challenging ideals or temporally extended goals, movement toward the ideal may rest on qualities such as commitment to the goal, the inclination to delay gratification, or adequate self-esteem, in that Jerry must regard himself as capable of achieving remote but desirable goals (Bandura, 2000; Mischel et al., 1996). Indeed, self-reports and partner reports of self-movement toward ideal are positively associated with self attributes such as self-esteem, self-respect, and promotion orientation (null or negative associations are evident for prevention orientation; see Table 1.2).

Whereas some ideals are pursued and attained chiefly as a result of the self's actions, selves frequently benefit from the backing of insightful, able, and motivated sculptors. Before turning to the partner per se, it is important to address a final class of self variable—qualities that elicit partner affirmation. Affirmation is facilitated to the extent that an individual (a) elicits partner insight, or clear understanding of the self's ideals (Jerry must make his ideals "visible" to Dorothy, sharing his most fervent dreams); (b) elicits partner ability, or calls forth the skills that are relevant to promoting the self's ideals (Jerry must effectively signal his needs and convey what types of assistance would be most helpful); and (c) elicits partner motivation, or genuine desire to promote the self's ideals (Jerry must be willing to make himself dependent upon Dorothy, inspire enthusiasm and commitment to his goals, and express gratitude for her efforts on his behalf). For example, when Rod Tidwell's professional prospects seem most bleak, Rod aggressively solicits Jerry's affirmation: "You bet on me like I bet on you!" Consistent with the claim that selves may be more or less adept in this regard, the receipt of partner affirmation is positively associated with the self's security of attachment, receptivity to affirmation, and expressions of gratitude for affirmation, as well as with the frequency with which the self and partner discuss the self's ideals (see Table 1.2, elicitation variables).

PARTNER PROCESSES AND THE MICHELANGELO PHENOMENON

All I really, really want our love to do/Is to bring out the best in me, and in you, too.

—Joni Mitchell, *All I Want*

Partner Affirmation: The Sculptor and the Slumbering Figure

In light of the inherently interpersonal character of the Michelangelo phenomenon, it is important to address the partner's role in promoting the self's movement toward ideal. By what mechanisms might partners "select" certain of the self's behaviors, motives, or dispositions? First, partners may engage in *retroactive selection* (selective reinforcement), wherein they reward (or punish) certain of the self's preferences, motives, and behaviors. For example, when Jerry enacts concerned caregiving behaviors with his client Rod, Dorothy reinforces such behavior by affectionately touching his arm. Second, partners may engage in *preemptive selection* (selective instigation), wherein they enact specific behaviors that elicit (or inhibit) certain preferences, motives, and behaviors on the part of the self. For example, in a situation wherein Jerry might normally behave in an acquisitive and self-centered manner, Dorothy displays his "ideal self" memo, thereby introducing a signal that instigates Jerry's caregiving behavior. And third, partners may engage in *situation selection* (manipulation of interdependence situations), wherein they create situations in which certain of the self's preferences, motives, and behaviors become more probable (or less probable). For example, at a critical meeting with a client, Dorothy preemptively steers conversation in such a manner as to elicit Jerry's most concerned and other-oriented behaviors.

Thus, affirmation does not entail treating the actual and ideal selves as one and the same. Rather, effective affirmation entails perceiving the self's potential to move closer to the self's ideal and behaving in such a manner as to elicit that ideal. Some forms of affirmation are active (steering the self toward situations in which the self will excel), whereas others are passive (providing unconditional support, a secure emotional environment); some forms are deliberate (offering information or instrumental support), whereas others are inadvertent (projecting one's own ideals onto the self; unconsciously serving as a model for the self). And, importantly, affirmation is not necessarily warm and gentle; sometimes affirming behavior is "tough." When Jerry affirms Rod Tidwell's goals as an athlete, he asserts:

> I'll tell you why you don't have your ten million dollars yet: Right now, you are a paycheck player—you play with your head, not your heart! When you get on the field, it's all about who's to blame, who underthrew the pass, who's got the contract that you don't have…. And you know what?—that is not what inspires people. Just shut up and play the game, play it from your heart!

Effective affirmation is not necessarily consciously controlled (Bargh & Chartrand, 1999): On some occasions Dorothy may consciously seek to promote Jerry's warm and caring behavior; on other occasions she may unconsciously and automatically exhibit affirming perception and behavior. For example, because Dorothy believes that "optimism is revolutionary," she may project her ideals onto Jerry, unconsciously behaving toward him as she, herself, would most like to be treated. Such unconscious and automatic compatibility of self-goals and partner goals for the self might result from any of several causes, including congruence of personal values (both Jerry and Dorothy place a high value on family and friends), compatible implicit personality theories (for both partners, caregiving is a central trait in person perception), or similarity of actual selves or ideal selves (Jerry and Dorothy possess similar dispositions or life goals; Byrne, 1971; Schneider, 1973; Wetzel & Insko, 1982).[4]

Role of the Partner in the Sculpting Process

Just as the self variables that are relevant to understanding movement toward an ideal can be characterized in terms of insight, ability, and motivation, so, too, can relevant partner variables. Table 1.2 summarizes empirical evidence regarding some of the partner variables that we have examined to date. First, effective affirmation is facilitated—and self-movement toward ideal is promoted—by partner insight, or a clear understanding of the self's actual and ideal selves. For example, Jerry is more likely to achieve his ideals when Dorothy intuits precisely when and how he needs her support, as well as when she engages in perspective taking and achieves a deeper understanding of his ideal self. As in *Beauty and the Beast* (Hahn, Trousdale, & Wise, 1991), when the actual and ideal selves are highly discrepant, special insight is required to see through the unpromising exterior to the inner potential and to perceive the possibilities for making that potential "real." Indeed, partner affirmation and self-movement toward ideal are positively associated with the partner's empathy and perspective taking, perceptual and behavioral attentiveness to the actual self, and accurate understanding of the self's goals and ideals (see Table 1.2, partner variables).

Second, the Michelangelo phenomenon is enhanced by *partner ability*, or possession of the skills and resources that are relevant to promoting the self's ideals. Jerry is more likely to achieve his ideals when Dorothy possesses unique knowledge of the elements that make up his ideals, proposes effective strategies for goal attainment, and delivers the precise types of assistance that are needed, including both instrumental and social-emotional support (actively participating in Jerry's goal pursuits, offering beer and a sandwich when Jerry is dejected). Indeed, partner affirmation and self-movement toward ideal are greater to the extent that partners exhibit competence and self-control, provide direct assistance or actively participate in the self's goal pursuits, and actually possess key components of the self's ideal (see Table 1.2).

And third, effective affirmation is facilitated—and self-movement toward ideal is promoted—by *partner motivation*, or genuine desire to promote the self's ideal. Jerry is more likely to achieve his ideals when Dorothy feels comfortable in situations wherein Jerry is dependent, employs her power over him in a benevolent manner, experiences genuine enthusiasm regarding his goal pursuits, and is willing to occasionally sacrifice her interests to promote his goals (exert effort, endure costs). Indeed, affirmation and self-movement toward ideal are positively associated with partner attributes such as promotion orientation, security of attachment, and responsiveness (see Table 1.2). Self-movement toward ideal is also promoted to the extent that partners offer encouragement, challenge, and unconditional support and regard the self's pursuits as a "team effort" (Jerry describes the company that he and Dorothy form as "our little project").

Partner Affirmation and Responsiveness

The interpersonal model of intimacy serves as a useful means of characterizing many of the processes on which effective partner affirmation rests (Reis & Shaver, 1988). According to this model, individuals feel supported—and relationships are strengthened—to the extent that a partner exhibits responsiveness. In parent–child interactions, responsiveness describes the caregiver's attentiveness to the signals a child uses to communicate his or her needs, sensitivity to the nature of the child's needs, and inclination to appropriately respond to the child's needs (Bowlby, 1969). The intimacy model proposes that among adults, responsiveness exists when a partner responds to the self in such a manner as to communicate (a) understanding, or accurate knowledge of the self's goals and needs; (b) validation, or approval of the self's goals and needs; and (c) caring, or genuine commitment to the self's goals and needs.

Understanding, validating, and caring do not necessarily require wholehearted endorsement of the self's ideal. Partners can be responsive even when their own ideals are not perfectly aligned with the self's ideals, and even when they do not believe that the self's goals and ideals constitute the "best" constellation for the self. Responsiveness also requires flexibility. To be truly responsive to his friend Rod, Jerry must recognize that Rod's ideal self is unlikely to be fixed—that Rod's ideals may evolve over the course of their friendship. Moreover, responsive behavior is characterized by contingencies: Some of Rod's needs may be well-defined and clearly attainable as a result of his own efforts, such that Rod simply needs approval, encouragement, and a buddy to share in his triumphs. Other needs may require relatively more instrumental support, such as advice or assistance. In short, responsiveness ideally is (a) contingent on the self's abilities, resources, circumstances, and signals of need; (b) affectively attuned to the partner's emotional state; (c) geared toward matching the self's needs in both type of support and timing of support; and (d) encouraging of autonomy rather than dependence.

For example, Avery did not understand Jerry's goals. She regarded Jerry as a shark in a suit rather than as the generous and caring person that he sought to become. When he revealed his ideal self to her, Avery was incapable of validating his goals and instead responded with disdain and ridicule. And when Jerry hit rock bottom and turned to Avery for consolation, Avery refused to respond to his need for reassurance: "Jerry, there is a sensitivity thing that some people have.... I don't have it—I don't cry at movies.... I don't tell a man who just screwed up both of our lives, 'Oh, poor baby.'" Instead, she communicated that her own goals and needs were unequivocally more important than Jerry's: "It's all about you, isn't it—soothe me, save me, love me. I have to finish *my* job!" In contrast, Dorothy understood Jerry's goals from the outset, fully apprehending the character of his ideals and comprehending their implications for his future. She also exhibited exceptional flexibility in the means she employed to affirm Jerry, skillfully validating Jerry's ideal self ("I think optimism is revolutionary") and communicating genuine caring for Jerry and his goals ("I loved that memo!" "I love this man!").

We have examined responsiveness—understanding, validation, and caring—in three components of our recent work (see Table 1.2): (a) In an interaction record study of everyday goal pursuits, as well as in an ongoing longitudinal study, we obtained self-reports and partner reports of each person's responsiveness; (b) in an ongoing longitudinal study, when participants review their videotaped interactions and provide online reports of their own and the partner's behavior, they report on the extent of each person's responsiveness; and (c) in an ongoing longitudinal study as well as in a previous study of marital relationships, measures of responsiveness are a component of the coding scheme used to rate partners' interaction behavior. Among the many predictors of affirmation and movement toward ideal, partner responsiveness stands out as a reliable and powerful component of the Michelangelo phenomenon.

HOW THE MICHELANGELO PHENOMENON DIFFERS FROM OTHER SELF-RELEVANT PHENOMENA

Before closing, it is important to distinguish the Michelangelo phenomenon from related interpersonal processes—processes to which it bears some similarity, or with which it shares some common themes. In the following paragraphs we distinguish partner affirmation from partner enhancement, partner verification, self-expansion, and the Pygmalion phenomenon.

Partner Affirmation and Partner Enhancement

How does partner affirmation differ from *partner enhancement*, or behavior that is exceptionally positive with regard to the self? Many studies have revealed that enhancement promotes couple vitality, demonstrating that selves whose partners view them favorably not only are more satisfied with their relationships but also develop increasingly positive self-images (Murray et al., 1996; Rusbult, Van Lange, Wildschut, Yovetich, & Verette, 2000). Might our findings regarding affirmation reflect the confounding of affirmation with enhancement?

To address this question, we must carefully distinguish between enhancement and affirmation. Empirically, these variables are likely to be positively associated, in that when partners exhibit "affirming" behavior, their behavior is also likely to be experienced as "enhancing." Indeed, when enhancement is defined in terms of attributes valued by the self, "enhancing" attributes may well be components of the self's ideal. To "unconfound" these variables, we define partner enhancement in terms of *normative desirability*, or the degree to which an elicited behavior is "desirable for people of your age and sex." For example, Avery believes that Jerry is physically courageous. This attribute is at least moderately positive from a normative point of view—many or most people would appreciate being viewed as intrepid. However, because being intrepid is not a part of Jerry's ideal self, Avery's behavior is disaffirming.

We have conducted two studies to unconfound affirmation and enhancement. In the study in which we developed within-participant correlation-based measures, we assessed both partner affirmation (correlation of partner-behavior ratings with ideal-self ratings) and partner enhancement (correlation of partner-behavior ratings with normative-desirability ratings). And in the experiment in which participants received information about potential dating partners' beliefs about them, this information concerned the participant's ideal, indifferent, or feared self, and was high, medium, or low in normative desirability. In both studies, analyses performed on key criteria revealed strong and reliable effects of affirmation and nonsignificant effects of enhancement (Drigotas et al., 1999; Kumashiro, Wolf, et al., 2003).

Thus, when push comes to shove, individuals prefer that their partners elicit behaviors that are positive and congruent with their ideals rather than behaviors that are merely normatively desirable. Of course, the key issue frequently is terminology: To the extent that researchers operationally define enhancement in terms of what the self regards as positive (as in Murray et al., 1996), enhancement is tantamount to affirmation (and, perhaps, should be described as such).

Partner Affirmation and Partner Verification

How does partner affirmation relate to *partner verification*, or behavior that elicits the actual self (or the self's beliefs about the actual self)? Many studies have revealed that people value social feedback that confirms their self-conceptions: Whereas positive partner regard is valued and enhances intimacy among people with high self-esteem, positive regard is unpleasant for those with low self-esteem (Swann, 1990; Swann, De La Ronde, & Hixon, 1994). How can we reconcile these findings with research regarding the benefits of affirmation?

First, we suspect that if partners are to competently affirm the self's ideal, they must develop an accurate understanding of the block of stone they seek to sculpt: What possibilities are inherent in the block, what flaws must be circumvented, and what glories might be highlighted? In short, effective affirmation rests on a partner's (reasonably accurate) understanding of the actual self. Second, although selves may appreciate partners who accurately perceive both their strengths and their limitations, they also hope that (a) they will be loved despite their limitations and (b) the partner will perceive the best that they can be, and behave in such a manner as to translate the actual self into the ideal self. In short, selves wish to be understood and validated.

We have conducted three studies to examine the simultaneous effects of affirmation and verification. First, in the study in which we developed correlation-based measures, we assessed both affirmation (correlation of partner-behavior ratings with ideal-self ratings) and verification (correlation of partner-behavior ratings with actual-self ratings). Second, in the experiment in which participants received information about potential partners' beliefs about them, this information concerned the participant's ideal, indifferent, or feared self and was highly descriptive, moderately descriptive, or not at all descriptive of the actual self. Third, in a study of marital relationships, we obtained self-report measures of both affirmation and verification. Analyses performed on key criteria revealed effects of affirmation in all three studies and revealed effects of verification in two of three studies (Drigotas et al., 1999; Kumashiro, Wolf, et al., 2003; Rusbult, Kumashiro, Finkel, et al., 2003).

Thus, there is no necessary inconsistency between eliciting another's actual self and eliciting that person's ideal self. These variables sometimes operate in concert, such that both tendencies contribute to growth and couple vitality. Future research should determine whether these variables exert additive effects because accurate understanding serves as the foundation for effective affirmation, because individuals wish to be both understood and validated, or both.

Partner Affirmation and Self-Expansion

How does the Michelangelo phenomenon differ from *self-expansion* (Aron & Aron, 2000)? Humans arguably are motivated by the need for self-expansion—for greater physical and social influence, cognitive complexity, and social identity. Some research suggests that close involvement provides a means of self-expansion, in that interdependence involves inclusion of other in the self, or incorporating a partner's attributes and resources (Aron & Aron, 2000). However, the precise nature of self–other merger is unclear: Do individuals acquire their partners' attributes in a wholesale manner, incorporating both desirable and undesirable partner qualities? And are the benefits of self–other merger attributable to the full panoply of acquired attributes, or are such benefits mainly attributable to the acquisition of desirable partner attributes?

We suggest that it is not straightforward self–other merger per se, but ideal-self expansion—or expansion toward the ideal self—that promotes personal well-being and couple vitality. Including Dorothy in his self benefits Jerry and their marriage mainly when such inclusion promotes Jerry's movement toward his ideal self; embracing Dorothy's less-than-ideal dispositions is unlikely to be helpful. By what mechanism(s) might such effects come about? Beneficial self–other merger may be at least partially attributable to circumstances wherein a partner possesses attributes that are components of the self's ideal. Under such circumstances, Dorothy should be better able to affirm Jerry's ideal, perceiving his potential for growth, encouraging ideal-congruent actions, and challenging him to achieve his ideals. Moreover, when Dorothy actually possesses qualities that Jerry regards as ideal, he can use her as a model and inspiration for movement toward his ideals.

We tested this logic in two studies that (a) assessed key variables using self-report measures, (b) assessed self–other merger using the inclusion of other in the self scale (Aron et al., 1992), and (c) included measures of the degree to which the partner possessed qualities that were important components of the self's ideal (e.g., using participants' ratings of 25 attributes to identify the five most important components of the ideal self and calculating the degree to which the partner actually possessed each of those attributes; Rusbult, Kumashiro, Coolsen, et al., 2003). Mediation analyses revealed that (a) Michelangelo model variables partially to wholly mediate associations of self–other merger with key criteria, (b) partner possession of the self's ideal partially mediates associations of Michelangelo model variables with key criteria, and (c) partner possession of the self's ideal partially to wholly mediates associations of self–other merger with key criteria.

Thus, self–other merger may be particularly beneficial when it promotes the Michelangelo phenomenon, or the acquisition of attributes that are components of the self's ideal. Moreover, such effects may be at least partially attributable to instances wherein a partner to some extent possesses the self's ideal. It would appear that when a partner actually possesses qualities that are important components of the self's ideal, the partner is better able to affirm the self's ideal (encourage ideal-congruent actions, challenge the self) and the self may be better able to use the partner as a model and inspiration for movement toward the ideal.

Partner Affirmation and the Pygmalion Phenomenon

How does the Michelangelo phenomenon differ from the *Pygmalion phenomenon*? Whereas the Michelangelo phenomenon describes a partner who sculpts the self's ideal, the Pygmalion phenomenon describes a partner who sculpts the partner's ideal. Some research provides indirect support for the Pygmalion phenomenon, revealing that individuals are attracted to people who are similar to their own ideal selves (Wetzel & Insko, 1982). Moreover—and as outlined in the preceding analysis of self–other merger—a partner who possesses important components of the self's ideal may be in a unique position to sculpt toward that ideal. At the same time, we suggest that the well-being of both self and couple will be enhanced to the extent that a partner perceives the self and behaves toward the self in a manner that is congruent with the self's ideal and will be degraded to the extent that a partner affirms qualities that are antithetical the self's ideal.

Thus, the question is: Whose ideal is sculpted—the self's or the partner's? Two longitudinal studies revealed evidence that effective sculpting is oriented toward the self's ideal: Analyses employing (a) self-report measures of the partner's inclination to sculpt toward his or her own ideal (rather than the self's ideal) and (b) online reports from couples' goal relevant interactions suggest that a partner's inclination to "foist his or her own ideals onto the self" yields negative consequences for selves and relationships (Rusbult, Coolsen, et al., 2003; Rusbult, Kumashiro, Finkel, et al., 2003). Thus, not all sculpting is beneficial: When partners sculpt one another toward their own ideals rather than the self's ideals—even when such sculpting is masterful and yields a lovely product—the consequences tend to be maladaptive for both personal well-being and couple adjustment.

CONCLUSIONS

Our goal in this chapter was to review theory and research regarding the Michelangelo phenomenon. This work incorporates concepts from the behavioral confirmation, self-discrepancy, and interdependence traditions to identify processes that are central to understanding the self in its relational context. The Michelangelo phenomenon describes a congenial pattern of interdependence in which close partners sculpt one another in such a manner as to bring each person closer to his or her ideal self. To date, empirical evidence suggests that the three components of this phenomenon—partner perceptual affirmation, partner behavioral affirmation, and self-movement toward the ideal self—relate to one another in predicted ways. The empirical evidence suggests that partner affirmation and self-movement toward ideal play strong and reliable roles in shaping both personal well-being and couple well-being. Recent findings also begin to identify the processes and mechanisms that underlie the Michelangelo phenomenon, including a variety of self and partner dispositions, motives, and behavioral tendencies. We hope that such findings may extend our understanding of the social nature of the self, highlighting one means by which adaptation to interdependence partners shapes everyday experience.

ACKNOWLEDGMENTS

The research reported in this chapter was supported by grants from the National Institute of Mental Health (BSR-1-R01-MH-45417), the National Science Foundation (BCS-0132398 and BNS-9023817), the Fetzer Institute, and the Templeton Foundation.

NOTES

1. The two members of a dyad may act as both target and observer—as (a) self, or the target of another's perception and behavior, and (b) partner, or the observer who perceives the target and directs behavior toward the target. We use *self* to describe the target, and *partner* to describe the observer; we speak of *self-perceptions of the self* (target perceptions of target), *partner perceptions of the self* (observer perceptions of target), and *partner perceptions of himself or herself* (observer perceptions of observer). Parallel structure is used to describe behavior (*self-behavior, partner behavior toward self,* and *partner behavior*).
2. The appendix at the end of the chapter includes citations and information regarding research that provides empirical evidence relevant to the Michelangelo phenomenon.
3. In a later section, we address whether empirical support might be attributable to self-relevant processes such as partner enhancement or verification.
4. In our ongoing research, we are using diverse procedures to determine whether partners are consciously aware of one another's ideals, whether they make active decisions to affirm one another, and whether affirmation of the self's ideal is an automatic or controlled process (e.g., using indirect measures to assess the accuracy

with which partners perceive one another's ideals; determining whether selves perceive acts of affirmation that their partners do not apprehend).

REFERENCES

Aron, A., & Aron, E. (2000). Self-expansion motivation and including other in the self. In W. Ickes & S. Duck (Eds.), *The social psychology of personal relationships* (pp. 109–128). New York: Wiley.

Aron, A., Aron, E. N., & Smollan, D. (1992). Inclusion of Other in the Self Scale and the structure of interpersonal closeness. *Journal of Personality and Social Psychology, 63*, 596–612.

Bandura, A. (2000). Social cognitive theory: An agentic perspective. *Annual Review of Psychology, 52*, 1–26.

Bargh, J. A., & Chartrand, T. L. (1999). The unbearable automaticity of being. *American Psychologist, 54*, 462–479.

Baumeister, R. F., & Vohs, K. D. (2003). Willpower, choice, and self-control. In G. Loewenstein & D. Read (Eds.), *Time and decision: Economic and psychological perspectives on intertemporal choice* (pp. 201–216). New York: Russell Sage.

Bowlby, J. (1969). *Attachment and loss: Vol. 1. Attachment*. New York: Basic Books.

Brooks, J. (Producer), & Crowe, C. (Director). (1996). *Jerry Maguire* [Film]. Culver City, CA: Tristar Pictures.

Byrne, D. (1971). *The attraction paradigm*. New York: Academic Press.

Campbell, J. D. (1990). Self-esteem and clarity of self-concept. *Journal of Personality and Social Psychology, 59*, 538–549.

Carver, C. S., & Scheier, M. F. (1998). *On the self-regulation of behavior*. New York: Cambridge University Press.

Coolsen, M., Kirchner, J., Kumashiro, M., Finkel, E., & Rusbult, C. E. (2003). *Promotion orientation, prevention orientation, and the Michelangelo phenomenon*. Unpublished manuscript, University of North Carolina at Chapel Hill.

Darley, J. M., & Fazio, R. H. (1980). Expectancy confirmation processes arising in the social interaction sequence. *American Psychologist, 35*, 867–881.

Davis, M. H. (1983). Measuring individual differences in empathy: Evidence for a multi-dimensional approach. *Journal of Personality and Social Psychology, 44*, 113–126.

Deci, E. L., & Ryan, R. M. (2000). The "what" and "why" of goal pursuits: Human needs and the self-determination of behavior. *Journal of Health and Social Behavior, 2*, 237–256.

Derogatis, L. R. (1994). SCL–90–R: *Symptom Checklist—90–R: Administration, scoring, and procedures manual* (3rd ed.). Minneapolis, MN: National Computer Systems.

Diener, E., Emmons, R. A., Larsen, R. J., & Griffin, S. (1985). The Satisfaction With Life scale. *Journal of Personality Assessment, 49*, 71–75.

Drigotas, S. M., Rusbult, C. E., Wieselquist, J., & Whitton, S. (1999). Close partner as sculptor of the ideal self: Behavioral affirmation and the Michelangelo phenomenon. *Journal of Personality and Social Psychology, 77*, 293–323.

Emmons, R. A. (2003). Personal goals, life meaning, and virtue: Wellsprings of a positive life. In C. L. Keyes & J. Haidt (Eds.), *Flourishing: Positive psychology and the life well-lived* (pp. 105–128). Washington: American Psychological Association.

Erikson, E. (1950). *Childhood and society* (2nd ed.). New York: Norton.

Fazio, R. H., Effrein, E. A., & Falender, V. J. (1981). Self-perceptions following social interactions. *Journal of Personality and Social Psychology, 41*, 232–242.

Freud, S. (1923). *The ego and the id* (J. Strachey, Trans.). New York: Norton.

Gombrich, E. H. (1995). *The story of art* (16th ed.). London: Phaidon.

Gotlib, I. H., & Whiffen, V. E. (1991). The interpersonal context of depression: Implications for theory and research. In W. H. Jones & D. Perlman (Eds.), *Advances in personal relationships* (Vol. 3, pp. 177–206). London: Kingsley.

Hahn, D. (Producer), Trousdale, G., & Wise, K. (Directors). (1991). *Beauty and the beast* [Film]. Burbank, CA: Disney Motion Pictures.

Harris, M. J., & Rosenthal, R. (1985). Mediation of interpersonal expectancy effects: 31 meta-analyses. *Psychological Bulletin, 97,* 363–386.

Higgins, E. T. (1987). Self-discrepancy: A theory relating self and affect. *Psychological Review, 94,* 319–340.

Higgins, E. T. (1996). The "self digest": Self-knowledge serving self-regulatory functions. *Journal of Personality and Social Psychology, 71,* 1062–1083.

Ickes, W., Stinson, L., Bissonnette, V., & Garcia, S. (1990). Naturalistic social cognition: Empathic accuracy in mixed-sex dyads. *Journal of Personality and Social Psychology, 59,* 730–742.

Isen, A. M. (1999). Positive affect. In T. Dagleish & M. Powers (Eds.), *Handbook of cognition and emotion* (pp. 521–539). Sussex, England: Wiley.

Karney, B. R., & Bradbury, T. N. (1995). The longitudinal course of marital quality and stability: A review of theory, methods, and research. *Psychological Bulletin, 118,* 3–34.

Kelley, H. H., & Thibaut, J. W. (1978). *Interpersonal relations: A theory of interdependence.* New York: Wiley.

Kirchner, M., Stocker, S., Kumashiro, M., Finkel, E., & Rusbult, C. E. (2003). *Security of attachment and the Michelangelo phenomenon.* Unpublished manuscript, University of North Carolina at Chapel Hill.

Kumashiro, M., Finkel, E. J., & Rusbult, C. E. (2002). Self-respect and pro-relationship behavior in marital relationships. *Journal of Personality, 70,* 1009–1049.

Kumashiro, M., Rusbult, C. E., & Estrada, M. J. (2003). *The Michelangelo phenomenon in everyday life: An interaction record study of self and partner processes.* Unpublished manuscript, University of North Carolina at Chapel Hill.

Kumashiro, M., Wolf, S., Coolsen, M., & Rusbult, C. E. (2003). *Partner affirmation, verification, and enhancement as determinants of attraction to potential dates: Experimental evidence of the unique effect of affirmation.* Unpublished manuscript, University of North Carolina at Chapel Hill.

Lockwood, P., Jordan, C. H., & Kunda, Z. (2002). Motivation by positive or negative role models: Regulatory focus determines who will best inspire us. *Journal of Personality and Social Psychology, 83,* 854–864.

Markus, H., & Nurius, P. (1986). Possible selves. *American Psychologist, 41,* 954–969.

Maslow, A. H. (1962). *Toward a psychology of being.* Princeton, NJ: Van Nostrand.

Mischel, W., Cantor, N., & Feldman, S. (1996). Principles of self-regulation: The nature of willpower and self-control. In E. T. Higgins & A. Kruglanski (Eds.), *Social psychology: Handbook of basic principles* (pp. 329–360). New York: Guilford.

Murray, S. L., Holmes, J. G., & Griffin, D. W. (1996). The self-fulfilling nature of positive illusions in romantic relationships: Love is not blind, but prescient. *Journal of Personality and Social Psychology, 71,* 1155–1180.

Paulhus, D. L. (1984). Two-component models of socially desirable responding. *Journal of Personality and Social Psychology, 46,* 598–609.

Pearlin, L., Lieberman, M., Menaghan, E., & Mullan, J. (1981). The stress process. *Journal of Health and Social Behavior, 22,* 337–356.

Reis, H. T. (2003). *Measuring responsiveness in close relationships*. Unpublished manuscript, University of Rochester, Rochester, NY.

Reis, H. T., & Shaver, P. (1988). Intimacy as an interpersonal process. In S. Duck (Ed.), *Handbook of personal relationships* (pp. 367–389). Chichester, England: Wiley.

Rempel, J. K., Holmes, J. G., & Zanna, M. P. (1985). Trust in close relationships. *Journal of Personality and Social Psychology, 49*, 95–112.

Rogers, C. R. (1961). *On becoming a person*. Boston: Houghton Mifflin.

Rosenberg, M. (1965). *Society and the adolescent self-image*. Princeton, NJ: Princeton University Press.

Rosenthal, R., & Jacobson, L. (1968). *Pygmalion in the classroom*. New York: Holt, Rinehart, & Winston.

Rusbult, C. E., Coolsen, M., Kirchner, J., Stocker, S., Kumashiro, M., Wolf, S., et al. (2003). *Partner affirmation in newly-committed relationships: A longitudinal study of partner affirmation and movement toward the ideal self*. Unpublished manuscript, University of North Carolina at Chapel Hill.

Rusbult, C. E., Kumashiro, M., Coolsen, M., Kirchner, J., & Stocker, S. (2003). *Self–other merger and the Michelangelo phenomenon: Partner possession of the self's ideal and the affirmation process*. Unpublished manuscript, University of North Carolina at Chapel Hill.

Rusbult, C. E., Kumashiro, M., Finkel, E., Kirchner, J., Coolsen, M., Stocker, S., & Clarke, J. (2003). *A longitudinal study of the Michelangelo phenomenon in marital relationships*. Unpublished manuscript, University of North Carolina at Chapel Hill.

Rusbult, C. E., Martz, J. M., & Agnew, C. R. (1998). The investment model scale: Measuring commitment level, satisfaction level, quality of alternatives, and investment size. *Personal Relationships, 5*, 357–391.

Rusbult, C. E., Reis, H. T., & Kumashiro, M. (2003). *Partner affirmation as responsiveness*. Unpublished manuscript, University of North Carolina at Chapel Hill.

Rusbult, C. E., & Van Lange, P. A. M. (2003). Interdependence, interaction, and relationships. *Annual Review of Psychology, 54*, 351–375.

Rusbult, C. E., Van Lange, P. A. M., Wildschut, T., Yovetich, N. A., & Verette, J. (2000). Perceived superiority in close relationships: Why it exists and persists. *Journal of Personality and Social Psychology, 79*, 521–545.

Schneider, D. J. (1973). Implicit personality theory: A review. *Psychological Bulletin, 79*, 294–309.

Snyder, M., Tanke, E., & Berscheid, E. (1977). Social perception and interpersonal behavior: On the self-fulfilling nature of social stereotypes. *Journal of Personality and Social Psychology, 35*, 656–666.

Spanier, G. B. (1976). Measuring dyadic adjustment: New scales for assessing the quality of marriage and similar dyads. *Journal of Marriage and the Family, 38*, 15–28.

Stocker, S., Coolsen, M., Kumashiro, M., Kirchner, J., Wolf, S., Estrada, M., & Rusbult, C. E. (2003). *Mechanisms underlying partner affirmation and movement toward the ideal self*. Unpublished manuscript, University of North Carolina at Chapel Hill.

Swann, W. B., Jr. (1990). To be adored or to be known: The interplay of self-enhancement and self-verification. In R. M. Sorrentino & E. T. Higgins (Eds.), *Foundations of social behavior* (Vol. 2, pp. 408–448). New York: Guilford Press.

Swann, W. B., Jr., DeLaRonde, C., & Hixon, J. G. (1994). Authenticity and positivity strivings in marriage and courtship. *Journal of Personality and Social Psychology, 66*, 857–869.

Tangney, J. P., & Baumeister, R. F. (2001). *High self-control predicts good adjustment, less pathology, better grades, and interpersonal success.* Unpublished manuscript, George Mason University, Fairfax, VA.

Wetzel, C. G., & Insko, C. A. (1982). The similarity–attraction relationship: Is there an ideal one? *Journal of Experimental Social Psychology, 18,* 253–276.

Appendix
Empirical Evidence Regarding the Michelangelo Phenomenon

	Research method				Measurement technique								Participant population		
	Experiment	Interaction record study	Longitudinal study	Survey study	Self-report	Partner-report	Friend-report	Indirect measures	Correlation based	Interaction records	Online ratings of interaction	Behavioral codings of interaction	Dating relationships	Marital relationships	Newly committed relationships
Coolsen et al. (2003)		✓			✓	✓				✓			✓		
			✓		✓	✓								✓	
			✓		✓	✓									✓
Drigotas et al. (1999)			✓		✓	✓							✓		
			✓		✓		✓						✓		
			✓		✓	✓								✓	
				✓	✓	✓				✓			✓		
Kirchner et al. (2003)		✓			✓	✓				✓			✓		
			✓		✓	✓								✓	
			✓		✓	✓									✓
Kumashiro, Rusbult, et al. (2003)		✓			✓	✓				✓			✓		
Kumashiro, Wolf, et al. (2003)	✓				✓								✓		
	✓				✓								✓		
Rusbult, Coolsen, et al. (2003)			✓		✓	✓		✓			✓	✓			✓
Rusbult, Kumashiro, Coolsen, et al. (2003)			✓		✓	✓								✓	
			✓		✓	✓									✓
Rusbult, Kumashiro, Finkel, et al. (2003)			✓		✓	✓	✓				✓	✓		✓	
Rusbult, Reis, et al. (2003)					✓	✓				✓			✓		
			✓		✓	✓					✓	✓		✓	
			✓		✓	✓					✓	✓			✓
Stocker et al. (2003)			✓		✓	✓					✓	✓		✓	
			✓		✓	✓					✓	✓			✓

Note. Check marks denote properties of studies in a given publication, with one row per study for each publication. Some studies are included in multiple publications—the publications listed include two experiments, one interaction record study, five longitudinal studies, and one survey study.

2

From Thought and Experience to Behavior and Interpersonal Relationships: A Multicomponent Conceptualization of Authenticity

MICHAEL H. KERNIS AND BRIAN M. GOLDMAN

We want our chocolate to be authentic ("made with real milk chocolate"). We want our pasta to be authentic ("authentic Italian recipe"). We want our leather to be authentic ("100% cowhide leather"). But, do we want our "selves" to be authentic? On the one hand, a vast literature documents people's willingness to profess opinions, modulate their emotional expressions, and tailor their behaviors to audiences, seemingly with little regard for the truth (Schlenker, 2002). The more skillful the portrayal, the more interpersonally successful the messenger is said to be (Snyder, 1987). Those most skillful at strategic fabrications of the truth are likely to be revered as television or film celebrities, or perhaps reviled as con or scam artists. On the other hand, many philosophers and psychologists place great value on acting in accord with one's true inclinations and place this type of congruence at the core of an individual's well-being and interpersonal functioning (Rogers, 1961). From this perspective, actions that do not resonate with one's true self, no matter how skillfully they are performed, will undermine one's well-being and erode one's interpersonal relationships over time. How can we account for these seemingly disparate views? We believe that one factor that may contribute to ambivalence about the value of authenticity is that it has both costs and benefits. Depending upon one's vantage point, the costs may appear to outweigh the benefits, or vice versa.

In this chapter we articulate some of these costs and benefits within a multi-component conceptualization of authenticity that incorporates (a) self-awareness and understanding, (b) the processing of self-relevant evaluative information, (c) behavior, and (d) relationship functioning. We argue that each component of authenticity comes with costs and benefits and is associated with its own barriers to fruition. We begin by presenting our conceptualization (see also Goldman

& Kernis, 2002; Kernis, 2003; Kernis & Goldman, in press) and then report data obtained from several recent studies that focus on the relationship of authenticity to various aspects of psychological and interpersonal functioning. These data suggest that, on average, authentic functioning confers many benefits toward individuals' psychological and interpersonal well-being. Following this, we consider the psychological and interpersonal costs and benefits associated with each component of authenticity and some factors that may inhibit authenticity. We close by examining the relationship between self-esteem and authenticity.

A MULTICOMPONENT CONCEPTUALIZATION OF AUTHENTICITY

Most perspectives of authenticity stress the extent to which one's thoughts, feelings, and behaviors reflect one's true or core self (for a brief history of these perspectives, see Kernis & Goldman, in press). Accordingly, we (Goldman & Kernis, 2002; Kernis, 2003; Kernis & Goldman, in press) define authenticity as the unobstructed operation of one's true or core self in one's daily enterprise. Rather than viewing this as a single unitary process, however, we assert that authenticity can be broken down into four discriminable components. Specifically, we suggest that authenticity involves *awareness*, *unbiased processing*, *behavior*, and *relational orientation*. As we describe in this chapter, each of these components focuses on an aspect of authenticity that, while related to each of the others, can operate independently.

Awareness

The awareness component refers to possessing, and being motivated to increase, one's knowledge of and trust in one's motives, feelings, desires, and self-relevant cognitions. It includes, for example, understanding one's likes and dislikes, strengths and weaknesses, goals and aspirations, dispositional characteristics, and emotional states. We believe that having awareness of one's true self promotes the integration of one's inherent polarities into a coherent multifaceted self-representation. As Perls, Hefferline, and Goodman (1951) suggested, people are not either masculine or feminine, either introverted or extroverted, either emotional or stoic, and so forth. Instead, although one aspect of these dualities (*figure*) generally predominates over the other (*ground*), individuals invariably possess both aspects to some degree. As people function with greater authenticity, they become more aware of the fact that they possess these multifaceted self-aspects and they strive to integrate them into a cohesive self-structure.

This view differs from the prevailing conceptualization of self-concept *clarity* (Campbell, 1990; Campbell et al., 1996) that holds that endorsing as self-descriptive adjectives that reflect both endpoints of bipolar trait dimensions (e.g., introversion, extraversion) reflects self-concept *confusion*. An assumption underlying this view of confusion, to which we take exception, is that these so-called endpoint traits are in fact mutually exclusive. In fact, data we collected (Kernis, Whitaker,

& Davies, 1997) indicate that laypeople view many of the trait pairs used by Campbell in her research as not mutually exclusive. In this research, we presented undergraduate respondents with each trait pair and asked, "If a person is *X*, to what extent can that person also be *Y*?" Ratings were made on 7-point scales (1 = *not at all*, 7 = *very much*). Mean ratings for the pairs ranged from a low of 2.8 to a high of 5.8.[1] Although multiple interpretations of these data admittedly are viable, they suggest to us that laypeople have a view of self-characteristics that is multifaceted rather than simple (see also Sande, Goethals, & Radloff, 1988). One focus of future research should be to develop techniques that offer sophisticated assessments of the *figure* and *ground* in personality and relate them to authenticity. Later in this chapter, we present our initial attempt to do so, utilizing Paulhus and Martin's (1988) operationalization of the construct of functional flexibility.

Unbiased Processing

The second component of authenticity involves the unbiased processing of self-relevant information. This component involves objectivity with respect to one's positive and negative self-aspects, emotions, and other internal experiences, information, and private knowledge. In addition, it involves not denying, distorting, or exaggerating externally based evaluative information. In short, unbiased processing reflects the relative absence of interpretive distortions (e.g., defensiveness and self-aggrandizement) in the processing of self-relevant information. It follows, then, that variables conceptually related to authenticity would predict the relative absence of self-serving biases and illusions. In fact, research has demonstrated that dispositionally autonomous and self-determining individuals (whom we expect to be relatively high in authenticity) do not engage in self-serving biases following success or failure (Knee & Zuckerman, 1996).

Our characterization of the unbiased-processing component of authenticity is consistent with recent conceptualizations of ego-defense mechanisms. Interest in defense mechanisms has been bolstered by findings linking them to a wide range of important outcomes. For example, Vaillant's longitudinal research has revealed that adaptive defense mechanism styles involving minimal reality distortions predict psychological and physical well-being many years into the future (see, e.g., Vaillant, 1992). In contrast, maladaptive or immature defenses, involving considerable reality distortion and/or failure to acknowledge and resolve distressing emotions, predict psychological and interpersonal difficulties, including poor marital adjustment (Ungerer, Waters, Barnett, & Dolby, 1997).

Behavior

The third component of authenticity involves behaving in accord with one's values, preferences, and needs as opposed to acting "falsely" merely to please others or to attain rewards or avoid punishments. This component can be thought of as the behavioral output of the awareness and unbiased-processing components. We acknowledge that instances exist in which the unadulterated expression of one's true self may result in severe social sanctions. In such instances, we expect authenticity to reflect sensitivity to the fit (or lack thereof) between one's true self and the dictates of the environment, and a heightened awareness of the potential implications of one's behavioral choices. In contrast, blind obedience to environmental forces typically reflects the absence of authenticity (cf. Deci & Ryan, 2000). Importantly, authenticity is reflected not in a compulsion to be one's true self but rather in the free and natural expression of core feelings, motives, and inclinations. When this expression stands at odds with immediate environmental contingencies, we expect that authenticity will be reflected in short-term conflict. How this conflict is resolved can have considerable implications for one's felt integrity and authenticity. This line of reasoning implies that it is not sufficient to focus exclusively on whether authenticity is or is not reflected in one's actions per se. Instead, it is important to focus also on the manner in which processes associated with the other authenticity components inform one's behavioral selection. For example, when a person reacts to pressure by acting in accord with prevailing social norms that stand in contrast with his or her true self, authenticity may still be operating at the awareness and processing levels. Understanding how people resolve these sorts of conflicts is likely to provide important keys to their functioning and well-being. In any event, sometimes the needs and values of the self are incompatible with those of the larger society (e.g., when an artist focuses on a highly controversial subject matter). We believe that in these instances, authenticity may be reflected in awareness of one's needs and motives and an unbiased assessment of relevant evaluative information. Sometimes the resulting behavior may also reflect authenticity, but sometimes it may not (as when the aforementioned artist "sells out"). Consequently, although the awareness, unbiased processing, and behavior components of authenticity are related to each other, they clearly are separable. We return to this issue shortly.

Relational Orientation

The fourth component of authenticity is relational in nature, in that it involves valuing and striving for openness and truthfulness in one's close relationships. Relational authenticity involves endorsing the importance of close others seeing the "real" you and relating to them in ways that facilitate their being able to do so. Authentic relationships involve a reciprocal process of self-disclosure and the development of mutual intimacy and trust (Reis & Patrick, 1996). In essence, relational authenticity means being genuine rather than fake in one's relationships with close others. Overall, we expect that people high in relational authenticity would be involved in healthier and more satisfying relationships than people low in relational authenticity. Later in the chapter, we report data linking relational authenticity to more secure and less insecure attachment styles.

More on the Separateness of These Components

We view these multiple components of authenticity as related to, but separable from, each other. For instance, situations invariably exist in which environmental pressures may inhibit the expression of one's true self (e.g., a person may not express his true opinion to a close friend who is highly depressed). Although behavioral (and perhaps relational) authenticity may be thwarted in such instances, authenticity at the levels of awareness and unbiased processing may be operative. Specifically, awareness may involve active attempts to resolve conflicting motives and desires involved in knowing one's true opinion and the implications expressing it may have for one's friendship and the well-being of one's friend. Unbiased processing may involve acknowledgment of the fragile underpinnings of one's attitude. In contrast, inauthenticity may involve actively ignoring or denying one's opinion or emphasizing the superiority of one's judgmental abilities. In short, it is possible for a person to be operating authentically at some levels but not at others. Therefore, it is important to examine the processes associated with each component of authenticity (for a more extended discussion of this issue, see Kernis, 2003).

In fact, each of these aspects of authenticity has received some attention in the past, although not usually with explicit reference to the construct of authenticity. For example, aspects of the awareness component have been studied in research on public and private self-consciousness (e.g., Fenigstein, Scheier, & Buss, 1975). Some implications of biased processing of self-relevant information have been examined in research on self-serving biases (e.g., Blaine & Crocker, 1993). Aspects of behavioral authenticity have been examined in research on personality–behavior and attitude–behavior consistency (Koestner, Bernieri, & Zuckerman, 1992; Snyder, 1987). Finally, aspects of relational authenticity have been studied in research on attachment processes and self-disclosure (Mikiluncer & Shaver, in press). Readers of this chapter undoubtedly will recognize aspects of our theory in this prior work. Importantly, however, our theory has the capacity to integrate these various strands of research to explicate the processes associated with the construct of authenticity in a way not done before.

OPERATIONALIZING INDIVIDUAL COMPONENTS OF AUTHENTICITY

At the outset, we acknowledge the inherent difficulty in assessing individual differences in authenticity. One problem is that people are unlikely to admit to being inauthentic (Weinberger, 2003). Recognizing this, we do not ask them to directly do so ("To what extent do you think you are not authentic in your relationships with important others?"). Instead, we ask people to respond to questions reflecting the degree to which (a) they possess self-knowledge and their motivation to achieve it (awareness), (b) they have difficulty dealing with accurate or negative self-relevant information (unbiased processing), (c) their behavior reflects their own needs and desires (behavior), and (d) they value and engage in self-expression within their close relationships (relational orientation). Questions similar to these have previously been incorporated into a number of important self-report measures with great success, including the Self-Consciousness Scale (Fenigstein, Scheier, & Buss, 1975), and the Self-Monitoring Scale (Snyder, 1987). Therefore, we have every reason to believe that we can develop a self-report measure of authenticity that, although not perfect, will yield interesting and important findings. Of course, we will continually assess its psychometric properties. For example, we will examine whether the responses our participants give reflect response biases such as social desirability. Moreover, we plan to introduce behavioral and behavioroid measures to demonstrate the scale's validity, as one of the challenges will be to accumulate findings that cannot be interpreted as merely reflecting response biases and the like.

Recognizing the difficulties inherent in studying authenticity, we have to start somewhere if we are to examine this important phenomenon empirically. Toward that end, for the last several years we have worked on a self-report measure of authenticity (the Authenticity Inventory; AI) and have now completed several iterations of it. In addition, we have collected construct and predictive validity data by correlating this measure with a range of theoretically relevant variables. The first hypothesis we tested was that authenticity scores would relate positively to other general indices of psychological health, well-being, and life satisfaction. Demonstrating these links would provide support for the contention that, in general, authentic functioning is beneficial.

Authenticity, Psychological Health, and Well-Being

We developed the AI to measure each of the four components of authenticity. The first version of the inventory (AI Version 1; Goldman & Kernis, 2001) contained a 15-item awareness subscale ($\alpha = .74$); a 10-item unbiased processing subscale ($\alpha = .51$); a 13-item behavior subscale ($\alpha = .73$); and a 6-item relational orientation subscale ($\alpha = .32$). The total scale thus contained 44 items ($\alpha = .83$). Subsequent revisions of the scale have produced different subscale compositions and accompanying changes in their psychometric properties. We discuss these as warranted throughout the chapter. In Table 2.1 we present a brief description of each authenticity component and sample items from the latest version of the AI (Version 2) used in studies discussed in this chapter.

In our first empirical venture using the AI (Version 1; Goldman & Kernis, 2002) we examined the relations between authenticity and various aspects of psychological well-being. The aspects of well-being we included were self-esteem level, contingent self-esteem (feelings of self-worth that are dependent upon the achievement of specific outcomes or evaluations, a form of fragile self-esteem; Deci & Ryan, 1995; Kernis, 2003; Kernis & Paradise, 2002), daily positive and negative affect, and life satisfaction. We expected that greater authenticity would relate to more favorable psychological health and subjective well-being.

Seventy-nine male and female introductory psychology students participated in exchange for credit toward fulfillment of a course research requirement (other options for completing the requirement were available). Participants completed the following measures: (a) Rosenberg's (1965) Self-esteem Scale, a well-validated measure of global self-esteem level; (b) Contingent Self-esteem Scale (CSS; Kernis & Paradise, 2003), a 15-item scale that assesses the extent to which individuals' self-worth depends upon meeting expectations, matching standards, or achieving specific outcomes or evaluations; (c) Life Satisfaction (Diener, Emmons, Larsen,

TABLE 2.1. Authenticity Components and Sample Items

Authenticity component	Description	Sample items
Awareness	Awareness and knowledge of, and trust in, one's motives, feelings, desires, and self-relevant cognitions Includes awareness of one's strengths and weaknesses, dominant–recessive aspects of personality, powerful emotions, and their roles in behavior	I actively strive to understand who I truly am. I am generally aware of times when my needs and/or motives are in conflict with one another.
Unbiased processing	Minimal, if any, denial, distortion, exaggeration, or ignoring of private knowledge, internal experiences, and externally based self-evaluative information Objectivity and acceptance with respect to one's strengths and weaknesses	I generally am capable of objectively considering my limitations and shortcomings. I do not exaggerate my strengths to myself.
Behavior	Actions congruent with one's values, preferences, and needs Not acting merely to please others or to attain rewards or avoid punishments	I find that my behavior typically expresses my values. I frequently pretend to enjoy something when in actuality I really don't (reverse scored).
Relational orientation	Values and makes efforts to achieve openness and truthfulness in close relationships Important for close others to see "the real you," those deep, dark, or potentially shadowy self-aspects that are not routinely discussed Relational authenticity means being genuine and not "fake" in one's relationships with others	My openness and honesty in close relationships are extremely important to me. I want close others to understand the real me rather than the public persona or "image."

& Griffin, 1985), a 7-item measure that assesses how satisfied individuals feel about their lives in general over the past few days; and (d) Positive Affect/Negative Affect Scale (Brunstein, 1993), a 20-item measure that assesses experiences of positive and negative affect over a recent few days. We computed a net negative affect index for the last measure by summing positive affect scores and subtracting that sum from the sum of negative affect scores.

We computed zero-order correlations between each of the measures of well-being, total AI scores, and subscale AI scores. Importantly, total AI scores significantly related to each of the psychological well-being measures. Specifically, greater self-reported authenticity related to higher levels of self-esteem and life satisfaction and to less contingent self-esteem and net negative affect.

In terms of the individual subscales, the awareness subscale related to three of the four well-being measures. Specifically, greater self-reported awareness related to higher life satisfaction and self-esteem and to lower net negative affect. The unbiased-processing subscale related only to life satisfaction, such that greater unbiased processing related to greater life satisfaction. The behavior subscale related to two well-being measures; specifically, greater behavioral authenticity related to higher levels of self-esteem and to less contingent self-esteem. Finally, the relational orientation subscale related to two well-being measures; specifically, greater relational authenticity related to higher life satisfaction and to less net negative affect. We present the relevant correlations in Table 2.2.

The findings from this study offer initial support for our conceptualization and assessment of multiple components of authenticity. To reiterate, total authenticity scale scores positively related to self-esteem level and life satisfaction but negatively related to contingent self-esteem and net negative affect. Importantly, these findings suggest that authenticity is related to feelings of self-worth that not only are positive but that are more secure as well (i.e., less contingent on specific outcomes). Thus, authenticity correlates with markers of *optimal* self-esteem (i.e., high self-esteem that is not contingent; Kernis, 2003); we return to this issue in a later section. Our findings also indicated that greater self-reported authenticity related inversely to the frequency of experiencing unpleasant emotions (i.e., less net negative affect), as well as positively to more global appraisals of individuals' perceived life satisfaction. Taken as a whole, these findings provide initial empirical support for the contention that authenticity relates to healthy psychological functioning and positive subjective well-being.

Two additional findings stand out with respect to the psychometric properties of the scale (AI Version 1) itself—namely, the unacceptably low internal reliabilities obtained for the unbiased processing and relational orientation subscales. We are continuing to rectify these shortcomings through item revisions. In fact, in the next scale version (AI Version 2), items pertaining to relational orientation were rewritten so that they would explicitly refer to relationships with close others rather

TABLE 2.2. Zero-Order Correlations of Authenticity Inventory With Psychological Well-Being Measures

Psychological well-being measures	Total (composite)	Awareness	Unbiased processing	Behavior	Relational orientation
Life satisfaction	.40**	.43**	.23*	.15	.41**
Self-esteem	.33**	.28*	.15	.33**	.18
Contingent self-esteem	−.27*	−.16	−.17	−.31**	−.14
Net negative affect	−.31**	−.36**	−.17	−.05	−.36**

Note. Reprinted from Goldman and Kernis (2002) with permission.
*$p < .05$. **$p < .01$.

than to others in general. This change alone produced more than a 100% increase in the obtained alpha coefficient (α = .66). Item revisions to the unbiased-processing subscale yielded an alpha of .60. Although these values reflect substantial improvements, additional room for improvement remains.

In our next study (Goldman, Kernis, Piasecki, Herrmann, & Foster, 2003), we sought to flesh out the implications of authenticity for a variety of realms of psychological and social functioning. First, we focused on the relation between authenticity and global measures of psychological adjustment. Ryff (1989) presented a multifaceted conceptualization of psychological well-being that has six core components: *self-acceptance*, characterized by holding positive attitudes toward oneself; *positive relations with others*, characterized by the capacity for love, friendship, and identification with others; *autonomy*, characterized by qualities such as self-determination, independence, and regulation of behavior from within; *environmental mastery*, characterized by the ability to choose or create environments suitable to one's characteristics; *purpose in life*, characterized by beliefs that promote the sense that purpose and meaning to life do exist; and *personal growth*, characterized by continued development of one's potential and self-realization. Our findings indicated that scores on the awareness, behavioral, and relational orientation subscales correlated positively and significantly with scores on each of these subscales, with the lone exception of the correlation between behavioral authenticity and Ryff's self-acceptance subscale. In addition, scores on the unbiased-processing subscale correlated positively with autonomy and (marginally) with positive relations with others.

We also measured the hedonic aspects of psychological well-being—specifically, depressive symptoms (Center for Epidemiological Studies Depression Scale; Radloff, 1977), positive and negative affectivity, and general life satisfaction. Awareness correlated positively with positive affectivity and life satisfaction (as did relational orientation) and inversely with negative affectivity (as did behavior) and depression. In addition, we replicated and extended several findings from Goldman and Kernis (2002). For example, the awareness, behavioral, and relational orientation subscales correlated positively with self-esteem level, and all the authenticity subscales negatively correlated with contingent self-esteem, again implying that optimal self-esteem and authenticity are linked.

AUTHENTICITY AND HEALTHY INTERPERSONAL FUNCTIONING

To examine how authenticity relates to healthy interpersonal functioning, we (Goldman et al., 2003) also had participants complete the Bartholomew and Horowitz (1991) attachment measure consisting of 30 items that assess four distinct attachment styles: secure, fearful, dismissive, and preoccupied. Scores on the awareness and relational orientation subscales correlated positively with the secure attachment style and negatively with both the fearful (as did behavior) and preoccupied attachment styles but were unrelated to scores on the dismissive attachment subscale. Why no relationships emerged for the dismissive style is unclear.

However, the significant findings that did emerge clearly link overall authenticity and some of its components to healthy interpersonal functioning.

AUTHENTICITY, FUNCTIONAL FLEXIBILITY, AND MINDFULNESS

Paulhus and Martin's (1988) concept of *functional flexibility* is relevant to the construct of *figure–ground* in personality and its relation to authenticity. Specifically, functional flexibility involves having confidence in one's ability to call into play multiple, perhaps contradictory, self-aspects in dealing with life situations. One who is high in functional flexibility believes that he or she would experience little anxiety or difficulty in calling forth these multiple selves, not avoid situations requiring their enactment, and would feel very capable of calling upon these multiple selves, presumably because they are well-defined and can be enacted with confidence. These aspects of multiple selves can be thought of as constituting figure-ground aspects of personality because the "selves" under consideration are arranged around the interpersonal circumplex (Wiggins, 1979). In this circumplex model, 16 interpersonal trait characteristics are arrayed around two orthogonal dimensions (in this case, dominance and warmth). Examples of trait pairs include ambitious–lazy, warm–cold, dominant–submissive, agreeable–quarrelsome, extroverted–introverted, and arrogant–unassuming. For each item constituting the eight pairs, respondents indicate the extent to which "they are *capable* of being [insert trait] if the situation requires it," "it is *difficult* for them to behave in a [insert trait] manner," "how *anxious* they are when they behave in a [insert trait] manner," and "the extent to which they attempt to *avoid* situations that require them to behave in a [insert trait] manner." We created summary indexes of *capable*, *difficulty*, *anxiety*, and *avoidance* scores by summing responses to the 16 traits. The instructions, traits, and response stems for the functional flexibility task were taken from Paulhus and Martin (1988).

In contrast, *situationality* involves the belief that one is not very capable of calling forth well-defined multiple self-aspects; moreover, this belief is accompanied by the sense that one's behaviors are not self-initiated but rather are "pulled out" by situational contexts absent personal control or endorsement. In short, situationality involves one's social behaviors being buffeted around rather haphazardly according to prevailing social winds. Following Paulhus and Martin (1988), to assess *situationality*, we summed the number of *it depends on the situation* responses to the question "Indicate whether each adjective accurately or inaccurately describes you using the following alternatives (*it depends on the situation, accurate, inaccurate, average, don't know,* and *don't understand word*). In Paulhus and Martin's (1998) research, functional flexibility was tied to a high sense of agency and other indices of adaptive psychological functioning. In contrast, situationality was marked by self-doubt and other manifestations of psychological difficulties. Thus, if grounded in functional flexibility, possessing a multifaceted self is based in strong self-beliefs, self-confidence, self-acceptance, and agency.

Conversely, if grounded in situationality, possessing a multifaceted self is reflected in self-doubt, confusion, and conflict.

Kernis, Goldman, Piasecki, and Brunnell (2003) administered the Functional Flexibility Inventory (Paulhus & Martin, 1988) and the AI (Version 2) to a sample of 84 individuals. Total authenticity scale scores correlated positively with *capability*, and negatively with *difficulty, anxiety, avoidance*, and (marginally) *situationality* scores. The marginal relationship involving situationality may reflect a disconnect between its conceptualization and operationalization. Specifically, a number of assumptions have to be made to characterize a response of *it depends on the situation* as necessarily reflecting passive acceptance of situational dictates. Additional research is needed, therefore, to fully explicate the construct of situationality. Other data obtained by Goldman et al. (2003) indicate that total authenticity scores correlate negatively with self-monitoring (Snyder, 1987) and public self-consciousness (Fenigstein et al., 1975). In sum, although authenticity relates to greater capability and comfortableness enacting various interpersonal behaviors, it is not associated with heightened concern over one's public presentation or with behavioral plasticity reflective of heightened passive responsiveness to situational cues.

We (Kernis et al., 2003) also examined the relation between authenticity and mindfulness, which refers to a state of relaxed, nonevaluative awareness of one's immediate experience (Brown & Ryan, 2003). A number of studies have linked mindfulness with more positive immediate experiences (i.e., eating chocolate; LeBel & Dubé, 2001), as well as greater psychological health and well-being (Brown & Ryan, 2003). Recently, Brown and Ryan developed the Mindful Attention Awareness Scale to measure individual differences in mindfulness. In a series of studies, high mindfulness related to higher psychological well-being and positive affect and to lower stress. Sample items, endorsement of which reflects low mindfulness, include: "I could be experiencing some emotion and not be conscious of it until some time later;" "I do jobs or tasks automatically, without being aware of what I am doing"; "I find myself listening to someone with one ear, doing something else at the same time." The capacity for mindfulness is an aspect of being fully functioning, and we therefore expected that it would be associated with greater authenticity. We found that it correlated significantly with total authenticity scores, as well as scores on each of the subscales.

Two issues deserve comment at this point. The first issue concerns the nature of the "self" that is authentic. We believe that it is multifaceted and complex, ever-growing and developing, yet possessing a core that contains one's basic psychological needs (e.g., autonomy, competence, meaning, self-determination), personality characteristics, relational schemas, and values. This core, albeit open to change, usually changes slowly and over the passage of time. Certain events (e.g., traumatic events), however, may be potent enough to instigate more immediate changes in one's core self.

The second issue involves the relative value of accurate versus flattering self-relevant information and the dynamics associated with seeking each type of information. We believe, as many have before us (e.g., Deci & Ryan, 2000; Rogers, 1961), that people are oriented toward growing, developing, and increasing in complexity. Importantly, we believe that these processes are inherently geared toward obtaining accurate, not necessarily flattering, information (we discuss this in some detail shortly). An assumption underlying this perspective is that people often seek out self-relevant information when they are feeling good about themselves and confident in their capabilities. Precisely because of their inner strength, they are able to cope with and integrate into their "selves" potentially unflattering information. Of course, people also seek out self-knowledge when they are unsure about themselves and insecure about their abilities. Under these circumstances, we would expect people to shy away from accurate, negative information, and instead focus their efforts on positive, flattering information, even if it is not completely accurate. In essence, we believe that positive self-illusions generally are less healthy than are accurate self-realities (in contrast to Taylor & Brown, 1988), even though the former may confer short-term benefits by helping individuals cope with unpleasant emotions (Crocker, 2002). In the long run, possessing and portraying accurate self-knowledge is more beneficial than is possessing and portraying positive but false self-knowledge (e.g., Crocker, 2002; Robins & Beer, 2001). We consider this issue again the section on costs and benefits associated with unbiased processing.

BENEFITS, COSTS, AND BARRIERS ASSOCIATED WITH EACH AUTHENTICITY COMPONENT

As noted at the beginning of the chapter, ambivalence over the benefits of authenticity exists. We believe that this is the case because authentic functioning is not always easy and it sometimes has costs that are consequential. The research reviewed so far empirically documents some of the benefits associated with authenticity. In this section, we focus on a conceptual explication of the benefits and costs associated with each authenticity component.

Awareness

A high awareness score signifies interest in, and knowledge of, one's internal states, including self-relevant cognition, affect, motives, goals, and so forth. As much literature on self-schemas has shown, these internalized structures, often activated as aspects of the *working self-concept* (Markus & Kunda, 1986), provide individuals with vital information that informs behavioral choices and reactions to evaluative information. Information in the form of *possible selves* (Markus & Nurius, 1986) provides temporally extended blueprints for goal-directed action. For example, individuals with the possible self of *academic* are likely to plan their activities around such things as working with a mentor, conducting research, taking classes, reading relevant material, and writing manuscripts for publication. In addition, quality of performance in these domains is likely to be of greater importance to these individuals than to individuals who have the possible self of landscaper or beautician. In essence, being in touch with oneself provides a wealth of information that helps individuals navigate through the many trials and tribulations associated with everyday life and with development.

What are the potential costs of such self-knowledge? First, it is the case that certain forms of self-knowledge may be painful. Knowing, for example, that one is not very socially skilled may be aversive for individuals who are at an age or in a context in which it is important for them to develop close interpersonal relationships. Second, experiencing powerful emotions per se may be unsettling and even threatening, particularly if they reflect unresolved conflict or if one is not well-versed in display rules. Third, the very act of self-reflection may activate unpleasant affect, depending upon the form it takes (Campbell et al., 1996). Fourth, possessing a multifaceted self-concept that affords awareness of a diverse set of possible selves may itself promote role strain (Thoits, 1986).

One of the premises underlying our conceptualization is that awareness of self is one component of healthy functioning. Awareness is really just a first step, however. Also important is that this awareness fosters self-integration and acceptance of self. An important issue, therefore, is how individuals attain self-knowledge in ways that foster integration and acceptance of self. A number of techniques are available, some of which stem from the Gestalt therapy framework developed by Perls, Hefferline, and Goodman (1951). These techniques emphasize deliberately attending to aspects of self without evaluating their implications. A similar principle underlies the use of techniques or strategies designed to enhance individuals' mindfulness. Through these exercises, people can become aware of currently ignored or unexamined self-aspects with which they often are uncomfortable. Other techniques then can be applied to understand and resolve the basis of the uncomfortableness, thereby fostering self-integration and acceptance.

At many steps along the way toward authenticity, however, obstructions may exist (Kernis, 2003). For instance, blockages may occur in the awareness component, as people may not be attuned to their motives, feelings, and self-relevant cognitions. People low in private self-consciousness (i.e., low in chronic tendencies to focus on one's internal states and other internal self-aspects; Fenigstein, Scheier, & Buss, 1975) may be particularly susceptible to this type of blockage, as may repressors and people with low implicit self-esteem. As these variables suggest, low awareness may reflect a skills deficit (i.e., people low in private self-consciousness may not possess the skills needed to self-reflect in a nonruminative manner), or it may reflect self-protective motivational processes (i.e., repressors or people low in conscious or nonconscious self-esteem may be motivated to avoid what they anticipate will be aversive self-reflection).

Unbiased Processing

Although related to the awareness component, the unbiased-processing component is more likely to involve the processing of new self-relevant information. This information is evaluative in nature, and it may pertain to performance outcomes, interpersonal interactions or feedback, or self-assessments of one's traits and characteristics. As much research has shown, many people are prone to selectively seek out or distort information so that it only reflects positively on the self and close others. For example, people routinely overemphasize their importance in social interactions and group products (Zuckerman, Kernis, Guarnera, Murphy,

& Rapaport, 1983), inflate their contributions to positive outcomes, and minimize their contributions to negative outcomes (Zuckerman, 1979).

Currently, a controversy exists over whether these illusions contribute to healthy psychological functioning (Robins & Beer, 2001; Taylor & Brown, 1988). It is beyond the scope of this chapter to address this controversy fully. However, we do want to note that we believe that often these distortions stem from insecurity rather then strength (Kernis, 2000). In support of this contention, research has shown that people who are highly autonomous and self-determining do not show such self-serving distortions (Knee & Zuckerman, 1996). In contrast, and as noted earlier, people who rely on defense mechanisms that involve major distortions of reality have relatively poor interpersonal and psychological outcomes throughout their lifetimes (Vaillant, 1992). As Crocker (2002) and others (e.g., Kernis, 2003; Robins & Beer, 2001) have argued, self-illusions may minimize negative affectivity in the short run and therefore may seem to be adaptive. However, this adaptiveness is itself an illusion, as it does not hold up over time and, in fact, may contribute to poorer outcomes in the end (as shown in Robins & Beer, 2001).

The major benefit of unbiased processing is that it contributes to an accurate sense of self. As we discussed earlier, this accuracy can then be utilized in behavioral choices that have either short- or long-term implications. Accuracy is valued the more one's outcomes depend upon it. Picking the right occupation, investing one's time in developing one's talents, and even asking another out on a date all benefit from accurate or unbiased processing of evaluative information. Conversely, engaging in biased processing may unwittingly limit one's options, as important self-knowledge may be ignored or distorted. As was the case for awareness, blockages to unbiased processing exist as well. These blockages may also reflect either skill deficits or motivational propensities. With respect to skills, people may not have the requisite defense mechanisms in their psychological repertoire. Motivationally, these blockages may be fueled by their short-term payoffs, such as minimizing unpleasant affect (Crocker, 2002). Simultaneously, however, they may close people off to opportunities to grow and develop in ways that will have long-term payoffs (Crocker, 2002). People who possess fragile self-esteem (defensive, contingent, or unstable self-esteem) may be particularly susceptible to a blockage of this authenticity component (Kernis, 2003).

Behavior

Behaving authentically often takes courage because one's true proclivities may be in conflict with prevailing environmental dictates. This is most likely to be the case in environmental settings or with people who have strong evaluative or controlling tendencies (Deci & Ryan, 1995). As a good deal of research shows, behaving in ways that are at odds with one's true self merely to satisfy controlling pressures often has deleterious effects (Deci & Ryan, 2000; Neighbors, Larimer, Geisner, & Knee, 2004). In contrast, behaving in ways that are authentic and self-determining promotes positive affect, well-being, and adjustment (Deci & Ryan, 2000).

Assessing the costs and benefits of behavioral authenticity is complex. Adding to this complexity is the fact that when people conform to environmental contingencies they are not always behaving in ways that conflict with their true selves. People can, and often do, internalize social contingencies, such that they freely adopt them as self-guides (Ryan & Connell, 1989). In such cases, conflict is minimal or absent and people function authentically.

When people do not behave authentically, distinguishing behavioral authenticity from awareness and unbiased processing takes on greater importance. That is, a person's experience of not behaving authentically is likely to be very different depending on whether authenticity is operative at the other levels. Blind obedience to environmental dictates does not stimulate personal growth; instead, it often stifles it. In contrast, internal conflict among the authenticity components can provide a real impetus for reflection and development. In short, authenticity at the awareness and unbiased-processing levels can promote growth and deepen one's self-knowledge even when authentic behavior is inhibited.

Blockages to behavioral authenticity include variables that are associated with heightened sensitivity to the interpersonal implications of one's behaviors. Some blockages may reflect motivational processes (e.g., contingent and unstable self-esteem, fragile forms of self-esteem), whereas others may reflect the absence of skills (e.g., lack of assertiveness skills). Still others may reflect a particular culturally based value orientation (e.g., the view that disagreements are construed as rudeness can undermine integrity) or personality processes with genetic underpinnings (e.g., self-monitoring; Snyder, 1987).

Relational Orientation

Relational authenticity can provide the foundation for deep, intimate, and fulfilling social interactions and relationships. Consistent with this assertion, earlier we reported findings indicating that authenticity relates positively to secure attachment styles and negatively to insecure attachment styles (fearful and preoccupied, but not dismissive; Goldman et al., 2003). People who are high on relational authenticity want their intimates to know them deeply, and they place a premium on being genuine and not fake in their close relationships. Healthy personal relationships are a very strong predictor of happiness (Diener & Diener, 1995), and this is true across cultures. Thus, the benefits of relational authenticity are difficult to ignore. Conversely, the potential costs of confrontations over relational authenticity are many, including self- and partner defensiveness, overreactivity, and lack of intimacy. In turn, these costs contribute to shallow, unsatisfying relationships that are prone to dissolve over time or be continually fraught with problems and challenges (Kernis, Goldman, & Paradise, 2003).

One of the hallmarks of relational authenticity is the desire for partners to see one for "who one really is, warts and all." This desire to be "transparent" makes one potentially vulnerable if one's partner is not in harmony. Relational authenticity thus has some risks, because rather than sweeping differences under the rug, the relationally authentic person seeks to bring differences out into the open so that they can be resolved. For relational authenticity to bring about positive outcomes reliably, one's partner must also be invested in relational authenticity. If not, conflicts may remain unresolved and potentially fester, serving to undermine relationship quality and eventually bring about the relationship's destruction. Thus, relational authenticity also has its costs. As before, blockages to authenticity may occur at the relational stage, perhaps related to such motivational factors as low or fragile self-esteem, fear of rejection (Downey, Freitas, Michaelis, & Khouri, 1998), or high public self-consciousness (Fenigstein et al., 1975) or to a skills deficit such as poor interpersonal skills.

Summary

Authenticity is not without potential costs. Accurate self-knowledge may be painful; acting in accord with one's true self may meet with disfavor; and opening oneself to an intimate may provide the grist for disappointment, scorn, or betrayal. These and other adverse consequences that sometimes are associated with authenticity are likely to undermine individuals' *hedonistic*, or subjective, well-being. In other words, authenticity may not always be pleasurable. Importantly, however, the benefits of authentic functioning to individuals' *eudaemonistic* well-being (i.e., the extent to which they are fully functioning; Ryan & Deci, 2000) are generally sufficient to offset these (often temporary) emotional setbacks. When functioning authentically, people are likely to think, feel, and behave in ways that promote the fulfillment of their needs and the degree to which they are fully functioning (Deci & Ryan, 2000; Rogers, 1961). These considerations suggest that people sometimes are faced with choosing between experiencing pleasure (or avoiding displeasure) and maximizing the extent to which they are fully functioning. How they resolve this dilemma has enormous implications, both short- and long-term.

AUTHENTICITY AND SELF-ESTEEM

The extent to which people function authentically has considerable implications for their self-esteem, and vice versa. Although research has shown that low self-esteem relates to low authenticity (Goldman & Kernis, 2002; Goldman et al., 2003), we believe that authenticity and high self-esteem are also related in interesting ways. Does high self-esteem invariably relate to greater overall authenticity, or to the individual components of awareness, unbiased processing, behavior, or relational orientation? In this regard, we revisit some relevant findings that we reported earlier. At the outset, however, we want to emphasize that we see the question as far more complex than "Is high self-esteem associated with greater authenticity than low self-esteem?" The reason for this complexity is that high self-esteem has multiple forms, some more closely related to psychological health and well-being (especially eudaemonistic) than are others (Kernis, 2003; Paradise & Kernis, 2002). Consequently, we believe that authenticity will relate more strongly to some forms of high self-esteem than to others.

Some forms of high self-esteem reflect *secure* high self-esteem, whereas other forms reflect *fragile* high self-esteem (Kernis, 2003). Specifically, *secure* high self-esteem involves the following:

- Feeling worthwhile and valuable
- Liking and being satisfied with oneself
- Accepting weaknesses
- Being built upon a solid foundation
- Not requiring continual validation or promotion

In contrast, *fragile* high self-esteem involves the following:

- Feeling very proud and superior to others
- Not liking to see weaknesses in oneself, or for others to see them
- Having exaggerated tendencies to defend against possible threats to self-worth
- Having a strong tendency to engage in self-promoting activities

Existing theory and literature provide four ways to distinguish between secure and fragile forms of high self-esteem. We list the markers reflecting these distinctions in Table 2.3.

Each of these forms has been discussed extensively elsewhere, along with supporting evidence (Kernis, 2003; Kernis & Paradise, 2002), so we only briefly discuss them here. *Unstable* (fragile) self-esteem reflects substantial short-term fluctuations in contextually based immediate feelings of self-worth, whereas *stable* (secure) self-esteem reflects minimal short-term fluctuations. *Contingent* (fragile) self-esteem is dependent upon achieving specific outcomes, meeting expectations, matching standards, and so forth, whereas *true* (secure) self-esteem is secure self-worth that arises naturally from satisfaction of basic psychological needs and is not in need of continual validation. A match between individual's *implicit* (nonconscious) and *explicit* (conscious) positive feelings of self-worth reflects secure high self-esteem. In contrast, a mismatch between individual's implicit (nonconscious) and explicit (conscious) feelings of self-worth (i.e., one is negative) reflects fragile high self-esteem. Finally, *defensive* (fragile) high self-esteem involves reporting high self-esteem but harboring negative feelings, to which a person is

TABLE 2.3. Markers of Secure and Fragile High Self-Esteem

Fragile High	Secure High
Unstable	Stable
Contingent	True
Low implicit	High implicit
Defensive	Genuine

Note. Kernis (2003).

unwilling to admit. In contrast, *genuine* (secure) high self-esteem involves the accurate reporting of inwardly held positive self-feelings.

Optimal self-esteem reflects the sum total of these secure self-esteem markers (Kernis, 2003). It arises naturally from (a) success in dealing with life challenges; (b) the operation of one's core, true, authentic self as a source of input to behavioral choices; and (c) relationships in which one is valued for whom one is, and not for what one achieves. We believe that authenticity and each aspect of secure (vs. fragile) high self-esteem likely are reciprocally related to each other. That is, authenticity may provide both the foundation for achieving secure (and ultimately optimal) high self-esteem and the processes through which secure (and optimal) high self-esteem relates to psychological and interpersonal adjustment. Recall that *self-esteem* refers to global feelings of self-worth and acceptance, whereas *authenticity* refers to the operation of one's true self in one's daily enterprise. Thus, self-esteem and authenticity are likely to feed off each other in ways that can either strengthen or weaken them. When breakdowns in authenticity occur, they are likely to reverberate through the self system and cause decreased or more fragile self-esteem. Conversely, possessing fragile self-esteem may undermine or interfere with various processes associated with authenticity. For example, to ease the sting associated with failure, people with fragile self-esteem may be more likely to engage in biased than unbiased processing or to modify their behavior merely to please a potential evaluator. Recall also that in two separate studies (Goldman & Kernis, 2002; Goldman et al., 2003), we found positive correlations between authenticity and self-esteem level and negative correlations between authenticity and contingent self-esteem. Taken together, these two correlations indicate that authenticity is more strongly related to secure than to fragile high self-esteem (based on the marker of contingent self-esteem). A number of other relations are likely to exist between authenticity and self-esteem processes. An important agenda for the future is to examine these relations.

An additional type of evidence (albeit indirect) supporting the link between authenticity and optimal self-esteem is research that has shown authenticity to be related to engaging in goal pursuits that provide opportunities for (a) self-determination, (b) expression of one's true self, (c) positive self-feelings, and (d) competence. In our view, engaging in goal pursuits that provide these opportunities provides the psychological nourishment that promotes the development of optimal self-esteem.

We (Goldman et al., 2003) examined how authenticity relates to the meanings people ascribe to their personal projects, defined as the "activities and concerns that people have in their lives." Respondents were given time to generate a list of personal projects that they were engaging in or intended to begin over the next month or so. Next, participants selected the eight projects that "together provide the most complete and informative overview of your life" and rated each on a total of 31 characteristics or dimensions. We took many of these dimensions from McGregor and Little (1998) and generated a few specifically for this study. Multiple items tapping into the same meaning dimension were combined to form categories that were deemed relevant to authenticity and optimal self-esteem. We now name these categories and provide sample items:

- *Opportunities for positive self-feelings (three items):* To what extent do you feel that being engaged in this project contributes to your sense of self-worth? How important or significant does this project make you feel when engaged in it?
- *Efficacy (six items):* How competent are you to complete this project? How much do you feel that you are in control of this project?
- *Fun–enjoyment (three items):* Some projects are intrinsically fun, whimsical, or delightful. How much fun is this project for you?
- *Commitment (two items):* How committed are you to the completion of this project? How important is this project to you at the present time?
- *Goal authenticity (four items):* Most of us have some projects that are "really us" and some others that we don't really feel "ourselves" when doing. To what extent does this project reflect who you really are? How much do you feel that it was your decision to take on this project?
- *Absorption (one item):* To what extent do you become engrossed or deeply involved in this project?

As noted earlier, we anticipated that participants high in authenticity would engage in projects where they felt competent and autonomous and that contributed to their sense of self-worth. The findings that emerged are reported in detail elsewhere (Goldman et al., 2003), so we focus here only on relations involving the awareness subscale. The sample consisted of 111 undergraduate students. First, scores on the awareness subscale correlated positively with goal authenticity ($r = .23, p < .02$). Thus, the higher individuals' awareness scores, the more individuals characterized their goal pursuits in terms of a composite consisting of reflecting their true selves, autonomy, personal meaning, and consistency with broad values. Second, awareness subscale scores correlated, though not significantly, with a higher amount of striving commitment ($r = .17, p < .08$). Third, awareness scores correlated positively with efficacy ($r = .27, p < .01$). Fourth, the higher individuals' awareness scores, the higher their goals' self-worth benefit to them ($r = .21, p < .05$). Finally, higher awareness scores related to higher ratings of project fun ($r = .20, p < .04$) and absorption ($r = .20, p < .04$). Taken as a whole, these correlations support the view that how individuals' construe their goal pursuits provides a way to link processes associated with authenticity with those associated with optimal self-esteem.

SUMMARY AND CONCLUDING COMMENTS

In this chapter, we presented a multicomponent conceptualization of authenticity. In our view, authenticity involves an awareness of one's self; unbiased processing of self-relevant information; behaving in accord with one's core values, inclinations, needs, and so forth; and relating to close others in genuine, trustworthy, and honest ways. On average, we expect that each authenticity component will be associated with a range of positive outcomes, both intrapersonal and interpersonal. At the same time, we acknowledge that authenticity often comes at a cost. Fortunately, these costs are not so powerful that they inevitably dampen people's investments in becoming more authentic. Moreover, as more people work to enhance their authenticity, many of these costs will diminish even further.

NOTE

1. Participants also made ratings for the adjectives used by Sande, Goethals, and Radloff (1988) in their investigation of self-concept complexity. The values reported here incorporate these ratings as well.

REFERENCES

Bartholomew, K., & Horowitz, L. (1991). Attachment styles among young adults: A test of a four-category model. *Journal of Personality and Social Psychology, 61,* 226–244.

Brown, K. W. & Ryan, R. M. (2003). The benefits of being present: Mindfulness and its role in psychological well-being. *Journal of Personality and Social Psychology, 84,* 922–848.

Brunstein, J. (1993). Personal goals and subjective well-being: A longitudinal study. *Journal of Personality and Social Psychology, 65,* 1061–1070.

Campbell, J. D. (1990). Self-esteem and clarity of the self-concept. *Journal of Personality and Social Psychology, 59,* 538–549.

Campbell, J. D., Trapnell, P. D., Heine, S. J., Katz, I. M., Lavallee, L. F., & Lehman, D. R. (1996). Self-concept clarity: Measurement, personality correlates, and cultural boundaries. *Journal of Personality and Social Psychology, 70,* 141–156.

Crocker, J. (2002). Contingencies of self-worth: Implications for self-regulation and psychological vulnerability. *Journal of Self and Identity, 1,* 143–149.

Deci, E. L., & Ryan, R. M. (1995). Human agency: The basis for true self-esteem. In M. H. Kernis (Ed.), *Efficacy, agency, and self-esteem* (pp. 31–50). New York: Plenum Press.

Deci, E. L., & Ryan, R. M. (2000). The "what" and "why" of goal pursuits: Human needs and the self-determination of behavior. *Psychology Inquiry, 11,* 227–269.

Diener, E., & Diener, M. (1995). Cross-cultural correlates of life satisfaction. *Journal of Personality and Social Psychology, 68,* 653–663.

Diener, E., Emmons, R., Larsen, R., & Griffin, S. (1985) The Satisfaction With Life scale. *Journal of Personality and Social Psychology, 49,* 71–75.

Downey, G., Freitas, A. L., Michaelis, B., & Khouri, H. (1998). The self-fulfilling prophecy in close relationships: Rejection sensitivity and rejection by close partners. *Journal of Personality and Social Psychology, 75,* 545–560.

Fenigstein, A., Scheier, M. G., & Buss, A. H. (1975). Public and private self-consciousness: Assessment and theory. *Journal of Consulting and Clinical Psychology, 43,* 522–528.

Goldman, B. M., & Kernis, M. H. (2001). *Development of the Authenticity Inventory.* Unpublished manuscript, University of Georgia, Athens.

Goldman, B. M., & Kernis, M. H. (2002). The role of authenticity in healthy psychological functioning and subjective well-being. *Annals of the American Psychotherapy Association, 5*, 18–20.

Goldman, B. M., Kernis, M. H., Piasecki, R., Herrmann, A., & Foster, J. (2003). *Multiple conceptualizations of authenticity and their relations to various aspects of psychological functioning and well-being.* Manuscript submitted for publication.

Kernis, M. H. (2000). Substitute needs and fragile self-esteem. Invited commentary of Deci & Ryan's target article. *Psychological Inquiry, 11*, 227–268.

Kernis, M. H. (2003). Toward a conceptualization of optimal self-esteem. *Psychological Inquiry, 14*, 1–26.

Kernis, M. H., & Goldman, B. M. (in press). Authenticity, social motivation, and well-being. In J. Forgas, K. Williams, & W. von Hippel (Eds.), *Social motivation: Conscious and unconscious processes.* New York: Cambridge University Press.

Kernis, M. H., Goldman, B. M., & Paradise, A. N. (2003). *Fragile self-esteem, overreactivity and satisfaction in close relationships.* Manuscript in preparation.

Kernis, M. H., Goldman, B. M., Piasecki, R., & Brunnell, A. (2003). *Authenticity, functional flexibility, and mindfulness.* Manuscript in preparation.

Kernis, M. H., & Paradise, A. W. (2002). Distinguishing between secure and fragile forms of high self-esteem. *In* E.L. Deci & R. M. Ryan (Eds.), *Handbook of self-determination research* (pp. 330–360). Rochester, NY: University of Rochester Press.

Kernis, M. H., & Paradise, A. W. (2003). *Contingent self-esteem: Scale development and relation to anger arousal.* Manuscript in preparation.

Kernis, M. H., Whitaker, D., & Davies, B. (1997). *Laypeople's perceptions of the mutual exclusivity of trait characteristics.* Unpublished manuscript, University of Georgia, Athens.

Knee, C. R., & Zuckerman, M. (1996). Causality orientations and the disappearance of the self-serving bias. *Journal of Research in Personality, 30*, 76–87.

Koestner, R., Bernieri, F., & Zuckerman, M. (1992). Self-regulation and consistency between attitudes, traits, and behaviors. *Personality and Social Psychology Bulletin, 18*, 52–59.

LeBel, J. L., & Dubé, L. (2001, June). *The impact of sensory knowledge and attentional focus on pleasure and on behavioral responses to hedonic stimuli.* Paper presented at the meeting of the American Psychological Society, Toronto, Ontario, Canada.

Markus, H., & Kunda, Z. (1986). Stability and malleability of the self-concept. *Journal of Personality and Social Psychology, 51*, 858–866.

Markus, H., & Nurius, P. (1986). Possible selves. *American Psychologist, 41*, 954–969.

McGregor, I., & Little, B. R. (1998). Personal projects, happiness, and meaning: On doing well and being yourself. *Journal of Personality and Social Psychology, 74*, 494–512.

Mikiluncer, M., & Shaver, P. (in press). Mental representations of attachment security: Theoretical foundation for a positive social psychology. In M. W. Baldwin (Ed.), *Interpersonal cognition.* New York: Guilford Press.

Neighbors, C., Larimer, M. E., Geisner, I. M., & Knee, C. R. (2004). Self-determination, contingent self-esteem, and drinking motives among college students. *Self and Identity, 3*, 207–224.

Paradise, A., & Kernis, M. H. (2002). Fragile self-esteem and its implications for psychological well-being. *Journal of Social and Clinical Psychology, 12*, 345–361.

Paulhus, D. L., & Martin, C. L. (1988). Functional flexibility: A new conceptualization of interpersonal flexibility. *Journal of Personality and Social Psychology, 55*, 88–101.

Perls, F., Hefferline, R. F., & Goodman, P. (1965). *Gestalt therapy.* New York: Dell Press. (Original work published 1951)

Radloff, L. S. (1977). The CES-D Scale: A self-report depression scale for research in the general population. *Applied Psychological Measurement, 1,* 385–401.

Reis, H. T., & Patrick, B. C. (1996). Attachment and intimacy: Component processes. In E. T. Higgins & A. W. Kruglanski (Eds.), *Social psychology: Handbook of basic principles* (pp. 523–563). New York: Guilford Press.

Robins, R. W., & Beer, J. S. (2001). Positive illusions about the self: Short-term benefits and long-term costs. *Journal of Personality and Social Psychology, 80,* 340–352.

Rogers, C. R. (1961). *On becoming a person: A therapist's view of psychotherapy.* Boston: Houghton Mifflin.

Rosenberg, M. (1965). *Society and the adolescent self-image.* Princeton, NJ: Princeton University Press.

Ryan, R. M., & Connell, J. P. (1989). Perceived locus of causality and internalization: Examining reasons for acting in two domains. *Journal of Personality and Social Psychology, 57,* 749–761.

Ryan, R. M., & Deci, E. L. (2002). An overview of self-determination theory: An organismic-dialectical perspective. In E. L. Deci & R. M. Ryan (Eds.), *Handbook of self-determination research* (pp. 3–36). Rochester, NY: University of Rochester Press.

Ryff, C. (1989). Happiness is everything, or is it? Explorations on the meaning of psychological well-being. *Journal of Personality and Social Psychology, 57,* 1069–1081.

Sande, G. N., Goethals, G. R., & Radloff, C. E. (1988). Perceiving one's own traits and others': The multifaceted self. *Journal of Personality and Social Psychology, 54,* 13–20.

Schlenker, B. R. (2002). Self-presentation. In M. Leary & J. Tangney (Eds.,), *Handbook of self and identity* (pp. 492–518). New York: Guilford Press.

Snyder, M. (1987). *Public appearances/private realities: The psychology of self-monitoring.* New York: Freeman.

Taylor, S. E., & Brown, J. D. (1988). Illusion and well-being: A social psychological perspective on mental health. *Psychological Bulletin, 103,* 193–210.

Thoits, P. A. (1986). Multiple identities: Examining gender and marital status differences in distress. *American Sociological Review, 51,* 259–272.

Ungerer, J. A., Waters, B., Barnett, B., & Dolby, R. (1997). Defense style and adjustment in interpersonal relationships. *Journal of Research in Personality, 31,* 375–385.

Vaillant, G. (1992). *Ego mechanisms of defense: A guide for clinicians and researchers.* Washington, DC: American Psychiatric Press.

Weinberger, J. (2003). Genuine, defensive, unconscious, and authentic: How do they all fit together? *Psychological Inquiry, 14,* 80–82.

Wiggins, J. S. (1979). A psychological taxonomy of trait-descriptive terms: The interpersonal domain. *Journal of Personality and Social Psychology, 37,* 395–412.

Zuckerman, M. (1979). Attribution of success and failure revisited, or: The motivational bias is alive and well in attribution theory. *Journal of Personality, 47,* 245–287.

Zuckerman, M., Kernis, M. H., Guarnera, S., Murphy, J., & Rapaport, L. (1983). The egocentric bias: Seeing oneself as cause and target of others' behavior. *Journal of Personality, 51,* 621–630.

$$3$$

Transportation Into Narrative Worlds: Implications for the Self

MELANIE C. GREEN

Most people have had the sensation of being "lost in a book" (Nell, 1988), swept up into the world of a story so completely that they forget the world around them. A reader nearing the end of the latest John Grisham thriller may be oblivious to the hustle and bustle of the crowded airport terminal around him; a child swept away by Harry Potter's adventures at Hogwarts may be constantly thinking about the magical world described there. Narratives may provide more than a temporary diversion from reality, however. Educators have long recognized that powerful stories can change the way we think about the world and even about ourselves. For instance, at Harvard Medical School, physician training includes a course in which students read selected fictional works (stories, novels). The goal of the course is not to deliver medical knowledge, but rather to produce graduate physicians whose treatment of patients will be caring and humane (Coles, 1987).

Becoming engaged in a story involves deep, yet subjectively effortless, concentration. Transported readers see the action of the story unfolding before them. They react emotionally to events that are described simply by words on a page or images on a screen. Their thinking is focused on the narrative. This phenomenological experience of being absorbed in a story—a process I call *transportation into a narrative world*—is a key mechanism underlying narrative impact. Transportation resembles flow, or optimal experience (e.g., Csikszentmihalyi, 1990). Indeed, individuals appear to seek out transportation experiences on a regular basis; book publishing and movie production are multimillion-dollar industries.

This chapter describes the concept of transportation into narrative worlds and briefly summarizes previous transportation research. I then explore four ways in which transportation into narrative worlds may be related to the self. First, I discuss the implications of transportation for construction of or change in the self, including the ways that transportation may create openness to change, and the active participation of readers in constructing the self. Second, I describe the interplay among emotions, transportation, and the self. Third, I explore relationships between transportation and the executive function of the self. Finally,

I consider the influences of the self on becoming transported. The chapter closes with a discussion of two future directions: transportation into personal narratives and the effects of interactive narratives on the self.

THE NATURE OF TRANSPORTATION INTO NARRATIVE WORLDS

A transported individual is cognitively and emotionally involved in the story and may experience vivid mental images (Green & Brock, 2000, 2002). Transportation can be measured with a 15-item paper and pencil scale that taps cognitive, affective, and imagery involvement (Green & Brock, 2000). Example items on the transportation scale include "While I was reading the narrative, I could easily picture the events in it taking place"; "I was emotionally involved in the narrative"; and the reverse-scored item, "I found my mind wandering while reading the narrative." Previous research showed that transportation can also be manipulated by varying the instruction sets given to readers. For example, instructions that tell readers to focus on surface aspects of a narrative such as grammar and sentence structure can reduce transportation relative to baseline (Green & Brock, 2000). (Manipulations that reliably increase transportation, without altering the target narratives, have proved more elusive.)

Like a literal traveler, individuals who are immersed in a story may lose access to aspects of the real world and can return changed by their experience (Gerrig, 1993). Specifically, narratives can lead to changes in how the individual views the real world (Prentice, Gerrig, & Bailis, 1997; Wheeler, Green, & Brock, 1999). Studies have shown that highly transported individuals report more story-consistent beliefs on both story-specific and general dependent measures (Green & Brock, 2000). For example, readers of a crime story think that crime is more likely and that the world is a less just place; similarly, readers of an uplifting tale about loyalty between a boy and his dog show more positive views about canines.

Mechanisms of Story Influence

There are at least three possible means by which transportation is likely to affect readers. First, transportation is associated with increased positivity toward sympathetic characters (Green & Brock, 2000). If an individual likes or identifies with a particular character, the events experienced by the character or assertions made by the character may carry special weight in shifting a reader's beliefs. Next, transportation leads to a reduction in negative cognitive responding, or counter-arguing of story assertions (Green & Brock, 2000). Transportation may reduce individuals' ability to counterargue story assertions because the reader's mental capacity is devoted to imaging story events. It may also reduce individuals' motivation to counterargue because interrupting the narrative flow to dispute the author's claims or descriptions would likely destroy the pleasure of the experience. If individuals are not refuting claims made in a narrative or disputing the realism of the narrative situations, the story events may become integrated into real-world belief structures. Finally, transportation may also make narrative experience seem more like real experience (Green, 2004). Direct experience with attitude objects is a powerful predictor of attitudes (see Fazio & Zanna, 1981, for a review). If the story seems more like an actual event, the plausibility and impact of the story are increased.

The Narrative as a Fundamental Mode of Thinking

Psychologists and literary critics have proposed different definitions of what constitutes a narrative, but common themes include episodes where some development occurs, or in which a protagonist moves toward a goal (e.g., Mandler, 1984). In other words, some change occurs from the beginning of the story to the end. Furthermore, stories often allow people to go beyond the information given and assess reasonable outcomes given the causal structure presented in the story.

Gaining information from narratives seems to be a fundamental process. Schank and Abelson (1995) made the strong claim that all knowledge is stories. While many are skeptical of the strong form of that hypothesis, the power of the narrative form has been demonstrated in the judgement and decision-making literature with Pennington and Hastie's (1988) story model of jury decision making, as well as in the consumer psychology literature (e.g., Adval & Wyer, 1998; Deighton, Romer, & McQueen, 1989). There is some developmental support for a weaker version of the claim that narratives are a basic cognitive structure; Mancuso (1986) reviewed evidence suggesting that people in most cultures have an internalized narrative grammar, or understanding of story structure, by age 3.

Responding to Narratives

Individuals not only easily recognize stories and think in terms of stories, they also tend to react to story characters and events as if they were real. Narratives do not need to be true to affect readers. For example, following Spinoza, Gilbert (1991) proposed that the default response to information is to believe every assertion encountered. His experiments (in a nonnarrative context) indicated that individuals may later discount information that is known to have come from a false source, but belief is a relatively automatic process in response to information comprehension. Correction for inaccurate information may generally occur without difficulty, but if a person is prevented from engaging in correction processes, the belief may persevere (Gilbert, Krull, & Malone, 1990; Gilbert, Tafadrodi, & Malone, 1993). Similarly, Gerrig (1993) proposed that there is no special psychological category for fictional information. Although readers can disengage from a narrative and tell themselves, "It's only a story," that may not be the default tendency.

In their discussion of new media (television and computers), Reeves and Nass (1996) suggested that "the automatic response is to accept what seems to be real as in fact real" (p. 8). They proposed that individuals respond socially and naturally to media, even without intending to, because humans evolved in a world where the only entities that exhibited social behaviors were real humans. Individuals today respond to puppets, story characters, and actors on a movie screen as real because of these evolved responses. Indeed, the ease with which individuals relate to story characters may be a natural extension of individuals' need to understand real others in their social world or their need to construct possible futures and possible selves in order to plan ahead.

Nell (2002) took a slightly different evolutionary approach, arguing that narratives serve the adaptive purpose of creating an "illusion of immortality" and preventing individuals from experiencing debilitating fear about mortality. Narratives provide a response to threats to the very existence of the self. This perspective is similar to that of terror management theory (Greenberg, Solomon, & Pyszcznski, 1997). In Nell's view, narratives, particularly the classic mythic structures, create hope.

The Scope of Transportation

Although most of the research on transportation has focused on it as an aspect of the situation (transportation into a particular narrative), research has also documented reliable individual differences in the tendency to become transported. There does not appear to be a consistent gender difference in transportation propensity, however. Men and women can become equally immersed in stories, although certain types of stories may appeal more to one gender than another (e.g., the audience for romance novels tends to be largely female; the reverse may be true for Westerns). Texts also vary in their ability to transport readers; best-sellers are rated as more transporting than stories written by amateurs (see Green & Brock, 2000). The best stories have the ability to transport readers again and again; readers are eager to return to the narrative world even if they already know the ending.

Because most of the research on transportation thus far has been conducted with written narratives, this chapter most often refers to "readers." However, transportation is not limited to written texts. An individual may also be transported into a film or a spoken story. In the extreme case, a narrative may not even need to include words; silent films or other purely visual media may also be able to convey a transporting story.

Furthermore, individuals may be transported into fictional or factual worlds; narratives do not need to be true (or even be thought to be true) to draw readers in, engage their emotions, and even transform them (see Green, Garst, & Brock, 2004). Readers confronted with a work of fiction may be less concerned with its objective truth status (whether the events described actually occurred) and more concerned with whether the work meets some plausibility criterion (realistic characters, settings, or sensible ideas). In Bruner's words, "A good story and a well-formed argument are different natural kinds.... The one [argument] verifies by eventual appeal to procedures for establishing formal and empirical proof. The other establishes not truth but verisimilitude" (1986, p. 11).

TRANSPORTATION AND THE BOUNDARIES OF THE SELF

A skeptic might ask how much a narrative, much less a fictional narrative, could possibly affect individuals' real lives and selves. One anecdotal answer comes from the documentary film *Trekkies* (Border & Nygard, 1997), which showcases people who are obsessed with the *Star Trek* universe. *Star Trek* began as a science fiction television series about a starship crew who "boldly go[es] where no man has gone before"; its popularity has continued over 30 years, and the original concept has spawned several feature films and television spin-offs. The documentary highlights not only individuals who spend thousands of dollars on *Star Trek* memorabilia and regularly attend *Star Trek* conventions, but even those who dress in *Trek*-style uniforms in their daily lives and one woman who insists on being called by her "Star Fleet" title even at her regular job. The film *Trekkies* provides an extreme case of individuals allowing a narrative universe to shape their behavior and sense of self. As a less extreme example, many children enjoy dressing like characters in the *Harry Potter* novels—the red and gold scarves worn by the Gryffindor characters were popular sellers around the release of the first and second *Harry Potter* films. Most adults do not go that far in trying to bring a story world to life, but when asked, many people can name a novel, story, or fictional character who has influenced their lives in some way.

I suggest that although transportation has primarily been investigated in the persuasion domain, it also has clear implications for the self. Specifically, transportation can provide a temporary escape from the self and self-awareness but, at the same time, can aid in learning about, expanding, and changing the self. Narratives have long been touted as a means to obtain personal insight into the nature of self and the world; transportation may be one mechanism by which this insight occurs.

Absorption and Transportation: Creating Openness to Change

Transportation is conceptually related to Tellegen's concept of absorption, defined as a tendency to "enter under conducive circumstances psychological states that are characterized by marked restructuring of the self and the phenomenal world" (1982, p. 1). Absorption tendencies are related to the imaginative involvement component of openness to experience (one of the Big Five personality dimensions), as well as to hypnotic susceptibility (Glisky, Tataryn, Tobias, Kihlstrom, & McConkey, 1991). Some authors have likened immersion in reading to a hypnotic trance (e.g., Nell, 1988). Both are altered states of consciousness that can allow for transformation. Individuals under hypnosis or immersed in stories may temporarily suspend their normal assumptions about the world (for instance, in a narrative world, trees may be purple and animals might converse with humans) and relinquish some control to the author or hypnotist.

Absorption and Possible Selves Empirically, transportation shows a moderate positive correlation with absorption, but transportation is specifically related to narratives, whereas individuals may become absorbed into a range of experiences (e.g., a beautiful sunset, a piece of music). Like absorption, however, transportation can open the doors to exploring other possible selves. Possible selves are those that individuals might become, wish to become, or fear becoming (Markus & Nurius, 1986). The repertoire of possible selves is influenced by social context, and narrative worlds can provide additional sources of influence beyond the individual's immediate social world. Narratives may be especially important for individuals whose actual worlds may be limited in some important way, such as a teenager growing up a in a small town who dreams of more excitement or independence, or a person with a stigmatized identity who does not know anyone else who shares that part of him- or herself.

Transportation, in a sense, may loosen the boundaries of the self. Green, Garst, and Brock (2004) proposed that fiction prompts a less critical approach to material. Individuals reading fictional narratives are not constantly comparing the narrative world with the real world. Just as individuals may relax their critical or evaluative standards when transported into a story, they may also be less defensive about the boundaries and qualities of the self. While immersed in a narrative, readers may take on role of characters and see through a new set of eyes. Because of this extension of the self, the lessons learned in a narrative world may become integrated into the actual self or may provide a blueprint toward a new possible self. Prentice and Gerrig (1999) noted that fiction has its greatest influence when approached experientially rather than rationally; narrative encourages an experiential mind-set.

Simulating Alternative Selves

Narrative worlds have the unique benefit of providing simulations of alternative personalities, realities, and actions without any real cost to the reader (besides, perhaps, the time spent reading). A reader doesn't have to take the risk of changing jobs or romantic partners or of moving to a different city to experience another kind of life. A viewer of *The Sopranos* can try on a life of crime and mob life, and play through some of the implications of those choices, without risking death or imprisonment.

In addition to providing a low-risk means of exploring alternative selves, stories also provide an organized and concrete means of simulating new lives. A narrative provides a model of human emotion and action, often focusing on the essential elements of the human condition. An individual sitting alone simply trying to think up different ways of acting or being may be too strongly anchored to his or her existing self-concept, whereas a reader of story has put that task in the author's hands. To the extent that the story can provide specific pathways to goals (e.g., showing how a character overcame a particular obstacle), it may be especially effective in motivating individuals to reach a desired future self and may increase individuals' optimism about their ability to achieve their goals (e.g., Taylor & Schneider, 1989). Future research could explore this possibility.

Active Construction of Self

The process by which readers adopt alternative selves from narratives is likely a complex one. There is some commonality in readers' reactions to particular texts; authors typically intend for readers to feel certain emotions or draw particular conclusions from their stories. However, individuals are not injected with new versions of self as a simplistic "hypodermic model" would predict (and as censors often seem to fear). Readers are not helpless slaves to the whims of writers. The cognitive response approach in persuasion suggests that individuals' reactions to persuasive messages, rather than the messages themselves, determine attitude change (Greenwald, 1968; Petty, Ostrom, & Brock, 1981). In a similar way, readers' thoughts about stories affect the type and extent of narrative impact. Individuals vary in their responses to narratives and may selectively adopt parts of them to fit their unique needs. Radway (2002) described this selective, sometimes critical approach to narratives as being "like wandering through an enormous attic filled with the cast-offs and hand-me-downs of others ... imagining how they might be put to work differently, gleaning from that miscellaneous collection those few tattered and worn habiliments and treasures that might be adapted for use in ... one's ordinary life" (p. 194). For example, a girl watching Disney's *The Little Mermaid* may try to model herself after the main character's independence, but not after her willingness to do anything for a man.

Remindings: Linking Narratives to Past Experience

One way in which a narrative might prompt self-examination and change is by reminding the reader of his or her own experiences that relate to those in the narrative. Following Schank and Abelson (1995), Strange and Leung (1999) high-lighted the role of "remindings" in narrative impact. Individuals who were more immersed in a story showed greater generalization of the beliefs implied by the story, but additionally, whether or not the story brought to mind events from the readers' real lives seemed to be important in determining narrative impact. Strange and Leung examined beliefs about social issues (specifically, the causes of students' dropping out of high school) rather than about the self, but the processes involved likely apply to self-relevant beliefs as well. Individuals recruit story-congruent memories while reading, and these memories can continue to exert influence beyond the story context.

Visual Imagery

Transportation can also recruit imagery systems (Green & Brock, 2002) and may make it easier for individuals to literally visualize alternative selves or contexts. Visual imagery has most often been investigated for its possible role in motor skill performance, as when athletes are told to visualize themselves performing at their best. However, individuals may also visualize themselves active with self-confidence, succeeding at interpersonal tasks, or completing other self-relevant behaviors. Research on the cognitive-experiential self theory suggests that visualized experience is similar to real experience in individuals' intuitive-experiential systems (Epstein & Pacini, 2001). The state of transportation is theoretically similar to the experiential mode, which involves concrete and emotional thinking. One avenue for future research might be to focus on how visual images may be especially powerful ways of thinking about the self because they tend to be relatively impervious to change via arguments or other forms of persuasion.

Subtle Persuasion

Although stories can have a powerful influence on readers, narratives rarely announce a persuasive intent. In fact, stories that have too strong a message risk being dismissed by readers as preachy or boring; they inspire reactance rather than transportation, and thus may fail at changing the minds of readers. The "backdoor" form of persuasion via narratives may also reduce defensiveness and allow us to apply lessons from stories to our own lives and possible selves. Because stories can be a subtle form of influence, they may be able to alter our thinking about ourselves more readily than direct attempts at change. Children may be more likely to want to be doctors when they grow up if their storybooks portray medical professionals as heroes than if their parents constantly try to push them toward medical school.

Social Comparison With Characters

Stories may provide means of simulating alternative lives, but additionally, individuals may view narrative characters as targets for social comparison. This possibility has been of interest to communication and media researchers, with particular attention paid to young women's social comparison to thin models presented on television (e.g., Cattarin, Thompson, & Williams, 2000). Comparisons to idealized media figures can lead to negative self-views and destructive behavior, such as eating disorders. Other research has focused on the more positive side of social comparison with media images; Mares and Cantor (1992) showed that lonely elderly people preferred to watch a portrayal of an unhappy, isolated elderly person. They suggested that the media image provided a target for downward social comparison, thus improving lonely participants' moods. Lockwood and Kunda (1997), although not focusing on media characters per se, provided a more differentiated view. They suggested that self-relevant "superstar" role models can have either positive or negative effects: Superstars inspire individuals when their success seems attainable but can cause self-deflation when similar achievements seem out of a person's grasp. Media and fiction may well be a potent source of these star role models and social comparison targets.

It may be that individuals are more likely to engage in social comparison processes when their exposure to media characters or figures is relatively non-transporting (attractive, thin models on beer commercials; a brief clip of a program shown in a laboratory). Readers or viewers who are transported may be more likely to merge the other with the self in some way, rather than treating that character as an external target.

Boundary Conditions

Not all stories are life-changing or self-changing. Oatley (1995) distinguished between assimilative and accommodative narratives. *Assimilative narratives* create suspense; individuals want to know what will happen next and thus "fill in the blanks" in a schema. Genre or plot-driven narratives might fall in this category—thrillers, mystery novels, and romances. *Accomodative narratives*, on the other hand, attempt to make the reader view familiar situations in new ways (see Miall & Kuiken, 1994, 2002). More artistic or literary narratives tend to have this quality. The surprise and violation of expectations leads the reader to consider the narrative and the situation more deeply and thus may lead to insight. (See Schank & Berman, 2002, for further discussion of the ways in which expectation failures can lead to learning.)

Narratives intended to cause self-reflection or change also have to contend with the fact that individuals likely have strong and well-established self-concepts in various domains. Strong attitudes are resistant to counterpersuasion, and a one-shot exposure to a particular story may be less likely to change beliefs or behaviors that have been established over a lifetime.

Finally, narratives may be used as a means to escape the self rather than to expand the self. Individuals who are dissatisfied with their current circumstances may retreat into story worlds, but not use those story worlds to improve their real lives or selves. Individuals may prefer imagined selves or fictional "happy endings" to the work of creating a desired actual self. Future research might explore moderating factors that determine whether narratives encourage or discourage personal growth (cf. Baumeister, 1997).

TRANSPORTATION, EMOTION, AND THE SELF

Narratives may be an especially effective means of bringing together emotion and cognition, especially as compared to rhetorical messages. Emotion flows naturally from readers' reactions to story events.

Transportation into a narrative world may provide an arena for working through emotional issues related to the self; Oatley (1999), following Scheff (1979), suggested that narratives provide a middle ground where emotions are experienced enough for their meaning to be understood, but where these emotions do not overwhelm the reader. Narratives provide a safe space for individuals to explore the implications of their emotional experiences. Because the emotions evoked through reading are a result of events happening to characters, rather than to the individual, readers may feel more free to express those emotions.

Oatley further suggested that during the reading process, identification occurs and the characters' goals become the readers' goals (see also Oatley, 1995). Stories take advantage of the natural cognitive machinery that allows individuals to make plans and set goals. The success or failure of the characters' pursuits then influences the emotions experienced by the reader. Transportation can evoke this process. Future research might test whether the reader maintains the goals from the story in consciousness even after story reading is completed, and how long these goals remain active, perhaps even at an unconscious level (e.g., Chartrand & Bargh, 2002).

TRANSPORTATION AND EMPATHY–SYMPATHY: EMOTIONAL LINKS BETWEEN SELF AND OTHERS

Transportation and Dispositional Empathy

Feeling close to another person may involve putting oneself in another person's shoes, or including others as part of the self (e.g., Aron, Aron, Tudor, & Nelson, 1991). Just as we can have a sense of "fellow feeling" for others in our social environment, we also react to fictional or narrative others. Therefore, I expected that transportation would be positively related to empathy. Although empathy is an interpersonal construct and transportation relates to a person's interaction with a text, both constructs involve taking the perspective of another person. In the case of narratives, the perspective might be that of the author or of a character in a story. Additionally, both constructs have an affective component, such that feelings are evoked in response to events that may not personally involve the individual. The Interpersonal Reactivity Index (IRI) contains four subscales (perspective taking, empathic concern, personal distress, and fantasy) tapping different components of dispositional empathy (Davis, 1983).

I have found significant and fairly sizable correlations with the empathy scale and three of the four subscales of the IRI (*rs* range from .43 to .73). The fantasy scale measures the tendency to transpose oneself into fictional situations and is theoretically and empirically the most highly related to transportation. An example item is "I really get involved with the feelings of characters in a novel." (Indeed, the shared meaning between the fantasy items and the transportation items likely accounts for some of this high correlation.) The one uncorrelated subscale, personal distress, consists of items assessing individuals' tendencies to become distressed in emergency situations (e.g., "When I see someone get hurt, I tend to remain calm"; reverse scored). Because narratives rarely involve such a need for immediate response, personal distress items would be the least theoretically relevant to transportation.

Relationships With Characters: Empathy or Sympathy?

In recent research, I have been attempting to investigate the nature of relationships with characters in stories; that is, how does the self enter a narrative world and respond to (perhaps fictional) others (cf. Zillman, 1994)? Assuming that the reader does in fact become transported into the narrative world, there are two broad ways that the self may be emotionally involved in a story (see Tan, 1996, for a more detailed discussion of emotions prompted by fiction). First, a reader may empathize with a character—that is, may put herself in the character's shoes, and experience the events as if she were the character. A reader (or viewer) of *The Wizard of Oz* might actually feel like he has traveled along the Yellow Brick Road. Alternatively, the reader may sympathize with the characters. *Sympathy* refers to feeling an emotion *for* the characters, rather than *with* the characters. A sympathetic reader would understand Dorothy's longing to return to her home in Kansas, and perhaps even feel sad or sorry for her, but would not feel homesick himself.

Participants in my study read a story called "Witches of Yazoo," about a boy, Will, who meets an eccentric old woman when sneaking around her "haunted" house. The story moves from Will's excitement at facing danger to his fright at encountering the woman, and then to a gradual liking for the woman as he learns more about her life.

It is possible that techniques used by the author could affect the type of engagement the reader experiences. Some writing styles invite the reader in; others allow the reader to keep his or her distance. In particular, the perspective adopted by the author might differentially evoke empathy versus sympathy. To test this idea, I varied the point of view of the story. Some participants read the story in third person ("Will walked up the hill …"), which might map better to sympathy, and others read it in first person ("I walked up the hill …"), which might be more likely to lead to empathy. Indeed, individuals themselves tend to adopt the more distant third-person perspective when describing past selves that no longer match current self-concepts (Libby & Eibach, 2002). Theoretically, stories could also be written in the second person ("You walk up the hill …"), but because this voice is used so rarely in narratives, and because the story seemed to be awkward with that construction, I did not test it.

I asked participants to simply choose which option best reflected their feelings while reading the narrative: "While reading, I felt scared, relieved, glad, or other feelings FOR Will because of the events that were happening," or "While reading, I felt scared, relieved, glad, or other feelings WITH Will, as if the events were happening to me." (Participants were also given the option "The story did not affect my feelings.") Participants also rated how much they were putting themselves in the characters' shoes while reading. Results suggested that the reader does not merge with the main character, even when the story is presented in the first person. Rather, individuals were feeling for the character, as a caring observer. Interestingly, responses did not differ by point of view. A reader is equally likely to sympathize (rather than truly empathize) with a character regardless of whether the narrative is told as "I" versus "he." It may be that true empathy with story characters is relatively rare or perhaps that only the most skilled writers can evoke it.

Fellow Feeling for Negative Versus Positive Events

Individuals do not always extend the self to feel for or with others, however. Royzman and Kumar (2001) suggested that it is easier and more common for individuals to empathize with others who are experiencing negative events than positive events; when watching the news, we feel a tug at our heartstrings for the family who lost their home in a fire but do not feel corresponding elation for the lottery winner. Royzman and Kumar further suggested that in order to experience empathy for another's good fortune, some type of relationship must have been previously established. That is, we feel happy for a friend's triumph more than a stranger's success (unless the domain is one relevant to our self-concept as described by self-evaluation maintenance theory; see, e.g., Tesser, 1988). This theory has two implications for the experience of empathy and sympathy for narrative characters. First, much of the world's great literature deals with human suffering; perhaps authors intuitively know that this is a way to engage the emotions of readers. Second, it suggests that transporting literature can indeed create a bond between a real person (the reader) and fictional characters. We are delighted when the hero vanquishes the villain not only because good has prevailed but because we have come to like and identify with the hero.

Additional complexities also arise because there are multiple characters in most stories, and readers may have feelings toward each of them. The reader may also have more knowledge than the characters, so emotions may be evoked that are not strictly sympathy or empathy for any particular character (Tan, 1996).

TRANSPORTATION AND SELF-AWARENESS

Through engagement with characters as well as other processes, transportation takes the reader to a different world. Because transportation is thought of as diminishing the impingement of the individual's current environment (including social demands), Brock and I (Green & Brock, 2002) suggested that transportation should be negatively correlated with self-awareness. If individuals are concentrating on self-evaluation or potential evaluations of others, they are less likely to become "lost" in a narrative world. Conversely, individuals transported into a narrative world not only leave the real world behind but they likely leave their worries and public self-consciousness behind as well. This aspect of transportation may prove critical in explaining individuals' motivation to seek transporting experiences; entering a narrative world may be a release from the stress of personal concerns, problems, and contexts that elicit social anxiety.

As an initial test of this idea, we administered the Self-Consciousness Scale (Fenigstein, Scheier, & Buss, 1975) to a small group of participants who had also rated their transportation into a narrative. The Self-Consciousness Scale contains three subscales, assessing private self-consciousness, public self-consciousness, and social anxiety. Example items include "I reflect about myself a lot" (private) and "I'm concerned about the way I present myself" (public). Transportation was moderately associated with private self-awareness but had no relationship with public self-awareness. Transportation showed a moderate inverse relationship to social anxiety; individuals who tend to be worried about their social interactions appeared to have a more difficult time entering a narrative world.

Self-focused attention can be negative, especially when one focuses on shortcomings or discrepancies from an ought or ideal self (e.g., Higgins, 1989). Transportation may be a particularly appealing route away from such self-focus. For example, Moskalenko and Heine (2003) found that watching television reduced individuals' self-discrepancies and that individuals who had received a threat to the self (failure feedback) watched more television. Although those authors suggest that any stimulus that engages the individual and provides a distraction from self-discrepancies may have the same effect, it remains an empirical question whether other activities would indeed provide the same benefit.

Television may be a particularly effortless means of transportation; future research might explore whether reading a narrative has similar, or perhaps even stronger, effects. Individuals may watch television at the same time as they are doing other tasks, chatting with friends, and so on, but it is rare to find individuals doing concurrent activities while reading. Reading demands full attention and therefore may be especially effective at releasing individuals from a self-focused state. An alternative possibility, though, is that it may be more difficult to become immersed in reading to begin with if one is ruminating about the self—television may be a better distractor because it provides visual and auditory stimulation, lessening the need for imaginative input from the individual.

TRANSPORTATION AND EGO DEPLETION

Self-awareness involves the reflexive self, the individual examining and evaluating himself. Baumeister, Bratslavsky, Muraven, and Tice (1998) highlighted another aspect of the self: the executive function, the self in the world that controls acts of volition and choice. They presented evidence that self-regulation resembles a muscle; it requires energy to exert self-control, and thus the executive function may become depleted after use. For example, participants who had to suppress unwanted thoughts showed reduced persistence on a later difficult task (anagrams; Muraven, Tice, & Baumeister, 1998). In this framework, self-control efforts draw upon a common resource.

Failures of self-regulatory ability can have real consequences for individuals. Recovering alcoholics trying to resist taking a drink or dieters trying to steer clear of rich desserts may be more likely to succumb to temptation when they're ego depleted. Academics summoning up the motivation to write a manuscript or dissertation may find this task more difficult when their self-regulatory resources are low. On the positive side, an array of studies indicate that self-control, as measured by ability to delay gratification, for example, is associated with success in a number of life domains. Developing strategies for restoring or maintaining self-regulatory strength can potentially yield a range of beneficial outcomes.

Acts that require effort involving the self are thought to deplete ego resources. However, Tesser and I (Green & Tesser, 2001) proposed that transportation, although demanding of cognitive capacity, may be more effective in restoring self-regulatory resources than simple rest. Individuals who are transported are removed from a self-focused state. Engagement in a narrative world likely has effects beyond mere distraction, however; the flowlike properties of transportation may provide a replenishing boost to ego functioning. Kant (1951) described this aspect of aesthetic judgment as a "feeling of life," which is subjectively experienced as enlivening and regenerating (see Kuiken, Busink, Miall, & Cey, 2003).

Although transportation is a pleasurable state, we expect that the effects of transportation on self-regulatory functioning would not simply be due to positive mood. However, emotional distress can be a cause of self-regulatory failure (e.g., Heatherton & Baumeister, 1991), and transportation may allow individuals to temporarily remove themselves from these negative emotions without otherwise impairing their functioning (in contrast to drinking alcohol, for instance).

Although becoming temporarily transported into a narrative world may increase self-regulatory resources, it may be harmful when individuals regularly retreat into an alterative world in order to avoid facing difficult real-world tasks. Transportation may lead to escapism rather than increased ability to act in the world. A person may decide to simply pick up another mystery novel rather than returning to an unpleasant but necessary task in the real world. Escaping from excessive self-focus may be restorative, but some degree of self-focus is likely needed for effective self-regulation. Ideally, individuals should be able not only to become engaged in a narrative world but also to know when to return from the narrative world to real life. Future research should attempt to distinguish between beneficial and harmful uses of transportation into a narrative world.

In addition to a temporary boost to self-regulatory ability, transportation experiences may also help individuals construct meanings or build resources for the future. Kuiken et al. (2003) suggested that an aesthetic approach to a text can help readers "clear a space" for a fuller understanding of both text and self. Csikszentmihalyi (1990) described flow experiences as increasing the complexity and integration of the self. According to his theory, the focus that is created when individuals are engaged in an all-consuming activity allows an individual's consciousness to become better ordered. This focus can then carry over into other activities. It is likely that such benefits would also accrue from becoming transported.

THE EFFECT OF THE SELF ON BECOMING TRANSPORTED

Much of our research to date has focused on effects that occur once individuals have been transported. However, individual differences may also play a role in whether individuals become transported into a particular narrative world in the first place. For example, television viewers are more likely to watch programs with content that matches their self-concept (Preston & Clair, 1994). There is suggestive evidence that individuals who share some similarity with characters or situations in a story become more transported into it. In one study (Green, 2003), undergraduate participants read a (slightly adapted) short story, "Just as I Am," by best-selling author E. L. Harris (1996). The story is told from the point of view of a gay man who returns to his college fraternity reunion, where none of his former fraternity brothers know that he is gay. The story highlights the difficulties faced by gay men, particularly in fraternity settings, and ends with the attempted suicide of a potential fraternity member who had been harassed by current members because of his sexual orientation.

Participants rated their transportation into the story and provided information on their own experiences relevant to the story, including friendships with gay men and lesbians. Results suggested that individuals who had friends or family members who were gay or lesbian were more transported into the narrative. The number of participants who classified themselves as gay or lesbian was too small to conduct meaningful analyses, but the pattern of means suggested that identifying as such also led to higher transportation into this particular story.

The view of gay people in the story was largely positive but also included negative aspects (e.g., the main character did not feel he could reveal his sexual orientation to people close to him). Therefore, the increased transportation does not appear to be a simple positivity effect, where readers like stories that present a rosy view of individuals who share traits with their significant others. It appeared that the link between the story and the self may have either increased individuals' motivation to enter the narrative world or made it easier for them to imagine the events in the narrative. Additionally, readers with a preexisting similarity to the protagonist on one dimension may also have assumed that he was more like themselves on other characteristics (although this was not measured in the current study; cf. Burnstein, Stotland, & Zander, 1961; Stotland, Zander, & Natsoulas, 1961).

Of course, individuals who did not have this relevant prior experience did not completely fail to be transported; they simply were less engaged than those who did have a preexisting link with the main character. It is likely that in the extreme case, readers will cease reading a story if they feel that they have nothing in common with the characters. Individuals may not be able to put themselves in the place of the characters if the story-world situations are completely removed from any experience the reader has had.

This finding seems to be in opposition to the claim that a typical literature teacher might make, that one of the great benefits of literature is that it can allow individuals to walk in someone else's shoes, to learn about life in different times or cultures. Indeed, superficial similarities may be less important than being able to relate to the basic conflicts, emotions, or situations experienced by the character. For example, in other data collected in my lab, participants read a first-person diary-style narrative about a high school student's experimentation with drugs, including her euphoric first experiences with hallucinogens and the later negative consequences (a selection adapted from the 1971 novel *Go Ask Alice*). Manipulating whether or not the main character was the same gender as the participant did not affect transportation, nor did manipulating whether the main character attended the same school as the participant or a rival school (Penn vs. Princeton; Green, Butler, & Britt, 2003). In the same study, however, there was a positive correlation between transportation and responses to an item asking whether "the experiences of the narrator are similar to ones that I have faced at some point."

Furthermore, aspects of self that differentiate individuals from one another tend to be the most salient (McGuire & McGuire, 1988), and people are especially influenced by social comparisons with individuals who are similar to themselves on a distinctive dimension (Miller, Turnbull, & McFarland, 1988). It may be that reading about a character who shares a relatively rare characteristic will lead to greater transportation (as well as perhaps greater liking and identification) than reading about a character who shares a relatively common aspect of self.

FUTURE DIRECTIONS

Transportation Into Personal Narratives

Although this chapter has focused primarily on public or external narratives, personality psychologists have also highlighted the importance of personal or autobiographical narratives. Individuals may view their lives or parts of their lives as stories (see, e.g., McAdams, 1985). Research by Pennebaker, King and Miner, and others has demonstrated the beneficial effects of writing about emotional events, both positive and negative, on health and well-being (see, e.g., King & Miner, 2000; Pennebaker, 1997). The moderators of these effects are still being explored. It may be that individuals who are more transported while writing these narratives experience greater benefits; stepping back into a past experience and reliving it may be a particularly powerful way of writing.

Becoming fully immersed in the past experience may allow individuals to release the emotions associated with that experience. Individuals who merely record the facts of past events may be engaging in a primarily cognitive task.

Narratives need not be real or true (in a literal sense) for individuals to become transported into them; interestingly, this appears to be the case for personal narratives as well. Individuals who wrote about an imagined trauma for 20 min showed the same kinds of benefits as those who wrote about their own memorable experiences (Greenberg, Wortman, & Stone, 1996). Greenberg et al. suggested that even fictional writing can spur self-regulation processes, but they noted that the experience of emotion is necessary for this self-regulatory enhancement to occur. (Specifically, they noted that negative affect is required, but this conclusion has been challenged by later researchers, such as King & Miner, 2000.)

Interactive Narratives

Rapid advances in technology are leading to the emergence of new forms of narrative, ones that blur the line between reader and author. How might the self be affected by becoming transported into interactive or virtual worlds? Interactive narratives (e.g., some video games or virtual reality simulations) require the active participation of the user. Interactive narratives existed before these recent technological advances—in the form of "choose your own adventure" books in which readers made choices at key points in the story and turned to different pages for new plot twists, or in dinner theater productions in which audience members were given small roles in the overall drama—but they were relatively rare. In contrast, interactive narrative games sell millions of copies, and in addition to the ability to exert control over the ongoing story, these products also provide a multisensory experience. This may lead to enhanced sensation or emotion. To illustrate, Schubert, Friedmann, and Rogenbrecht (2001) gave the example that if someone reads about a narrow suspension bridge, they may be able to clearly imagine the setting, but they rarely feel any actual anxiety; an individual walking over a shaky bridge in a virtual reality world would experience physiological symptoms of fear. Because of this potentially more immediate and powerful evocation of emotions and environments, these narratives may have even greater implications for changes in the self-image.

Engineering and human–computer interaction researchers use the term *presence* to describe the state where "our awareness of the medium disappears and we are pushed through the medium to sensations that approach direct experience" (Biocca, 2002, p. 102; in film, this experience is called the *diegetic effect*). Although presence is often defined or measured with more explicit reference to interactive technology (e.g., Schubert et al.'s, 2001, presence scale included items about individuals' ability to explore the virtual space, such as examining objects close up), it is conceptually similar to transportation. Presence is a psychological and phenomenological state, not a property of a particular technology. Poor technology can impair the experience of presence, however. If the virtual reality device is difficult to use, or the users' movements do not cause corresponding changes or movements in the virtual world, users may not feel fully present in the virtual environment. (Of course, these problems are not unique to virtual reality environments, though they are perhaps more common—the same distraction effects could occur with a movie that is not in focus, or a book where words are blurred or missing.) It is generally believed that increasing user embodiment—that is, involving more of the user's sensory and motor capacities in the medium—will lead to a greater sense of presence (Biocca, 2002).

One of the most basic definitions of the self distinguishes that which is "inside the skin" (the self) from that which is outside the skin (others, the environment). Research in virtual reality domains suggests that even individuals' schemas about their own bodies can be changed, at least temporarily, by taking on a different form in the virtual world. Biocca and Rolland (1998) showed changes in users' hand–eye coordination that continued even after users left the virtual world. The mental representation users had of their own bodies, which one might expect would be a relatively stable feature of the self, had been changed. It is likely that other self-schemata could be similarly altered, especially with repeated exposure to the virtual world.

As noted above, transportation into a narrative world can create strong feelings for characters, and individuals may feel like story characters are friends or companions. Virtual reality narratives take this feeling a step further by allowing actual interaction with either narrative characters or other individuals engaged in the same narrative world. On the one hand, this ability might make the narrative experience even more powerful; individuals can provide actual responses rather than just "as if" participatory responses (Polichak & Gerrig, 2002). On the other hand, however, allowing users and characters the freedom to interact requires a looser narrative structure (Biocca, 2002). There is a trade-off between a well-constructed plot and allowing interactive freedom for the user.

Interactive narratives can also be especially good at creating empathy for characters, or allowing users to (almost literally) walk in the shoes of another person. This kind of narrative immersion becomes like role playing (see, e.g., Janis & King, 1954). Individuals can improvise their own responses to situations within the limits of the game. For example, the HeartSense game (Silverman, Holmes, & Kimmel, 2002), designed to teach individuals to recognize symptoms of a heart attack and seek treatment quickly, puts players in the position of convincing other characters in the game to call 911 when they have heart attack symptoms. This practice may increase players' feelings of self-efficacy about dealing with real-life medical emergencies.

Interactive, user-created narratives are also a fertile ground for identity play; individuals can switch genders, races, or ages with relative ease, as well as exploring new personalities. Turkle (1995, chapter 7) presented ethnographic case studies of individuals who use the Internet to create new (virtual) identities. In particular, she examined individuals who participate in multi-user dungeons (MUDs). The earliest MUDs were based on role-playing games such as Dungeons and Dragons; today, the term refers to a variety of multiuser games and virtual spaces, typically text-based, where individuals can play characters, adopt roles, or simply observe. MUDs tend to have an overarching narrative context (adventure, science fiction, exploration), which makes them especially relevant to investigating the role of transportation. There are almost certainly important differences between individuals who try out a temporary identity for fun versus those who become immersed or invested in the online world.

The online personae that individuals create allow them to explore personal issues in another context and may substitute for a perceived lack of affection, social skills, or other qualities in their real lives. Unfortunately for Turkle's participants, the lessons learned about interacting confidently with others in the virtual world did not always carry over into the real world. Perhaps this failure of behavior generalization is related to what Gerrig (1993) termed the *paradox of fiction*: People may exhibit strong affective responses but generally will not show the types of behavioral changes that would occur if those emotions had corresponded to actual events. In other words, the people in the movie theater may scream in reaction to a frightening monster, but they will generally not flee the theater. Virtual selves may temporarily satisfy emotional or self-esteem motives rather than leading to enduring behavior change. Alternatively, it may be that individuals are prevented from expressing those aspects of self because of constraints in their real environments. For example, an individual working at a fast-food restaurant may rarely have opportunities to be heroic. An important question for future research is to determine when selves created in virtual narratives will carry over to the real world and when they will not.

MUDs may also provide outlets for individuals to express aspects of themselves that may be more inhibited in everyday life. (See also Bargh, McKenna,

& Fitzsimons, 2002, for a discussion of how this process may occur in computer-mediated communication more generally and McKenna & Bargh, 1998, for examples of how expressing aspects of identity online can lead to expression of that identity in real life as well.) Rather than creating entirely new identities, individuals may simply change their self-presentation to emphasize some qualities rather than others.

CONCLUSION

Transportation into narrative worlds fundamentally involves the self, and may even change the self. Individuals who are immersed in story worlds may relax the boundaries of the self, identifying with characters and sympathizing with them. Reading narratives may provide a replenishing boost to self-regulatory ability, and characters and narrative events can provide blueprints for possible selves. On the other hand, similarities between readers and characters may make it easier to enter a narrative world.

REFERENCES

Adaval, R., & Wyer, R. S., Jr. (1998). The role of narratives in consumer information processing. *Journal of Consumer Psychology, 7*, 207–245.

Anonymous. (1971). *Go ask Alice*. Englewood Cliffs, NJ: Prentice-Hall.

Aron, A., Aron, E. N., Tudor, M., & Nelson, G. (1991). Close relationships as including other in self. *Journal of Personality and Social Psychology, 60*, 241–253.

Bargh, J. A., McKenna, K. Y. A., & Fitzsimons, G. M. (2002). Can you see the real me? Activation and expression of the "true self" on the Internet. *Journal of Social Issues, 58*, 33–48.

Baumeister, R. F. (1997). Esteem threat, self-regulatory breakdown, and emotional distress as factors in self-defeating behavior. *Review of General Psychology, 1*, 145–174.

Baumeister, R. F., Bratslavsky, E., Muraven, M., & Tice, D. M. (1998). Ego depletion: Is the active self a limited resource? *Journal of Personality and Social Psychology, 74*, 1252–1265.

Biocca, F. (2002). The evolution of interactive media: Toward "being there" in nonlinear narrative worlds. In M. C. Green, J. J. Strange, & T. C. Brock (Eds.), *Narrative impact: Social and cognitive foundations* (pp. 97–130). Mahwah, NJ: Erlbaum.

Biocca, F., & Rolland, J. (1998). Virtual eyes can rearrange your body: Adaptation to visual displacement in see-through, head-mounted displays. *Presence: Teleoperators and Virtual Environments, 7*, 262–277.

Border, W. K. (Producer) & Nygard, R. (Director). (1997). *Trekkies* [Motion picture]. Los Angeles: Neo Motion Pictures.

Bruner, J. (1986). *Actual minds, possible worlds*. Cambridge, MA: Harvard University Press.

Burnstein, E., Stotland, E., & Zander, A. (1961). Similarity to a model and self-evaluation. *Journal of Abnormal and Social Psychology, 62*, 257–264.

Cattarin, J. A., Thompson, J. K., & Williams, R. (2000). Body image, mood, and televised images of attractiveness: The role of social comparison. *Journal of Clinical and Social Psychology, 19*, 220–239.

Chartrand, T. L., & Bargh, J. A. (2002). Nonconscious motivations: Their activation, operation, and consequences. In A. Tesser, D. Stapel, & J. Wood (Eds.), *Self and motivation: Emerging psychological perspectives* (pp. 13–41). Washington, DC: American Psychological Association Press.

Coles, R. (1987). The humanities in postgraduate training. *Journal of the American Medical Association, 257,* 1644.

Csikszentmihalyi, M. (1990). *Flow: The psychology of optimal experience.* New York: Harper & Row.

Davis, M. H. (1983). Measuring individual differences in empathy: Evidence for a multi-dimensional approach. *Journal of Personality and Social Psychology, 44,* 113–126.

Deighton, J., Romer, D., & McQueen, J. (1989). Using drama to persuade. *Journal of Consumer Research, 16,* 335–343.

Epstein, S., & Pacini, R. (2001). The influence of visualization on intuitive and analytical information processing. *Imagination, Cognition, and Personality, 20,* 195–216.

Fazio, R. H., & Zanna, M. P. (1981). Direct experience and attitude–behavior consistency. In L. Berkowitz (Ed.), *Advances in experimental social psychology* (Vol. 14, pp. 161–202). San Diego, CA: Academic Press.

Fenigstein, A., Scheier, M. F., & Buss, A. H. (1975). Public and private self-consciousness: Assessment and theory. *Journal of Consulting & Clinical Psychology, 43,* 522–527.

Gerrig, R. J. (1993). *Experiencing narrative worlds.* New Haven, CT: Yale University Press.

Gilbert, D. T. (1991). How mental systems believe. *American Psychologist, 46,* 107–119.

Gilbert, D. T., Krull, D. S., & Malone, P. S. (1990). Unbelieving the unbelievable: Some problems in the rejection of false information. *Journal of Personality and Social Psychology, 59,* 601–613.

Gilbert, D. T., Tafarodi, R. W., & Malone, P. S. (1993). You can't not believe everything you read. *Journal of Personality and Social Psychology, 65,* 221–233.

Glisky, M. L., Tataryn, D. J., Tobias, B. A., Kihlstrom, J. F., & McConkey, K. M. (1991). Absorption, openness to experience, and hypnotizability. *Journal of Personality and Social Psychology, 60,* 263–272.

Green, M. C. (2004). Transportation into narrative worlds: The role of prior knowledge and perceived realism. *Discourse Processes, 38,* 247–266.

Green, M. C., & Brock, T. C. (2000). The role of transportation in the persuasiveness of public narratives. *Journal of Personality and Social Psychology, 79,* 701–721.

Green, M. C., & Brock, T. C. (2002). In the mind's eye: Transportation-imagery model of narrative persuasion. In M. C. Green, J. J. Strange, & T. C. Brock (Eds.), *Narrative impact: Social and cognitive foundations* (pp. 315–341). Mahwah, NJ: Erlbaum.

Green, M. C., Butler, D., & Britt, L. (2003). [Effect of character and reader similarity on transportation into narrative worlds]. Unpublished raw data.

Green, M. C., Garst, J., & Brock, T. C. (2004). The power of fiction: Persuasion via imagination and narrative. In L. J. Shrum (Ed.), *The psychology of entertainment media: Blurring the lines between entertainment and persuasion* (pp. 161–176). Mahwah, NJ: Erlbaum.

Green, M. C., & Tesser, A. (2001). Effect of transportation into a narrative world on self-regulatory ability (ego depletion). Unpublished data, University of Pennysylvania.

Greenberg, J., Solomon, S., & Pyszczynski, T. (1997). Terror management theory of self-esteem and cultural worldviews: Empirical assessments and conceptual refinements. In M. P. Zanna (Ed.), *Advances in experimental social psychology* (Vol. 29, pp. 61–139). San Diego: Academic Press.

Greenberg, M. A., Wortman, C. B., & Stone, A. A. (1996). Emotional expression and physical health: Revising traumatic memories or fostering self-regulation? *Journal of Personality and Social Psychology, 71,* 588–602.

Greenwald, A. G. (1968). Cognitive learning, cognitive response to persuasion, and attitude change. In A. G. Greenwald, T. C. Brock, & T. M. Ostrom (Eds.), *Psychological foundations of attitudes* (pp. 147–170). New York: Academic Press.

Harris, E. L. (1996). Just as I am. In S. S. Ruff (Ed.), *Go the way your blood beats: An anthology of lesbian and gay fiction by African-American writers* (pp. 487–498). New York: Holt.

Heatherton, E. F., & Baumeister, R. F. (1991). Binge eating as an escape from self-awareness. *Psychological Bulletin, 110,* 86–108.

Higgins, E. T. (1989). Self-discrepancy theory: What patterns of self-beliefs cause individuals to suffer? In L. Berkowitz (Ed.), *Advances in experimental social psychology* (Vol. 22, pp. 93–136). San Diego, CA: Academic Press.

Janis, I. L., & King, B. T. (1954). The influence of role-playing on opinion change. *Journal of Abnormal and Social Psychology, 49,* 211–218.

Kant, I. (1951). *Critique of judgment* (J. H. Bernard, Trans). New York: Hafner Press.

King, L. A., & Miner, K. N. (2000). Writing about the perceived benefits of health traumas: Implications for physical health. *Personality and Social Psychology Bulletin, 26,* 220–230.

Kuiken, D., Busink, R., Miall, D., & Cey, R. (2003, June). *Withdrawing to engage: How literary reading penetrates consciousness.* Paper presented at the workshop How Literature Enters Life, Utrecht, the Netherlands.

Libby, L. K., & Eibach, R. P. (2002). Looking back in time: Self-concept change affects visual perspective in autobiographical memory. *Journal of Personality and Social Psychology, 82,* 167–179.

Lockwood, P., & Kunda, Z. (1997). Superstars and me: Predicting the impact of role models on the self. *Journal of Personality and Social Psychology, 73,* 91–103.

Mancuso, J. C. (1986). The acquisition and use of narrative grammar structure. In T. R. Sarbin (Ed.), *Narrative psychology: The storied nature of human conduct* (pp. 91–125). New York: Praeger.

Mandler, J. M. (1984). *Stories, scripts, and scenes: Aspects of schema theory.* Hillsdale, NJ: Erlbaum.

Mares, M. L., & Cantor, J. (1992). Elderly viewers' responses to televised portrayals of old age: Empathy and mood management versus social comparison. *Communication Research, 19,* 459–478.

Markus, H., & Nurius, P. (1986). Possible selves. *American Psychologist, 41,* 954–969.

McAdams, D. P. (1985). *Power, intimacy, and the life story: Personological inquiries into identity.* Homewood, IL: Dorsey.

McGuire, W. J., & McGuire, C. V. (1988). Content and process in the experience of the self. In L. Berkowitz (Ed.), *Advances in experimental social psychology* (Vol. 20, pp. 97–144). New York: Academic Press.

McKenna, K. Y. A., & Bargh, J. A. (1998). Coming out in the age of the Internet: Identity "demarginalization" through virtual group participation. *Journal of Personality and Social Psychology, 75,* 681–694.

Miall, D. S., & Kuiken, D. (1994). Foregrounding, defamiliarization, and affect: Response to literary stories. *Poetics, 22,* 389–407.

Miall, D .S., & Kuiken, D. (2002). A feeling for fiction: Becoming what we behold. *Poetics, 30,* 221–241.

Miller, D. T., Turnbull, W., & McFarland, C. (1988). Particularistic and universalistic evaluation in the social comparison process. *Journal of Personality and Social Psychology, 55*, 908–917.

Moskalenko, S., & Heine, S. J. (2003). Watching your troubles away: Television viewing as a stimulus for subjective self-awareness. *Personality and Social Psychology Bulletin, 29*, 76–85.

Muraven, M., Tice, D. M., & Baumeister, R. F. (1998). Self-control as limited resource: Regulatory depletion patterns. *Journal of Personality and Social Psychology, 74*, 774–789.

Nell, V. (1988). *Lost in a book: The psychology of reading for pleasure.* New Haven, CT: Yale University Press.

Nell, V. (2002). Mythic structures in narrative: The domestication of immortality. In M. C. Green, J. J. Strange, & T. C. Brock (Eds.), *Narrative impact: Social and cognitive foundations* (pp. 17–37). Mahwah, NJ: Erlbaum.

Oatley, K. (1995). A taxonomy of the emotions of literary response and a theory of identification in fictional narrative. *Poetics, 23*, 53–74.

Oatley, K. (1999). Why fiction may be twice as true as fact: Fiction as cognitive and emotional simulation. *Review of General Psychology, 3*, 101–117.

Pennebaker, J. W. (1997). Writing about emotional experiences as a therapeutic process. *Psychological Science, 8*, 162–166.

Pennington, N., & Hastie, R. (1988). Explanation-based decision making: Effects of memory structure on judgement. *Journal of Experimental Psychology: Learning, Memory, and Cognition, 14*, 521–533.

Petty, R. E., Ostrom, T. M., & Brock, T. C. (1981). Historical foundations of the cognitive response approach to persuasion. In R. E. Petty, T. M. Ostrom, & T. C. Brock (Eds.), *Cognitive responses in persuasion* (pp. 1–29). Hillsdale, NJ: Erlbaum.

Polichak, J. W., & Gerrig, R. J. (2002). Get up and win: Participatory responses to narrative. In M. C. Green, J. J. Strange, & T. C. Brock (Eds.), *Narrative impact: Social and cognitive foundations* (pp. 71–96). Mahwah, NJ: Erlbaum.

Prentice, D. A., & Gerrig, R. J. (1999). Exploring the boundary between fiction and reality. In S. Chaiken & Y. Trope (Eds.), *Dual-process theories in social psychology* (pp. 529–546). New York: Guilford.

Prentice, D. A., Gerrig, R. J., & Bailis, D. S. (1997). What readers bring to the processing of fictional texts. *Psychonomic Bulletin & Review, 5*, 416–420.

Preston, J. M., & Clair, S. A. (1994). Selective viewing: Cognition, personality, and television genres. *British Journal of Social Psychology, 33*, 273–288.

Radway, J. (2002). Girls, reading, and narrative gleaning: Crafting repertoires for self-fashioning within everyday life. In M. C. Green, J. J. Strange, & T. C. Brock (Eds.), *Narrative impact: Social and cognitive foundations* (pp. 183–204). Mahwah, NJ: Erlbaum.

Reeves, B., & Nass, C. (1996). *The media equation: How people treat computers, television, and new media like real people and places.* New York: Cambridge University Press.

Royzman, E. B., & Kumar, R. (2001). On the relative preponderance of empathic sorrow and its relation to commonsense morality. *New Ideas in Psychology, 19*, 131–144.

Schank, R. C., & Abelson, R. P. (1995). Knowledge and memory: The real story. In R. S. Wyer, Jr. (Ed.), *Advances in social cognition* (Vol. 8, pp. 1–85). Hillsdale, NJ: Erlbaum.

Schank, R. C., & Berman, T. R. (2002). The pervasive role of stories in knowledge and action. In M. C. Green, J. J. Strange, & T. C. Brock (Eds.), *Narrative impact: Social and cognitive foundations* (pp. 287–314). Mahwah, NJ: Erlbaum.

Scheff, T. J. (1979). *Catharsis in healing, ritual, and drama*. Berkeley: University of California Press.

Schubert, T., Friedmann, F., & Rogenbrecht, H. (2001). The experience of presence: Factor analytic insights. *Presence, 10*, 266–281.

Silverman, B. G., Holmes, J., & Kimmel, S. (2002). Computer games may be good for your health: Shifting healthcare behavior via virtual reality simulators. *Journal of Healthcare Information Management, 16*(2), 80–85.

Stotland, E., Zander, A., & Natsoulas, T. (1961). Generalization of interpersonal similarity. *Journal of Abnormal and Social Psychology, 62*, 250–256.

Strange, J. J., & Leung, C. C. (1999). How anecdotal accounts in news and in fiction can influence judgments of a social problem's urgency, causes, and cures. *Personality and Social Psychology Bulletin, 25*, 436–449.

Tan, E. S. (1996). *Emotion and the structure of narrative film: Film as an emotion machine*. Mahwah, NJ: Erlbaum.

Taylor, S. E., & Schneider, S. K. (1989). Coping and the simulation of events. *Social Cognition, 7*, 174–194.

Tellegen, A. (1982). *Brief manual for the Differential Personality Questionnaire*. Unpublished manuscript. University of Minnesota, Minneapolis.

Tesser, A. (1988). Toward a self-evaluation maintenance model of social behavior. In L. Berkowitz (Ed.), *Advances in experimental social psychology* (Vol. 21, pp. 181–227). New York: Academic Press.

Turkle, S. (1995). *Life on the screen: Identity in the age of the Internet*. New York: Touchstone.

Wheeler, S. C., Green, M. C., & Brock, T. C. (1999). Fictional narratives change beliefs: Replications of Prentice, Gerrig, & Bailis (1997) with mixed corroboration. *Psychonomic Bulletin & Review, 6*, 136–141.

Zillman, D. (1994). Mechanisms of emotional involvement with drama. *Poetics, 23*, 33–51.

4

Conflict and Habit:
A Social Cognitive Neuroscience
Approach to the Self

MATTHEW D. LIEBERMAN
AND NAOMI I. EISENBERGER

But that's how biographies are. I mean, who's going to read about the peaceful
life and times of a nobody employed at the Kawasaki Municipal Library?

—Haruki Murakami (1994), *Dance, Dance, Dance*

Novelist Haruki Murakami's claim is hardly contentious. We all prefer to read a
biography full of unexpected events, tragic downfalls, and hard-won victories. They
take us on a journey through which we hope to glean the character of the individual
and perhaps some insight into human nature more generally. It is not that
the simple life of the librarian has any fewer events filling the days or years but
rather that those events follow an expected repetitive pattern with little variation
over time. Indeed, there are no more hours in the day for a head of state than
for Murakami's librarian, just more memorable ones.

Just as we prefer the miraculous to the mundane, the tragic to the trivial, and
conflict over commonplace in choosing which biographies to read, we often rely
on similar distinctions in understanding and defining ourselves. We look to those
moments in our past when we were faced with obstacles for which our daily
routine, and the mental habits formed through this routine, could not guarantee
safe passage. Should I be a lawyer or a doctor? Should I be a Democrat or
Republican? Should I stand up for the student who is being picked on or keep
quiet? If these situations have not been a part of one's routine, how is one to go
forward? There seems to be no alternative but to "assert oneself" in these cases
and use one's "free will," or at least that is how these episodes are often experienced
in retrospect. These are the moments when the self seems to burst onto the scene,

and thus these are the moments that we often take as self-defining in our own private autobiographies (Baumeister, 1986).

Why do these moments of conflict and the way we resolve them figure so prominently into our self-concepts? The main purpose of this chapter will be to suggest that a neural system (the *C-system*) specialized for controlled self-regulation processes can provide an explanation for the critical role of conflict and conscious choice in self-concept formation. That is to say that the computational properties of this neural system are biased toward encoding our mental and behavioral responses to conflicts rather than our habitual thoughts and behaviors. Because of the importance of facilitating timely and adaptive responses to future episodes of conflict or choice points, we hypothesize that our solutions to conflicts will be more easily accessed for solving future conflicts and more strongly identified as part of our self-concept. Though we will focus a great deal on the neural system responsible for encoding postconflict thoughts and behaviors, there is also ample data to suggest this is not the only type of self-knowledge. We will also review the evidence for a second self-knowledge system, including data suggesting that there is a second neural system (the *X-system*) that supports this second kind of self-knowledge. This type of self-knowledge system does not rely on discrete episodes of conflict; rather, it is built up gradually over time through the integration of habitual thoughts, action patterns, and behavioral sequences.

In this chapter, we will first delve into the historical and functional accounts of the self in order to build the foundation for answering why moments of conflict or choice points constitute the most recognizable determinants of our self-concept. We will then expand on the neural structures underlying our explicit (*evidence-based*) self-knowledge system. Finally, we will review the less recognizable determinants of our self-concept as well as the neural correlates of this implicit (*intuitive*) self-knowledge system.

HISTORICAL CHANGES IN SELF-CONCEPT FORMATION

Baumeister (1986, 1987) proposed a radical hypothesis about the nature of the self-concept and how it has been transformed throughout history. He suggested that not only are there qualitatively distinct forms of self-definition processes that can shape the self-concept but that these processes have different effects on self-concept formation and have also been differentially present in Western civilization over the past millennium. As a result, self-concepts of people living in the past 2 centuries may be qualitatively different from those of people living in the middle ages. This is not just a matter of content, with medieval dwellers pondering their resilience to plagues and modern folks pondering over which character on television they are most like. Rather, Baumeister argued that only in the past few centuries has self-definition become problematic in such a way that the self, rather than being transparently equated with status and behavior in a rather simple fashion, is now something to be pondered and probed by all individuals—psychologists included. In essence, though people presumably have always had personalities and other defining characteristics, by this argument complex mental autobiographies are relatively modern psychological phenomena.[1]

Baumeister (1986) suggested that the distinct forms of self-definition processes, namely *given*, *achieved*, and *choice-driven* self-definition processes, differ in the difficulty they pose for the individual and the likelihood that the self-definition process will turn reflective such that the individual becomes aware of the process and its implications for self-definition. *Given* aspects of self-definition, including family lineage and gender, are present at birth and thus require no effort or decision making. *Achievement* aspects may be effortful or effortless processes (gaining wealth vs. becoming a parent) and typically only involve clear societal prescriptions. Until the 20th century, few people had internal conflicts over the prospect of achieving wealth or parenthood—it is simply what was done to the extent that one was capable. *Choice-driven* self-definition processes emerge when there are either no clear criteria or conflicting criteria for making a decision. For instance, how does one decide whether to be a professor or a doctor? Neither is objectively better, nor does society clearly value one more than the other. Each is better on some dimensions (doctors make more money and save lives, whereas professors choose their own avenue of study and advance human knowledge), but which dimensions are more important? Baumeister argued that when confronted with these conflicts, we look to our *self* to determine which is more important. It is unclear whether we find the answer in ourselves or construct an answer, which then becomes a defining part of our self. Either way, these choice points, for which behavior-guiding criteria are absent, are often in the highlights reel of our own *True Hollywood Story*.

An analysis of the changing social structure from the medieval period to our own reveals a shift in the landscape of self-definitional processes available. Baumeister (1986) showed that changes in the structure of society closely parallel the increasing frequency of people's reflecting on the nature of their identities. Medieval identity was simple and stable, defined primarily by givens such as social rank and gender. Many facets of identity that today are choice-driven or complex achievement processes were essentially givens in medieval life. One's occupation was most often determined by family lineage, and marriage was often arranged without any choice on the part of the betrothed. During this time period there is little evidence of self-reflection in existing cultural artifacts and almost no recovered autobiographies. In the centuries that followed, however, Protestantism provided people with religious alternatives, and later, industrialization and urbanization increasingly brought new opportunities for achievement and ultimately a variety of life choices that could only be made by assessing and asserting one's self. Accordingly, these centuries saw a boom in the number of artifacts indicating time devoted to self-reflection, such as personal diaries, autobiographies, and the development of an "inner life" in the characters of novels. It is of interest to note that during the same time period that Baumeister reviewed, mirrors changed from being rarely seen religious accoutrements to being the implicit enforcers of social norms and equipment used for self-discovery (Melchior-Bonnet, 1994).

FUNCTIONS OF THE SELF

Baumeister's (1987) historical account suggests that choices that produce the most internal anguish, as a result of lacking or conflicting criteria available for deciding, spur on the development of identity and become disproportionately salient in our resulting self-concepts. On the one hand, this seems obvious because experiences meeting these criteria are easy to bring to mind. Moreover, numerous theories of identity have suggested that these "nuclear episodes" that include "high points, low points, and turning points" and often focus on a sense of agency or the lack thereof (McAdams, 1993, p. 296) are important contributors to our identity as containing both continuity and change (Erikson, 1968; Harter, 1999; P. J. Miller, 1994; Prout & Prout, 1996; Thorne & McLean, 2002).

On the other hand, it is not clear from a mechanistic standpoint why these experiences should be more accessible than others. Eventually we will conclude that this is the case because conflicts engage the C-system, which produces robust episodic memories in order to facilitate the speedy dissolution of similar conflicts in the future. A discussion of one major function of the self, that of self-regulation, will provide a bridge between the phenomenology of choice conflicts and the neural bases of self-concept.

Ramachandran (1995) publicly declared that humans do not have free will but suggested instead that we may have "free won't." This play on words harkens to the age-old discussion of the duality of the self as both the controller and the thing controlled (Baumeister, 1998; Lakoff & Johnson, 1999; Turner, 1976). When one says "I made myself keep studying," there seem to be two separate entities involved—one that wants to keep working and one that would prefer to bang on a drum all day. This can be partially resolved by considering the joint action of automatic and controlled cognitive processes. In this context, automatic processes are the habits and impulses that guide us through daily life with little effort or intention on our part (Bargh & Chartrand, 2001; Langer, 1989; Lieberman, 2000). These processes often run relatively autonomously, and because they have largely evolved or become conditioned to help us achieve our goals, they are often quite adaptive. When driving down the road, one hardly needs to think at all about all the various aspects of driving; with minimal attention, it just seems to happen. Such automaticities have their limitations, including spontaneous deployment at inappropriate times. For instance, it is adaptive to have our automatic driving habits guiding our behavior when we are driving up the street to the video store. Those same habits can be hazardous to one's health if they guide one's driving unchecked while in a foreign country with different driving laws (including driving on the "other" side of the road).

When our habits take us astray, we are then in need of "free won't," the capacity to stop our habits from running their course and possibly running us into oncoming traffic. Under optimal conditions, controlled processes are reasonably successful in correcting our behavior in light of the current context (Gilbert, 1989; Lieberman, 2003). Controlled processes typically involve effort, awareness, and intention—all the characteristics necessary to make these processes feel self-willed (Lieberman, Gaunt, Gilbert, & Trope, 2002) regardless of whether this phenomenological assessment is accurate (Wegner, 2002; Wilson, 2002) or even coherent (Dennett, 1984). Controlled processes are enormously flexible, limited only to the amount of information that can be processed at any one time, but not to the range of information that can be considered together or to the originality of new representations generated. Because of this flexibility, it is easy to forget why controlled processes probably evolved: control.

Carver and Scheier (1981) developed an influential model of self-control guided by the insight that if controlled processes exist for the purpose of control, external or internal, then engineering models of control implemented in physical systems might shed light on human self-control. They drew on cybernetic models of self-regulation (Wiener, 1948) most simply exemplified in *test–operate–test–exit* (TOTE) units discussed by G. A. Miller, Galanter, and Pribram (1960). TOTE describes any computational mechanism with the capacity to (a) assess whether the current state of the world (limited to the world as detectable by the TOTE unit) deviates from the TOTE's standard of comparison or desired state of the world and (b) effect some change on the world until the current state matches the standard of comparison. Essentially the TOTE is a system that performs "tests" on the world, and when deviations from standards occur, the TOTE unit performs an "operation" on the world. The test–operate cycle continues until the test result indicates a match between the current state and the standard, at which point the TOTE unit "exits" until it is scheduled to begin new tests.

The beauty of the TOTE unit is that it is equally applicable to self-correcting systems as different as thermostats, individual humans, and complex governments. Within humans, there are many self-correcting systems for regulating bodily processes that could be described with TOTE units without any connection to consciousness or controlled processing. However, the TOTE units associated with our controlled processes are special because we are aware of their activity and experience TOTE functioning as coming from the self. Carver and Scheier (1981) and Duval and Wicklund (1973) have demonstrated in numerous experiments that state and trait self-awareness are intimately linked to the test function of controlled-processing TOTE units. Self-focused attention is typically either a response to a test indicating a mismatch from a standard or is involved in performing the test itself. The response to the mismatch can involve an assortment of reactions including self-evaluation (Higgins, 1987), generating reflected appraisals in which one infers the evaluations others are making of oneself (Lieberman & Rosenthal, 2001; Mead, 1934), and controlled processing operations to remove the mismatch. Each of these responses to the self-perceived mismatch is experienced as self-related.

If the TOTE units involved in controlled processing are typically experienced as generated "by the self and for the self," then a clear account can be given of why the increasing number of choices and conflicts presented in recent time periods would lead to greater reflection on the nature of the self than in earlier time periods. To the extent that goals, standards, and expectations are given at birth, TOTE units should be called upon less frequently. Under those conditions, the habits acquired while growing up would continue to be adaptive because they would remain in a relatively unchanging context. If the rules are set and constant, habits will perform exceptionally well. The modern world has opened up more and more aspects of life that involve rule changes, and the more those changes occur the more frequently TOTE units will be called upon in the service of overriding contextually inappropriate habits and keeping track of the self-assertions needed to guide behavior. To summarize, the more often habits conflict with current goals and expectations, the more often that TOTE units are called up for duty, and the more people should be cognizant of themselves as having an active self.

MULTIPLE MEMORY SYSTEMS

The preceding logic explains why the self should take up a greater part of the cultural consciousness as the presence of choice and conflict increases. This logic still does not explain why our mental and behavioral responses to these conflicts should be such salient aspects of our mental autobiographies. One can imagine that with a greater cultural emphasis on the self, people might be more likely to attend to and form more robust memories for their behavior in general without any special advantage for the kind of events that were catalysts for the greater emphasis.

The best explanation for this proposed memorial advantage for conflict-related events comes from the cognitive neuroscience of memory. We have known for almost half a century (Milner, Corkin, & Teuber, 1968)—since patient H.M. had most of his medial temporal lobes (MTLs), including the hippocampus, removed to treat his epilepsy—that there are multiple memory systems that are sensitive to different kinds of stimuli and have different operating characteristics. H.M., and many other patients with MTL damage, are dramatically impaired in their ability to form and retain new episodic memories. H.M. can meet new people several times, each time believing it to be the first time because he cannot retrieve a memory of the episode of the earlier meeting. This is because the MTL is critical to forming memories for particular episodes and for storing them, at least for several years (Squire, 1992). As bad as H.M.'s episodic memory is, he can form new habits, which comprise memory for procedures and conditioned associations. Since his surgery, H.M. has been trained to use a computer, but he does not know why he knows how to use it and he does not remember the learning episodes themselves. Conversely, patients with damage to the basal ganglia often have severe deficits in forming and using habits but are relatively spared in their capacity to form new episodic memories (Knowlton, Mangels, & Squire, 1996). Moreover, a number of studies suggest that the basal ganglia, critical for habit use, and the MTL, critical for episodic memory, may inhibit one another such that the activation of one system tends to deactivate the other (Lieberman, Chang, Chiao, Bookheimer, & Knowlton, 2004; Packard, Hirsh, & White, 1989; Poldrack et al., 2001).

The relation of these memory systems to one another suggests that as long as habits are successfully guiding our behavior, we are less likely to form strong robust episodic memories. This would account to some extent for the autobiographical salience of our reactions to choice and conflict, as habitual behavior will be relatively deemphasized in episodic memory.

NEURAL CORRELATES OF THE TOTE

In order to determine whether the salience of our memories for choice conflicts is due to the nonsalience of habits in episodic memory or because of something about choice reactions that actually increases the salience of these in episodic memory, we must determine the relation of TOTE-like self-regulation processes to episodic memory. Strictly speaking, there are no studies directly assessing this relationship. However, there are several findings suggestive of a special relationship between human TOTE-like processes and episodic memory.

First, it is well-established that successful encoding of episodic memories is related to depth of processing (Craik & Tulving, 1975). The more an individual mentally elaborates on the meaning of a stimulus, the more likely the individual will be able to recall the stimulus later. Paralleling these depth-of-processing effects, recent neuroimaging studies (Brewer, Zhao, Desmond, Glover, & Gabrieli, 1998; Wagner et al., 1998) have shown that the extent to which the lateral prefrontal cortex (LPFC) is active during encoding significantly predicts retrieval success later.

The LPFC has been associated with linguistic (Bookheimer, 2002), working memory (Smith & Jonides, 1999), and causal processes (Satpute et al., 2004), among others. These processes all share the requirement of operating on and holding distinct multiple symbols and the capacity to flexibly and asymmetrically combine, compare, and sequence those symbols. For instance, "John loves Mary" is asymmetric because it does not imply that Mary loves John (although John might hope that it does). The fact that the LPFC possesses relatively sparsely coded representations (O'Reilly, Braver, & Cohen, 1999), using a relatively small number of neurons for each representation, may promote the ability to hold the representations separate from one another and thus keep track of the asymmetric relations between them (Holyoak & Hummel, 2000).[2]

This capacity for propositional representations that represent asymmetrical relations and implications between the different "objects" of a proposition could promote the capacity to hold context specific goals and rules in mind. These context-specific rules could temporarily bind symbols that ordinarily are not associated with one another. Instead of merely being able to represent that A goes with B, this capacity allows us to represent that A goes with B, but only right now in context C. This flexibility would allow the LPFC to "think outside the box," overcoming automatic habits and associations by incorporating contextually relevant information into goals and action plans. In other words, the LPFC could guide behavior toward current standards. We have suggested elsewhere (Lieberman, Jarcho, & Satpute, 2003; Lieberman et al., 2002) that the LPFC along with the anterior cingulate cortex (ACC), posterior parietal cortex (PPC), and MTL together perform the TOTE functions of human controlled processes. We call this group of four structures the C-system (for the C in *reflective consciousness*).

There are numerous functional magnetic resonance imaging (fMRI) and event-related fMRI studies suggesting that the ACC is sensitive to discrepancies between perceptions and impulses, on the one hand, and current expectations and goals on the other hand (Braver, Barch, Gray, Molfese, & Snyder, 2001; Kiehl, Liddle, & Hopfinger, 2000). It is sensitive to conflicts as minor as the automatic impulse to read a color word (*r-e-d*) during the Stroop task when the goal is to say the color of the ink that the word is written in (*blue*). It is also sensitive to major conflicts such as physical pain (Lieberman, Jarcho, et al., 2004; Rainville, Duncan, Price, Carrier, & Bushnell, 1997) and social exclusion (Eisenberger & Lieberman, 2004; Eisenberger, Lieberman, & Williams, 2003). In a series of elegant studies, Botvinick, Braver, Barch, Carter, and Cohen (2000) and Carter et al. (2000) have shown that the ACC acts as a conflict monitor, performing the test component of the TOTE unit. Rather than performing the subsequent TOTE operations itself, the ACC acts as an alarm that signals the LPFC to begin performing operations (see Hunter et al., 2003, for research demonstrating the temporal sequencing of ACC and LPFC operations).

If the ACC performs the test and the LPFC handles the operations, what role is left for the MTL? A comparison between the TOTE units implemented in thermostats and human controlled processing will suggest an answer that will also address the larger question of the overrepresentation of choice conflicts in our mental autobiographies. Thermostats have a single goal or standard to test for—the temperature level set by the occupant of the room. In addition, in any given season there is typically only one way the temperature can deviate from the standard: it can be too cold in winter and too warm in summer. In the summer, then, each and every time a mismatch is detected, the thermostat automatically triggers the air conditioning to come on. For humans, things are not so simple—not even close. At any one time, there are virtually an infinite number of standards that might not be met. Everything from uncomfortable clothes, aches and pains, hunger, negative nonverbal feedback from friends, and subpar performance at work or on a test can all grab the attention of the ACC.

Leaving aside the issue of how the standards are formed and maintained (Higgins, 1987; Mead, 1934), it is no simple matter for the LPFC to perform the appropriate operation to fix the problematic situation. This is especially unfortunate because one of the defining and unique features of the LPFC is that its functions are severely limited by processing constraints. LPFC computations, characterized by the constraints of working memory (Smith & Jonides, 1999), seem to operate on symbolic representations in serial fashion with only seven, plus or minus two, bits of information in use at a time in the service of a single thought at a time (James, 1890/1950; G. A. Miller, 1956). Attempts to handle more information simultaneously lead to a degradation in performance as evidenced by dual-task and cognitive-load studies (Gilbert, 1989). Moreover, sustained use of working memory, even within its constraints, can deplete working memory effectiveness for short periods (Baumeister, Bratslavsky, Muraven, & Tice, 1998; Vohs & Heatherton, 2000). Given the limitations of the LPFC, the less work it performs in general the better able it will be to perform when it is really needed.

The fragility of LPFC processing helps explain why the ACC performs the TOTE tests. The LPFC is able to effectively rest until it is called upon by a mismatch detected in the ACC. The MTL also serves to compensate for LPFC fragility by preserving a record of how previous conflicts were resolved by the LPFC. When the same situation arises in the future, automatic habits are likely to be little changed. For instance, driving for 5 min in a country where driving on the left side of the road is the norm will have little effect on one's preexisting habit to drive on the right side of the road. Indeed, what good would our habits be if they were upended so easily (McClelland, McNaughton, & O'Reilly, 1995)? Instead, habits are decontextualized representations that are insensitive to the constraints of the particular situation and change only with numerous instances of a new behavior, perception, or contingency. Because of the habit system's intransigence, renewed exposure to the situation that activated the ACC before is likely to activate it again.

Recall that episodic memories in the MTL are better encoded to the extent that there is deeper processing associated with LPFC operations. In the context of TOTE functions this means that as the number and complexity of LPFC operations performed in response to an ACC mismatch increases, so too does the strength of the episodic memory laid down in the MTL. In other words, we have good episodic memories for big problems that were difficult to solve. Why? Because those who cannot remember—recall how they solved a problem in—the past are doomed to repeat it (and thus must figure out the solution again). If the LPFC can retrieve a solution from the MTL's records of past responses to conflicts, then it can focus on implementing the solution rather than on rediscovering it. Thermostats only need to "remember" a single solution and thus would not benefit from a memory bank. A thermostat's memory bank would have line after line of "At 3:42 on a Wednesday afternoon, turned on air conditioning. At 6:07 on a Tuesday evening, turned on air conditioning. At 10:15 on a Saturday night, turned on air conditioning." For humans, however, this database of solutions to past problems (which have not occurred frequently enough to change our habits) is invaluable. Tommy may not mind putting in the effort to figure out the answer to a math problem once ($288,499 \times 25 + 1,462,834 = 8,675,309$), but it would be nice to have an episodic memory of the answer to turn to if asked again seconds later.

This brings us to the solution of the major question of this chapter. Why are our mental autobiographies filled more with memories of our responses to difficult choices and conflicts than with memories of banal everyday activity? It seems that there are at least two complementary reasons for this. In part, this occurs because the successful deployment of our automatic habits may directly interfere with the formation of new episodic memories given the competitive relationship between the basal ganglia and MTL (Poldrack & Packard, 2003). More important, however, is that episodic memory may be an integral part of the TOTE functions of the C-system, forming new episodic representations to the extent that LPFC operations occur, and serving as a shortcut to the previous solution when the situation arises again. Thus, if the computations of the C-system involve looking to the self and constructing new solutions to conflicts for which habits of mind and behavior are ineffectual, these self-infused solutions will be recorded in episodic memory.

EXPERIENCING THE SELF IN THE C-SYSTEM

Now that we have addressed the question of why reactions to conflicts should be overrepresented in autobiographical memory, we would like to backtrack and address one of our earlier assumptions in greater detail. Earlier, we noted that one way the TOTE-like processes of humans and thermostats differ is that we experience our TOTE processes as coming from the self and (certain Buddhist doctrines notwithstanding) thermostats do not. This is a critical assumption because otherwise the solutions to our choice conflicts might be recorded into episodic memory without their being linked to the self. We might have memories of this and that having happened without having a sense that we were the agent at the center of the action. Recent research in cognitive neuroscience has begun to shine a light on the link between experienced self-processes and the structures of the C-system in terms of self-awareness, self-control, and self-knowledge. We address each of these topics in turn.

Self-awareness. Self-awareness refers to the ability to turn one's attention and thoughts to oneself. A nuanced understanding of self-awareness would fill volumes and even then would most likely leave us feeling that something basic about self-awareness was still not addressed. In the meantime, a number of neuroimaging studies have implicated the ACC in self-awareness across a variety of domains. When individuals are asked to reflect on their emotions (Lane, Fink, Chua, & Dolan, 1997) or their actions (Jueptner et al., 1997), rather than merely experiencing them, there is greater activity in the ACC. Additionally, when individuals are asked to consider a scenario and reflect on how they would feel and act, the ACC is again more active (Vogeley et al., 2001). Finally, ACC activity is found when individuals are asked to reflect on their physical traits (Kjaer, Nowak, & Lou, 2002).

Though brain localization is an important first step in understanding the neural bases of any mental process (Lieberman & Pfeifer, in press), it is unsatisfactory as an end in itself (Willingham & Dunn, 2003). After determining that the ACC is related to self-awareness, the next obvious question to ask is why. Which aspects of ACC computations are critical for self-awareness? We recently addressed this question in an fMRI study (Eisenberger, Lieberman, & Satpute, 2004). Given that the ACC's mismatch detection function is a good candidate for the TOTE test function in human controlled processing and given that self-awareness has been theoretically linked to TOTE processes, we hypothesized that the reactivity of the ACC to mismatches would predict the frequency and accuracy of self-awareness processes outside the scanner. We reasoned that more reactive ACC's should produce TOTE tests that are more sensitive to mismatches leading to more frequent episodes of self-awareness as well as more sensitive, or accurate, self-awareness.

In this study, participants were first scanned while performing an "oddball" task during which they were presented with a sequence of letters on the screen. Eighty percent of the letters were the letter X, but participants were instructed only to press a button whenever they saw a letter other than X. Because the base-rate expectation of seeing an X is 80%, seeing other letters violates this expectation and leads to activation of the ACC (Braver et al., 2001; Menon, Adleman, White, Glover, & Reiss, 2001; Weissman, Giesbrecht, Song, Mangun, & Woldorff, 2003). A week or more after the scanning session, participants returned to the behavioral lab, where frequency and accuracy of self-awareness were assessed. First, participants filled out questionnaires including a self-consciousness scale that measures, among other things, frequency of self-awareness (Fenigstein, Scheier & Buss, 1975). Participants then exercised vigorously for 1 min and then reported on how physiologically aroused they thought they were, from 0% (perceived arousal before exercising) to 100% (perceived arousal after exercising) every 2 min until 10 min postexercise. We measured actual physiological arousal at the same time points in terms of a gender-neutral measure of arousal, rate pressure product (Pham, Taylor, & Seeman, 2001), which combines heart rate and systolic blood pressure. We found that ACC reactivity to the oddball trials, relative to nonoddball trials, predicted the accuracy of arousal self-awareness extremely well ($r^2 = .50$) even after covarying out individual differences in arousal curves. Additionally, ACC reactivity correlated highly with the self-report measure of self-awareness ($r = .76$). Interestingly, ACC reactivity predicted arousal self-awareness better than self-reported self-awareness predicted this behavioral measure. Finally, ACC reactivity also correlated highly with neuroticism ($r = .69$), which can also be seen as related to dispositional self-awareness.

This study, like several before it, demonstrates a link between self-awareness and the ACC. Unlike previous studies, it helps explain why this link exists by connecting self-awareness to a particular neurocognitive process in the ACC—namely, reactivity to mismatches. Additionally this study provides some of the best evidence to date supporting the contention that self-awareness is linked to the TOTE unit's test function.

Discrepancy detection as a trigger for self-awareness and subsequent self-control is, generally speaking, an adaptive mechanism that goes well beyond the limitations of simple habits. We would not want to leave the reader with the impression that self-focused attention in all forms is always a good thing. In fact, several psychological disorders, including clinical depression and anxiety, are associated with elevated levels of self-focus (Ingram, 1990). Consistent with our account of self-focus and ACC activity, these self-focus-related disorders typically involve abnormal ACC functioning (Benkelfat et al., 1995; Davidson, Pizzagalli, Nitschke, & Putnam, 2002; Kimbrell et al., 1999; Pizzagalli et al., 2001; Ursu, Stenger, Shear, Jones, & Carter, 2003). Thus, although self-focused attention may be useful under various conditions, it can be problematic in its extreme forms.

Self-control. It is commonly believed that the LPFC is central to working memory processes most clearly aligned with effortful top–down processes that regulate behavior (E. K. Miller & Cohen, 2001; Smith & Jonides, 1999). The LPFC is believed to perform at least three types of processes that would greatly facilitate self-control. First, the ventral LPFC is involved in the suppression or disruption of unwanted cognitive, affective, or behavioral responses (Aron, Fletcher, Bullmore, Sahakian, & Robbins, 2003; Eisenberger, Lieberman, & Williams, 2003; Iversen & Mishkin, 1970; Monchi, Petrides, Petre, Worsley, & Dagher, 2001; Ochsner, Bunge, Gross, & Gabrieli, 2002; Preibisch et al., 2003; Small, Zatorre, Dagher, Evans, & Jones-Gotman, 2001). Second, the dorsal LPFC is involved in boosting the strength of weaker, but contextually appropriate, representations and action plans (Kosslyn, Thomson, & Alpert, 1997; E. K. Miller & Cohen, 2001; Tomita, Obayashi, Nakahara, Hasegawa, & Miyashita, 1999). Third, the LPFC along with the frontopolar region of the prefrontal cortex (PFC) can flexibly combine symbolic representations using propositional rules to consider novel courses of action and ultimately set one in motion (Kroger et al., 2002; Waltz et al., 1999; Zysset, Huber, Ferstl, & von Cramon, 2002).

Though each of these processes contribute to self-control, it is the phenomenological experience of being the author of these acts of self-control, the feeling that "I am planning" or "I am suppressing an impulse" that links them to self-concept. Despite the fact that all experience is produced by our own neural activity, the great majority of these experiences are attributed to something external to oneself. When faced with an American flag, only patriots, poets, and philosophers would be expected to say that a bit of their consciousness is red, white, and blue. When we see John shove Michael (because Mary loves Michael, not John), we believe the aggressiveness of the act is out there in the world, not an aspect of our conscious experience dependent on our goals, beliefs, and values (Griffin & Ross, 1991). When we engage in acts of self-control, be it holding our breath under water, fasting for a religious holiday, or rehearsing a nine-digit number, we almost always feel a sense of authorship for the act. It feels like no mere accident happening to us but instead feels intentional—intended by us. Indeed, it is hard to imagine ever finding oneself accidentally rehearsing a nine-digit number, for as soon as we stop intending to do so, active rehearsal stops (though a trace may have been laid down in long-term memory).

A number of studies have implicated the PPC in assessing whether oneself or another was responsible for an action (Chaminade & Decety, 2002; Farrer & Frith, 2002; Ruby & Decety, 2001; Taylor, 2001), although its exact role is unclear. In other words, it has not been determined whether the PPC participates in all judgments of authorship or just those involving the perception of actions. For example, Gusnard, Akbudak, Shulman, and Raichle (2001) found that when individuals were differentiating their emotional reaction from the emotional reaction of others, the dorsomedial PFC (adjacent to the ACC) rather than the PPC was involved. Apart from neuroimaging studies, a number of neuropsychological investigations also implicate the PPC in the experience of authorship for one's body and its actions. *Anosognosia* refers to a condition in which patients have some kind of impairment but do not recognize that they have it (Galin, 1992). When patients have had a stroke that has paralyzed one side of their body as well as damaged inferior parietal cortex they will sometimes, and often only temporarily, become anosognosic. Ramachandran (1995) provided a vivid case history of such a patient who believed that her paralyzed left arm was just as able as her right arm. Despite incontrovertible evidence that she cannot control this arm in any way, she continues in her belief. This suggests that the PPC may play an important role in the experience of self-efficacy, control, and authorship. Similarly, when individuals have alien hand syndrome and experience their arm movements as controlled by an external force, there is increased PPC activity (Spence et al., 1997), which drops off with symptom reductions.

Self-knowledge.   In the first neuroimaging study of self-knowledge, Craik et al. (1996) found that self-knowledge judgments activated the right PFC. This is consistent with a number of neuropsychological investigations suggesting a link between this area and self-knowledge (B. L. Miller et al., 2001; Stuss, Picton, & Alexander, 2001). To date, there have now been at least seven neuroimaging studies, including three positron emission tomography (PET) studies (Craik et al., 1999; Fink et al., 1996; Kjaer, Nowak, & Lou, 2002) and four fMRI studies (Johnson et al., 2002; Kelley et al., 2002; Kircher et al., 2000; Lieberman, Jarcho, & Satpute, in press), each using relatively similar paradigms in which participants had to judge whether words were self-descriptive. As seen in Table 4.1, six of the seven studies found activation in the medial aspect of PPC, called the precuneus, and adjacent posterior cingulate. The precuneus, along with the MTL, is associated with successful episodic recall (Cabeza & Nyberg, 2000). In one rodent study (Izquierda et al., 1997), the precuneus was the only structure examined that if ablated any time after learning would prevent successful recall. MTL structures were critical for the first month after encoding, but eventually retrieval could function without the MTL. This supports the basic assumption that the self-concept is dependent on memory for autobiographical episodes. TOTE test functions associated with the ACC bring self-awareness online when conflicts occur that our habits cannot handle. Self-control is then exerted in its varied forms, implemented by the LPFC and labeled as self-authored by the PPC and perhaps medial PFC. To the extent that the LPFC is engaged in the conflict resolution, these operations should be encoded more robustly in the MTL and later retrieved during self-knowledge judgments by the precuneus and the PFC.

INTUITION-BASED SELF-KNOWLEDGE

If things were so simple as the previous summary suggests, we would be on to the reference section by now. For better or for worse, the story of self-concepts has a second act. Though the account of self-concepts as drawing on episodic memories of our reactions to important choice points fits very well with our folk theory of self-concepts and is consistent with much of the existing imaging data, there is a growing body of work suggesting that this account of self-knowledge is incomplete in important ways.

The problem, in a nutshell, is that episodic memory is not critical for many kinds of self-judgments. Imagine Jerry Seinfeld, a famous comedian, being asked to judge whether or not he is funny. At this point in his career, with all the success

TABLE 4.1. Neural Correlates of Self-Knowledge Retrieval From Seven Studies

Brain region	Brodmann area(s)	Side	Kircher et al. (2000)	Johnson et al. (2002)	Craik et al. (1999)	Kelley et al. (2002)	Fink et al. (1996)	Lieberman et al. (2003)	Kjaer et al. (2002)	Total
Precuneus and posterior cingulate	7/31	Both	✓	✓		✓	✓	✓	✓	6/7
Medial and ventromedial prefrontal	9/10/11	Both		✓	✓			✓	✓	4/7
Inferotemporal	21/38	Right		✓			✓	✓		3/7
Inferior parietal	40	Both	✓					✓	✓	3/7
Ventrolateral prefrontal	44/45/47	Right			✓			✓		2/7
Basal ganglia		Left	✓					✓		2/7
Insula		Both	✓				✓			2/7

Note. Check marks indicate areas of activation.

and laughter his comedy has produced, it seems possible that he would just know this without having to reflect on and evaluate memories of discrete comedic performances from the past. True, barring a nasty bump on the head, he could engage C-system processes to consult all those episodic memories, evaluate them, and construct what we have called *evidence-based* self-knowledge (Lieberman, Jarcho, & Satpute, in press). But does he need to?

In a series of behavioral and neuropsychological studies, Klein and his colleagues have shown that evidence-based self-knowledge does not appear to be necessary for various self-knowledge judgments. In one series of studies (Klein, Loftus, Trafton, & Fuhrman, 1992), participants showed no reaction time advantage when making self-knowledge judgments immediately after the activation of relevant autobiographical memories, relative to when no autobiographical memories were preactivated. If episodic retrieval is used in making self-knowledge judgments, one would expect that making the relevant memories more accessible would facilitate those judgments, but here it did not. The activation of autobiographical memories only improved reaction times when participants were making judgments about themselves in a domain that was relatively new to them. This suggests that early in the development of any area of self-knowledge, particular episodes are important elements of the self-concept in that domain. With growing experience, however, Klein's data suggests that the knowledge is recompiled in such a manner as to render the link to the particular episodes unnecessary.

From behavioral data alone, it is unclear whether a single representation undergoes a transformation from being evidence-based to being something else or whether there are multiple distinct self-knowledge representations forming in parallel. Klein and colleagues used neuropsychological case studies to shed light on the issue of single versus multiple self-knowledge systems (for a review of all of these case studies, see Klein, Rozendal, & Cosmides, 2002). A series of patients with congenital or acquired deficits in episodic memory have proved able to produce self-knowledge judgments as accurate as those of healthy controls. In the best known of these cases, patient W.J. suffered a traumatic head injury that temporarily rendered her incapable of retrieving memories of events that had occurred in the previous 12 months. Despite this impairment in episodic memory, W.J. was able to produce personality ratings for herself that were highly correlated with the ratings she produced after she regained access to her episodic memories (Klein, Loftus, & Kihlstrom, 1996).

These studies make a compelling case for the multiple self-knowledge systems position. However, they primarily shed light on what the second self-knowledge system is not rather than illuminating what it is. We know that representations from the second system do not depend on evidence from the autobiographical record generated in the C-system, at least once these representations have fully matured. However, we do not know what type of self-related information this second self-knowledge system is dependent upon.

Because of the independence from autobiographical evidence, we have characterized the second system as an *intuition-based* self-knowledge system. In other unrelated research on judgment and decision making, attribution, and prejudice (Lieberman, 2000; Lieberman Chang, et al., 2004; Lieberman, Eisenberger, &

Crockett, 2003; Lieberman et al., 2002; Lieberman, Hariri, Jarcho, Eisenberger, & Bookheimer, 2004), we have found evidence of a second neurocognitive system called the X-system (for the *x* in *reflexive*; it includes the basal ganglia, ventromedial PFC, amygdala, and lateral temporal cortex), which is typically the automatic social-cognitive counterpart to the C-system's controlled processes.[3] We hypothesized that the same relation would hold with regard to self-knowledge such that intuition-based self-knowledge would be subserved by the X-system. If supported, this is a case where merely finding where in the brain a process occurs can yield theoretical fruit, because there is already a reasonable understanding of the characteristics of the X-system (e.g., associative learning, parallel processing). Given that we mostly know what intuition-based self-knowledge is not, this link would suggest some answers to what it is.

Lieberman, Jarcho, and Satpute (in press) tested the hypotheses that there were two distinct self-knowledge systems, evidence-based and intuition-based, and that these depended on two neurocognitive systems, the C-system and X-system, respectively. Each participant was an experienced athlete or actor. The athletes and actors were asked to make self-knowledge judgments regarding the applicability of traits words relevant to each domain (athleticism and acting). Thus, participants made judgments in both a high-experience domain and a low-experience domain. When the neural activity was compared across these different judgments, all but one of the regions more active for high-experience judgments than low-experience judgments were X-system regions. In this comparison all regions of the X-system were more active, including the basal ganglia, ventromedial PFC, amygdala, and lateral temporal cortex. The only C-system region active in this comparison was the PPC. The dorsolateral PFC was the only region of the brain that was significantly more active for low-experience judgments, although the right hippocampus in the MTL was also significant once reaction times were controlled for.

We believe this study clearly shows two self-knowledge systems at work in distinct neural systems. The C-system produced greater activation when making low-experience domain self-judgments presumed to rely on evidence-based self-knowledge, whereas the X-system produced greater activation when making high-experience domain self-judgments presumed to rely on intuition-based self-knowledge. So what do these results buy us? They help us to make inroads into the operating principles of intuition-based self-knowledge based on what is already known about the characteristics of the X-system.

The X-system (again, the amygdala, basal ganglia, ventromedial PFC, and lateral temporal cortex) is hypothesized to automatically generate the affective and social components of the stream of consciousness and produce a great deal of the habits and impulses that guide our daily activity (for full reviews, see Lieberman et al., 2002; Lieberman, Hariri, et al., 2004; Lieberman, Jarcho, & Satpute, in press). The basal ganglia and ventromedial PFC have both been identified as playing a role in learning abstract relationships between features of the environment and the affective significance of these feature without conscious awareness or intention (Bechara, Damasio, Tranel, & Damasio, 1997; Cromwell & Schultz, 2003; Knowlton, Mangels, & Squire, 1996; Lieberman, 2000). The amygdala is also strongly identified with automatic affective responses, in particular responding to the threat value of environmental stimuli (LeDoux, 1996), even without the conscious perception of these stimuli (Whalen et al., 1998). The lateral temporal cortex has been more frequently associated with semantic associations than affect (Burton, Diamond, & McDermott, 2003; Copland et al., 2003; Mummery, Shallice, & Price, 1999), but it may store various social-cognitive associations that would modulate the automatic affective responses in other parts of the X-system. This suggests that intuition-based self-knowledge is more affect-based than evidence-based self-knowledge. C-system representations may be about affect, but they are still likely to be propositions. X-system representations are much closer to the primitives of affective experience. This is a new positive piece of information about intuition-based self-knowledge that can be inferred from simply knowing what structures in the brain are responsible for this type of self-knowledge.

Another critical feature of all the X-system structures is that the formation of new representations is typically slow and incremental (Damasio, 1994; McClelland, McNaughton, & O'Reilly, 1995), whereas C-system structures typically form complete representations quickly based on single trials.[4] This has two major implications for our understanding of evidence-based and intuition-based self-knowledge. First, it is likely to require numerous repetitions in a domain before intuition-based self-knowledge will mature enough to dominate cognition and behavior when it is needed. Though the work by Klein et al. (1992) demonstrated that evidence-based self-knowledge was guiding behavior most when individuals made low-experience domain self-knowledge judgments, it was not clear why this should be the case. The fact that intuition-based self-knowledge is implemented in a neural system that is well-documented as having a slow incremental learning algorithm helps to explain Klein's findings. The second implication that this finding has is that it suggests that most intuition-based self-knowledge cannot be updated quickly. Convincing individuals with longstanding low self-esteem that they are deserving of greater self-esteem may lead to the modification of some linguistic propositions in the C-system, but it will probably have little effect on the X-system. The X-system seems to be less sensitive to linguistic input, whether it be a friend's, a therapist's, or even one's own interior thoughts, and more sensitive to repeated exposure to an environment with a stable set of underlying relationships between stimuli.

INTUITION-BASED SELF-KNOWLEDGE AND IMPLICIT SELF-PROCESSES

There is a natural desire to identify intuition-based self-knowledge with implicit self-processes (see Spencer, Jordan, Logel, & Zanna, this volume), and we suspect that there is some overlap between the two. We do, however, hesitate to suggest they are synonymous. Implicit representations are typically those that cannot be brought to mind explicitly and are instead revealed through various other responses that imply that a representation must be present and guiding cognition even though it is not consciously accessed (Schacter, 1992).

In all of Klein's work, as well as our own imaging work, subjects explicitly and successfully answered questions about their own self-concepts. Clearly, this knowledge does not pass the litmus test for being implicit. What may appear to be implicit is the evidentiary basis for intuitive self-knowledge; however, we believe this is not the case. There is no reason to believe that there are links from intuition-based self-knowledge to implicit representations of the evidence supporting that knowledge (Lieberman et al., 2002). Rather, as long as each episode that provides evidence incrementally alters intuition-based self-knowledge as it happens, it would have its effect without leaving a representational trace of itself in the X-system. Every time a hammer hits a nail, it will be embedded further into a piece of wood. In so doing, the hammer incrementally changes the status of the nail but the nail does not require a memory of the hammer in order to maintain its new status.

MEDIAL PREFRONTAL CORTEX AND SELF-PROCESSES

A number of studies suggest that the medial prefrontal cortex (mPFC) also plays a role in self-processes (see Table 4.1). It is unclear at this time for multiple reasons what this role is and where mPFC would fit with respect to the X- and C-systems. Although future reviews may well include this region of the brain as a major component of self-processing, it is too soon to make such a claim. The mPFC is a very large area of cortex comprising no less than three Brodmann's areas (9, 10, 11). It is likely that different areas are involved in different kinds of computations, but for now there is no agreed upon nomenclature for dividing the mPFC into its constituent parts. The upshot of this is that self studies reporting activity in mPFC appear to be talking about the same area of the brain as one another when in fact these studies are reporting activations that are quite distinct.

A second issue is that the mPFC has been identified with social cognition more generally and not just self-processes. It is more active when we are trying to understand the intentions of others (Gallagher & Frith, 2002) or even just imputing intention to moving cartoon objects (Schultz et al., 2003). It is also more active when processing information related to a person than an object (Mitchell, Heatherton, & Macrae, 2002). Thus, it is difficult to draw any conclusions about whether the mPFC is playing a specific role in self-processing.

Finally, the mPFC has an unusual property that makes drawing inferences about its role even more difficult. A review of dozens of neuroimaging studies (Raichle et al., 2001) indicates that the mPFC is more active at rest than during almost any kind of mental activity a person engages in. In other words, engaging in almost any kind of mental activity seems to interfere with whatever it is the mPFC does when the rest of the brain is at rest. Most previous studies ostensibly showing mPFC increases are really only showing smaller decreases during self- or social cognition than during some control task (Kelly et al., 2002; Mitchell, Heatherton, & Macrae, 2002). We have recently shown true mPFC increases relative to a resting baseline when participants were watching realistic social interactions between two people (Iacoboni et al., 2004); however, it is unclear at this point exactly which features of the social interaction led to this increase. All these issues taken together suggest that it would be premature to make any claims about the specific role of the mPFC in self-processes.

CONCLUSION

To be sure, this was meant to be a review of research on self-processes, specifically those involved in defining our "selves." We hope that we have provided some insight into why conflict and the response to it plays such a prominent role in our autobiographical stories. Moreover, we hope we have provided a framework for understanding the multiple self-knowledge systems and their neurocognitive bases.

In essence, we have reviewed two self-knowledge systems with two separate underlying neural subcomponents. The evidence-based self-knowledge system, which contributes to the importance of conflict in our self-definition, is composed of C-system structures (the LPFC, ACC, PPC, and MTL), involved in the controlled regulation of behavior when something goes wrong or no clear behavioral response is available. The intuition-based self-knowledge system, which is built up gradually over time through repeated habits and behaviors, is comprised of X-system structures (the basal ganglia, ventromedial PFC, amygdala, and lateral temporal cortex), involved in the automatic enactment of behavioral responses. An important purpose of the C-system is to exert control when no clear habitual response exists and to record these new behavioral responses should a similar situation arise again. Thus, the conflicts that we face (deciding whether to become a doctor or lawyer) become the basis for our evidence-based self-knowledge, whereas our habitual behavioral responses (how we respond to our patients or clients) become the basis for our intuition-based self-knowledge.

The subtext of this chapter, however, was meant to demonstrate the value of cognitive neuroscience research and neuroimaging tools in advancing social psychological theories of the self. By understanding the neural components involved in automatic and controlled processes, we can begin to disentangle the complexity of self-processes such as those involved in self-knowledge, self-esteem, self-enhancement, or self-regulation. Neural activity in specific structures provides us with clues about the type of cognition that occurs there, and the interactions between structures tells us about how these types of processes support or interfere with each other. As neural data continue to inform us of the different types of processes involved in self-knowledge, so too should social psychological theories of the self be updated to accommodate the implications of cognitive neuroscience data. If, through a better understanding of the neural processes involved in self-knowledge, readers have had to rethink their theories of the self, then we have done our job.

NOTES

1. Baumeister did not suggest that the nature of self-concept processes is the same for everyone at a certain point in history. Rather, he suggested that generalizations can be made about the typical experience from the different time periods.

2. Though we have not yet reached the discussion of posterior parietal cortex, it is worth noting here that it works in concert with the LPFC for working memory tasks and also has very sparse representations (Gottlieb, Kusunoki, & Goldberg, 1998).

3. We do not mean to imply these structures are all necessarily coordinated with each other neurally. Rather, we believe they serve a common set of functions which bind them even if "one hand doesn't know what the other is doing." Though there is some evidence of neural connectivity for some of the structures within each system and especially the C-system, the full extent of this connectivity is beyond the scope of this chapter and is still largely unknown.

4. Though the amygdala often forms representations of threat cues incrementally, it is also capable, at least in rodents, of single-trial learning. This makes sense in light of the differential need to learn threat-versus-reward cues quickly; however, it does make the amygdala somewhat anomolous within the X-system.

REFERENCES

Aron, A. R., Fletcher, P. C., Bullmore, E. T., Sahakian, B. J., & Robbins, T. W. (2003). Stop-signal inhibition disrupted by damage to right inferior frontal gyrus in humans. *Nature Neuroscience, 6*, 115–116.

Bargh, J. A., & Chartrand, T. L. (1999). The unbearable automaticity of being. *American Psychologist, 54*, 462–479.

Baumeister, R. F. (1986). *Identity.* New York: Oxford University Press.

Baumeister, R. F. (1987). How the self became a problem: A psychological review of historical research. *Journal of Personality and Social Psychology, 52*, 163–176.

Baumeister, R. F. (1998). The self. In D. T. Gilbert, S. T. Fiske, & G. Lindzey (Eds.), *The handbook of social psychology* (pp. 680–740). Boston: McGraw-Hill.

Baumeister, R. F., Bratslavsky, E., Muraven, M., & Tice, D. M. (1998). Ego depletion: Is the active self a limited resource? *Journal of Personality and Social Psychology, 65*, 317–338.

Bechara, A., Damasio, H., Tranel, D., & Damasio, A. R. (1997). Deciding advantageously before knowing the advantageous strategy. *Science, 275*, 1293–1295.

Benkelfat, C., Bradwejn, J., Meyer, E., Ellenbogen, M., Milot, S., Gjedde, A., & Evans, A. (1995). Functional neuroanatomy of CCK4-induced anxiety in normal healthy volunteers. *American Journal of Psychiatry, 152*, 1180–1184.

Bookheimer, S. Y. (2002). Functional MRI of language: New approaches to understanding cortical organization of semantic processing. *Annual Review of Neuroscience, 25*, 151–188.

Botvinick, M. M., Braver, T. D., Barch, D. M., Carter, C. S., & Cohen, J. D. (2000). Conflict monitoring and cognitive control. *Psychological Review, 108*, 624–652.

Braver, T. D., Barch, D. M., Gray, J. R., Molfese, D. L., & Snyder, A. (2001). Anterior cingulate cortex and response conflict: Effects of frequency, inhibition, and errors. *Cerebral Cortex, 11*, 825–836.

Brewer, J. B., Zhao, Z., Desmond, J. E., Glover, G. H., & Gabrieli, J. D. E. (1998). Making memories: Brain activity that predicts how well visual experience will be remembered. *Science, 281*, 1185–1187.

Burton, H., Diamond, J. B., & McDermott, K. B. (2003). Dissociating cortical regions activated by semantic and phonological tasks: An fMRI study of blind and sighted people. *Journal of Neurophysiology, 90*, 1965–1982.

Cabeza, R., & Nyberg, L. (2000). Imaging cognition: II. An empirical review of 275 PET and fMRI studies. *Journal of Cognitive Neuroscience, 12*, 1–47.

Carter, C. S., MacDonald, A. W., Botvinick, M. M., Ross, L. L., Stenger, V. A., Noll, D., et al. (2000). Parsing executive processes: Strategic vs. evaluative functions of the anterior cingulate cortex. *Proceedings of National Academy of Sciences, 97*, 1944–1948.

Carver, C. S., & Scheier, M. F. (1981). *Attention and self-regulation: A control theory approach to human behavior.* New York: Springer-Verlag.

Chaminade, T., & Decety, J. (2002). Leader or follower? Involvement of the inferior parietal lobule in agency. *NeuroReport, 13*, 1975–1978.

Copland, D. A., de Zubicaray, G. I., McMahan, K., Wilson, S. J., Eastburn, M., & Chenery, H. J. (2003). Brain activity during automatic semantic priming revealed by event-related functional magnetic resonance imaging. *NeuroImage, 20*, 302–310.

Craik, F. I. M., Moroz, T. M., Moscovitch, M., Stuss, D. T., Winocur, G., Tulving, E., et al. (1999). In search of the self: A positron emission tomography study. *Psychological Science, 10*, 26–34.

Craik, F. I. M., & Tulving, E. (1975). Depth of processing and retention of words in episodic memory. *Journal of Experimental Psychology: General, 104*, 268–294.

Cromwell, H. C., & Schultz, W. (2003). Effects of expectations for different reward magnitudes on neuronal activity in primate striatum. *Journal of Neurophysiology, 89*, 2823–2838.

Damasio, A. R. (1994). *Descartes' error: Emotion, reason, and the human brain.* New York: Putnam.

Davidson, R. J., Pizzagalli, D., Nitschke, J. B., & Putnam, K. (2002). Depression: Perspectives from affective neuroscience. *Annual Review of Psychology, 53*, 545–574.

Dennett, D. C. (1984). *Elbow room: The varieties of free will worth wanting.* Cambridge, MA: MIT Press.

Duval, S., & Wicklund, R. A. (1973). Effects of objective self-awareness on attribution of causality. *Journal of Experimental Social Psychology, 9*, 17–31.

Eisenberger, N. I., & Lieberman, M. D. (2004). "Why it hurts to be left out": The neurocognitive overlap between physical and social pain. *Trends in Cognitive Sciences, 8*, 294–300.

Eisenberger, N. I., Lieberman, M. D., & Satpute, A. B. (2004). *Individual differences in the neural reactivities underlying cognitive control: An fMRI study of neuroticism, extraversion, and self-conciousness.* Manuscript submitted for publication.

Eisenberger, N. I., Lieberman, M. D., & Williams, K. D. (2003). Does rejection hurt? An fMRI study of social exclusion. *Science, 302*, 290–292.

Erikson, E. H. (1968). *Identity, youth, and crisis.* New York: Norton.

Farrer, C., & Frith, C. D. (2002). Experiencing oneself vs another person as being the cause of an action: The neural correlates of the experience of agency. *NeuroImage, 15*, 596–603.

Fenigstein, A., Scheier, M. F., & Buss, A. H. (1975). Public and private self-consciousness: Assessment and theory. *Journal of Consulting and Clinical Psychology, 43*, 522–527.

Fink, G. R., Markowitsch, H. J., Reinkemeier, M., Bruckbauer, T., Kessler, J., & Heiss, W. (1996). Cerebral representation of one's own past: Neural networks involved in autobiographical memory. *Journal of Neuroscience, 16*, 4275–4282.

Galin, D. (1992). Theoretical reflections on awareness, monitoring, and self in relation to anosognosia. *Consciousness and Cognition, 1*, 152–162.

Gallagher, H. L., & Frith, C. D. (2002). Functional imaging of "theory of mind." *Trends in Cognitive Sciences, 7*, 77–83.

Gilbert, D. T. (1989). Thinking lightly about others: Automatic components of the social inference process. In J. S. Uleman & J. A. Bargh (Eds.), *Unintended thought* (pp. 189–211). New York: Guilford Press.

Griffin, D. W., & Ross, L. (1991). Subject construal, social inference, and human misunderstanding. In M. P. Zanna (Ed.), *Advances in experimental social psychology* (Vol. 24, pp. 319–359). San Diego, CA: Academic Press.

Gottlieb, J. P., Kusunoki, M., & Goldberg, M. E. (1998). The representation of visual sailence in monkey parietal cortex. *Nature, 391*, 481–484.

Gusnard, D. A., Akbudak, E., Shulman, G. L., & Raichle, M. E. (2001). Medial prefrontal cortex and self-referential mental activity: Relation to a default mode of brain function. *Proceedings of the National Academy of Science, USA, 98*, 4259–4264.

Harter, S. (1999). *The construction of the self: A developmental perspective.* New York: Guilford Press.

Higgins, E. T. (1987). Self-discrepancy: A theory relating self and affect. *Psychological Review, 94*, 319–340.

Holyoak, K. J., & Hummel, J. E. (2000). The proper treatment of symbols in a connectionist architecture. In E. Dietrich & A. B. Markman (Eds.), *Cognitive dynamics: Conceptual and representational change in humans and machines* (pp. 229–263). Mahwah, NJ: Erlbaum.

Hunter, M. D., Farrow, T. F., Papadakis, N. G., Wilkinson, I. D., Woodruff, P. W., & Spence, S. A. (2003). Approaching an ecologically valid functional anatomy of spontaneous "willed" action. *NeuroImage, 20*, 1264–1269.

Iacoboni, M., Lieberman, M. D., Knowlton, B. J., Molnar-Szakacs, I., Moritz, M., Throop, C. J., & Fiske, A. P. (2004). Watching social interactions produces dorsomedial prefrontal and medial parietal BOLD fMRI signal increases compared to a resting baseline. *NeuroImage, 21*, 1167–1173.

Ingram, R.E. (1990). Self-focused attention in clinical disorders: Review and a conceptual model. *Psychological Bulletin, 107*, 156–176.

Iversen, S. D., & Mishkin, M. (1970). Perseverative interference in monkeys following selective lesions of the inferior prefrontal convexity. *Experimental Brain Research, 11*, 376–386.

Izquierda, I., Quillfield, J. A., Zanatta, M. S., Quevedo, J., Schaeffer, E., Schmitz, P. K., et al. (1997). Sequential role of hippocampus and amygdala, entorhinal cortex and parietal cortex in formation and retrieval of memory for inhibitory avoidance in rats. *European Journal of Neuroscience, 9*, 786–793.

James, W. (1890/1950). *The principles of psychology.* New York: Dover.

Johnson, S. C., Baxter, L. C., Wilder, L. S., Pipe, J. G., Heiserman, J. E., & Prigatano, G. P. (2002). Neural correlates of self-reflection. *Brain, 125*, 1808–1814.

Jueptner, M., Stephan, K. M., Frith, C. D., Brooks, D. J., Frackowiak, R. S., & Passingham, R. E. (1997). Anatomy of motor learning: I. Frontal cortex and attention to action. *Journal of Neurophysiology, 77*, 1313–1324.

Kelley, W. M., Macrae, C. N., Wyland, C. L., Caglar, S., Inati, S., & Heatherton, T. F. (2002). Finding the self? An event-related fMRI study. *Journal of Cognitive Neuroscience, 14*, 785–794.

Kiehl, K. A., Liddle, P. F., & Hopfinger, J. B. (2000). Error processing and the rostral anterior cingulate: An event-related fMRI study. *Psychophysiology, 37*, 216–223.

Kimbrell, T. A., George, M. S., Parekh, P. I., Ketter, T. A., Podell, D., M., Danielson, A. L., et al. (1999). Regional brain activity during transient self-induced anxiety and anger in healthy adults. *Biological Psychiatry, 46*, 454–465.

Kircher, T. T. J., Senior, C., Phillips, M. L., Benson, P. J., Bullmore, E. T., Brammer, M., et al. (2000). Towards a functional neuroanatomy of self-processing: Effects of faces and words. *Cognitive Brain Research, 10*, 133–144.

Kjaer, K. W., Nowak, M., & Lou, H. C. (2002). Reflective self-awareness and conscious states: PET evidence for a common midline parietofrontal core. *NeuroImage, 17*, 1080–1086.

Klein, S. B., Loftus, J., & Kihlstrom, J. F. (1996). Self-knowledge of an amnesic patient: Toward a neuropsychology of personality and social psychology. *Journal of Experimental Psychology: General, 125*, 250–260.

Klein, S. B., Loftus, J., Trafton, J. G., & Fuhrman, R. W. (1992). Use of exemplars and abstractions in trait judgments: A model of trait knowledge about the self and others. *Journal of Personality and Social Psychology, 63*, 739–753.

Klein, S. B., Rozendal, K., & Cosmides, L. (2002). A social-cognitive neuroscience analysis of the self. *Social Cognition, 20*(2), 105–135.

Knowlton, B. J., Mangels, J. A., & Squire, L. R. (1996). A neostriatal habit learning system in humans. *Science, 273*, 1399–1402.

Kosslyn, S. M., Thompson, W. L., & Alpert, N. M. (1997). Neural systems shared by visual imagery and visual perception: A positron emission tomography study. *NeuroImage, 6*, 320–334.

Kroger, J. K., Sabb, F. W., Fales, C. L., Bookheimer, S. Y., Cohen, M. S., & Holyoak, K. J. (2002). Recruitment of anterior dorsolateral prefrontal cortex in human reasoning: A parametric study of relational complexity. *Cerebral Cortex, 12*, 477–485.

Lakoff, G., & Johnson, M. (1999). *Philosophy in the flesh: The embodied mind and its challenge to Western thought.* New York: Basic Books.

Lane, R. D., Fink, G. R., Chau, P. M.-L., & Dolan, R. J. (1997). Neural activation during selective attention to subjective emotional responses. *NeuroReport, 8*, 3969–3972.

Langer, E. J. (1989). *Mindfulness.* Reading, MA: Addison-Wesley.

LeDoux, J. E. (1996). *The emotional brain: The mysterious underpinnings of emotional life.* New York: Simon & Schuster.

Lieberman, M. D. (2000). Intuition: A social cognitive neuroscience approach. *Psychological Bulletin, 126*, 109–137.

Lieberman, M. D. (2003). Reflective and reflexive judgment processes: A social cognitive neuroscience approach. In J. P. Forgas, K. Williams, & W. von Hippel (Eds.), *Social judgments: Implicit and explicit processes* (pp. 44–67). New York: Cambridge University Press.

Lieberman, M. D., Chang, G. Y., Chiao, J. Y., Bookheimer, S. Y., & Knowlton, B. J. (2004). An event-related fMRI study of artificial grammar learning in a balanced chunk strength design. *Journal of Cognitive Neuroscience, 16*, 427–438.

Lieberman, M. D., Eisenberger, N. I., & Crockett, M. (2003). *An fMRI study of automatic behavior: A disruption account.* Manuscript in preparation.

Lieberman, M. D., Gaunt, R., Gilbert, D. T., & Trope, Y. (2002). Reflection and reflexion: A social cognitive neuroscience approach to attributional inference. *Advances in Experimental Social Psychology, 34*, 199–249.

Lieberman, M. D., Hariri, A., Jarcho, J. J., Eisenberger N. I., & Bookheimer, S. Y. (2004). *Amygdala responses to race-based categorization: Processing mode and participant race effects.* Manuscript submitted for publication.

Lieberman, M. D., Jarcho, J. M., Berman, S., Naliboff, B., Suyenobu, B. Y., Mandelkern, M., et al. (2004). *The neural correlates of placebo effects: A disruption account.* Neuroimage, 22, 447–455.

Lieberman, M.D., Jarcho, J. M., & Satpute, A. B. (in press). Evidence-based and intuition-based self-knowledge: An fMRI study. *Journal of Personality and Social Psychology*.

Lieberman, M. D., & Pfeifer, J. H. (in press). The self and social perception: Three kinds of questions in social cognitive neuroscience. In A. Easton & N. Emery (Eds.), *Cognitive neuroscience of emotional and social behavior*. Philadelphia: Psychology Press.

Lieberman, M. D., & Rosenthal, R. (2001). Why introverts can't always tell who likes them: Multitasking and nonverbal decoding. *Journal of Personality and Social Psychology, 80*, 294–310.

McAdams, D. P. (1993). *The stories we live by: Personal myths and the making of the self.* New York: Guilford Press.

McClelland, J. L., McNaughton, B. L., & O'Reilly, R. C. (1995). Why there are complementary learning systems in the hippocampus and neocortex: Insights from the successes and failures of connectionist models of learning and memory. *Psychological Review, 102*, 419–457.

Mead, G. H. (1934). *Mind, self, and society.* Chicago: University of Chicago Press.

Melchior-Bonnet, S. (1994). *The mirror.* New York: Routledge.

Menon, V., Adleman, N. E., White, C. D., Glover, G. H., & Reiss, A. L. (2001). Error-related brain activation during a go/no go response inhibition task. *Human Brain Mapping, 12*, 131–143.

Miller, B. L., Seeley, W. W., Mychack, P., Rosen, H. J., Mena, I., & Boone, K. (2001). Neuroanatomy of the self: Evidence from patients with frontotemporal dementia. *Neurology, 57*, 817–821.

Miller, E. K., & Cohen, J. D. (2001). An integrative theory of prefrontal cortex function. *Annual Review of Neuroscience, 24*, 167–202.

Miller, G. A. (1956). The magical number seven, plus or minus two: Some limits on our capacity for processing information. *Psychological Review, 63*, 81–97.

Miller, G. A., Galanter, E., & Pribram, K. (1960). *Plans and the structure of behavior.* New York: Holt, Rinehart & Winston.

Miller, P. J. (1994). Narrative practices: Their role in socialization and self-construction. In U. Neisser & R. Fivush (Eds.), *The remembering self* (pp. 158–179). New York: Cambridge University Press.

Milner, B., Corkin, S., & Teuber, H. L. (1968). Further analysis of the hippocampal amnesic syndrome: Fourteen year follow-up study of H.M. *Neuropsychologia, 6*, 215–234.

Mitchell, J. P., Heatherton, T. F., & Macrae, C. N., (2002). Distinct neural systems subserve person and object knowledge. *Proceedings of the National Academy of Sciences, 99*, 15238–15243.

Monchi, O., Petrides, M., Petre, V., Worsley, K., & Dagher, A. (2001). Wisconsin card sorting revisited: Distinct neural circuits participating in different stages of the task identified by event-related functional magnetic resonance imaging. *Journal of Neuroscience, 21*, 7733–7741.

Murakami, H. (1994). *Dance, dance, dance: A novel.* New York: Vintage Books.

Mummery, C. J., Shallice, T., & Price, C. J. (1999). Dual-process model in semantic priming: A functional imaging perspective. *NeuroImage, 9*, 516–525.

O'Reilly, R. C., Braver, T. S., & Cohen, J. D. (1999). A biologically based computational model of working memory. In A. Miyake & P. Shah (Eds.), *Models of working memory: Mechanisms of active maintenance and executive control* (pp. 375–411). New York: Cambridge University Press.

Ochsner, K. N., Bunge, S. A., Gross, J. J., & Gabrieli, J. D. (2002). Rethinking feelings: An FMRI study of the cognitive regulation of emotion. *Journal of Cognitive Neuroscience, 14*, 1215–1229.

Packard, M. G., Hirsh, R., & White, N. M. (1989). Differential effects of fornix and caudate nucleus lesions on two radial maze tasks: Evidence for multiple memory systems. *Journal of Neuroscience, 9*, 1465–1472.

Pham, L. B., Taylor, S. E., & Seeman, T. E. (2001). Effects of environmental predictability and personal mastery on self-regulatory and physiological processes. *Personality and Social Psychology Bulletin, 27*, 611–620.

Pizzagalli, D., Pascual-Marqui, R. D., Nitschke, J. B., Oakes, T. R., Larson, C. L., Abercrombie, H. C., et al. (2001). Anterior cingulate activity as a predictor of degree of treatment response in major depression: Evidence from brain electrical tomography analysis. *American Journal of Psychiatry, 158*, 405–415.

Poldrack, R. A., Clark, J., Pare-Blagoev, E. J., Shohamy, D., Creso Moyano, J., Myers, C., et al. (2001). Interactive memory systems in the human brain. *Nature, 414*, 546–550.

Poldrack, R. A., & Packard, M. G. (2003). Competition among multiple memory systems: Converging evidence from animal and human brain studies. *Neuropsychologia, 41*, 245–251.

Preibisch, C., Neumann, K., Raab, P., Euler, H. A., Gudenberg, A. W. von, Lanfermann, H., et al. (2003). Evidence for compensation for stuttering by the right frontal operculum. *NeuroImage, 20*, 1356–1364.

Prout, H. T., & Prout, S. M. (1996). Global self-concept and its relationship to stressful life conditions. In B. A. Bracken (Ed.), *Handbook of self-concept: Developmental, social and clinical considerations* (pp. 259–286). New York: Wiley.

Raichle, M. E., MacLeod, A. M., Snyder, A. Z., Powers, W. J., Gusnard, D. A., & Shulman, G. L. (2001). A default mode of brain function. *Proceedings of the National Academy of Sciences, 98*, 676–682.

Rainville, P., Duncan, G. H., Price, D. D., Carrier, B., & Bushnell, M. C. (1997). Pain affect encoded in human anterior cingulate but not somatosensory cortex. *Science, 277*, 968–971.

Ramachandran, V. S. (1995). Anosognosia in parietal lobe syndrome. *Consciousness and Cognition, 4*, 22–51.

Ruby, P., & Decety, J. (2001). Effect of subjective perspective taking during simulation of action: A PET investigation of agency. *Nature Neuroscience, 4*, 546–550.

Satpute, A. B., Sellner, D., Waldman, M. D., Tabibnia, G., Holyoak, K. J., & Lieberman, M. D. (2004). *An fMRI study of causal judgments.* Manuscript submitted for publication.

Schacter, D. L. (1992). Understanding implicit memory: A cognitive neuroscience approach. *American Psychologist, 47*, 559–569.

Schultz, R. T., Grelotti, D. J., Klin, A., Kleinman, J., Van der Gaag, C., Marois, R., et al. (in press). The role of the fusiform face area in social cognition: Implications for the pathobiology of autism. *Philosophical Transactions of the Royal Society of London (Series B).*

Small, D. M., Zatorre, R. J., Dagher, A., Evans, A. C., & Jones-Gotman, M. (2001). Changes in brain activity related to eating chocolate: From pleasure to aversion. *Brain, 124*, 1720–1733.

Smith, E. E., & Jonides, J. (1999). Storage and executive processes in the frontal lobes. *Science, 283*, 1657–1661.

Spence, S. A., Brooks, D. J., Hirsh, S. B., Liddle, P. F., Meehan, J., & Grasby, P. M. (1997). A PET study of voluntary moevement in schizophrenic patients experiencing passivity phenomena (delusions of alien control). *Brain, 120*, 1997–2011.

Squire, L. R. (1992). Memory and the hippocampus: A synthesis from findings with rats, monkeys, and humans. *Psychological Review, 99*, 195–231.

Stuss, D. T., Picton, T. W., & Alexander, M. P. (2001). Consciousness, self-awareness, and the frontal lobes. In S. P. Salloway & P. F. Malloy (Eds.), *The frontal lobes and neuropsychiatric illness* (pp. 101–109). Washington, DC: American Psychiatric Publishing.

Taylor, J. G. (2001). The central role of the parietal lobes in consciousness. *Consciousness and Cognition, 10*, 379–417.

Thorne, A., & McLean, K. C. (2002). Gendered reminiscence practices and self-definition in late adolescence. *Sex Roles, 46*, 267–277.

Tomita, H., Ohbayashi, M., Nakahara, K., Hasegawa, I., & Miyashita, Y. (1999). Top–down signal from prefrontal cortex in executive control of memory retrieval. *Nature, 401*, 699–701.

Turner, R. H. (1976). The real self: From institution to impulse. *American Journal of Sociology, 81*, 989–1016.

Ursu, S., Stenger, V. A., Shear, M. K., Jones, M. R., & Carter, C. S. (2003). Overactive action monitoring in obsessive–compulsive disorder: Evidence from functional magnetic resonance imaging. *Psychological Science, 14*, 347–353.

Vogeley, K., Bussfeld, P., Newen, A., Hermann, S., Happe, F., Falkai, P., et al. (2001). Mind reading: Neural mechanisms of theory of mind and self-perspective. *NeuroImage, 14*, 170–181.

Vohs, K. D., & Heatherton, T. F. (2000). Self-regulatory failure: A resource-depletion approach. *Psychological Science, 11*, 249–254.

Wagner, A. D., Schacter, D. L., Rotte, M., Koutstaal, W., Maril, A., Dale, A. M., et al. (1998). Building memories: Remembering and forgetting of verbal experiences as predicted by brian activity. *Science, 281*, 1188–1191.

Waltz, J. A., Knowlton, B. J., Holyoak, K. J., Boone, K. B., Mishkin, F. S., de Menezes Santos, M., et al. (1999). A system for relational reasoning in human prefrontal cortex. *Psychological Science, 10*, 119–125.

Wegner, D. T. (2002). *The illusion of conscious will.* Cambridge, MA: MIT Press.

Weissman, D. H., Giesbrecht, B., Song, A. W., Mangun, G. R., & Woldorff, M. G. (2003). Conflict monitoring in the human anterior cingulate cortex during selective attention to global and local object features. *NeuroImage, 19*, 1361–1368.

Whalen, P. J., Rauch, S. L., Etcoff, N. L., McInerney, S. C., Lee, M. B., & Jenike, M. A. (1998). Masked presentations of emotional facial expressions modulate amygdala activity without explicit knowledge. *Journal of Neuroscience, 18*, 411–418.

Wiener, N. (1948). *Cybernetics: Control and communication in the animal and the machine.* Cambridge, MA: MIT Press.

Willingham, D. B., & Dunn, E. W. (2003). What neuroimaging and brain localization can do, cannot do, and should not do for social psychology. *Journal of Personality and Social Psychology, 85*, 662–671.

Wilson, T. D. (2002). *Strangers to ourselves: Discovering the adaptive unconscious.* Cambridge, MA: Harvard University Press.

Zysset, S., Huber, O., Ferstl, E., & von Cramon, D. Y. (2002). The anterior frontomedian cortex and evaluative judgment: An fMRI study. *NeuroImage, 15*, 983–991.

5

Ideal Agency: The Perception of Self as an Origin of Action

JESSE PRESTON AND DANIEL M. WEGNER

It is chiefly my will which leads me to discern that I bear a certain image and similitude of Deity.

—René Descartes, 1641/1901 "Meditations IV"

Each of us has ideals, things we would like to be. We would like to be happy, pretty, smart, brave, kind, or honest. Such desired characteristics are often appreciated in psychology as facets of a person's ideal self (Cooley, 1902; Rogers, 1961), and studies of the ideal self commonly focus on the particular selection of such ideals that an individual embraces. These ideals are all descriptions of the "good person." In this sense, they all skip right over an important point. There is a far more fundamental ideal that often goes unnoticed, a basic prerequisite for even being a person at all. This is the ideal of agency. Quite simply, we would rather be agents than objects.

Yes, of course, anyone would rather do things than be a block of wood. It turns out, though, that the ideal of agency is far more subtle, pervasive, and even insidious than a mere desire to be active. This chapter is about how the desire to be an agent influences human psychology. As suggested by Wegner (2002), aspiration to the ideal of agency is a profound force that underlies and connects many patterns of human thought and behavior. Ideal agency is involved in how people come to believe they consciously will their actions, it operates in the processes (usually understood in terms of cognitive dissonance) that underlie the perception and confabulation of intentions, and it functions as well to produce the misperception of actions as successful. It takes a lot of work not to be a block of wood, and the aspiration to the ideal of agency prompts an unsettling array of psychological distortions in service of this goal.

To examine the influences of ideal agency, we will consider first what it means to be an agent of any sort. There are basic properties of agency that can inform the analysis of how humans aspire to this goal. This analysis allows us to understand how an agent could be more or less ideal. With a grasp on the dimension of ideal agency, then, we will examine each of three essential paths toward the ideal—the confabulation of intention, the experience of an illusion of conscious will, and the misperception of action.

AN ANATOMY OF AGENCY

Agents are entities that cause events through self-movement. By this definition, humans, dolphins, gerbils, grasshoppers, robots, bean sprouts, certain artificial intelligence (AI) programs, and God Almighty all hold in common the property of agency. Agents can be contrasted with objects—entities that do not cause events. Objects include the billiard ball, as well as the aforementioned block of wood, and many other items in the universe that appear to move only when moved upon. In a sense, the unique property of agents is the inscrutability of their motion. Agents are first causes or uncaused causes. Authorship is ascribed to agents as the origin of action because their prior causal history is unclear.

The notion of agency is so central to human psychology that it is regularly assumed rather than examined. We readily perceive agents all around us and seldom mistake them for objects. The philosophy of mind reveals agency to be a major human preoccupation. Much thought and theory is aimed at understanding agent causation and how it can be understood as distinct from object causation (e.g., Anscombe, 1957; Brand, 1984; Davidson, 1980). And psychologists have long believed that the perception of persons is dominated by the theme of agency rather than by a theme of mechanism or simple physical causation (DeCharms, 1968; Heider, 1958; Heider & Simmel, 1944).

The fundamental character of agency perception is suggested by the finding that judgments of agency appear to be snap decisions, based on visual cues such as biological motion (Blakemore & Decety, 2001) and agentlike appearance, such as eye spots (Baron-Cohen, 1994). The perception of agents is deeply ingrained in our minds, a property of our early perceptual systems that is amplified and refined as we grow to develop mature "theories of mind" (Premack & Woodruff, 1978; Wellman, 1992). We not only perceive the real agents around us but we also make up a spirit world of angels, devils, gods, and other supernatural agents to account for events that we cannot otherwise explain (Barrett, 2000; Boyer, 2001). Indeed, Guthrie (1980) suggested that we have evolved to perceive agency because it is of crucial importance to detect other agents in order to survive. After all, it is much better to mistake a boulder for a bear than to mistake a bear for a boulder.

When we perceive agency in ourselves, others, or imagined others, what is it that we think we are seeing? Are there common features of things that cause themselves to behave? What, then, makes up an agent? In a discussion of the characteristics of artificially intelligent agents (computer programs that "do things"), Russell and Norvig (2003) provided a useful three-part architecture of agency that applies broadly to both natural and artificial agents. In essence, agents can be described in terms of the operation of three key features: sensors, processors, and actuators (Russell & Norvig, 2003). Agents input information through sensors, operate on the information through processors, and output behavior through actuators.

Sensors are the means by which the agent knows about its environment. Just as people sense and come to know their environment through sight, smell, hearing, taste, and touch, an AI agent such as a robot could sense its environment by detecting variation in heat and light, for example. The *processor* is the mechanism by which the agent chooses a course of action based on the input. Russell and Norvig discussed three different kinds of processors with which an AI agent could be programmed: if–then rules (e.g., if the car in front of you is braking, then initiate braking), goal-based processors (which are based on trying to get to a set goal), and utility-based processors (which select actions that are "good" for the agent—have high utility—without having a specific goal). The human mind might potentially implement any of these sorts of processors (Carver & Scheier, 1998; Newell, 1973; Powers, 1990), whereas software agents are typically programmed with just one, as appropriate to their specific task. Regardless of the specific programming, however, the AI processor, like the human, uses the sensed input to select some actions over others, and that selection is based on criteria applied by the agent. The *actuator*, the third property of the agent, is the means by which the agent acts upon the environment. People have the limbs, nerves, and muscles of their bodies to get what they want. An AI agent could have mechanical limbs or other tools at its command that provide the same function. In the simplest AI agent, the actuator could merely be some computational function that changes stored information in memory or turns on a pixel on the computer screen.

Despite the proficiency of computer programs to calculate and even outplay chess masters, AI researchers have yet to actually build an AI agent that approaches the sophistication of human agents. To be sure, there is a hierarchy among agents, in that some agents are better than others. The hierarchy is not a matter of who is flesh and who is metal. The hierarchy of agents involves agents that are better or worse at the three defining features of agency: sensing, processing, and actuating. The best possible agent would be the one that performs all three functions most effectively.

IDEAL AGENCY

The ideal agent thinks about the situation and action, chooses what will enhance its happiness (or achieve its goal), and then successfully performs the action that is needed. The ideal agent, in other words, senses ideally, processes ideally, and actuates ideally.

There are agents all around us that fall short of this ideal. There is the copy machine that can nicely sense the presence of an original to be copied, can process the input when we press the button for five copies, but that then actuates the copies into a serious paper jam. There is the dollar-bill changer that can't sense our rumpled bill and keeps spitting it back. There is the Web site that accepts our order and successfully sends us the item we have purchased but also processes the order repeatedly and sends us the item again and again. Modern life is filled with simple agents gone wrong, and this is before we even get to the errors of flesh-and-blood agents. There are dogs who won't fetch; parrots who only repeat vile language; and all the bad drivers, incompetent waiters, and insolent store clerks who populate our daily lives. Their breakdowns of agency can be traced alternately to poor sensing, poor processing, or poor actuating.

In contrast to all these bad agents, there is the perfect agent. In some cultures, this ideal is human, but in many it is God. The dominant Western concept of God portrays an agent that is omniscient, benevolent, and omnipotent. To be omniscient means that God knows all and is aware of everything. God's sensors are therefore perfect. To be benevolent means that God wills good things to happen. God's will is therefore perfect in that God knows exactly what the right thing is that should be done in order to cause events that achieve the best possible goals. In this sense, God's processor has perfect utility. And to be omnipotent means that God can do anything—can affect anything and change it in any way that God likes. God's actuators are therefore perfect, in that the outcome desired is exactly the outcome that God achieves. Deities with lesser talents appear in religions around the world, but their godliness is typically accompanied by a heightened level of one of these characteristics—lesser gods can sometimes at least sense more acutely, will more benevolently, or act more powerfully than mere mortals. Thus, the concept of God is an agent more ideal than the human, and sometimes perfectly ideal.

We humans fall somewhere between faulty vending machines and the God of infinite perfection. More often than we would like to admit, we behave without full knowledge of our situation and how it pertains to what we are doing. Thoughts about our situation and what should cause us to act would require perfect sensors, and we don't always have them. We also may have knowledge and perform an action but fail to choose the proper course. Willing our actions correctly would require perfect processors, and we don't always have them. Finally, although we may have the thought and the will, our capacities to act may fail us. The ability to perform the actions we envision would require perfect actuators and, sadly, we don't always have these, either. However, we know what ideal agency should be, and we are motivated by our conception of this ideal to assimilate our actions to it. Thus, we fill in the blanks: When possible, we assume that we have thought, will, and action that exemplify ideal agency.

IDEALIZATION PROCESSES

The fact that our humble bodies and minds do not always follow the ideal thought–will–action model means that we often find ourselves with only some fragments of the ideal. However, these failures of agency could have the effect of making the agent more likely to fail in the future. Experiences of loss of control and expectations of failure can lead to learned helplessness (Abramson, Seligman, & Teasdale, 1978; Dweck & Leggett, 1988) and self-handicapping behavior (Arkin & Baumgardner, 1985; Berglas & Jones, 1978), turning judgments of the self as a faulty agent into a self-fulfilling prophecy. It may be better for the agent to not pay too much attention to the "blips" in the system and believe that everything is operating as it should. In aspiring to the ideal of agency, then, we infer that the missing components of ideal agency are actually in place. People do more than merely deduce that the aspects of ideal agency are present; they also actually perceive them to be there. If we cannot directly observe any one of the components, we may infer that it has functioned and fill it in with the relevant information, just as the blind spot is filled with the appropriate background by the visual system.

Certainly there are times when we are content to be objects. Agency is not even an issue for whole classes of behavior (e.g., knee reflexes, eye saccades, sneezes, autonomic nervous system responses), and it also is not a concern when our bodies are moved about by external forces (e.g., lifted by an elevator, bumped by a door). And for events that occur far from our bodies, we may have an initial filtering system that screens out those for which we could not be agents at all. However, for a range of actions of our bodies that we commonly understand as voluntary (Passingham, 1993), possibilities of agency are always present. For such actions, we attempt to apply a template of ideal agency, and when it seems to fit, we assume that thought, will, and action are all in place.

This means that whenever any of the components of ideal agency is absent, we tend to feel a certain tension and incompleteness. Something seems amiss. For example, when you walk into the kitchen and realize on arrival that you don't remember what you intended to do when you got there ("Was I coming in here for cookies? Milk? A double whiskey with beer chaser?"), something seems wrong. You performed an action (walking into the room), it somehow felt willed (you know you weren't pushed, anyway), and yet you don't have the thoughts that would tell you what you had sensed to lead you in this direction. You don't know what you were doing. The case of less-than-ideal agency feels somehow distressing. This observation can be generalized to a wide range of action: We usually assume that all three components of ideal agency will be present, and we find it discomfiting when any one is absent.

Beyond a basic feeling that something is wrong, the ideal of agency prompts people to make motivated inferences. Specifically, whenever some component of ideal agency is missing, the person is motivated to infer that the component is indeed present. This inference engine is weakest when all three components of ideal agency are missing. Thus, when a person has no relevant thought, will, or action, the person is quite unlikely to infer that any or all of these are present. Only rarely do people assume they were the agents of actions performed by others, which they did not conceive of in advance, and which they did not feel that they willed. Admittedly, some alien-control hallucinations in schizophrenia may have these properties (Stephens & Graham, 2000), but they are rare. Claiming authorship of environmental events at a distance is not the normal human proclivity and only occurs when there are serious breakdowns in the brain and mind processes responsible for authorship processing (Frith, Blakemore, & Wolpert, 2000; Wegner & Sparrow, in press).

When one component of agency is present, somewhat stronger inferences of ideal agency are made. A person who thinks about an action (say, telling off the boss) may have a tendency to perceive that the action happened (noticing, e.g., that she actually had said something the boss might not have liked) and may also feel that she willed this action (even to the point of feeling guilty about her imagined slur)—when these idealized accompaniments of the thought actually did not occur. By the same token, perceiving that an action has occurred (such as having hurt someone) might lead the person to infer that this action was thought about in advance and even that it was willed. And feelings of will ("I want to do better in school") might bring about the inference that relevant thoughts had crossed one's mind ("I studied for the test") and even lead to a tendency to perceive that the action had happened (as in the case of a C grade misremembered as an A).

These motivated inferences become far more likely, and far more powerful, when multiple components of ideal agency are already in place and just one is missing. Thought, will, and action are presumed to co-occur so profoundly that when we get two out of three, we assume we've won the whole match. When will and action are present, we infer thought; when thought and action are present, we infer will; and, when thought and will are present, we infer action. Each of these three patterns of motivated inference leads to a different range of distortions in self-perception, some of which are already widely known and studied in psychology and others of which are only beginning to be discerned. Different circumstances may lead to different inferences' being made. However, whatever is most ambiguous and unclear will typically be altered to match the more unambiguous components of the ideal.

The three strong inferences from ideal agency are the focus of the remainder of the chapter. As shown in Table 5.1, these inferences each follow when evidence of ideal agency is present for two components of the ideal and is not present for the third. They include *intention confabulation* (inference of premeditative thought), *apparent mental causation* (inference of the will), and *action misperception* (inference of action).

Intention confabulation occurs when we can observe that we have performed an act and feel as though it was willed but cannot access the thoughts or intentions

TABLE 5.1. Strong Inferences of Ideal Agency

	Component of ideal agency		
Type of inference	Thought	Will	Action
Intention confabulation	Inferred	Observed	Observed
Apparent mental causation	Observed	Inferred	Observed
Action misperception	Observed	Observed	Inferred

that led us to perform the act. An intention is then inferred after the fact that suitably explains why we would have wanted to perform the action in the first place. Apparent mental causation occurs when we observe that we have performed an act and had intention to perform the act but do not have access to willing that act. Knowing that we had prior thoughts and sensations that suggested the intention, and seeing that the action was indeed performed, leads to the feeling that the act arose out of our will. Action misperception occurs when we have intention to perform an act and feel as though we have willed the act but do not have access to the act itself. Whether or not the action occurred as intended may be altered in our minds so that we view the outcome to be more successful. In what follows, we discuss each of these inferences in turn and review the evidence indicating some of the conditions under which each of the inferences has been observed.

INFERENCE OF PREMEDITATION: INTENTION CONFABULATION

In a scene in the 1985 film *Pee-Wee's Big Adventure* (Shapiro, Abramson, & Burton, 1985), the title hero is seen riding his beloved bicycle through the streets, doing a number of daring tricks. At one point, a trick goes awry, and Pee-Wee is catapulted off his bike. He flies hundreds of feet through the air, landing in front of a group of neighborhood kids. Dusting himself off, our hero dryly comments "I meant to do that," and walks off.

We all fly through the air in our own special ways only to land on the ground and claim that we meant to do that. A wealth of research has caught people making this particular inference of ideal agency in a variety of situations. But we should not be too quick to chastise ourselves for such selfish delusions; we also have an astounding lack of insight into the reasons for all sorts of actions—good, bad, or neutral. What is particularly interesting is that despite the fact that the reasons for what we do are often hidden from ourselves, the tendency to report reasons for what we do remains unimpaired (Wilson, Hodges, & LaFleur, 1995; Wilson & Schooler, 1991).

It appears as though we are unable to admit or understand that we may have acted without knowing why. Apparently, it is unpleasant to think that the things we do might not emerge from our personal resolutions to do them. Making ourselves do things is how we get all the things in the world we cherish, how we interact with the people with whom we have our most meaningful relationships, and how we do the jobs and the hobbies that define our identities. All these activities should begin from our desires and intentions to do them; otherwise, what could all of these behaviors be for? Thus, if we have performed some behavior, it surely must be for a reason, even if we only make that reason explicit after the act. The motivated inference of reasons and thoughts relevant to action has been termed *intention confabulation* (Wegner, 2002), and it occurs whenever we generate reasons to explain our actions post hoc and believe that those reasons were our intentions all along.

Confabulation by Children

There is evidence that young children are particularly prone to confabulate memory for intentions. Schult (1997) observed this in a study in which children tossed a beanbag toward three colored buckets. They were asked to name in advance which color bucket they wanted to hit and were given a color chip to remind them of their choice. Hidden at the bottom of one bucket was a prize—a picture signaling that they had "won" (and that they could mark on a score sheet). After each time they hit a bucket, the children were asked, "Which one were you trying to hit?" The interesting case here, of course, is when the child "wins" by hitting a bucket other than the color they had said they wanted. And, indeed, when the intended bucket was missed but a picture was found, the 3-year-olds answered incorrectly more often than the 4- and 5-year-olds. Like Pee-Wee, the youngest children often claimed they had been "trying to hit" the winner all along. Similar results have been reported by Abbott and Flavell (1996).

Cognitive Dissonance and Self-Perception

A wealth of evidence demonstrating intention confabulation comes from research on the theories of cognitive dissonance and self-perception. The phenomenon at the heart of these theories is that people report their attitudes to be consistent with the actions they perform, even if their prior attitude was in fact inconsistent with the action (Bem, 1972; Bem & McConnell, 1970; Cohen, 1962; Festinger, 1957; Wicklund & Brehm, 1976). The theories differ in the mechanism they use to explain this phenomenon. According to cognitive dissonance theory, the change in attitude results from the conflict a person feels when he or she holds two inconsistent cognitions. Festinger (1957) argued that people believe that their actions ought to arise from their attitudes. If their actions and attitudes are incongruent, this causes tension. As a result, one of the two cognitions is altered to match the other. In general, it is easier to deny an attitude than an action, so people change their attitude to match the behavior. According to self-perception theory (Bem, 1967, 1972) there need not be a prior attitude at all. Bem suggested that we often are in the same position as an observer of actions; we don't know how we feel until we see ourselves acting in some way. We believe that our attitudes and actions should be consistent, but sometimes it is only our actions that inform us of our attitudes. The conflict between these theories is not critical for our purposes, and in fact it has been quite nicely resolved (Cooper & Fazio, 1984). What matters is the common point—the idea that people will confabulate prior intentions based on their actions. This confabulation relies on the feeling that the action was freely willed by the actor, not induced by others.

In one of the first experiments on cognitive dissonance, Festinger and Carlsmith (1959) had research participants engage in an extremely dull task—turning pegs on a board. The participants were then asked to tell the next participant that this dull activity was fun and interesting. For their PR work, participants were paid either $1 or $20. Following this, participants were then asked to report their true feelings about the joy of peg turning. The people who were paid $20 reported that the activity was actually quite dull and boring, despite what they had told the confederate. But apparently being poorly paid has its benefits, because the people who were paid $1 reported that turning pegs was enjoyable. Being paid $1 to do anything is not a very good justification for anything, certainly not for telling a lie to a stranger who has never caused you any harm; $20, on the other hand, is much more motivating, and one could justify telling a lie in order to get a healthy amount of cash in hand. What is interesting is that in no case did anyone refuse to lie for the experimenter. Compliance is very easily induced in participants, and people are remarkably eager to go along with the polite requests of a scientist. It appears, then, that in all cases participants confabulated an inaccurate intention for their action. In the case of participants paid $1, they believed that their endorsement of the activity stemmed from their true enjoyment of the activity. In the case of participants paid $20, they believed their endorsement stemmed from the generous monetary compensation. However, in all cases, their endorsement was simply compliance with the experimenter, possibly to be helpful to the experimenter or because they were submitting to authority. However, none of the participants were aware of the powerful forces of social pressure, and so they confabulated an intention to explain their behavior.

Induced compliance turned out to be very useful in this line of research, for it made the participants feel that they were acting of their own free will. In another study, Linder, Cooper, and Jones (1967) had students write an essay that contradicted their held attitude (to ban speakers at their college). As in the Festinger and Carlsmith (1959) study, the payment for this task varied. For some participants, the pay for writing the essay was announced as 50¢, whereas for others it was $2.50—a tidy sum back then. A further variation in the experiment manipulated the perception of choice: Some participants were led to believe that they had considerable personal choice with respect to whether to write an essay—the experimenter explained at the outset that after he had described the study they could decide for themselves whether or not to write the essay. For others, there was no such emphasis placed on choice.

As expected, everyone complied with the request. The effect of payment was also replicated: Those who wrote the essay that ran against their own opinion for 50¢ endorsed it more afterward than did those who wrote for the larger sum of $2.50. However, compared to participants who were not given the sense of choice (an illusory sense, because everyone did write the essay), those who perceived choice showed a classic cognitive dissonance effect. Performing a dissonant act under conditions designed to arouse a feeling of choice made people become more positive toward the topic they were paid less to espouse. When the coercion of the experimenter was overt and the experience of willing the action was thus undermined, the participants did not need to confabulate an intention to write the essay. Their action was accounted for by the experimenter's will. However, when participants were given an illusory sense of choice, they came to feel as though they were in favor of the attitude they presented in the essay. Why else would they "choose" to write such an essay?

These studies and many others demonstrate that people change or create their attitude to match the behavior they have performed. But does this necessarily mean that they have confabulated a prior intention? It may very well be that behaving in a way has made them see the error of their ways and persuaded them to change their views. However, the researchers in the early dissonance studies reported that not only do people report a new inconsistent attitude but they also fail to recall that their prior attitude was different from their present one. Bem and McConnell (1970) addressed the issue of prior-attitude awareness. They asked people who had written counterattitudinal essays to report not their final (post-essay) opinion on the issue but their prior opinion. People couldn't do this. Instead, these reports of prior attitudes mirrored faithfully the standard dissonance effect: Participants led to believe that they had a high degree of choice in whether to write the essay reported that they had agreed with the essay all along, whereas those led to believe they had a low degree of choice reported no such agreement. What happened, apparently, was that people looking back after they had written the essay had no conscious memory of their pre-essay attitudes. It is as though the confabulation of intention erases its tracks, leaving people with no memory of ever having wanted other than what they currently see as their intention.

It is important to note that the success of cognitive dissonance and self-perception paradigms relies on the participants' impression that they are acting of their own choice. We do not confabulate reasons for our actions unless we also feel as though the actions were willed. For this reason we do not confabulate intentions for reactions that we understand don't require will, such as jerking a hand away from a hot stove. We know that such things will happen without our choice and do not originate from our desires or beliefs. It is only for actions that are willed that we apply a model of ideal agency and for which we need to have thoughts that precede our actions. Although the perception of choice has long been known as a key precondition for the phenomena of dissonance and self-perception (Wicklund & Brehm, 1976), it is only through an appreciation of these phenomena in the context of ideal agency that the role of this variable in making action seem willful can be understood. With action observed and will apparent, the person infers prior thoughts consistent with what was done.

Posthypnotic Suggestion

In the late 19th century, hypnotism reached the peak of its popularity. The public and the scientific community alike were fascinated with understanding hypnosis and its implications for medicine, psychoanalysis, and party games. Hypnosis also yields excellent illustrations of people confabulating intentions, as this is a common response to behaviors performed as the result of posthypnotic suggestion. Moll (1889) observed one such instance when he gave a woman the posthypnotic suggestion to take a book from the table and put it on the bookshelf when she woke up. He woke her, and she did as Moll had suggested. Moll asked her why she did this, and she reported that she did not like to see things untidy, and so she put the book away. She did not remember the suggestion that Moll had given her, and so she created a (very sensible) reason for her action in the form of a confabulated prior intention.

But hypnotism is no fun at all if you just make people put books on shelves. The woman in that case may well have been a tidy person and could have genuinely wanted to put that book away regardless of Moll's suggestion. The real power of hypnotism is that people can be persuaded to do very strange things that they might otherwise never do. It is easy to find a reason for a mundane action such as putting a book away, but it may not be so easy to find reasons for less sensible behaviors. Nevertheless, reasons can be found. In another case, Moll gave a man a posthypnotic suggestion to take a flowerpot from the window, wrap it in cloth, put it on the sofa, and bow to it three times. The man awoke and did as Moll had suggested. When asked why he did this, the man responded that the plant was probably cold. So, he wrapped it in cloth and put it near the fire (on the sofa) to keep it warm. This pleased him, so he bowed to the plant to show his happiness about the whole idea. He also added that this was not foolish, because he had reasons for doing it.

Left-Brain Interpreter

In the examples of posthypnotic suggestion and in the research on cognitive dissonance and self-perception, people confabulated a prior intention for their actions because they were unaware that the true cause for their action was created by others. Intention confabulation can also result when our true intentions originate within the self but remain concealed. Some fascinating examples of this emerge from "split brain" patients—people who have had the corpus callosum surgically severed as a treatment for severe epilepsy. The corpus callosum connects the left and right sides of the brain and is the means by which the two halves communicate with each other. As a result, people who have undergone this kind of procedure have two "minds," each partially unaware of what the other is thinking. Studies conducted by Gazzaniga (1983, 1988; Gazzaniga & LeDoux, 1978) have shown that if the intentions of the right half of the brain are concealed from the left, the person may confabulate an intention to match the action.

In these studies, the patient is presented with words or pictures to one visual field but not the other. Consequently, the information is only available to one half of the brain. The resulting actions must be quickly explained by the other side. For example, the patient J.W.'s left visual field (which corresponds to the right brain) was presented with the word *walk*. He obeyed and began to leave. When asked why, he responded that he was going to get a Coke. Prior testing had indicated that his right brain lacked the verbal sophistication to come up with such a response, so this answer must have been a quick interpretation of his behavior, provided by his left brain. In another instance, the word *laugh* was presented to his right brain, and J.W. laughed. When asked why he laughed, he replied, "You guys come up and test us every month. What a way to make a living" (Gazzaniga, 1983). Another explanation for laughter came when the patient N.G.'s right brain was presented with a nude picture of a woman. She laughed at the picture, but when asked why she did so, she responded that she thought the machine presenting the pictures was funny (Gazzaniga & LeDoux, 1978).

A telling example was found with the patient P.S., who was shown two pictures. One was shown to the left brain, and one to the right . Also in front of him was an array of pictures that were perceived by both visual fields. His task was to select the picture that best matched the picture he was shown. In one instance, a picture of a chicken was flashed to the left side of his brain at the same time that a snow scene was flashed to the right side of his brain. P.S. selected a picture of a claw with his right hand (left brain) to go with the picture of the chicken. He also selected a picture of a shovel with his left hand (right brain) to go with the snow scene. He was then asked to explain these choices. The left brain understood the choice of the claw; it matched the picture of the chicken it just saw. However, it did not know the reason for the choice of the shovel, which was selected by the right brain. It quickly improvised a reason for the choice—the shovel is used to clean out the chicken coop! The choice of the shovel was interpreted by the left brain in a way that was consistent with its own intentions and knowledge.

Gazzaniga (Gazzaniga & LeDoux, 1978) emphasized that the explanations that the patients give are offered as the reason for behavior, not merely as guesses at the reason. This is true despite the patients' awareness that their surgery has resulted in their having a "split brain." Even though they could say that it must be the result of their surgery, they are not inhibited from confabulating a different reason and feeling as though that reason is veridical. Gazzaniga (1988) accounted for these findings by suggesting that the left brain, in addition to its verbal duties, is responsible for interpreting our actions. The brain is made up of various modules that are responsible for specific functions and operate outside of our conscious awareness. Gazzaniga argued that there is a left-brain system (the interpreter) that monitors the actions that result from all these functional modules and comes up with the reasons for those actions. The interpreter considers all the outputs of the functional modules as soon as they are made and immediately constructs a hypothesis as to why a particular action occurred. In fact, the interpreter may not be privy to why a particular module responded. Nonetheless, it will take the behavior at face value and fit the event into the large outgoing mental schema (belief system) that it has already constructed.

According to Gazzaniga (Gazzaniga & LeDoux, 1978) this interpretation happens on a regular basis in the left side of the brain, which raises the question of how many of the intentions that we feel are ever the true reason for our actions. Even if people constantly confabulate their intentions, it is almost impossible to know because intentions are generally kept private. If we always had to make our intentions explicit before acting, like calling shots in a pool game, we might find a whole lot of actions that weren't as successful as we wanted and a whole lot of unexplained actions left over. As unpleasant as failure may be, having performed actions with no reason may be much more disconcerting. The left-brain interpreter provides a seamless connection between our thoughts and actions that makes us feel like effective, sensible, ideal agents.

INFERENCE OF THE WILL: APPARENT MENTAL CAUSATION

The feeling that we will many of our actions is an inescapable part of human life. We feel that we cause our actions when we think of going out to lunch and then do so, for example, and it is difficult in the face of this compelling feeling to subscribe to mechanistic theories of human behavior that suggest our actions are caused by psychological processes—not by our agent selves. The experience of willing an action is a variable one, however—something that is not inevitable in the action's occurrence—and this observation suggests that the feeling is separable from the processes whereby the action is caused. Quite simply, our "feeling of doing" any action is an inference, an interpretation that arises from specific conditions. The conditions that produced this feeling have been explored in the theory of apparent mental causation (Wegner, 2002; Wegner & Wheatley, 1999).

In essence, this theory says that we experience conscious will when we infer that our thought has caused our action. Thus, when you think of going to lunch and then do so, there's no telling what really caused the lunch going—but you nonetheless are likely to experience the strong sense that you consciously willed it. There are three principles guiding our inferences about the relationship between thought and action: priority, consistency, and exclusivity (Wegner 2002; Wegner & Wheatley, 1999). These principles suggest that we are most inclined to experience conscious will for an action when our thoughts immediately precede the action (priority), when these thoughts are consistent with the action (consistency), and when the thoughts occur exclusive of other salient potential cause of the action (exclusivity).

Thus, if you think that ice cream is tasty just before you lean over and have a bite of a cone, you are more likely to feel that you willed that action than if you think ice cream is tasty only after you take a bite (priority violated). You are more inclined to experience willing the action if you think that ice cream is tasty than if you think it is unhealthy when you take that bite (consistency violated). And you are more likely to think you willed the bite if your thought accompanies the action alone—and is not accompanied by the ministrations of a pushy friend who is encouraging you to try the cone (exclusivity violated). To the extent that thoughts about an action have all these aspects, the thoughts provide a preview of the action of the agent, and it feels as though the will has operated by transforming the goals of the agent into reality.

Evidence on the Principles

Evidence for apparent mental causation comes from studies that demonstrate that giving people a preview of action does increase their feelings of authorship for that action. In a study inspired by the Ouija board, the role of the priority of thought was investigated (Wegner & Wheatley, 1999). A participant and a confederate were seated facing each other across a small table, both wearing headphones. Between them was a computer mouse and on a computer screen beside them was a page from the book *I Spy,* displaying about 50 small objects, such as a swan, a dinosaur, a car, and the like. The participant and the confederate were told that they were to move the mouse together by both placing their fingertips on it, and that they should stop moving the mouse every 30 s or so when music played. When they made a stop, they rated how intentional each stop was—how much they personally intended to make the stop independent of their partner's actions. They were also played words through the headphones during the study, which was ostensibly to provide some distraction, and were told that their partner would hear different words than they would.

All this was designed to create a situation in which the participant would have a thought about the action before it was actually performed. Moreover, the action would not be his or her own. The confederate was instructed to guide the motion of the mouse on some trials and to make specific stops on certain objects (e.g., the swan). Some of the words that the participants heard corresponded to the objects on the screen (e.g., *swan*). Each of the stops was timed to occur at specific intervals from when the participant heard the corresponding word, so the participant was primed with a thought of the action either 30 s before the stop, 5 s before, 1 s before, or 1 s after. Participants rated the stop as much more intentional when they heard the prime either 5 s before or 1 s before the stop. When the prime was given 30 s before or 1 s after, they felt the stop was less intentional on their part. When the thought and the action were consistent in a timely fashion, people came to feel that the action was their own choice, even though in all cases the stops were controlled by the confederate.

Part of the reason why magic tricks and optical illusions capture the fascination of eager audiences is that they persist despite the watcher's knowing that they can't be so. If apparent mental causation really is an illusion, then the feeling of conscious will could be induced even in cases in which people logically know that they did not create the action. Wegner, Sparrow, and Winerman (2004) looked at just this. People in a lab setting rated how much control and intention they felt about moving someone else's arms, but under conditions that paralleled real self-generated action. To promote the illusion, the experimenters made it look as though the other person's arms were the participant's own arms. Participants watched themselves in a mirror as another person hidden immediately behind them extended arms forward on each side of them. This is the pantomime routine sometimes known as *helping hands*. The person behind the participant then followed a series of instructions for hand movement delivered over headphones (e.g., "clap three times"). In some cases, the participant heard these same instructions and so knew what actions were to follow. In other cases, the participant did not hear any instructions. Afterward, participants were asked to rate on a 7-point scale how much control they felt over the other person's arms. The people who heard the previews felt a greater degree of control over the arms than those who did not, even though they knew that they were not actually controlling any of the movement.

Research has also examined how apparent mental causation can give rise to magical thinking (Pronin & Wegner, 2003). In two studies, participants were led to have evil thoughts about another person, who then came to experience a negative outcome. Would participants feel as though their ill thoughts produced an ill will? Participants were told they were participating in a study on voodoo with another person (actually a confederate). The participant was selected to play the role of witch doctor, and the confederate played the role of the victim. The participant and confederate went to separate rooms, and the participant said a brief voodoo chant (written by the experimenter, not a genuine chant). In one condition, the chant was neutral; in the other condition, the chant was malevolent and specifically wished harm against the confederate. After the chant, the participant was instructed to stick pins in a voodoo doll (with the confederate's name on it) in the presence of the confederate. Following the voodoo ritual, the confederate reported that she now had a headache that she did not have before. Participants who were instructed to recite the malevolent chant felt more responsible for the confederate's headache than those who just said a neutral chant. In a second study, negative thoughts about the confederate were manipulated by having the confederate act in an obnoxious and irritating manner. In this condition the confederate arrived 10 min late to the study, littered on the floor, chewed gum with his mouth open, and wore a T-shirt that read "Stupid people shouldn't breed." In a neutral condition the confederate acted normally and wore an inoffensive shirt. Again, the participant was selected to be the witch doctor and the confederate was the victim. Rather than say a chant, the participant was instructed to focus his or her thoughts on the confederate. As expected, participants reported more negative thoughts toward the confederate when he acted offensively and also felt more responsible for the confederate's feigned headache.

Illusion of Control

Evidence for apparent mental causation also comes from Langer's (1975; Langer & Roth, 1975) work on the illusion of control. She observed that people often feel that they have personal control over the outcome of events in which control is impossible. For example, they may feel that a game of chance (e.g., throwing dice) is actually a game of skill. However, the illusion of control does not arise universally and equally for all events. Certain factors such as choice, familiarity, and involvement may increase feelings of control in cases where no control exists. Performing the actions one normally performs in cases of skill may, in chance tasks, lead to the illusory sense that one actually can control the outcome.

In one study (Langer, 1975) participants bought raffle tickets for $1. Half the participants were allowed to choose which ticket they wanted; others were simply given a ticket. Familiarity was also manipulated. Half the tickets had a letter of the alphabet on it; the other half had a novel symbol. Participants were later called and asked whether they would be willing to swap the ticket they bought for a ticket in another lottery, one with the same prize but with better odds. People were more attached to their ticket if they had selected the ticket themselves—despite the better odds, they were less likely to trade their ticket. Familiarity also affected the decision to swap; people were less inclined to trade if it had a letter of the alphabet than a novel symbol. Another study examined the role of involvement. People at a racetrack were entered into a lottery as part of their admission fee. They were approached throughout the day and asked about the likelihood that they would win. Confidence increased as time went by. Langer reasoned that this was a result of the time that people had to think about winning. With more time, they had more opportunity to think about their "strategies" for winning.

The illusion of control is fostered when one behaves in a way that resembles what one would do in a skill situation. Thus, just acting like one has control has the side effect of feeling that one is in control. Becoming involved in the task by choosing a card or some other action gives a person opportunity to think about winning, even if by a random action. Such thoughts promote apparent mental causation. Familiarity and time to think about the event can increase intentionality because they direct a person's thoughts toward the event. Thoughts about action make people feel as though they are consciously willing the desired outcome, even when influence over that event is impossible.

For the ideal agent, will is the servant of thought. If the will of the agent does not reflect the thoughts and intentions of the agent, something has gone wrong. Thus, when one feels the intention to have a certain outcome, one also feels that one is doing things that can control that outcome. This association is strong even in cases in which actual control is not possible. The more one thinks about an outcome, the more one feels that outcome is within personal control when it happens. Thought and action lead to an inference that the action was willed.

INFERENCE OF ACTION: ACTION MISPERCEPTION

During his campaign for the U.S. presidency, then Vice President Al Gore was interviewed on the CNN program *Late Edition*. In that interview he made his famous claim that he "took the initiative in creating the Internet." The statement was altered in the retelling, and soon his claim to have "invented the Internet" was being ridiculed by the press and public. Some people who opposed the vice president's campaign called him a liar, and those who were more sympathetic suggested that he was merely exaggerating. It is true that while in the Senate, Gore had introduced bills that promoted the growth of the Internet, but did his actions actually result in the Internet as we know it today? Perhaps Gore was neither lying nor boasting but simply expressing his pursuit of ideal agency. He perceived his actions to be somewhat grander and more successful than they were.

This may be easy to understand if we assume that Gore had both thought about seeing the Internet develop and was willfully attempting to contribute to that development. For the ideal agent, action is the culmination of thought and will. Thought and will should naturally lead to a consistent action and, most important, to an outcome that matches the original intention reflected in the person's thoughts. To an outside observer who does not remember Al Gore wanting or trying to develop the Internet, his claim seems like an outrageous leap. However, to Gore, his intention and will were consistent with creating the Internet—and it happened! It is a relatively small step to feel that his actions did produce the outcome.

Such misperception can also happen when there is not even an outcome to claim. A person playing tennis could "see" the ball fall inside the line when everyone else sees it fall outside, for instance, or a person telling a joke could think it was a hit when everyone else thought it was a flop. When our best plans go awry, we may feel that the result was more successful than it was, so much so that we misperceive the actual outcome. This is a matter of action misperception, and it happens when we revise our actions to be consistent with our thoughts and our will.

Because actions are less open to interpretation than are thought or will, misperceiving action may be a more difficult maneuver for an agent than either intention confabulation or apparent mental causation. Yet, there is evidence that people distort what they think of their behavior when information about the action is somewhat ambiguous. For example, people who are incompetent in humor, grammar, or logic tend to overestimate their own skills in those respective domains (Kruger & Dunning, 1999). Children with poor social skills seem unaware of their difficulty and judge themselves as socially competent (Fagot & O'Brien, 1994) as do adults in the same predicament (Bem & Lord, 1979). Research on the "above-average effect" shows that people judge themselves to be better than most other people on many different attributes, a bias that increases when the attribute itself is loosely defined (Dunning, Mcyerowitz, & Holzberg, 1989).

The ambiguity of an action increases as the action is further away in time, so past actions are more susceptible to misperception. In a classic demonstration of memory distortion, Hastorf and Cantril (1954) found that people who watched the same college football game remembered the game differently depending on which college they went to, judging the opposing team to be playing less fairly than their own. In a related study, Ross and Sicoly (1979) found that husbands and wives claimed responsibility for a greater proportion of the housework than they attributed to their spouse, accounting for more than 100% between the couples. Such distortions tend to be of the self-serving variety and so can be explained by the need to maintain self-esteem (Tesser, 1988). In these various cases, people may recall that they wanted to be funny, work hard, be smart or socially competent, be good at tests, and have other positive attributes, so they perceive themselves to be successful at these efforts. Although it remains to be seen whether such effects indeed become more pronounced when both prior thought and feelings of will are present, it makes sense that these action misperceptions occur as a result of strivings for ideal agency.

Dissonance Revisited

Most cognitive dissonance studies focus on attitude change. However, it may not always be possible to change a prior attitude if the person is acutely aware of this prior attitude. People are less free to alter their intentions and prior thoughts when these are explicit beforehand—at least not without recognizing that it is indeed an alteration. If the memory of prior thoughts and a prior attitude cannot be changed, other cognitions could be changed, including cognitions about their actual behavior. In one study, Scheier and Carver (1980) made people's prior attitude salient to them through self-attention. Half the participants were put in front of a mirror, which directed the participants' thoughts toward themselves. Other participants were not put in this self-focused situation. The researchers then had participants write a counterattitudinal essay. When prior attitudes were made salient in this way, participants did not revise their prior attitudes to match their essay. Rather, they distorted what they thought of the essay they wrote. Participants who were initially made to focus on themselves later judged the counterattitudinal essay they penned as being closer to their own attitude. However, this judgment was inaccurate; raters blind to condition did not think the essays reflected the original attitude. Action misperception occurred to bring the perceived action into line with prior thoughts.

Action Misperception Studies

Although there is considerable evidence that people misperceive their own actions in a self-flattering way when they are given the chance, the role of intention and conscious will in that misperception has not been specifically examined. Preston and Wegner (2003) conducted two studies to investigate this relationship. In a first study, we looked at the effect of exerting will over an action. Participants came into the lab to do a study on typing. A seven-letter word appeared on the computer screen before them, and their task was to type the word as accurately as possible without looking at the keys. To prevent them from cheating, the letters on the keyboard were covered. The degree of conscious will people felt over this act was manipulated by giving some degree of choice over what to type. On some trials, there was no choice—one word was presented that the participant had to type. On other trials, two words were presented side by side and participants selected which one they wanted to type. After typing each word, participants had to report how many of the letters they thought they had typed correctly. Participants felt they had done a better typing job when they were given a chance to exert their will; they thought they had typed more letters correctly when they were given a choice of word to type, as compared to the trials in which they had no choice.

In another study, Preston and Wegner (2003) manipulated both thoughts about action and the experience of will. Participants fired a toy gun at a target 10 ft (approximately 3 m) away. The gun shot a foam bullet that hit the target and fell to the ground. The task of the participants was to judge how close (in inches) they were to hitting the bull's-eye of the target after each shot. The participants could not see it from where they were standing, but the target had a faint grid of 1-in. (approximately 2.6-cm) squares, allowing the experimenter surreptitiously to record the actual distance of each shot from the bull's-eye. Will was manipulated by the type of firing instruction that the participant received before each shot. On some trials, the experimenter counted down from three before instructing the participant to fire ("3–2–1–Go!"); on other trials, the instruction to fire came with no countdown (Go!). Pretests revealed that giving people a countdown before an action increases the degree to which the action feels personally willed.

The intention to be accurate was manipulated by what the target represented. Slides of famous faces were projected onto the target, some of which were pictures of people who were well-liked (e.g., Mahatma Gandhi) and others of which were of people who were disliked (e.g., Adolf Hitler) with the assumption that people would be more motivated to hit a person they despised. The bull's-eye was centered directly between the eyes of each famous face. Both motivation to be accurate (i.e., shooting at someone they hate) and the conscious will to fire contributed to people's flattering estimates of their own accuracy. Controlling for actual distance from the bull's-eye, people judged themselves to be most accurate in cases in which they were shooting at someone they disliked.

These studies provide some hints about the possible influence that thought and will may have on action misperception. It may well be that many of the most brazen, self-aggrandizing judgments of action occur not because people are generally egomaniacal. Instead, the tendency to misperceive action may follow primarily when people think about an action in advance of its occurrence and feel they have willed that action. Then, it begins to make sense that the action, too, should fall into line. We only start distorting our view of what we have done when we have thought about doing it and feel that we chose to do it.

CONCLUSION

All agents are not created equal. The hallmark of a good agent is its ability to manipulate the environment in a self-serving way. Such manipulation in humans involves three components—thought, will, and action. Having thoughts before acting allows an agent to sense the features of the environment relevant to action and so to select more favorable and more complex actions. The experience of will allows the agent to feel "in charge" of the specific actions and attribute agency for the action to the self. And of course, if the actions themselves are successful, the agent is successful as well. An ideal agent possesses all of these characteristics working together—thoughts create a goal for the agent to achieve, the agent experiences willing itself to pursue this goal, and its actions then satisfy the goal. This is what we aspire to be in our own agency, emulating this model for many of our actions each day.

These components of agency are not always easy to see. Action is observable some of the time, of course, but thoughts occur and then disappear, and the will is simply an experience that occurs on the way from thought to action. The model of an ideal agent leads us to believe that when we start to make out the image of an agent in some way—through thoughts, will, or action—the complete picture may soon come into view. We go beyond the information given and infer the remaining facets of ideal agency.

Anyone who has spent much time as a human knows quite well that ideal agency is not always possible. When we fall short of the ideal, we infer that the missing components of ideal agency are actually in place. As we have seen, such distortions take three forms: intention confabulation (when we have will and action but must infer thought), apparent mental causation (when we have thought and action and so infer will), and action misperception (when we have will and thought but must infer action). The evidence we have presented suggests that people can distort their perceptions in these three ways in order to maintain a conception of self as an ideal agent.

Ultimately, of course, all of these processes lead us away from reality; they involve changes in self-perception that may carry the person far from a veridical view. At the extreme, these sources of error and illusion in self-understanding may be responsible for psychological disorders and maladaptive behavior. A person who always insisted that every action was premeditated, who believed that every thought about action that happened to predict the action meant that the action was willed, or who perceived all willed actions as successful, after all, would qualify for a variety of psychiatric diagnoses. For the normal person, ideal agency guides inferences about the self within the constraints provided by reality.

ACKNOWLEDGMENTS

This chapter was prepared with the support of National Institute of Mental Health Grant MH 49127. We thank Ricardo Alanis, Marie Baldwin, and Michael Berkovits for their assistance in data collection.

REFERENCES

Abbott, K., & Flavell, J. H. (1996). *Young children's understanding of intention.* Unpublished manuscript, Stanford University, Stanford, CA.

Abramson, L. Y., Seligman, M. E. P., & Teasdale, J. D. (1978). Learned helplessness in humans: Critique and reformulation. *Journal of Abnormal Psychology, 87,* 49–74.

Anscombe, G. E. M. (1957). *Intention.* London: Blackwell.

Arkin, R. M., & Baumgardner, A. H. (1985). Self-handicapping. In J. H. Harvey & G. W. Weary (Eds.), *Attribution: Basic issues and applications* (pp. 169–202). Orlando, FL: Academic Press.

Baron-Cohen, S. (1994). How to build a baby that can read minds: Cognitive mechanisms in mindreading. *Cahiers de Psychologie Cognitive, 13,* 513–552.

Barrett, J. L. (2000). Exploring the natural foundations of religion. *Trends in Cognitive Sciences, 4,* 29–34.

Bem, D. J. (1967). Self-perception: An alternative interpretation of cognitive dissonance phenomena. *Psychological Review, 74,* 183–200.

Bem, D. J. (1972). Self-perception theory. In L. Berkowitz (Ed.), *Advances in experimental social psychology* (Vol. 6, pp. 1–62). New York: Academic Press.

Bem, D. J., & Lord, C. G. (1979). Template matching: A proposal for probing the ecological validity of experimental settings in social psychology. *Journal of Personality and Social Psychology, 37,* 833–846.

Bem, D. J., & McConnell, H. K. (1970). Testing the self-perception explanation of dissonance phenomena: On the salience of premanipulation attitudes. *Journal of Personality and Social Psychology 14,* 23–31.

Berglas, S., & Jones, E. E. (1978). Drug choice as a self-handicapping strategy in response to noncontingent success. *Journal of Personality and Social Psychology, 36,* 405–417.

Blakemore, S. J., & Decety, J. (2001). From the perception of action to the understanding of intention. *Nature Reviews: Neuroscience, 2,* 561–567.

Boyer, P. (2001). *Religion explained.* New York: Basic Books.

Brand, M. (1984). *Intending and acting.* Cambridge, MA: MIT Press.

Carver, C. S., & Scheier, M. F. (1998). *On the self-regulation of behavior.* Cambridge, England: Cambridge University Press.

Cohen, A. R. (1962). An experiment on small rewards for discrepant compliance and attitude change. In J. W. Brehm & A. R. Cohen (Eds.), *Explorations in cognitive dissonance* (pp. 73–78). New York: Wiley.

Cooley, C. H. (1902). *Human nature and the social order.* New York: Scribners.

Cooper, J., & Fazio, R. H. (1984). A new look at dissonance theory. In Berkowitz (Ed.), *Advances in experimental social psychology* (Vol. 17, pp. 229–266). San Diego, CA: Academic Press.

Davidson, D. (1980). Agency. In *Actions and events* (pp. 43–62). Oxford, England: Clarendon Press.

DeCharms, R. (1968). *Personal causation.* New York: Academic Press.

Descartes, R. (1901/1989). *Discourse on method and mediations* (J. Veitch, Trans.). New York: Prometheus. (Original work published 1641)

Dunning, D., Meyerowitz, J. A., & Holzberg, A. D. (1989). Ambiguity and self-evaluation: The role of idiosyncratic trait definitions in self-serving assessments of ability. *Journal of Personality and Social Psychology, 57,* 1082–1090.

Dweck, C. S., & Leggett, E. L. (1988). A social cognitive approach to motivation and personality. *Psychological Review, 95,* 256–273.

Fagot, B. I., & O'Brien, M. (1994). Activity level in young children: Cross-age stability, situational influence, correlates with temperament, and perception of problem behaviors. *Merrill-Palmer Quarterly, 40,* 378–398.

Festinger, L. (1957). *A theory of cognitive dissonance.* Stanford, CA: Stanford University Press.

Festinger, L., & Carlsmith, J. M. (1959). Cognitive consequences of forced compliance. *Journal of Abnormal and Social Psychology, 58,* 203–210.

Frith, C., Blakemore, S. J., & Wolpert, D. M. (2000). Abnormalities in the awareness and control of action. *Philosophical Transactions of the Royal Society of London, Series B, 355,* 1771–1788.

Gazzaniga, M. S. (1983). Right hemisphere language following brain bisection: A 20-year perspective. *American Psychologist 38,* 525–537.

Gazzaniga, M. S. (1988). Brain modularity: Towards a philosophy of conscious experience. In A. J. Marcel & E. Bisiach (Eds.), *Consciousness in contemporary science* (pp. 218–238). Oxford, England: Clarendon Press.

Gazzaniga, M. S., & LeDoux, J. E. (1978). *The integrated mind.* New York: Plenum Press.

Guthrie, S. E. (1980). A cognitive theory of religion. *Current Anthropology, 21,* 181–203.

Hastorf, A. H., & Cantril, H. (1954). They saw a game: A case study. *Journal of Abnormal and Social Psychology, 49,* 129–134.

Heider, F. (1958). *The psychology of interpersonal relations.* New York: Wiley.

Heider, F., & Simmel, M. (1944). An experimental study of apparent behavior. *American Journal of Psychology, 57,* 243–259.

Kruger, J., & Dunning, D. (1999). Unskilled and unaware of it: How difficulties in recognizing one's own incompetence lead to inflated self-assessments. *Journal of Personality and Social Psychology, 77*, 1121–1134.

Langer, E., & Roth, J. (1975). Heads I win, tails it's chance: The illusion of control as a function of the sequence of outcomes in a pure chance task. *Journal of Personality and Social Psychology, 32*, 951–955.

Langer, E. J. (1975). The illusion of control. *Journal of Personality and Social Psychology, 32*, 311–328.

Linder, D. E., Cooper, J., & Jones, E. E. (1967). Decision freedom as a determinant of the role of incentive magnitude in attitude change. *Journal of Personality and Social Psychology, 6*, 245–254.

Moll, A. (1889). *Hypnotism*. London: Walter Scott.

Newell, A. (1973). Production systems: Models of control structures. In W. G. Chase (Ed.), *Visual information processing* (pp. 463–526). New York: Academic Press.

Passingham, R. E. (1993). *The frontal lobes and voluntary action*. Oxford, England: Oxford University Press.

Powers, W. T. (1990). Control theory: A model of organisms. *System Dynamics Review, 6*, 1–20.

Premack, D., & Woodruff, G. (1978). Does the chimpanzee have a theory of mind? *Behavioral & Brain Sciences, 1*, 515–526.

Preston, J., & Wegner, D. M. (2003). *Action misperception as a consequence of intention and will to act*. Unpublished manuscript, Harvard University, Cambridge, MA.

Pronin, E., Wegner, D. M., & McCarthy, K. (2004). *Everyday magical powers: The role of apparent mental causation in the overestimation of personal influences*. Unpublished manuscript, Harvard University, Cambridge, MA.

Rogers, C. R. (1961). *On becoming a person*. Boston: Houghton Mifflin.

Ross, M., & Sicoly, F. (1979). Egocentric biases in availability and attribution. *Journal of Personality and Social Psychology, 37*, 322–336.

Russell, S. J., & Norvig, P. (2003). *Artificial intelligence: A modern approach* (2nd ed.). Englewood Cliffs, NJ: Prentice Hall.

Scheier, M. F., & Carver, C. S. (1980). Private and public self-attention, resistance to change, and dissonance reduction. *Journal of Personality and Social Psychology, 39*, 390-405.

Schult, C. A. (1997). *Intended actions and intentional states: Young children's understanding of the causes of human actions*. (Doctoral dissertation, University of Michigan, 1997). *Dissertation Abstracts International, Section B: The Sciences and Engineering, 57*, 11-B.

Shapiro, R., & Gilbert Abramson, R. (Producers), & Burton, T. (Director). (1985). *Pee-Wee's big adventure* [Motion picture]. United States: Warner Brothers.

Spiegel, L. (Executive Producer). (1999, March 9). *Late edition* [Television broadcast]. Washington, DC: Cable News Network.

Stephens, G. L., & Graham, G. (2000). *When self-consciousness breaks: Alien voices and inserted thoughts*. Cambridge, MA: MIT Press.

Tesser, A. (1988). Toward a self-evaluation maintenance model of social behavior. In L. Berkowiz (Ed.), *Advances in experimental social psychology* (Vol. 21, pp. 181–227). San Diego, CA: Academic Press.

Wegner, D. M. (2002). *The illusion of conscious will*. Cambridge, MA: MIT Press.

Wegner, D. M., & Sparrow, B. (in press). Authorship processing. In M. Gazzaniga (Ed.), *The new cognitive neurosciences* (3rd ed.). Cambridge, MA: MIT Press.

Wegner, D. M., Sparrow, B., & Winerman, L. (2004). Vicarious agency: Experiencing control over the movements of others . *Journal of Personality and Social Psychology, 86*, 838–848.

Wegner, D. M., & Wheatley, T. P. (1999). Apparent mental causation: Sources of the experience of will. *American Psychologist, 54*, 480–492.

Wegner, D. M., Winerman, L., & Sparrow, B. (2003). *Action at a distance: Experiencing control over the movements of others*. Manuscript submitted for publication.

Wellman, H. M. (1992). *The child's theory of mind*. Cambridge, MA: MIT Press.

Wicklund, R. A., & Brehm, J. W. (1976). *Perspectives on cognitive dissonance*. Hillsdale, NJ: Erlbaum.

Wilson, T. D., Hodges, S. D., & LaFleur, S. J. (1995). Effects of introspecting about reasons: Inferring attitudes from accessible thoughts. *Journal of Personality and Social Psychology, 69*, 16–28.

Wilson, T. D., & Schooler, J. W. (1991). Thinking too much: Introspection can reduce the quality of preferences and decisions. *Journal of Personality and Social Psychology, 60*, 181–192.

6

Reflections in Troubled Waters: Narcissism and the Vicissitudes of an Interpersonally Contextualized Self

FREDERICK RHODEWALT AND
CAROLYN C. MORF

The *self* is one of the most discussed and researched constructs in personality and social psychology. Leary and Tangney (2003) contended that it is one of psychology's unifying concepts in that it serves as an umbrella for a diverse array of content areas spanning basic cognition and emotion to motivation and interpersonal and group behavior. People think about themselves; have feelings about the self; and are motivated to attain goals that enhance, defend, and expand the self. Moreover, they react to and structure their social worlds as a function of self-concerns and needs. The construct's breadth is also one of its weaknesses. By obtaining the status of *über-construct*, the self's various subelements often appear disjointed and unrelated. Thus, an overarching challenge to self researchers is to address the question of how the cognitive, affective, motivational, behavioral, and interpersonal components of the self cohere within the individual.

In an attempt to meet this challenge, Mischel and Morf (2003) recently advocated that the self be reconceptualized as a *psycho-social dynamic processing system*. This framework defines the self as a coherent, organized connectionist-like meaning system of cognitive–affective representations that become activated in the dynamic self-regulatory processes individuals employ to construct and maintain their desired psychological conceptions of themselves. Much of this self-construction unfolds in the social arena, and the self-regulatory processes are transacted at both automatic and more effortful levels. This system emerges through a process of motivated social self-construction in which there are continuous reciprocal interactions between the dynamics of the system and the demands and affordances of the particular social context. This self-system thus conceived is a social-interpersonal system: It develops from infancy on, within social relationships, and its self-regulatory functions are sustained and carried out largely in interpersonal contexts throughout life.

The Mischel and Morf (2003) framework was inspired, in part, by our recently proposed *dynamic self-regulatory processing model of narcissism* (Morf & Rhodewalt, 2001a, 2001b; Rhodewalt, 2001). Based on more than a decade of research with our colleagues and students, this dynamic processing model characterizes narcissism as a unique pattern of intra- and interpersonal self-esteem regulation processes in service of constructing and maintaining the narcissist's desired self. We contend that in addition to helping untangle some of the paradoxical behaviors of narcissism, the model also serves as a prototype for conceptualizing and investigating the coherence among self-constructs and processes within the people in general.

Like others, we argue that chronically accessible self-schemas form the core of personality: They affect the interpretation of self-relevant information, lead to particular expectations about other's behaviors, and produce the characteristic response tendencies personality researchers recognize as traits (Kihlstrom & Hastie, 1997). What is added to this perspective by our dynamic social construction approach is that intra- and interpersonal self-regulatory processes are key to the study of personality, in that it is these processes that give a distinctive form to the self's underlying mental system. That is, they shape its content (e.g., cognitions, emotions, needs, and motives and their interrelations) and influence which parts of the self-system become more frequently (or "chronically") activated, and under what conditions.

In this chapter, we begin with a description of the dynamic self-regulatory model of narcissism and briefly highlight some supporting research. One of the model's most exciting contributions, in our estimation, is that it connects the internal workings of the self with the interpersonal context in which the self resides. It is within those interactions that the individual's self-theory is constructed, validated, and revealed. Thus, we believe that in order to understand a person's self, one needs to understand that person's identity strivings through their expressions in social interaction. The goal of this chapter is to elaborate on this connectedness of the narcissistic self to its interpersonal context by drawing on recent and ongoing research. By so doing, we hope to provide the bases for openings of new areas of research and to illustrate how our approach might be of value to other self and personality researchers.

THE DYNAMIC SELF-REGULATORY MODEL OF NARCISSISM

Narcissism Defined

Although the term *Narcissus-like* was introduced into the lexicon of psychology over a century ago (Ellis, 1898), it was Freud's (1914/1953) seminal essay on early development and narcissistic investment in the self that took Narcissus from the pages of Greek mythology and placed him squarely on the stage of clinical psychology. Freud contended that as the ego develops in the young child it becomes invested with emotional significance or libido, a state he termed *primary narcissism*. As the child continues to develop, libido becomes invested more in others, and only in pathological instances does it become reattached to the ego, what Freud referred to as *secondary narcissism*.

In the decades following the Freud essay, psychodynamic theorists, most notably Kernberg and Kohut, argued and debated narcissism's causes and forms. Although a thorough review of this debate is beyond the scope of the current chapter, suffice it to say that despite important divergences between the various theoretical treatments, the major psychodynamic theorists appear to agree that adult narcissism results from a childhood history of problematic interpersonal relationships. As a consequence, narcissistic adults possess the appearance of a grandiose self-concept and invulnerability on the outside but harbor feelings of emptiness and isolation on the inside. This circumstance leads to a highly con-flicted overdependence on others to maintain self-esteem. In short, there appears to be clear convergence among these clinical theorists that narcissism is energized by concerns about self-worth—or what in the contemporary self literature is termed *self-esteem maintenance and enhancement*. Moreover and most important, narcissists' self-esteem concerns are played out and satisfied or frustrated through their social interactions.

Just as there is emerging accord about some of the core issues for narcissists, there is also consensus about its clinical manifestations. According to the *Diagnostic and Statistical Manual of Mental Disorders* (text rev.; *DSM–IV–TR*; American Psychiatric Association, 2000), narcissists exhibit a pervasive pattern of grandiosity, self-importance, and perceived uniqueness and are preoccupied with fantasies of unlimited success and power. Interpersonally, narcissists engage in exhibitionism and attention seeking but at the same time demonstrate emotional lability, particularly in response to criticism or threats to self-esteem. The *DSM–IV–TR* specifies the following:

> Self-esteem is almost invariably very fragile; the person may be preoccupied with how well he or she is doing and how well he or she is regarded by others.... In response to criticism, he or she may react with rage, shame, or humiliation. (p. 350)

In addition, narcissists are also described as prone to interpersonal difficulties. They display entitlement and expect special treatment from others without the need to reciprocate or show empathy. In fact, they exploit others for their own needs. Interestingly, these difficulties most likely arise from their own doing, as we expand on in later sections of this chapter.

The Process Model of Narcissism

Despite the theoretical and definitional convergence, many aspects of narcissism remain a puzzle in which the pieces do not quite fit. How can the self be simul-taneously grandiose and vulnerable? Why do narcissists experience such extreme emotional peaks and valleys? Why is social feedback of paramount importance to them? And yet, why are they so neglectful or abusive of those interpersonal relationships upon which they are so reliant for self-definition and self-worth? We have taken as our challenge the task of fitting together the pieces of the puzzle by casting narcissism as a coherent set of social-cognitive units and self-regulatory processes, both intra- and interpersonal. The dynamic self-regulatory processing model that we employ to study narcissism is displayed in Figure 6.1. It analyzes narcissism in social-cognitive personality process terms rather than in static individual differences or syndrome terms (Morf & Rhodewalt, 2001a, 2001b; Rhodewalt, 2001; Rhodewalt & Sorrow, 2003).

In line with clinical theorizing, regulation of the **Self** is the core of our model for the narcissistic self-system depicted in Figure 6.1. It is the narcissist's self-concept and self-worth that are being regulated, maintained, and defended through a set of intra- and interpersonal strategies. The system incorporates both the content and process of self-esteem regulation. Narcissists are seen as individuals who possess transient, overblown, and fragile self-images that can only be sustained through social validation.

The narcissistic self-concept incorporates both the cognitive and affective or evaluative components of the self. Similar to the Jamesian *me*, the *cognitive self* component (Linville & Carlston, 1994) is the mental repository of autobiographical information, reflected appraisals, self-ascribed traits and competencies, and self-schemata including possible selves, self-with-others, and undesired selves. It also contains the attendant evaluations of what is known about the self or—collectively—self-esteem. The model addresses both the valence and stability of self-esteem.

This self-concept interconnects with the social environment through a set of self-regulatory units that include both intra- and interpersonal strategies enacted to protect or enhance positive self-views. Narcissists are active manipulators of social feedback, both at the point of its generation (interpersonal regulation) and

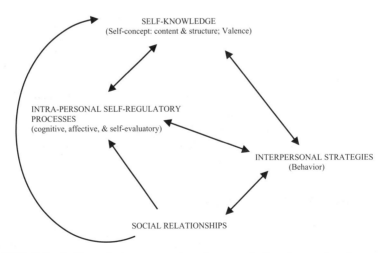

FIGURE 6.1. Self-regulatory processing framework for the study of personality dispositions (types). Adapted with permission from Morf and Rhodewalt (2001).

at the point of its interpretation (intrapersonal regulation). Intrapersonal strategies include distorted interpretations of outcomes and selective recall of past events. Interpersonal regulation covers a multitude of self-presentational gambits and social manipulations also in the service of engineering positive feedback or blunting negative feedback about the self.

We have found that the model has heuristic value in terms of focusing questions and guiding research. It should be evident that the elements in the model are neither discrete nor static entities but, rather, dynamic and recursive personality process units that intertwine and interact with one another. Narcissistic self-esteem regulation is characterized as shaped and guided by ongoing and changing self-concerns and social contexts. Narcissistic concerns about self-definition and worth guide interpersonal behaviors, which shape the narcissist's social contexts. The social context, in turn, makes salient, intensifies, or rechannels current self-concerns. In fact, it can be argued that the narcissist's self is context bound and that transitions from one social context to another contribute to the fragility and vulnerability of self-views.

We focus our review on a sampler of this research in order to illustrate a process approach to the study of individual differences (for more detailed discussion of the model, see Morf & Rhodewalt, 2001a; Rhodewalt, 2001; Rhodewalt & Sorrow, 2003). For example, with regard to the self-knowledge component, if narcissism at its core represents pathological self-love, then narcissists should have overly positive and inflated self-evaluations. However, according to Akhtar and Thompson's (1982) review of the clinical literature, this veneer of grandiosity covers underlying fragility and feelings of worthlessness. A goal for researchers has been to account for the coexistence of grandiosity and vulnerability within the narcissistic self.

There is consistent evidence that narcissism is related to self-reported high self-esteem (Emmons, 1984, 1987; Kernis & Sun, 1994; Morf & Rhodewalt, 1993; Raskin, Novacek, & Hogan, 1991a; Raskin & Terry, 1998; Rhodewalt & Eddings, 2002; Rhodewalt, Madrian, & Cheney, 1998; Rhodewalt & Morf, 1995, 1998). However, not only are narcissists' self-views quite positive but their self-evaluations are also inflated compared to objective reality. For example, Gabriel, Critelli, and Ee (1994) asked individuals to rate their intelligence and physical attractiveness. Compared to less narcissistic individuals, narcissists overestimated their intelligence and attractiveness compared to objective standards (IQ test scores, raters' evaluations of attractiveness).

Our model contains two elements that bridge narcissists' self-concepts to their social world. One component, *interpersonal self-regulatory processes*, involves behaviors and strategies designed to control the impressions and responses of other individuals. Such processes are also employed to diffuse or eliminate threats to the self. A classic example of interpersonal self-regulation was provided by Morf and Rhodewalt's (1993) investigation of narcissism and self-evaluation maintenance responses (Tesser, 1988). The focus of this investigation was on the extent to which narcissists would respond to such threatening comparisons with self-protective behaviors that came at the expense of their interaction partners. The key finding was that those narcissists who were threatened by another individual negatively evaluated that individual even when they expected to have to do so in a face-to-face interaction with that person, indicating that they placed self-needs over relationship concerns. In another example, Morf, Ansara, and Shia (2004) found that in a situation that required modesty, narcissists, compared to nonnarcissists, engaged in unmitigated grandiose self-presentations—presumably because their egos were on the line. What is striking in these examples is that narcissists' concerns about maintaining positive self-views triggered interpersonal behaviors that ultimately should contribute to disturbances in interpersonal relationships, a hallmark of the narcissistic syndrome.

Narcissists' interpersonal behaviors have consequences in terms of shaping outcomes and interpersonal reactions that feed back onto the self. This feedback is not passively received but rather passes through a set of *intrapersonal self-regulatory processes* that include cognitive, affective, and motivational components. Our model maintains that collectively these intrapersonal processes contribute to the self-enhancing distortions described previously. A core intrapersonal strategy appears to be the propensity to make self-aggrandizing attributions for positive outcomes (Rhodewalt & Morf, 1995, 1998; Rhodewalt, Tragakis, & Finnerty, 2003). We observe this most clearly in studies that provide participants with response- noncontingent success feedback. Narcissists persistently attribute such feedback to superior ability or competency. We have suggested that this self-aggrandizing attributional style has profound repercussions for the narcissist's self-conceptions, affect, and interpersonal behavior. Our studies reveal that narcissists stake out claims that they cannot meet (Rhodewalt & Morf, 1998; Rhodewalt et al., 2004). Thus, failure or the threat of failure has greater impact on their feelings of self-worth and behavior than it has on the feelings and behavior of less narcissistic individuals, presumably because of the uncertainty upon which narcissistic self-worth is based. As is evident in all of these examples, narcissists' intra- and interpersonal self-regulatory processes are closely intertwined. This entanglement is most clearly displayed when narcissists distort personal romantic memories (recalling self-enhancing past interpersonal experiences) to diffuse threats to the self after interpersonal rejection (Rhodewalt & Eddings, 2002) or when they hold negative views of (or even derogate!) those individuals who pose a threat, either because they provide negative feedback or because they outperform the narcissist (Kernis & Sun, 1994; Morf & Rhodewalt, 1993).

Finally, the model includes the social relationships and contexts in which narcissists function. We contend that through their actions, interpretations, and choices of interaction partners, narcissists create social environments that are objectively different from those of less narcissistic individuals. For example, narcissists prefer romantic partners who are admiring of them (Campbell, 1999). In addition, Buss and Chiodo (1991) found that perceivers describe their narcissistic acquaintances as acting in ways to impress others, such as bragging about their accomplishments and putting others down. In the short term, narcissists' attempts to mine their relationships appear to be successful, but over time result in rejection and hostility (Paulhus, 1998). We flesh out these early findings in terms of their theoretical relevance and likely connections to other processes in the sections to come.

This brief overview of our dynamic self-regulatory processing model of narcissism highlights its main components and illustrates their dynamic interdependencies. We believe that the model offers much in terms of integrating a set of disparate features into a coherent set of interacting elements and linking processes. The model also provides the architecture for addressing many of the paradoxes with which we began this section. By viewing narcissistic self-regulation as inseparable from the social context in which it transpires, one can begin to understand the combination of grandiosity and fragility, emotional lability, and interpersonal insensitivity that characterizes these individuals. For example, it makes sense that their selves can be grandiose and vulnerable at the same time because narcissists find ways of putting self-enhancing spins on events, and yet their strategic role in the generation of such feedback simultaneously undermines its validity. We suggest it is at the interface between the person and his or her interpersonal world where many of the paradoxes may be understood. The remainder of this chapter is devoted to the expansion of this proposition and to explication of the nature of this interface.

NARCISSISM AND INTERPERSONAL RELATIONS

In its essence, then, the model views narcissism in terms of motivated self-construction, in which the narcissistic self is shaped by the dynamic interplay of cognitive and affective intrapersonal self-processes and the interpersonal self-regulatory strategies that are embedded in the social arena. This is a stark departure from earlier theorizing on narcissism that, although allowing for social influences on personality development, concentrated primarily on intrapsychic processes and dynamics. In contrast, our approach has as its focal point the contextualized nature of the self-system in its social world.

All self-systems are fundamentally interpersonal: The self-system evolves from and depends on interpersonal experiences, and these interpersonal experiences are at the same time shaped and in part created by the self-system. Thus, narcissism represents a special case of interpersonal self-construction (see Mischel & Morf, 2003, for a detailed discussion of the more general case of interpersonal self-construction). As we have laid out, narcissists are preoccupied with building, buttressing, and defending a desired grandiose self, and they use their social environment as a vehicle for this endeavor. A particularly interesting consequence of narcissists' efforts to build a desired self through interpersonal maneuvers is that narcissists appear to employ strategies that may ultimately render these self-construction attempts ineffective. For example, they brag, show off, compete with and dominate others, derogate others when others perform better, express anger, and even engage in hostile retaliatory acts. These indiscriminant and aggressive self-promotion attempts, while perhaps successful in certain situations, most certainly will backfire in others and negatively affect narcissists' interpersonal relationships. At the same time, to the extent that narcissists are successful in manipulating others to provide feedback that confirms a positive self-image, this quite likely produces private doubt about such feedback because of their role in soliciting it. Thus, even their successful attempts at self-construction may ultimately maintain their underlying vulnerability and necessitate continued interpersonal self-construction. Moreover, deficits in the interpersonal domain may render many of narcissists' strategies ultimately self-defeating if, in order to preserve their positive self-views, they depend on consistent social affirmation—thus making affirming the grandiose narcissistic self potentially endless labor.

In the sections that follow, we examine more closely the interface between narcissists' socially constructed self-conceptions and the social environment upon which they rely. In particular, we focus on narcissists' underlying interpersonal motives, how they think they are perceived by others and their beliefs about their interpersonal relationships. What is known (or can be extrapolated from other findings) about how others actually perceive and react to narcissists is also considered. We then examine what may be the consequences of narcissists' characteristic intra- and interpersonal self-regulation strategies for their relationships with others. Romantic relationships are particularly self-involving and thus may offer an especially useful window into the narcissistic interpersonal world. Finally, we close the circle to consider the consequences of these interpersonal events for narcissists' self-knowledge and clarity.

Narcissism and Interpersonal Motivation

If narcissism is to be conceived of as interpersonal self-esteem regulation, then there should be an association between narcissists' social relationships and their self-esteem. In a series of daily diary studies (Rhodewalt, in press; Rhodewalt, Madrian, & Cheney, 1998) we have established that the self-esteem of narcissists is more unstable and more highly entrained to qualities of their social interactions than is the self-esteem of less narcissistic individuals. For example, Rhodewalt et al. (1998) reported that narcissists indicated that 25% of their daily interactions, on average, were negative compared to 16% for less narcissistic individuals, supporting the claim that narcissism is characterized by difficult interpersonal relationships—at least from the narcissist's perspective. The critical finding was that daily interactions—specifically, the extent to which they were cumulatively negative or problematic—were negatively related to self-esteem for all participants. However, level of narcissism predicted the magnitude of the relationship; as the percentage of negative interactions increased on any given day, self-esteem decreased, and this relationship was particularly descriptive of narcissists.

We have followed this research with attempts to identify those specific dimensions of social exchange to which narcissistic self-esteem is responding (Rhodewalt, Tragakis, & Hunh, 2000; Rhodewalt, in press). Participants evaluated each daily interaction for the extent to which they felt like their true self in the interaction and the degree of social inclusion, influence, and conflict they experienced in the interaction. Scores were computed from the daily interaction records so that we could examine, on average, the qualities of the participants' interactions for each day of the assessment period. Hierarchical linear modeling revealed that for all individuals, self-esteem rose and fell with the extent to which their interactions supported their self-concepts, made them feel included and engendered a sense of intimacy, were satisfying and positive, and were free of conflict. Who initiated and influenced the interaction was not related to daily self-esteem for the sample in general. More important, the relation between fluctuations in the extent to which the interactions supported one's sense of self and the extent to which one felt socially included in the social interactions was significantly stronger for narcissists than it was for less narcissistic individuals.

This emotional dependency on other people was also observed in an independent investigation that found a significant relationship between the emotional reliance subscale of the Interpersonal Dependency Inventory and the entitlement–exploitativenss component of narcissism (Davidov & Morf, 2004). Example items from this subscale are as follows: "Disapproval by someone I care about is very painful to me," "As a child, pleasing my parents was very important to me," and "I do my best work, when I know it will be appreciated." Thus, this subscale seems to tap needing others' emotional support and endorsement in order to maintain one's sense of well-being and self-worth, as well as a wish to please others. Collectively, these studies then illustrate two general points relevant to understanding the dynamics of narcissism. First, narcissists' self-esteem is dependent on and derived online from the responses of others. And, second, one of the paradoxes of narcissism, emotional lability, can be understood only when narcissism is placed in its interpersonal context.

Returning to the issue of social motivation, we were surprised by the finding that narcissists' daily self-esteem was also strongly influenced by how much they felt included and accepted by their interaction partners. Given that narcissistic self-esteem appears to be based more on the degree to which others admire them than on the degree to which others approve of them (Raskin et al., 1991), one might expect that social inclusion, if it is merely an index of approval and acceptance, would have less impact on narcissists' self-esteem than it would for others. However, it is possible that social inclusion or integration means something different to narcissists than it does to others. Social inclusion can mean approval-based acceptance, but it might also indicate admiration-based acceptance. That is, narcissists may feel more "included" in a group or relationship to the extent that the group or partner validates their self-concept or admires them.

This latter possibility was explored via a questionnaire designed to assess the layperson's understanding of what it means to feel socially included (Rhodewalt, in press). Pilot testing suggested six categories of ways in which people might feel part of a group that went beyond social acceptance and included the possibilities that people felt more a part of the group or interaction if it made them feel admired or influential, if it validated and respected their opinions, if it made them feel influential or helpful, or if it directly bolstered their self-esteem. We attempted to distinguish between social approval (i.e., acceptance) and self-esteem support (i.e., the provision of positive self-evaluations). This questionnaire was then administered to a sample of respondents who had also been assessed for narcissism. Narcissists, compared to less narcissistic individuals, reported that they felt significantly more included and accepted by the group or interaction partner when they were admired, had their self-esteem supported, and felt influential. It is noteworthy and consistent with past research that narcissists reported that social approval was less a source of feelings of inclusion and acceptance than did less narcissistic respondents. We replicated these findings in an independent sample that also indicated that these relationships were independent of trait self-esteem (Rhodewalt, Tragakis, & Finley, 2002).

An additional daily diary study was conducted in which participants evaluated their daily interactions in terms of intimacy, feelings about the self and interaction partners, social integration, influence, and conflict; participants also indicated how much others benefited and how admired by the other they were (Rhodewalt, Tragakis, & Finley, 2002). The results indicated that fluctuations in the extent to which these interactions affected feelings about the self, social integration, admiration, influence, and conflict were significantly related to fluctuations in self-esteem. Changes in the extent to which the interactions made one feel admired had a greater impact on the daily self-esteem of narcissists than the daily self-esteem of less narcissistic participants.

In brief, narcissists enter social interactions with the goal of being admired rather than liked, and their momentary sense of self-worth is based on the degree to which they believed that they were successful in pursuit of this goal. This conclusion is further corroborated by Emmons's (1989) analyses of written narratives, which revealed that narcissism was associated with high power and low intimacy strivings. Narcissists' narratives expressed desires to dominate, to have an impact on and influence over others, but they did not contain much reference to concerns about wanting to establish or maintain warm interpersonal relations. This was very different from nonnarcissists' narratives that centered around helping others, trying to minimize interpersonal conflict, and getting along with others.

Consequences of Narcissists' Intra- and Interpersonal Strategies for Their Relationships

If narcissists enter social relationships with the goal of gaining admiration and verification of grandiose self-images with little concern about acceptance or the feelings and wishes of others, then there must be consequences of this goal striving for all aspects of their interpersonal relations. We examine this issue from the perspective of both the narcissists as well as that of their interaction partners and significant others.

Narcissists' Perceptions of Their Relationships With

Others By their own account, narcissists generally report that they are perceived positively, in that they are valued and admired within their social networks. Rhodewalt and Morf (1995) found that in describing their sources of social support, narcissists were significantly more likely to report that their social networks provided them with self-esteem support than were less narcissistic individuals. Self-esteem support was reflected through the endorsement of items such as "Most people I know think highly of me." As noted previously, part of narcissists' conviction that others admire and are attracted to them comes from self-aggrandizing interpretations of social feedback. For example, Rhodewalt and Eddings

(2002) found that in response to structured interactions with a woman whom male narcissists believed was attractive and seeking a romantic relationship, the narcissistic men concluded that the woman was more attracted to them than did less narcissistic men. Remarkably, these perceptions had no basis in reality because (though unbeknownst to the men) the woman's responses were completely scripted so that each interaction was identical with regard to social feedback!

In addition to believing that they are generally perceived positively, narcissists also are significantly more likely to report experiencing interpersonal interactions that are positive and result in their feeling admired (Rhodewalt, in press). They are also more likely to believe that they were more integrated into the group and that others benefited from interacting with them. Although these findings characterize interpersonal relationships in general, romantic relationships provide a particularly revealing glimpse of narcissistic self-esteem regulation because such relationships are typically central and important to the self. Rhodewalt and Eddings (2002) asked participants to describe their past experiences in romantic relationships. Compared to less narcissistic men, narcissists described a history of romantic interactions in which it had been easy for them to meet women and the women had been receptive to their advances. They reported almost continuous romantic involvement, often dating more than one woman at a time. In fact, narcissists reported having had more serious romantic relationships than did less narcissistic men.

However, like other aspects of narcissistic functioning, narcissists' views of their social interactions are not straightforward but rather are somewhat paradoxical. As noted previously, narcissists report that a significantly higher proportion of their daily interactions are unsatisfactory and conflictive compared to less narcissistic individuals (Rhodewalt, in press; Rhodewalt et al., 1998). Similarly, people high on the entitlement–exploitativeness factor of narcissism compared to individuals lower on this component report feeling less satisfaction with their relationships in general. Moreover, when asked to evaluate the quality of their relationships compared to those of other people, they appraise them as being of lesser quality (Davidov & Morf, 2004).

In sum, narcissists perceive their interactions and relationships as meeting their self-regulatory goals, but not without also experiencing some conflict and some dissatisfaction. An interesting challenge for the next wave of research is to understand the course of these relationships as they meet or fail to meet the narcissist's interaction goals. The next few sections attempt to lay the foundation for addressing this question.

How Others See the Narcissist We begin by examining how narcissists are likely to be perceived by others. Given that narcissists' prime social motivation is to seek admiration from others, one measure of their success is how others view them. Although there is little research to date that addresses this question directly for narcissistic individuals, we can piece together what we know about narcissism with other research on self-enhancement and self-esteem in order to shed some light on this issue. As mentioned previously, acquaintances describe narcissists as exhibiting aggressive displays of self-centered and self-enhancing compulsions

(Buss & Chiodo, 1991). That is, narcissists were described as trying to "show off"—for example, by bragging about accomplishments, flaunting money and possessions, or dressing extravagantly to attract attention. Moreover, this was coupled with acts of condescension, such as insulting others' intelligence and otherwise putting people down, refusing to go out with someone who was not "good enough," and associating mostly with high-status people. Though perceptions and reactions to these behaviors were not assessed in that study, there is a growing body of research showing that overly positive self-presentations can engender unfavorable interpersonal perceptions. For example, Colvin, Block, and Funder (1995) demonstrated that individuals who self-enhanced were perceived by unacquainted observers as hostile, boastful, deceitful, and defensive. Similarly, Joiner, Vohs, Katz, Kwon, and Kline (2003) found that an excessive self-enhancement style (at least for men) predicted less favorable impressions from college roommates over time. Finally, Heatherton and Vohs (2000) found that, following an ego threat, high-self-esteem people were rated as arrogant, antagonistic, and unlikable by an unacquainted dyad partner, whereas low-self-esteem people, or those who had not experienced a threat to the self, were rated as more likable. As much of narcissistic behavior seems to be driven by actual or implied ego threat, these findings may provide useful insights into possible mechanisms for narcissism as well.

So, what about narcissism? As mentioned, to our knowledge, there are only a handful of studies that begin to address how narcissists may be perceived by others. One early investigation explored the choice of self-presentational tactics used by narcissists to get another person to like them during a dyadic conversation (Morf, 1994). Narcissists were found to have a pervasive preference for self-aggrandizing statements, rather than self-effacement or social approval seeking. For example, they chose to use sentence stems like "People look up to me because _____" rather than "Sometimes I get embarrassed, when _____." Moreover, they also completed these stems in more self-aggrandizing ways (e.g., "People look up to me, because I always know the right thing to do"), and they even found ways of completing stems that had been independently validated to form self-effacing or social approval statements when completed by most people, in such a way that they switched into the self-aggrandizing category. Independent coders who later rated the audiotaped conversations had significantly more negative impressions of those high than of those low in narcissism, although this study was inconclusive with regard to the exact processes that were contributing to these negative impressions.

Consistent with these findings, Paulhus (1998) showed that in small discussion groups narcissists exaggerated their positive personality characteristics, which had a direct impact on how they were perceived by their interaction partners. Upon first encounter, narcissists were rated agreeable, competent, intelligent, confident, and entertaining, but by the seventh interaction they were seen as arrogant, overestimating their abilities, tending to brag, and hostile. The largest change was on warmth, which correlated positively with narcissism at the first meeting but correlated negatively at the last meeting. Thus, whereas people viewed narcissists especially favorably on an initial encounter, these impressions became reversed over repeated interactions.

There is also recent evidence that suggests that narcissists' peers can discern up some of the same characteristics provided in the *DSM–IV–TR* for the definition of narcissism. People identified as narcissistic by a self-report scale were perceived by their peers as domineering and controlling as well as vindictive and self-centered on the Inventory of Interpersonal Problems (Clifton, Turkheimer, & Oltmanns, 2004b). The former is described by the inventory as controlling, manipulating, aggressing toward, and trying to change others; the latter is described as distrust and suspicion of others and an inability to care about others' needs and happiness. In addition, narcissists were rated as struggling against others and being unable to join collaboratively in either work or love and as engaging in active hostile and aggressive behaviors.

Interestingly, despite the fact that there is high consensus across peer judges about narcissistic traits, narcissists' self-descriptions diverge from how they are seen by their peers. Peer-nominated narcissists—who are described as reckless, insensitive, unsympathetic, and unkind to others; lacking in sincerity; and irresponsible—describe themselves as outgoing, gregarious, flirtatious, energetic, and quick and lively, so much so that others can't keep up with their pace (Clifton, Turkheimer, & Oltmanns, 2004a). Thus, narcissists provide ringing endorsements of themselves, almost as if to say, "You cannot believe how cool it is to be me," but their peers do not agree. Narcissists also believe that their contributions to a group product are greater than what other group members perceive them to be (John & Robins, 1994)—further illustrating a discrepancy between narcissists' self-perceptions and others' views of them.

In sum, it appears that despite narcissists' desperate efforts to obtain attention and admiration, they fool few, or at least not for very long. Sooner or later their peers and acquaintances see them for what they are. In addition, excessive self-enhancement has been shown across various investigations to have negative interpersonal consequences. There is also some evidence that these negative effects are greater over time, and that they may get worse in conditions of ego threat. Thus, as narcissists' egos are easily and often threatened, the likelihood is high that they damage (or at the very least, place in jeopardy) their relationships through their self-enhancement maneuvers.

Specific Costs to Interpersonal Mechanisms in Narcissists' Relationships

Now let us take a closer look at narcissists' relationships per se. Do these negative impressions they create mean that narcissists have fewer friends? It appears not. Even though nominated by peers as having *DSM–IV–TR* symptoms of narcissism, they were not less likely to be nominated as being a close friend by these same individuals (Oltmanns, Melley, & Turkheimer, 2002). Of course, these data do not tell us anything about the actual nature of these relationships. It is quite probable that narcissists, because of their social allure (e.g., being extraverted and entertaining), have a good many friends. Interdependent interaction partners find attractive the narcissists' confidence, extraversion, and assertiveness, at least initially (Morf, 1994; Paulhus, 1998). Yet this attraction may be primarily for instrumental reasons, in that narcissists' air of superiority and assertiveness might instill in others beliefs about their competence and social success. Thus, affiliating with narcissists may be a means to an end in order to incur certain benefits. However, it is also quite possible that these friendships are rather superficial and that difficulties arise when narcissists participate in relationships where closeness and reciprocity are the expected norms. True relatedness means more than simply having lots of friends and admirers or believing others are available to one for support (Rhodewalt & Morf, 1995); it means being able to form and maintain mutually beneficial, supportive, and satisfying relationships with other people. In other words, it is when relationships are pursued primarily for emotional benefits (e.g., nurturance, caring, and feelings of safety), and the interaction with the other person is more a goal in itself rather than a means to an end, that narcissists are expected to falter. This raises the question, then, of whether in addition to the negative impressions that narcissists create there are also concrete deficits in interpersonal functioning. Such information would help us understand where and how relatedness breaks down for narcissists.

We have already discussed some of the obvious and direct negative behavioral strategies narcissists engage in when in the pursuit of self-esteem, such as derogating the other, blaming the other, and overt hostility and aggression. However, there likely are also less obvious, more subtle, and perhaps more indirect ways in which narcissists impede their relationships. Some of the possible mechanisms are implicated in the *DSM–IV–TR* definition of narcissism—for example, narcissists' inability or unwillingness to empathize with others.

Apart from some correlational data that are consistent with this proposition (Watson, Biderman, & Sawrie, 1994), the question has, to our knowledge, not been investigated systematically, though Robins and John (1997) reported a finding that informs this discussion. A person's general tendency to see oneself as causal can be reversed if the person's perspective is switched from actor to observer. However, Robins and John found that for narcissists, taking the perspective of an observer of their own behavior leads them to become more, and not less, biased in their self-aggrandizing evaluations. To the extent that empathy involves perspective taking, narcissists seem incapable of moving the spotlight from themselves and seeing the other person's role in an outcome.

To return to romantic relationships, we note how Campbell (1999) asked participants to describe and select their ideal romantic partners. Narcissists, compared to less narcissistic respondents, said they are most attracted to a partner who is highly appealing with regard to appearance, personality, and accomplishments. They were particularly attracted to such partners if the partners were also admiring of them. Narcissists were also less attracted to caring targets or those who are emotionally needy. Similarly, Rhodewalt and Shimoda (2001) conducted a replication of the Hazan and Shaver (1987) "love quiz" study. Participants were asked to complete a quiz in which they described "the most important love relationship you ever had." Narcissistic respondents were significantly more likely to state that their most significant romantic relationship was characterized by love at first sight, sexual attraction, jealousy, and a fear of closeness.

Moreover, Campbell (1999) demonstrated that this preference for attractive others was indicative of an interpersonal self-enhancement strategy: Associating with such people made narcissists feel popular and provided them with a sense of importance. Choosing partners for self-esteem benefits may prove to be a dangerous gamble, however. Identification with idealized others and the seeking of admiration are both narcissistic interpersonal self-regulatory strategies that may lead to the selection of relationship partners who are not viable for long-term relationships.

For one, it is unlikely that these partners can live up to these perfect images with any consistency; and when the partners' attractiveness wanes, then the boost to the self through identification is no longer present in the relationship. Conversely, if the partner exceeds the narcissist on a dimension of self-worth enough to pose a threat, the narcissist is likely to respond with self-regulatory behaviors that undermine the relationship (e.g., Morf & Rhodewalt, 1993). This may be why narcissists report paying more attention to alternative partners even while in a stable relationship, seemingly forever on the lookout for a "better deal" (Campbell & Foster, 2002). In terms of the dynamics within the relationship, this study also showed that narcissists perceived less self-, and especially less partner, accommodation, which refers to constructive efforts to cope with conflict (e.g., discussing the conflict, instead of leaving or ignoring it, as well as remaining loyal to the partner). Interestingly, this lowered sense of accommodation was itself driven by a lack of commitment of narcissists to relationships. These speculations are consistent with the finding that narcissists report having been involved romantically with more partners than do less narcissistic individuals (Rhodewalt & Eddings, 2002; Rhodewalt & Shimoda, 2001).

As a whole, these studies demonstrate that narcissists are drawn to romantic partners for all the wrong reasons. Narcissists describe their emotional relationships as being based on immediate attraction and a need to be admired, not on friendship, trust, and closeness. Then, while in relationships, narcissists engage in behaviors that are detrimental to their relationships: They lack commitment, pay attention to alternative partners, and do not engage in constructive efforts in coping with conflict. It comes as little surprise then, that narcissists are not particularly satisfied with their relationships. However, these data beg the question of why it is that narcissists have so much difficulty in nurturing their intimate relationships. That is, what goes on in the intrapsychic dynamics that moves narcissists to behave the way they do?

Some inkling is provided in Rhodewalt and Shimoda (2001). Although narcissists did not differ from less narcissistic respondents in their ratings of overall happiness, friendship, or love, they did report more emotional highs and lows, jealousy, and a fear of closeness. Moreover, although on first look they also did not differ from their less narcissistic counterparts in perceived trust in and acceptance of their romantic partners, these null effects are likely misleading. Some of the trust items reflect being able to talk about oneself to the other, and as one would expect, narcissists score higher on these than less narcissistic people; but they scored lower in trust through dependence on the other. Likewise, narcissists scored higher on acceptance items reflecting the ability to see something special in their partners but lower in being able to accept faults than their less narcissistic counterparts.

Further insights are provided from some preliminary findings on the Inventory for Interpersonal Problems (Davidov & Morf, 2004). These indicate that individuals high on the entitlement–exploitativeness component of narcissism find it harder to be sociable, as well as have more difficulty with being intimate, compared with those lower on this component. Simultaneously, narcissists give higher reports of being too controlling and finding it harder to be submissive. This latter component primarily assesses one's ability to get along with those in authority positions, but it also includes items of getting along with others more generally. In a different sample, high entitlement–exploitativeness individuals also tended to score higher on a measure assessing fear of intimacy. Taken together, the findings from the two different intimacy scales suggest that narcissists experience difficulty both in providing and in seeking support and care from others in times of need. They also point to a reduced ability to open up to another person and become close, and to feeling less comfortable with this closeness and togetherness. Problems with sociability tap difficulty in trusting others, opening up, and sharing one's feelings and instead having a tendency to be suspicious of others and to keep them at a distance. This fits well with the finding discussed earlier that narcissists are distrustful and suspicious of others' motives and struggle against them, unable to join in collaborative work or love (Clifton et al., 2004b).

In short, the picture one gets from these data is one of narcissists in general having great difficulty opening up to others and allowing the self to become vulnerable even in intimate relationships. Instead, their emotional relationships are based on immediate attraction, and are characterized by emotional highs and lows and a tendency to be controlling and domineering over others. Albeit still preliminary, these findings provide further support for the notion that through their acquaintances, friends, and romantic partners narcissists pursue self-enhancement goals. They seek admiration and to be identified with attractive and successful others. This selfish focus is accompanied by an inability or unwillingness to appreciate the perspective and feelings of their interaction partners. They interact with others so as to channel and constrain social feedback to elicit admiring responses. At the microlevel, narcissists' goal pursuits directly or indirectly impact others through self-aggrandizing interpretations of relationship outcomes and hostile and derogatory responses to perceived threats.

The Nature of the Socially Constructed Narcissistic Self

For the most part, narcissists believe that they are successful in the goal of seeking admiration and enhancement from their interaction partners. At the same time, when this success is in question, they react with behaviors that in many cases undermine relationships. The relatedness and connectedness that develop naturally in most social relationships are not prime concerns for most narcissists. In many respects, narcissists view people as objects in the psychodynamic sense in that they fulfill a need within the individual but do not possess value or uniqueness in and of themselves. For narcissists, then, social interactions represent self-enhancement opportunities and little more. From our perspective, the narcissistic self is socially contextualized in that it is bounded by the self-enhancement opportunities afforded in a particular interaction and thus is continually defined by the immediate online context. One implication is that the socially contextualized self should be fragile and overly dependent on social feedback. Thus, although everyone's self is socially contextualized according to the social self-construction view that has been adopted, what is unique about the narcissistic self is that its internal dynamics are such that they create a more chronic need to reaffirm the self over and over again, in a somewhat endless fashion. In this final section of the chapter we consider the bases and implications of having a value of self that is so dependent upon and inseparable from the social context in which it exists.

The Contextualized Self of the Narcissist The general conclusion we wish to highlight is that the unique characteristics of the narcissistic self are a product of its interpersonal self-regulation attempts. Akhtar and Thompson (1982) concluded from their review of the clinical literature on narcissism that the narcissistic self-concept is overtly grandiose but covertly fragile and permeated with feelings of inferiority and self-doubt. Specifically, the clinical literature describes feelings of worthlessness, self-loathing, ambivalence, and ego fragility. It further suggests that narcissists, as a result, engage in the "splitting" of positive and negative self-images, so as not to have to face the negative parts of the self (e.g., Kernberg, 1976). We have documented research findings on the grandiose and inflated side of the narcissistic self, but examination of the negative or vulnerable side of narcissism has proved more daunting. Although the precise nature of this vulnerability has been difficult to isolate, its manifestations can be found in our daily diary studies of narcissism and self-esteem (Rhodewalt, Madrian, & Cheney, 1998; Rhodewalt, Tragakis, & Hunh, 2000). As mentioned previously, these studies reveal that although narcissists possess higher average levels of self-esteem than do less narcissistic individuals, they also experience greater fluctuations in self-esteem across time and context. There is also laboratory evidence that narcissists are hyperresponsive to threats to the self, reacting with anger and reductions in self-esteem (Rhodewalt & Morf, 1998). These reactions belie the conclusion that their positive self-views are confidently held, although when asked directly narcissists report they are (Rhodewalt & Morf, 1995).

Parallels between narcissism and high but unstable self-esteem have been discussed elsewhere (Kernis, 2001, 2003; Rhodewalt, 2001; Rhodewalt & Sorrow, 2002), but it is important to note here that like the narcissist depicted in our model, the individual of high unstable self-esteem displays an enhanced sensitivity to evaluative events, increased concern about self-image, and an overreliance on social sources of evaluation. Although there are important differences between narcissists and individuals of high unstable self-esteem, both seem to share the (perhaps implicit) striving for more stable self-views and to enhance positive self-feelings. Thus, like individuals of unstable, high self-esteem, narcissists are also more likely to display antagonism toward, and a cynical mistrust of, others (Bushman & Baumeister, 1998; Rhodewalt & Morf, 1995; Ruiz, Smith, & Rhodewalt, 2001). They react to self-esteem threats by derogating the source of that threat (Morf & Rhodewalt, 1993) and devaluing the negative feedback (Kernis & Sun, 1994) while viewing positive feedback as more valid and the evaluator as more competent than do less narcissistic individuals (Kernis & Sun, 1994; Rhodewalt & Eddings, 2002).

Our point is that the narcissistic self appears to be context dependent and shaped by the interplay between its self-regulation attempts and the interaction-based results of these attempts. This is in part the result of underlying vulnerability, but it also further feeds this vulnerability in a somewhat vicious cycle. Presumably, narcissists view social relationships as generic opportunities to elicit self-enhancing feedback. The connection between the feedback and specific self-views is less important than the feedback's enhancing properties. Thus, different self-aspects become more or less salient as they have relevance to the enhancement opportunities available in any given social context. It is likely that they learned this relevance and use of the social context over the course of their developmental history.

Early Interpersonal Relationships and the Narcissistic

Self   As mentioned herein, major psychodynamic theorists appear to agree that adult narcissism results from a childhood history of problematic interpersonal relationships. As adults, narcissists consequently possess grandiose self-concepts that incorporate a conflicted psychological dependence on others. Kohut (1971) proposed that normal development of the self occurs through interactions with others who provide the child with opportunities to gain approval and enhancement and simultaneously allow the child to identify with positive or perfect models. When significant others (parents) fail to provide these opportunities for approval and enhancement or are unempathetic, children undergo developmental arrest in which they childishly view the social world as being there to fulfill their needs instead of internalizing the self-standards by which to conduct their behaviors. Although they appear grandiose and invulnerable on the outside, narcissists, according to Kohut, are empty and isolated on the inside and, thus, are overly dependent on others to maintain self-esteem through mirroring and association. In contrast, Kernberg (1976) viewed narcissism as a defense against cold and rejecting parents. The child focuses on some aspect of the self that the parents do value and develops a grandiose self-concept around these core aspects and "splits" off or denies perceived weakness. In Kernberg's view, narcissism is a fixation in which the individual is unable to differentiate actual self-representations, ideal self-representations, and ideal significant-other representations. In both accounts, however, the bottom line appears to be a lack of clear self-knowledge that causes the narcissist to depend so heavily on others for a sense of self.

Borrowing from Linehan's (1993) work with borderline personality disorder (BPD), Strauman (2001) proposed that narcissists may have grown up in invalidating environments. Invalidating environments are ones in which the child's expressions of private experiences are trivialized, punished, or otherwise met with inappropriate responses by significant others in the child's life. In other words, as in Kohutian theory, parents did not provide the opportunities for approval and enhancement required for healthy development of the self. Although Linehan's model describes BPD, Strauman suggested that some of the same parental interaction patterns may be present in narcissism. He noted that such invalidating environments result in children who (a) do not adequately understand emotional reactions, (b) do not form realistic goals and expectations, and (c) search the social environment for cues about how to feel and act as well as for information about self-worth. All are, in slightly altered form, characteristics of adult narcissism.

In a study of romantic relationships, Rhodewalt and Shimoda (2001) included the Epstein and O'Brien Mother–Father–Peer (MFP) Scale. The MFP Scale asks respondents to recall and evaluate their childhood interactions with their mothers, fathers, and friends and provides measures of the extent to which mothers and fathers encouraged independence versus overprotection and were accepting versus rejecting and the extent they as children idealized their parents. There were a number of effects for levels of narcissism, but all were qualified by the sex of the respondent. Narcissistic men, compared to less narcissistic men, reported that their mothers and fathers were rejecting and that their mothers were overly protective. Narcissistic women, compared to less narcissistic women (and narcissistic men) reported that their mothers and fathers encouraged independence and that their mothers were more accepting (less rejecting). Regardless of sex, however, narcissists recalled their childhood friendships as containing more rejection than did their less narcissistic counterparts. Thus, we have preliminary evidence that at least for men, narcissists recall their mothers as rejecting but smothering, perhaps one manifestation of an invalidating environment. Much research remains to link problematic early child–parent interactions with adult narcissism, but it appears to be a meaningful and potentially fruitful area to research.

Linking the Past to the Present If it is the case that narcissism is a compensation for failures of early parent–child interactions to meet the needs of a developing self, is it plausible that these early interactions influence narcissists' reactions to current interpersonal contexts? This intriguing possibility was suggested by Anderson, Miranda, and Edwards (2001). Based on their past work, which indicates that people possess mental representations of significant others and of themselves when with these significant others, Andersen et al. proposed that such representations, when primed, may lead narcissists to react defensively. The logic underlying this proposition is based on the assumption that narcissists have represented in memory significant others (presumably neglectful mothers and fathers) who made them feel bad about themselves. Characteristics of current interaction partners may automatically trigger the negative and vulnerable feelings that were elicited in the earlier relationship. That is, the present social context primes the *self with negative significant other* and the feeling associated with that earlier important—but troubling—relationship. One interesting finding is that when people are primed with a negative significant other they react defensively by inflating or emphasizing aspects of the self that are independent of the self with significant other. In the case of narcissism, the Andersen hypothesis provides a mechanism by which grandiosity and vulnerability may coexist within the individual and suggests a process by which threat promotes self-aggrandizement.

Preliminary analyses of a test of this hypothesis offer some tentative insights (Sorrow & Rhodewalt, 2003). In terms of transference, narcissists appeared to be more reactive to their negative significant others than to their positive significant others, whereas the opposite was true for less narcissistic individuals. Although narcissists could distinguish their positive significant others from someone else's, the anticipation of interacting with a positive person, regardless of whether that person primed a significant other, resulted in a boost in the positivity of their own working self-concepts. In addition, narcissists showed the greatest defensive self-enhancement when exposed to targets who shared features with their negative significant others. Much research remains to be conducted in this area. However, if the predicted patterns are obtained, we will begin to have a map linking early relationships to current vulnerabilities and defensive behaviors.

There is yet another way in which the narcissistic self is embedded in and perpetuated by the social context. From the clinical literature, it can be concluded that narcissism is a compensation for this noncontingent social environment. Whether early significant others were neglectful or invalidating, they deprived the narcissists of behaviorally contingent information about who they were. Adult narcissists, then, are presumably concerned with establishing and protecting a positive self-image about which they are not confident. They are continuously invested in maneuvering through their interpersonal contacts so as to produce the feedback that shows they are who they desire and hope to be. This "self-solicitation" (Rhodewalt & Tragakis, 2002) in all likelihood contributes to ongoing uncertainty about the self and the need for continued interpersonal self-regulation. In channeling the interpretations of their behaviors and others' reactions to them through their intra- and interpersonal self-regulatory strategies, narcissists must suspect at some level (perhaps implicitly) that the social feedback was, in fact, the product of their own doing. This social feedback, then, is suspect with regard to unambiguous support of a desired self-image, and thus the insecurity is perpetuated. As a consequence, narcissists must continue to seek feedback from others that they are who they wish to be. Of course, they return to the well far too often, which no doubt contributes to the interpersonal difficulties that are a hallmark of narcissism.

CONCLUSION: HEURISTIC VALUE OF THE MODEL FOR THE STUDY OF THE SELF

We conclude by locating this work and discussion about narcissism within the broader conceptualization of self and discuss what this approach has to offer for other areas of self and personality research. The dynamic self-regulatory model of narcissism is a more specific instantiation of the broader psycho-social dynamic processing self-system framework outlined by Mischel and Morf (2003). To recap, according to this framework, the self is thought of as a coherent, organized connectionist-like meaning system of cognitive–affective representations that become activated in the dynamic self-regulatory processes individuals employ to construct and maintain their desired psychological identities and conceptions of themselves. Moreover, the self is inherently interpersonal in that much of these regulatory self-construction attempts (be they automatic or more deliberate) are transacted in the social context. Thus, an interpersonally contextualized self is not unique to narcissism; rather, it is common to all individuals. Through its specification of the elements of the self and how they interact with each other, the framework offers a guide for where to look for the unique features and unique dynamics of different self-construction types. That is, one needs to come to understand the distinctive cognitive–affective representations and dynamics within the person in his or her relation to—and in constant, seamless interchange with—elements that are "outside" the individual physically, but not psychologically. As we come to uncover these unique features and dynamics, they begin to form a distinctive signature of a particular type. Understanding this signature in turn makes possible the development of specific predictions about the features likely to activate and maintain the distinctive pattern.

As we saw with narcissistic people, for example, their intra- and interpersonal self-regulatory efforts appear to be aimed primarily at building and shaping contents of the self so as to promote perceptions of being extraordinary. Narcissists spend their time in continuous interpersonal maneuvers motivated toward garnering admiration and in intrapersonal strategic interpretations that put self-enhancing spins on events. For reasons we have speculated about, even when narcissists manage to generate self-affirming responses, however, these do not "stick," leaving them more dependent on online interpersonal feedback than is the case for most other people. Moreover, as a result of some of their internal dynamics (e.g., distrust and suspiciousness of others), narcissists engage in interpersonal behaviors that are ultimately detrimental to their self-affirmation goals. Many of these interpersonal behaviors appear paradoxical on the surface but become unmysterious when their role within self-construction endeavors is understood. In addition, thinking of narcissism in terms of a dynamic self-construction process within the psychosocial processing system framework allows one to generate predictions about the specific cognitive and affective representations that both contribute to and result from these endeavors. In this chapter we have also begun to touch on features likely to activate and maintain the pattern, such as certain ego-threatening situations or interactions with others that share feature resemblance with earlier significant—but troubling—relationships. Fleshing out the multiple features and dynamics of narcissism is far from done, of course, but the model provides a map that can be filled in and become increasingly elaborated over time.

Beyond narcissism, this motivated dynamic self-construction processing framework can also be applied to help unravel other individual differences and personality disorders by an analysis of their characteristic intra- and interpersonal self-regulatory dynamics. An exhaustive discussion is obviously impossible here, except to mention one potentially very interesting case in point: paranoid personality disorder. This construct is noteworthy because it is, like narcissism, a diagnostic category in the *DSM–IV–TR*. Yet, although it has a very different definition and symptomatology, the construct is also very highly correlated with narcissism (with correlations in the range of .60 to .70; see, e.g., Joiner, Petty,

Perez, & Sachs-Ericsson, 2004; T. F. Oltmanns, personal communication, November 2002). Examining distinctive self-regulatory attempts and dynamics may offer a way of distinguishing between the two constructs.

Finally, we note in closing that although our main interest has been in elaborating the dynamic self-regulatory processing model in order to understand which distinctive self-construction processes give rise to consistent individual differences in social behavior, our model also speaks to basic work on the self-system more broadly. The model offers a framework to examine how the intricate interplay between intra- and interpersonal self-regulatory processes is utilized—sometimes in paradoxical ways—for identity maintenance and change in a variety of contexts. Without this framework, it would be virtually impossible to make sense of some of the most fascinating observations in self-regulation—for example, how people can engage so persistently in apparently self-defeating behaviors. As we have emphasized, when one understands how someone's (in this case the narcissist's) cognitions, affects, and motivations interrelate within his or her self-system, the internal logic and coherence of these seemingly paradoxical behaviors become apparent (Morf & Rhodewalt, 2001a, 2001b).

REFERENCES

Akhtar, S., & Thompson, J. A. (1982). Overview: Narcissistic personality disorder. *American Journal of Psychiatry, 139,* 12–20.

American Psychiatric Association. (2000). *Diagnostic and statistical manual of mental disorders* (text rev.) Washington, DC: Author.

Andersen, S. M., Miranda, R., & Edwards, T. (2001). When self-enhancement knows no bounds: Are past relationships with significant others at the heart of narcissism? *Psychological Inquiry, 12,* 197–202.

Bushman, B., & Baumeister, R. F. (1997). Threatened egotism, narcissism, self-esteem, and direct and displaced aggression: Does self-love or self-hate lead to violence? *Journal of Personality and Social Psychology, 75,* 219–229.

Buss, D. M., & Chiodo, L. M. (1991). Narcissistic acts in everyday life. *Journal of Personality, 19,* 179–215.

Campbell, W. K. (1999). Narcissism and romantic attraction. *Journal of Personality and Social Psychology, 77,* 1254–1270.

Campbell, W. K., & Foster, C. A. (2002). Narcissism and commitment in romantic relationships: An investment model analysis. *Personality and Social Psychological Bulletin, 28,* 484–495.

Cantor, N. (1990). From thought to behavior: "Having" and "doing" in the study of personality and cognition. *American Psychologist, 45,* 735–750.

Cantor, N., & Kihlstrom, J. F. (1987). *Personality and Social Intelligence.* Englewood, NJ: Prentice Hall.

Clifton, A., Turkheimer, E., & Oltmanns, T. F. (2004a). Contrasting perspectives on personality problems: Descriptions from self and others. *Personality and Individual Differences, 136,* 1499–1514.

Clifton, A., Turkheimer, E., & Oltmanns, T. F. (2004b). *Self and peer perspectives on pathological personality traits and interpersonal problems.* Manuscript submitted for publication.

Colvin, R., Block, J., & Funder, D. (1995). Overly positive self-evaluations and personality: Negative implications for mental health. *Journal of Personality and Social Psychology, 68*, 1152–1162.

Cooper, A. (1959). Narcissism. In S. Arieti (Ed.), *American handbook of psychiatry* (pp. 297–316). Oxford, England: Basic Books.

Davidov, M., & Morf, C. C. (2004). *Narcissism and interpersonal relationships: Pushing away the ones we need.* Unpublished manuscript, University of Toronto, Ontario, Canada.

Downey, G., & Feldman, S. I. (1996). Implications of rejection sensitivity for intimate relationships. *Journal of Personality and Social Psychology, 70*, 1327–1343.

Downey, G., Freitas, A. L., Michaelis, B., & Khouri, H. (1998). The self-fulfilling prophecy in close relationships: Rejection sensitivity and rejection by romantic partners. *Journal of Personality and Social Psychology, 75*, 545–560.

Ellis, H. (1878). Autoeroticism: A psychological study. *Alienist and Neurologist, 19*, 260–299.

Emmons, R. A. (1984). Factor analysis and construct validity of the Narcissistic Personality Inventory. *Journal of Personality and Social Psychology, 48*, 291–300.

Emmons, R. A. (1987). Narcissism: Theory and measurement. *Journal of Personality and Social Psychology, 52*, 11–17.

Emmons, R. A. (1989). Exploring the relations between motives and traits: The case of narcissism. In D. M. Buss and N. Cantor (Eds.), *Personality psychology: Recent trends and emerging directions* (pp. 32–44). New York: Springer-Verlag.

Freud, S. (1953). On narcissism: An introduction. In J. Strachey (Ed. & Trans.), *The standard edition of the complete psychological works of Sigmund Freud* (Vol. 14, pp. 69–102). London: Hogarth Press. (Original work published 1914)

Gabriel, M. T., Critelli, J. W., & Ee, J. S. (1994). Narcissistic illusions in self-evaluations of intelligence and attractiveness. *Journal of Personality, 62*, 143–155.

Hazan, C., & Shaver, P. (1987). Romantic love conceptualized as an attachment process. *Journal of Personality and Social Psychology, 52*, 511–524.

Heatherton, T. F., & Vohs, K. D. (2000). Interpersonal evaluations following threat to self. *Journal of Personality and Social Psychology, 78*, 725–736.

John, O. P., & Robins, R. (1994). Accuracy and bias in self-perception: Individual differences in self-enhancement and the role of narcissism. *Journal of Personality and Social Psychology, 66*, 206–219.

Joiner, T. E., Petty, S., Perez, M., & Sachs-Ericsson, N. (2004). *The trajectory from narcissism to paranoid symptoms runs "down-hill": Depressive symptoms induce paranoid symptoms in narcissistic personalities (but not narcissistic symptoms in paranoid personalities).* Unpublished manuscript, Florida State University.

Joiner, T. E., Vohs, K. D., Katz, J., Kwon, P., & Kline, J. P. (2003). Excessive self-enhancement and interpersonal functioning in roommate relationships: Her virtue is his vice? *Self and Identity, 2*, 21–30.

Kernberg, O. F. (1976). *Borderline conditions and pathological narcissism.* New York: Aronson.

Kernis, M. (2003). Toward a conceptualization of optimal self-esteem. *Psychological Inquiry, 14*, 1–26.

Kernis, M. H. (1993). The roles of stability and level of self-esteem in psychological functioning. In R. Baumeister (Ed.), *Self-esteem: The puzzle of low self-regard* (pp. 167–182). New York: Plenum Press.

Kernis, M. H. (2001). Following the trail from narcissism to fragile self-esteem. *Psychological Inquiry, 12*, 223–225.

Kernis, M. H., & Sun, C.-R. (1994). Narcissism and reactions to interpersonal feedback. *Journal of Research in Personality, 28*, 4–13.

Kihlstrom, J. F., & Hastie, R. (1997). Mental representations of persons and personality. In R. Hogan, J. Johnson, & S. Briggs (Eds.), *Handbook of personality psychology* (pp. 711–735). San Diego, CA: Academic Press.

Kohut, H. (1971). *The analysis of the self.* New York: International Universities Press.

Leary, M. R., & Tangney, J. P. (2003). The self as an organizing construct in the behavioral sciences. In M. R. Leary & J. P. Tangney (Eds.), *Handbook of self and identity* (pp. 3–14). New York: Guilford Press.

Linehan, M. M. (1993). *Cognitive–behavioral treatment of borderline personality disorder.* New York: Guilford Press.

Linville, P. W., & Carlston, D. (1994). Social cognition and the self. In P. Devine, D. L. Hamilton, & T. Ostrom (Eds.), *Social cognition: Its impact on social psychology* (pp. 143–193). San Diego: Academic Press.

Mischel, W., & Morf, C. C. (2003). The self as a psycho-social dynamic processing system: A meta-perspective on a century of the self in psychology. In M. R. Leary & J. P. Tangney (Eds.), *Handbook of self and identity* (pp. 15–43). New York: Guilford Press.

Morf, C. C. (1994). Interpersonal consequences of narcissists' continual efforts to maintain and bolster self-esteem. (Doctoral dissertation, University of Utah, 1994). *Dissertation Abstracts International, 55(6-B)*, 2430.

Morf, C. C., Ansara, D., & Shia, T. (2004). *The effects of audience characteristics on narcissistic self-presentation.* Manuscript in preparation, University of Toronto, Toronto, Ontario, Canada.

Morf, C. C., & Rhodewalt, F. (1993). Narcissism and self-evaluation maintenance: Explorations in object relations. *Personality and Social Psychology Bulletin, 19*, 668–676.

Morf, C. C., & Rhodewalt, F. (2001a). Expanding the dynamic self-regulatory processing model of narcissism. *Psychological Inquiry, 12*, 243–251.

Morf, C. C., & Rhodewalt, F. (2001b). Unraveling the paradoxes of narcissism: A dynamic self-regulatory processing model. *Psychological Inquiry, 12*, 177–196.

Oltmanns T. F., Melley, A. H., & Turkheimer, E. (2002). Impaired social functioning and symptoms of personality disorders in a non-clinical population. *Journal of Personality Disorders, 16*, 438–453.

Raskin, R., Novacek, J., & Hogan, R. (1991). Narcissism, self-esteem, and defensive self-enhancement. *Journal of Personality, 59*, 20–38.

Raskin, R., & Terry, H. (1988). A principal-components analysis of the Narcissistic Personality Inventory and further evidence of its construct validity. *Journal of Personality and Social Psychology, 54*, 890–902.

Reich, A. (1960). Pathologic forms of self-esteem regulation. *Psychoanalytic Study of the Child, 18*, 218–238.

Rhodewalt, F. (2001). The social mind of the narcissist: Cognitive and motivational aspects of interpersonal self-construction. In J. P. Forgas, K. Williams, & L. Wheeler (Eds.), *The social mind: Cognitive and motivational aspects of interpersonal behavior* (pp. 177–198). New York: Cambridge University Press.

Rhodewalt, F. (in press). Social motivation and object relations: Narcissism and interpersonal self-esteem regulation. In. J. Forgas, K. Williams, & W. Von Hippel (Eds.), *Social motivation.* New York: Cambridge University Press.

Rhodewalt, F., & Eddings, S. (2002). Narcissus reflects: Memory distortion in response to ego relevant feedback in high and low narcissistic men. *Journal of Research in Personality, 36*, 97–116.

Rhodewalt, F., Madrian, J. C., & Chency, S. (1998). Narcissism, self-knowledge organization, and emotional reactivity: The effect of daily experiences on self-esteem and affect. *Personality and Social Psychology Bulletin, 24*, 75–87.

Rhodewalt, F., & Morf, C. C. (1995). Self and interpersonal correlates of the Narcissistic Personality Inventory: A review and new findings. *Journal of Research in Personality, 29*, 1–23.

Rhodewalt, F., & Morf, C. C. (1998). On self-aggrandizement and anger: A temporal analysis of narcissism and affective reactions to success and failure. *Journal of Personality and Social Psycholgy, 74*, 672–685.

Rhodewalt, F., & Shimoda, (2001). *What's love got to do with it?: Narcissism and romantic relationships*. Unpublished data, University of Utah, Salt Lake City.

Rhodewalt, F., & Sorrow, D. (2002). Interpersonal self-regulation: Lessons from the study of narcissism. In M. Leary & J. P. Tangney (Eds.), *Handbook of self and identity* (pp. 519–535). New York: Guilford Press.

Rhodewalt, F., & Tragakis, M. (2002). Self-handicapping and the social self: The costs and rewards of interpersonal self-construction. In J. Forgas & Kip Williams (Eds.), *The social self: Cognitive, interpersonal, and intergroup perspectives* (pp. 121–143). Philadelphia: Psychology Press.

Rhodewalt, F., Tragakis, M., & Finley, E. (2002). *Narcissism, social interaction, and self-esteem: II. The meaning of social inclusion*. Unpublished data, University of Utah, Salt Lake City.

Rhodewalt, F. Tragakis, M., & Finnerety, J. (2004). *Narcissism and self-handicapping: Linking self-aggrandizement to behavior*. Manuscript submitted for publication, University of Utah, Salt Lake City.

Rhodewalt, F., Tragakis, M., & Hunh, S. (2000). *Narcissism, social interaction, and self-esteem*. Unpublished manuscript. University of Utah, Salt Lake City.

Robins, R. W., & John, O. P. (1997). Effects of visual perspective and narcissism on self-perception: Is seeing believing? *Psychological Science, 8*, 37–42.

Ruiz, J., Smith, T. W., & Rhodewalt, F. (2001). Distinguishing narcissism from hostility: Similarities and differences in interpersonal circumplex and five-factor correlates. *Journal of Personality Assessment, 76*, 537–555.

Sorrow, D. L., & Rhodewalt, F. (2003). *Narcissism and defensive self-enhancement: The role of significant others*. Manuscript in preparation, University of Utah, Salt Lake City.

Strauman, T. J. (2001). Self-regulation, affect regulation, and narcissism: Pieces of the puzzle. *Psychological Inquiry, 12*, 239–242.

Tesser, A. (1998). Toward a self-evaluation maintenance model of social behavior. In L. Berkowitz (Ed.), *Advances in experimental social psychology* (Vol. 21, pp. 181–227). New York: Academic Press.

Vohs, K. D., & Heatherton, T. F. (2001). Self-esteem and threats to self: Implications for self-construals and interpersonal perceptions. *Journal of Personality and Social Psychology, 81*, 1103–1118.

Watson, P. J., Biderman, M. D., & Sawrie, S. M. (1994). Empathy, sex role orientation, and narcissism. *Sex Roles, 30*, 701–723.

7

Nagging Doubts and a Glimmer of Hope: The Role of Implicit Self-Esteem in Self-Image Maintenance

STEVEN J. SPENCER, CHRISTIAN H. JORDAN, CHRISTINE E. R. LOGEL, AND MARK P. ZANNA

As we first began studying implicit self-esteem, we were faced with two fundamental problems. First, what is it? Second, how is it measured? These questions, which point to the theoretical and methodological challenges that are faced in using implicit measures in research, were not easy to answer. Fortunately, a number of other people had already begun to answer them and we were able to draw on what they had learned. We review each of these questions in turn.

WHAT IS IMPLICIT SELF-ESTEEM?

Early theorizing on implicit self-esteem by Farnham, Greenwald, and Banaji (1999); Greenwald and Banaji (1995); and Greenwald and Farnham (2001) proposed that implicit measures of self-esteem tap automatic associations of the self-concept to positive and negative stimuli and reflect underlying attitudes about the self that are not affected by socially desirable responding. For example, Greenwald and Farnham (2001) found that people of high implicit self-esteem were less affected by feedback on a test than were people of low implicit self-esteem. They also found that implicit self-esteem predicted reactivity to feedback better than explicit self-esteem, suggesting that it might, in some way, be more authentic than explicit self-esteem.

One way to think about this perspective is that implicit self-esteem and explicit self-esteem are both proposed to measure the same underlying construct (i.e., self-esteem). Implicit self-esteem measures are, however, presumably more covert and less susceptible to response biases. The advantage of implicit self-esteem, therefore, from this perspective is that it better taps the "real" underlying feelings that people have about themselves.

In contrast to this perspective, Wilson, Lindsey, and Schooler (2000) proposed that our implicit evaluations and our explicit evaluations often reflect different underlying constructs. They proposed that for any attitude object we can have (at least) two attitudes: an implicit attitude that operates at a relatively automatic and unconscious level and an explicit attitude that operates at a relatively deliberative and conscious level. Both attitudes are "real" attitudes from this perspective and can influence people's thoughts, motivations, and behavior. For example, people may have genuinely positive explicit attitudes toward minority groups, but these explicit attitudes can be accompanied by genuinely negative implicit attitudes toward these same groups.

The model of dual attitudes has important implications for how we understand implicit and explicit self-esteem. If, indeed, implicit and explicit self-esteem reflect different underlying attitudes about the self, and thus implicit self-esteem is more than just a purer measure of people's self-esteem, then it becomes important to understand and measure both people's implicit self-esteem (i.e., their implicit attitude about the self) and their explicit self-esteem (i.e., their explicit attitude about the self) if we are to provide a full account of how self-esteem operates in influencing people's motives, thoughts, and behaviors.

Drawing on this dual attitude model, we have proposed that implicit self-esteem functions as a preconscious attitude toward the self (Jordan, Spencer, & Zanna, 2002; Jordan, Spencer, Zanna, Hoshino-Browne, & Correll, 2003). Although we agree that implicit self-esteem might often operate at the automatic and unconscious level, we have emphasized that at times these implicit views of the self are likely to seep into consciousness. It is at these times, we argue, that implicit self-esteem, which may be experienced as nagging doubts (if it is negative) or a glimmer of hope (if it is positive), may have a particularly strong effect on self-image maintenance.

What might lead preconscious thoughts about the self to seep into consciousness? At the present we can only offer a speculative account. It may be that when people focus on general affective reactions, these thoughts seep into consciousness more than when they deliberate on the meaning of their actions. Such an account would be consistent with Wilson's (Wilson, Hodges, & LaFleur, 1995; Wilson et al., 2000) account of how implicit attitudes influence evaluations and with Epstein's (1973) model of the experiential and rational self, but regardless of how implicit views of the self seep into consciousness, we predict that when they do, it is the discrepancy between implicit and explicit self-views that will be particularly potent in determining behavior.

If someone has high explicit self-esteem (i.e., conscious positive feelings about the self) but he or she experiences nagging doubts as low implicit self-esteem comes into consciousness, then what are the consequences? Conversely, what happens if someone has low explicit self-esteem (i.e., conscious negative feelings about the self) but he or she experiences a glimmer of hope as high implicit self-esteem comes into consciousness? We reasoned, following the argument laid out by Newby-Clark, McGregor, and Zanna (2002), that it was in these instances when people become aware of the ambivalence in their self-views that they would become motivated to reduce this ambivalence by altering their thoughts and behaviors.

Specifically, we predicted that if people have high explicit self-esteem, then implicit self-esteem may differentiate how they respond to threat. Those who have low implicit self-esteem may experience nagging doubts in the face of threat and react with defensiveness to maintain their positive explicit self-esteem. On the other hand, those who have high implicit self-esteem may be reminded of their positive feelings about themselves and respond with less defensiveness. In contrast, if people have low explicit self-esteem, then implicit self-esteem may differentiate how they respond to potential success. Those who have high implicit self-esteem may experience a glimmer of hope and react with increased efforts to succeed. On the other hand, those who have low implicit self-esteem may be reminded of their negative views about the self and respond with self-protective strategies.

Most of our research, which we review below, has addressed people with high explicit self-esteem, but we provide a bit of evidence for our predictions for people with low explicit self-esteem as well. Before we review this research, however, we still need to answer one more question.

HOW IS IMPLICIT SELF-ESTEEM MEASURED?

In the last 10 years there has been an explosion of implicit measures in social psychology, yet despite this growth our understanding of such measures is far from complete (see Fazio & Olson, 2003 for an excellent review). One of the vexing questions is whether implicit measures capture processes that are outside of awareness (i.e., that are implicit) or whether people are aware of the psychological processes but are only unaware that these processes are being measured. Put another way, do implicit measures tap implicit processes, or are they simply a covert measure of explicit processes? Distinguishing between these two possibilities has not proven to be a very tractable problem.

A second problem related to implicit measures is more empirical: Implicit measures typically show little correlation with explicit measures—and little correlation with other implicit measures. This problem is clearly evident for measures of implicit self-esteem. One study (Bosson, Swann, & Pennebaker, 2000) investigated the relation between seven implicit measures of self-esteem, three explicit measures of self-esteem, and three criterion variables (positive vs. negative feedback seeking, positive vs. negative interpretation of ambiguous statements, and independent evaluators' ratings of the positivity of participants' essays about themselves). None of the implicit measures were significantly correlated with each other or with any of the explicit measures. Only two of the measures showed significant (though modest) test–retest reliability: the Implicit Associates Test (IAT) developed by Greenwald and Farnham (2001) and preference for the initials in one's name and the numbers that make up one's birthday. In addition, these were the only measures that showed consistent relations with the criterion variables: The IAT predicted independent evaluators' ratings of the participants' essays, and preference for one's own initials and birthday numbers predicted feedback seeking and interpretation of ambiguous statements.

In an independent effort, we (Jordan et al., 2002) obtained very similar results. We examined the relation between four implicit self-esteem measures, three explicit self-esteem measures, and two criterion variables (participants' performance-related self-esteem after negative feedback on a test and perseverance on a similar test). We found that none of the implicit measures significantly correlated with one another or with any of the explicit self-esteem measures. In addition, only the IAT predicted participants' state self-esteem after negative feedback and their perseverance on a difficult task.

Clearly, much work is needed in the development of implicit measures of self-esteem. It is unclear whether current measures capture implicit processes or whether they are covert measures of explicit processes. In addition, past research cannot explain why implicit measures do not correlate with one another.

One possible reason for the lack of correlations between the IAT and name-letter preferences is that name-letter preferences may be a covert measure of people's vague and diffuse feelings about themselves—feelings about which they are nevertheless aware—whereas the IAT may measure feelings about the self about which people are less aware and may only experience fleetingly in response to stimuli in the environment. There is some evidence that people are at least vaguely aware of the self-related affect associated with name-letter preferences. In a series of studies Koole, Dijksterhuis, and van Knippenberg (2001) found that name-letter preferences were more related to conscious trait ratings when people made the trait ratings under time pressure and under cognitive load. One interpretation of this pattern of data is that when people have more time and cognitive resources they correct their conscious ratings, but without such corrections their conscious ratings would more closely match their name-letter preferences.

Despite these theoretical ambiguities and empirical shortcomings, we decided to plough ahead and use the IAT—which seemed in our earlier research (Jordan et al., 2002) to hold the most promise for measuring the preconscious self-views about which we hypothesized and, on balance, seemed to have the best psychometric properties—as a measure of implicit self-esteem in our research. We reasoned that if we could take as a temporary given that the IAT provides a measure of implicit self-esteem that captures preconscious self-views, then we could test our idea that implicit self-esteem and explicit self-esteem interact to predict defensiveness and optimism.

The IAT for self-esteem has participants make a series of judgments on the computer. Participants begin by categorizing a set of target words (e.g., *holiday, cockroach*) as pleasant or unpleasant using two response keys (one mapped to each category). They then categorize a second set of target words as self and not-self words (e.g., *me, it*), using the same response keys as before. During the two critical blocks of trials, participants make both types of judgments on separate trials using only a single pair of response keys. In one critical block, participants respond to self and pleasant words using one response key and not-self and unpleasant words using the other key; in the other critical block, self and unpleasant words share a single response key, whereas not-self and pleasant words share the other key.

A person is deemed to have high implicit self-esteem if he or she is faster at performing the task when self and pleasant share the same response than when self and unpleasant share a common response, because the positive affect associated with self presumably interferes with the processing of unpleasant words in the latter (but not the former) case. Average response latencies during the trials in which self and pleasant share a response are subtracted from average response latencies during the trials in which self and unpleasant share a response to create an index of implicit self-esteem.

We made one significant change when developing the version of the IAT that we used in our studies: For the category that was distinct from the self we selected not-self words that reflected neutral concepts (e.g., *it*, *that*), rather than words that represent the concept of "other" (e.g., *them*, *other*; as suggested by Farnham et al., 1999; Greenwald & Farnham, 2001). We did so because we felt that contrasting the self with others makes IAT scores very difficult to interpret. Do high scores reflect positive associations with the self, negative associations with others, or a combination of the two? In addition, attachment theory (Bartholomew & Horowitz, 1991; Bowlby, 1973) suggests that secure people are likely to have positive views of themselves and positive views of others. If this theorizing is correct, then people who have a secure attachment style might not show high implicit self-esteem on a measure of relative feelings of self versus others. Given that we predicted that implicit self-esteem would differentiate high explicit self-esteem people such that those who had high implicit self-esteem would be secure, whereas those who had low implicit self-esteem would be defensive, it seemed to us that a change in the IAT procedure was necessary.

NAGGING DOUBTS: HIGH EXPLICIT SELF-ESTEEM AND DEFENSIVENESS

We began our research by testing our predictions for individuals with high explicit self-esteem (see Jordan et al., 2003, for a complete description of the first three studies).[1] Specifically, as noted, we expected individuals with high explicit but low implicit self-esteem to be particularly defensive in many situations, and to show more self-enhancement and self-esteem maintenance activities than individuals with high explicit and high implicit self-esteem. The first indicator of defensiveness we examined was narcissism, an individual-differences measure known to be closely related to defensiveness (Paulhus, 1998; Raskin, Novacek, & Hogan, 1991). Narcissists react poorly when their positive self-views are challenged by criticism or negative evaluations—they respond, for example, by lashing out with hostility (Bushman & Baumeister, 1998) and by belittling other people (Morf & Rhodewalt, 1993). We thus expected that individuals with high explicit but low implicit self-esteem would be particularly narcissistic.

In the context of a larger study, we measured participants' explicit self-esteem using the Rosenberg Self-Esteem Scale (RSES; Rosenberg, 1965) and their implicit self-esteem using the IAT. We then measured participants' levels of narcissism, using the Narcissistic Personality Inventory (NPI; Raskin & Hall, 1988), a well-validated measure of narcissism intended for use in subclinical populations. With these measures, we examined whether narcissism could be predicted from explicit self-esteem; implicit self-esteem; and the interaction between the two, representing the degree of correspondence between explicit and implicit self-esteem. As can be seen in Figure 7.1, the interaction was a significant predictor—participants with high explicit but low implicit self-esteem showed the highest levels of narcissism overall, significantly higher than individuals with high explicit and high implicit self-esteem. In fact, these latter individuals showed levels of narcissism no higher than participants who reported low levels of (explicit) self-esteem.

We were encouraged by these findings and next turned to testing whether the correspondence between explicit and implicit self-esteem could predict a defensive reaction—namely, cognitive dissonance reduction. Cognitive dissonance reduction is viewed by many theorists as a means of maintaining positive self-views in the face of behavior or cognition that could contradict those self-views. When people behave in ways that could be construed as foolish or immoral, they may rationalize their behavior by reconstruing it in ways that make it appear more reasonable and ethical. These views are consistent with both Aronson's (1968) self-consistency theory of cognitive dissonance and Steele's (1988) self-affirmation theory. They are also consistent with the finding that people are less apt to engage in dissonance reduction when their positive self-views have been independently affirmed (Steele, Spencer, & Lynch, 1993). In other words, when the need to evaluate the self positively has been placated, people no longer engage in dissonance-reducing behavior to the same extent. We thus predicted that individuals with high explicit but low implicit self-esteem would engage in more dissonance

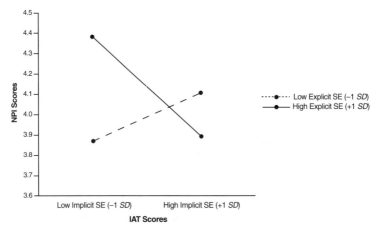

FIGURE 7.1. Narcissism as a function of explicit self-esteem and implicit self-esteem (from Jordan et al., 2003). NPI = Narcissistic Personality Inventory; SE = self-esteem; IAT = Implicit Associates Test.

reduction than individuals high in both types of self-esteem. We tested this prediction in the classic free-choice dissonance paradigm, borrowing materials developed and successfully employed by Hoshino-Browne, Zanna, Spencer, and Zanna (in press).

We examined whether we could predict dissonance reduction in the form of the spread of alternatives (the degree to which participants increased their rating of the item they chose and decreased their rating of the item they did not choose) from explicit self-esteem, implicit self-esteem, and the interaction between the two. We observed a marginal tendency for participants with high explicit self-esteem to show more dissonance reduction; however, as can be seen in Figure 7.2, a significant interaction revealed that this tendency was true only among participants with relatively low implicit self-esteem. In other words, the correspondence between explicit and implicit self-esteem predicted dissonance reduction as we had anticipated. Participants with high explicit but low implicit self-esteem showed the highest levels of dissonance reduction overall, and significantly more dissonance reduction than participants with high explicit and high implicit self-esteem. These latter individuals showed about the same amount of dissonance reduction as participants who reported having low self-esteem.

We have also explored whether discrepancies between explicit and implicit self-esteem predict a rather different form of self-enhancement—in-group bias. Tajfel and Turner (1979) first suggested that in-group bias (i.e., the robust tendency for people to favor members of their own groups over members of out-groups) represents a self-enhancement strategy. By favoring in-group members over out-group members, one can create a positive distinctiveness for one's own group, making it appear superior to contrasting out-groups. Then, by dint of membership in the in-group, one can feel more positively about the self, enhancing personal

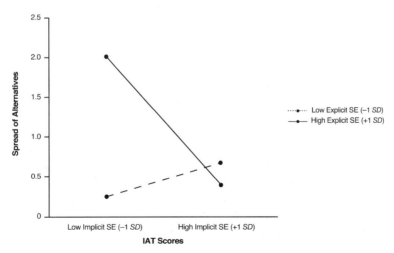

FIGURE 7.2. Spread of alternatives dissonance reduction as a function of explicit self-esteem and implicit self-esteem. SE = self-esteem; IAT = Implicit Associates Test (from Jordan et al., 2003).

self-esteem, because of the in-group's apparent superiority. Indeed, the available evidence does suggest that engaging in in-group bias results in boosts to state self-esteem (Rubin & Hewstone, 1998). We thus expected that individuals with high explicit but low implicit self-esteem would show more in-group bias than individuals high in both explicit and implicit self-esteem. We tested this prediction in the familiar minimal group paradigm.

Participants were invited to participate in a study of social decision making. We first measured their levels of explicit and implicit self-esteem and then had them complete a dot estimation task (based on the procedure of Tajfel, Flament, Billig, & Bundy, 1971). Participants viewed three arrays of dots and indicated how many dots they believed were in each array. Ostensibly based on their performance, each participant was told that he or she had a strong tendency toward over- or underestimation. This procedure served to create two novel groups for each participant, one of which was an in-group and the other an out-group. Participants were then asked to use Tajfel's (1981) matrices to allocate points to two other individuals who they believed were other participants in the study, and who were identified only by their group membership status. Participants thus allocated points to one in-group member and one out-group member. They believed their point allocations would determine which participant in the study would win a monetary prize, and they believed that other participants would be allocating points to them. This served to make the exercise more meaningful and engaging. Although space limitations preclude an in-depth discussion of Tajfel's matrices here (see instead Bourhis, Sachdev, & Gagnon, 1994), it is noteworthy that across the set of matrices, complete fairness in point allocations is quite difficult. Thus, participants typically show some degree of bias in their allocations, although this bias need not be in the direction of in-group favoritism. Our measure of in-group bias was thus the extent to which participants awarded more points to the in-group member relative to the out-group member.

As in the previously described studies, we examined whether explicit self-esteem, implicit self-esteem, and the interaction between the two could predict defensiveness—in this case, in-group bias. There was a tendency for participants with low implicit self-esteem to show more in-group bias, but this main effect was qualified by a significant interaction, as expected. Although in-group bias and implicit self-esteem were not strongly related among participants with low explicit self-esteem, there was a significant negative relationship between in-group bias and implicit self-esteem among participants with high explicit self-esteem. In other words, participants with high explicit but low implicit self-esteem allocated more points to the in-group member relative to the out-group member than did participants with high explicit and high implicit self-esteem. Indeed, these latter individuals were the only participants in the study who did not show any in-group bias at all, suggesting they may be particularly secure in their self-views, or at least not prone to self-enhance through in-group favoritism.

One final piece of evidence we have collected suggests that low implicit self-esteem may contribute to defensiveness among individuals with high explicit self-esteem. In light of the fact that implicit self-esteem predicted in-group bias in the minimal group paradigm, we thought it might similarly be related to racial discrimination. The minimal group paradigm is designed specifically to rule out preexisting histories of prejudice or antipathy between groups as an explanation of bias—after all, the groups are completely novel and so have no history what-soever—so we cannot extrapolate directly from the minimal group finding. Nevertheless, there is reason to expect that racial discrimination, at least in some circumstances, could serve a self-image maintenance function. Perhaps the most direct evidence of this comes from a series of studies by Fein and Spencer (1997). These studies demonstrated that people are more likely to use derogatory stereo-types when their self-views have been threatened by a negative evaluation, and to the extent that people stereotype in this context, it mediates subsequent gains in state self-esteem. In other words, people stereotype more when under threat, and to the extent that they do so, they come to feel better about themselves. Thus, discrimination can, in some cases, serve a self-image maintenance function. We examined whether people with high explicit but low implicit self-esteem are particularly likely to use racial discrimination in this capacity.

In this study, we invited only participants with high explicit self-esteem to participate—we premeasured explicit self-esteem and included only individuals who scored in the top third of the self-esteem distribution to participate. We then measured their levels of implicit self-esteem when they arrived at the lab. Next, we had all of our participants complete a computer-based verbal intelligence test that was described as a valid indicator of academic and career success. The test was derived primarily from the verbal section of the Graduate Record Examination, and included difficult questions from five areas, such as syllogisms, analogies, and verbal–picture matching. Each question was timed, and some questions did not include a correct response, making the test quite difficult and frustrating. Once finished, participants received feedback that they had scored at the 32nd to 56th percentile on each of the five parts of the test. This is discouraging and threatening feedback for undergraduate students (see Fein & Spencer, 1997). Thus, all of our participants had high explicit self-esteem and all were under self-threat.

We next had participants complete a social decision-making task for which they read a series of cases of student misconduct, ostensibly based on actual cases that had come before the university's disciplinary committee. The case of interest involves a student sleeping on a couch outside a campus bar late on a Friday night. It is unclear whether the student has been drinking. A group of students exit the bar and begin talking loudly near the protagonist, disturbing him. The student exchanges words with the group, and things begin to escalate to the point that a student in the group hurls a particularly nasty epithet at the protagonist. The protagonist retaliates by punching the student twice in the face. Our protagonist thus is clearly culpable of violence but has also clearly been provoked. Participants indicated the severity of punishment they believed the student offender deserved. They did so by indicating subjectively the severity of punishment they believed was appropriate, by indicating how much they believed the student offender should be forced to take an anger management class, and by choosing an objective punishment from a list of punishments of escalating severity (from reprimand to expulsion). We combined these ratings into a single index of the severity of the recommended punishment.

Unbeknownst to our participants, there were two versions of this final case. Half of our participants read about John Pride as the student offender, and the remaining half read about John Proudfoot, meant to indicate that the student offender was American Indian. We expected that participants with low implicit self-esteem, among our participants with high explicit self-esteem, would recommend a more severe punishment for John Proudfoot than John Pride, particularly compared to participants with high explicit and high implicit self-esteem.

As can be seen in Figure 7.3, our analyses revealed that implicit self-esteem was unrelated to the severity of punishment recommended for John Pride. Regardless of their level of implicit self-esteem, our participants with high explicit self-esteem under self-threat recommended an average severity of punishment for John Pride. In stark contrast, there was a strong negative relationship between implicit self-esteem and the severity of punishment recommended for John Proudfoot. Among our participants with high explicit self-esteem under threat, those with relatively low implicit self-esteem reported that they believed John Proudfoot deserved a much more severe punishment. Indeed, the severity of punishment these participants recommended for John Proudfoot was more severe than the severity of punishment they recommended for John Pride, a pattern of responses indicating racial discrimination. Participants with high implicit self-esteem showed no such tendency and, if anything, recommended a less severe punishment for John Proudfoot. Thus—though preliminary—this finding suggests that individuals with high explicit but low implicit self-esteem may be most likely to use racial discrimination as a means of maintaining threatened self-images.

Research in other labs is consistent with our findings. McGregor and Marigold (2003) have found that when participants high in explicit self-esteem and low in implicit self-esteem experience a self-image threat, they respond by hardening their attitudes (i.e., they hold their attitudes with more certainty and believe their

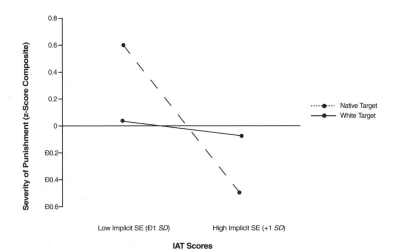

FIGURE 7.3. Severity of recommended punishment as a function of implicit self-esteem and target ethnicity. SE = self-esteem; IAT = Implicit Associates Test (from Jordan, 2003).

attitudes are more consensual); they do not do this when there is no self-image threat. In contrast, participants high in both types of self-esteem, and participants with low explicit self-esteem regardless of their implicit self-esteem, do not show evidence of this defensive tendency. Bosson, Brown, Zeigler-Hill, and Swann (in press) also found defensive tendencies among participants high in explicit self-esteem and low in implicit self-esteem, demonstrating that these participants engage in a number of self-enhancement strategies more than do people high in both types of self-esteem.

Together these studies, combined with our own, provide compelling evidence that implicit self-esteem can help differentiate defensive high explicit self-esteem from secure high explicit self-esteem. People with high explicit self-esteem and low implicit self-esteem appear to be more defensive than people who are high in both types of self-esteem. We argue that this defensiveness may well arise from nagging doubts that people high in explicit self-esteem and low in implicit self-esteem experience as they encounter threat. Although we find this theoretical account compelling, we must acknowledge that we still have not provided evidence of the proposed process. We hope to address this issue in future research.

A GLIMMER OF HOPE: LOW EXPLICIT SELF-ESTEEM AND SELF-PROTECTION

We have only begun to examine how implicit self-esteem may affect the motives, thoughts, and behaviors of people with low explicit self-esteem. Following our reasoning that implicit self-esteem may function as a preconscious view of the self, we propose that low explicit self-esteem people with high implicit self-esteem may, when thinking about future performance, experience a glimmer of hope that may cause them to respond with optimism and avoid the self-protective strategies often seen among low explicit self-esteem people. Three studies appear to be supportive of this interpretation.

In one study in our lab (Jordan et al., 2002), participants completed the IAT for self-esteem as an implicit measure of self-esteem and the RSES as an explicit measure of self-esteem. After participants completed these measures they took a difficult intellectual test and received negative feedback. They were then given the opportunity to take a similar test and work to improve their performance or take a test in a different domain. Among participants high in explicit self-esteem, we found results consistent with the results reported above: Participants with high implicit self-esteem were more likely to choose the similar task and continued effort in the threatened domain than were low implicit self-esteem participants. Interestingly, we found exactly the same pattern for participants with low explicit self-esteem. In fact, explicit self-esteem had no effect at all on participants' perseverance on the task. Thus, participants with low explicit and high implicit self-esteem showed an equally strong tendency to persevere on the task, as did participants high in explicit and implicit self-esteem. High implicit self-esteem might have served both participants with high and low explicit self-esteem by providing them with hope that they could do well despite the negative feedback they received.

Spalding and Hardin (2000) also found evidence consistent with our glimmer-of-hope hypothesis. They measured participants' explicit self-esteem with the RSES and participants' implicit self-esteem with a subliminal evaluative priming task. On this task, self-related words (i.e., *me*, *myself*) were flashed subliminally for some trials and self-irrelevant words (i.e., *two*, *manners*) were flashed subliminally for other trials. On each trial, after the subliminal word was flashed, participants evaluated whether a supraliminal stimulus word was a positively or negatively valenced adjective. The extent to which self-related primes (as compared to self-irrelevant primes) sped up judgments of positively valenced adjectives and slowed down judgments of negatively valenced adjectives was used as an implicit measure of self-esteem. After completing these measures, participants were told that they would be given an "emotional health" interview either about themselves or their best friends, but before completing this interview, participants had an opportunity to complete a self-handicapping index.

Consistent with previous research (Tice, 1991), participants with low explicit self-esteem engaged in considerably more self-handicapping than did those with high explicit self-esteem. What is perhaps more relevant to the present discussion, however, is that among those with low explicit self-esteem, implicit self-esteem predicted self-handicapping. Participants with low explicit self-esteem and high implicit self-esteem engaged in less self-handicapping than did participants with low explicit self-esteem who were also low in implicit self-esteem. These findings suggest that people with low explicit self-esteem who have high implicit self-esteem may have faced the impending interview with a greater sense of hope than their low implicit self-esteem counterparts and therefore were less likely to engage in self-protective strategies.

A final study by Bosson et al. (2003) provides additional support for our glimmer-of-hope hypothesis. They measured explicit self-esteem with the self-liking subscale of the Self-Liking, Self-Competence Scale (Tafarodi & Swann, 1995), and they measured implicit self-esteem with name-letter preferences. They then had participants complete Weinstein's (1980) measure of unrealistic optimism, which has people estimate how likely it is that they will experience five pleasant future events (e.g., liking their job) and five unpleasant future events (e.g., developing a drinking problem) during their life. Among people high in explicit self-esteem, those with low implicit self-esteem displayed more unrealistic optimism than those high in implicit self-esteem. More important for our hypothesis here, however, was that among participants low in explicit self-esteem, implicit self-esteem showed a strong relationship to their level of optimism for future events. Participants low in explicit self-esteem and high in implicit self-esteem showed about as much optimism as participants high in both explicit and implicit self-esteem, and a more realistic level of optimism than participants high in explicit self-esteem and low in implicit self-esteem. In contrast, participants low in both explicit and implicit self-esteem showed much less optimism.

Notably, these three studies used three different measures of implicit self-esteem, and yet each provided evidence consistent with our glimmer-of-hope hypothesis. Typically these different measures of implicit self-esteem do not correlate with one another, and yet they seem to predict the reactions of low explicit self-esteem people in the same way in these studies. How can this be? Do they all measure the same underlying construct but capture different and unrelated manifestations of that construct (e.g., amount of time spent running, biking, and swimming might be essentially uncorrelated, yet all measure cardiovascular exercise)? Do they measure different constructs that all interact with explicit self-esteem in the same way? Do they measure the same constructs in some situations, but different constructs in other situations? Perhaps future research will be able to sort between these possibilities.

Nevertheless, together these studies provide initial evidence to support our hypothesis that among people with low explicit self-esteem, high implicit self-esteem may function as preconscious views about the self that provide a glimmer of hope. When low self-esteem people think about future performance, this glimmer of hope may allow them to be more optimistic and to avoid self-protective and possibly counterproductive strategies. If this reasoning is correct, then it may have important implications for our understanding of depression. Considerable evidence suggests that self-esteem and depression are highly correlated (Crocker & Wolfe, 2001). However, implicit self-esteem might play an important role in the onset and sequelae of depression. If those with low explicit self-esteem and high implicit self-esteem experience a glimmer of hope when looking to the future, they may be less likely to fall into depression and more likely to come out of depression quickly if they do.

DISCUSSION

We have reviewed evidence that implicit self-esteem can provide important information in addition to explicit self-esteem in understanding how people maintain their self-images. Among people high in explicit self-esteem, those low in implicit self-esteem respond to threat with increased defensiveness, whereas those who are high in both types of self-esteem show less defensiveness and appear to be more secure. Among people low in explicit self-esteem, those who are high in implicit self-esteem appear to approach future performance with at least a modicum of optimism, whereas those low in both types of self-esteem appear to approach future performance with self-protective strategies.

In our view, implicit self-esteem functions in self-image maintenance in this way because it represents preconscious views of the self that seep into consciousness in specific situations. When people with low implicit self-esteem experience threat, nagging doubts representing their preconscious self-views may well become at least vaguely conscious. For those low in explicit self-esteem, this is likely to have little influence on their behavior. These preconscious views that have become conscious are, after all, largely consistent with their more chronic, conscious self-views. For those high in explicit self-esteem, however, these nagging doubts are likely to be disconcerting, as they will conflict with more positive chronic, conscious self-views. In this way, such nagging doubts may motivate people high in explicit self-esteem to strive for self-enhancement, resulting in defensive reactions to threat.

Our account is broadly consistent with Wilson's dual-attitude model (Wilson et al., 2000) that suggests that explicit attitudes and implicit attitudes are different attitudes that exist at different levels of consciousness. We add to this account that situations can bring implicit views of the self into consciousness, and when these formerly implicit self-views conflict with explicit self-views, people will be motivated to resolve the discrepancy.

We must admit, however, that we cannot completely rule out the possibility that the implicit measures in our studies were simply capturing self-esteem as a more authentic measure, as suggested by Greenwald and Banaji (1995). The discrepancies between implicit and explicit self-esteem in this account might result because the implicit measures capture true self-esteem whereas the explicit measures capture motivated and potentially defensive responding. Thus, people who are truly low in self-esteem but respond by exaggerating their self-esteem on explicit self-esteem scales are broadly defensive on a number of measures, whereas people who are truly high in self-esteem are not. Although plausible, we feel this explanation is less than compelling because people who are high in explicit self-esteem and low in implicit self-esteem score higher in self-deception (but not impression management) than do people high in both types of self-esteem. Thus defensively high self-esteem people do not seem to be merely inflating their self-esteem to others but also at some level seem to believe their highly positive explicit self-views. (See Jordan et al., 2003 for a more detailed description of this argument.)

In addition, the view that implicit self-esteem captures people's true level of self-esteem does not fare as well at explaining the glimmer-of-hope hypothesis. It is less clear why people who are truly high in self-esteem but who systematically lower their reported self-evaluations on explicit self-esteem measures would respond to the prospect of future performance by making optimistic interpretations. Nevertheless, at present there is only limited evidence that supports the glimmer-of-hope hypothesis, and it remains to be seen whether further testing will continue to support it.

Our account also seems to be broadly consistent with the work of Kernis and his colleagues (Kernis & Pardise, 2002; Kernis & Waschull, 1995) in which they find that among those high in explicit self-esteem, those who have unstable self-esteem display more defensiveness. If people with high explicit self-esteem and low implicit self-esteem experience nagging doubts when threatened but chronically are unaware of these doubts, then it seems that these people would also evidence more unstable self-esteem as these nagging doubts enter and recede from consciousness. Indeed, low implicit self-esteem among those with high explicit self-esteem might well be the source of the self-esteem instability that Kernis has repeatedly shown is related to insecurity and defensiveness.

But how does positive implicit self-esteem operate in self-image maintenance? We are proposing that when people look to the future and think about how they might fare, high implicit self-esteem may create a glimmer of hope, fostering a sense of optimism. For people high in explicit self-esteem, this glimmer of hope is likely to have little influence, as it is consistent with their chronic self-views, but for those who have low explicit self-esteem, these thoughts might well motivate them to seek self-enhancement and avoid the self-protective and potentially counterproductive strategies that are often seen among people with low explicit self-esteem.

This reasoning is at least broadly consistent with research on attributional styles and depression (Metalsky, Joiner, Hardin, & Abramson, 1993; Needles & Abramson, 1990; Seligman, 1991), which finds that among people who fall into depression, those who have a more optimistic attributional style are more likely to quickly recover. If people with low explicit self-esteem—who are likely to be prone to depression—have high implicit self-esteem, then they may face the future with a glimmer of hope that fosters a sense of optimism. In this way high implicit self-esteem may account for the more optimistic attributional style that allows some depressed people to more easily recover from depression.

Although we are encouraged by the empirical support that we have obtained for our understanding of the role of implicit self-esteem in self-image maintenance, we recognize that our results are quite preliminary. Important conceptual and empirical questions remain. Are people aware of their implicit self-esteem? Why are different measures of implicit self-esteem often uncorrelated? How does implicit self-esteem develop? What is the causal relationship between implicit self-esteem and the motives, thoughts, and behavior associated with it? The former two questions we have dealt with extensively already, but the latter two questions deserve further discussion.

The origin of implicit self-esteem is an intriguing problem, and several theoretical traditions offer interesting accounts. Attachment theory (Bowlby, 1973) suggests that our formative interpersonal relationships in infancy foster internal working models of ourselves and others. Perhaps implicit self-esteem represents these internal working models of ourselves. This perspective would suggest that implicit self-esteem is learned early in life and is relatively stable. The model of dual attitudes developed by Wilson et al. (2000) might also suggest that implicit self-esteem is an attitude about the self that is learned early in life and is stable. In contrast, recent research demonstrating the malleability of implicit constructs (Blair, 2002) suggests the possibility that implicit self-esteem might be less stable than these theories posit.

Related to this issue is the question of the direction of causality between implicit self-esteem and the motives, thoughts, and behaviors that are associated with it. In this chapter we have presented evidence that people high in explicit self-esteem and low in implicit self-esteem are defensive, but do their levels of these types of self-esteem lead to defensiveness, or does their defensiveness lead to their levels of self-esteem? Or, does some third variable create both responses? The data we have presented does not really address these important issues. It is plausible that people high in explicit self-esteem and low in implicit self-esteem had low self-esteem early in life (as attachment theory and the dual attitudes model would suggest) and later consciously challenged these self-views. Through this process, they might thus have developed high explicit self-esteem, and it is these new self-beliefs that lead to defensiveness. On the other hand, we must acknowledge that the opposite direction of causality is also plausible. Perhaps people who regularly engage in defensiveness develop positive explicit views of themselves as a result of defensiveness but develop negative implicit views of themselves because these defensive tendencies cause others to dislike them. These issues of causality will be important to address in future research.

Despite these questions, as we look to the future of this research, we experience more than a glimmer of hope. (Dare we say this is the influence of high implicit self-esteem?) The research we have reviewed demonstrates that our understanding of implicit self-esteem adds an important dimension to our understanding of self-image maintenance processes. However, this research is clearly in its infancy. Future research on implicit self-esteem holds the promise of advancing our understanding of the nature of implicit thoughts more generally and, in addition, may provide important insights to how the self-concept develops.

ACKNOWLEDGMENTS

This research was supported by grants from the Social Sciences and Humanities Research Council to the first and fourth authors, by a doctoral fellowship from the Natural Sciences and Engineering Research Council to the second author, and by an Ontario Graduate Scholarship to the third author.

NOTE

1. Implicit and explicit self-esteem were not significantly correlated in any of the studies reported below. In addition, we analyzed all of the results including gender as a factor, and because it was never a significant predictor we collapsed across it in all the analyses.

REFERENCES

Aronson, E. (1968). Dissonance theory: Progress and problems. In R. Abelson, E. Aronson, W. McGuire, T. Newcomb, M. Rosenberg, & P. Tannenbaum (Eds.), *Theories of cognitive consistency: A sourcebook* (pp. 5–27). Chicago: Rand McNally.

Bartholomew, K., & Horowitz, L. (1991). Attachment styles among young adults: A test of a four category model. *Journal of Personality and Social Psychology, 61*, 226–244.

Blair, I. V. (2002). The malleability of automatic stereotypes and prejudice. *Personality and Social Psychology Review, 6*, 242–261.

Bosson, J. K., Brown, R. P., Zeigler-Hill, V., & Swann, W. B. (2003). Self-enhancement tendencies among people with high explicit self-esteem: The moderating role of implicit self-esteem. *Self and Identity, 2*, 169–187.

Bosson, J. K., Swann, W. B., & Pennebaker, J. W. (2000). Stalking the perfect measure of implicit self-esteem: The blind men and the elephant revisited? *Journal of Personality and Social Psychology, 79*, 631–643.

Bourhis, R. Y., Sachdev, I., & Gagnon, A. (1994). Intergroup research with the Tajfel matrices: Methodological notes. In M. P. Zanna & J. M. Olson (Eds.), *The psychology of prejudice: The Ontario Symposium* (Vol. 7, pp. 209–232). Hillsdale, NJ: Erlbaum.

Bowlby, J. (1973). *Attachment and loss: Vol. 2. Separation: Anxiety and anger.* New York: Basic Books.

Bushman, B. J., & Baumeister, R. (1998). Threatened egotism, narcissism, self-esteem, and direct and displaced aggression: Does self-love or self-hate lead to violence? *Journal of Personality and Social Psychology, 75,* 219–229.

Crocker, J., & Wolfe, C. (2001). Contingencies of self-worth. *Psychological Review, 108,* 593–623.

Epstein, S. (1973). The self-concept revisited: Or a theory of a theory. *American Psychologist, 28,* 404–416.

Farnham, S. D., Greenwald, A. G., & Banaji, M. R. (1999). Implicit self-esteem. In D. Abrams & M. A. Hogg (Eds.), *Social identity and social cognition* (pp. 230–248). Oxford, England: Blackwell.

Fazio, R. H., & Olson, M. A. (2003). Implicit measures in social cognition research: Their meaning and use. *Annual Review of Psychology, 54,* 297–327.

Fein, S., & Spencer, S. J. (1997). Prejudice as self-image maintenance: Affirming the self through derogating others. *Journal of Personality and Social Psychology, 73,* 31–44.

Greenwald, A. G., & Banaji, M. R. (1995). Implicit social cognition: Attitudes, self-esteem, and stereotypes. *Psychological Review, 102,* 4–27.

Greenwald, A. G., & Farnham, S. (2001). Using the implicit association test to measure self-esteem and self-concept. *Journal of Personality and Social Psychology, 79,* 1022–1038.

Hoshino-Browne, E., Zanna, A. S., Spencer, S. J., & Zanna, M. P. (in press). Investigating attitudes cross-culturally: A case of cognitive dissonance among East Asians and North Americans. In G. R. Maio & G. Haddock (Eds.), *Perspectives on attitudes for the 21st century: The Cardiff Symposium.* London: Psychology Press.

Jordan, C. H. (2003). *Secure and defensive types of high self-esteem: Discrepancies between explicit and implicit self-esteem predict defensiveness.* Unpublished doctoral dissertation, University of Waterloo, Waterloo, Ontario, Canada.

Jordan, C. H., Spencer, S. J., & Zanna, M. P. (2002). "I love me … I love me not": Implicit self-esteem, explicit self-esteem, and defensiveness. In S. J. Spencer, S. Fein, M. P. Zanna, & J. M. Olson (Eds.), *Motivated social perception: The Ontario Symposium* (Vol. 9, pp. 117–145). Mahwah, NJ: Erlbaum.

Jordan, C. H., Spencer, S. J., Zanna, M. P., Hoshino-Browne, E., & Correll, J. (2003). Secure and defensive self-esteem. *Journal of Personality and Social Psychology, 85,* 969–978.

Kernis, M. H., & Paradise, A. W. (2002). Distinguishing between secure and fragile forms of high self-esteem. In E. L. Deci & R. M. Ryan (Eds.), *Handbook of self-determination research* (pp. 339–360). Rochester, NY: University of Rochester Press.

Kernis, M. H., & Waschull, S. B. (1995). The interactive roles of stability and level of self-esteem: Research and theory. In M. P. Zanna (Ed.), *Advances in experimental social psychology* (Vol. 27, pp. 93–141). San Diego, CA: Academic Press.

Koole, S. L., Dijksterhuis, A., & van Knippenberg, A. (2001). What's in a name: Implicit self-esteem and the automatic self. *Journal of Personality and Social Psychology, 80,* 669–685.

McGregor, I., & Marigold, D. C. (2003). Defensive zeal and the uncertain self: Conviction as repression. *Journal of Personality and Social Psychology, 85,* 838–852.

Metalsky, G. I., Joiner, T. E., Jr., Hardin, T. S., & Abramson, L. Y. (1993). Depressive reactions to failure in a naturalistic setting: A test of the hopelessness and self-esteem theories of depression. *Journal of Abnormal Psychology, 102,* 101–109.

Morf, C. C., & Rhodewalt, F. (1993). Narcissism and self-evaluation maintenance: Explorations in object relations. *Personality and Social Psychology Bulletin, 19,* 668–676.

Needles, D. J., & Abramson L. Y. (1990). Positive life events, attributional style, and hopefulness: Testing a model of recovery from depression. *Journal of Abnormal Psychology, 99,* 156–165.

Newby-Clark, I. R., McGregor, I., & Zanna, M. P. (2002). Thinking and caring about cognitive inconsistency: When and for whom does attitudinal ambivalence feel uncomfortable? *Journal of Personality and Social Psychology, 82,* 157–166.

Paulhus, D. L. (1998). Interpersonal and intrapsychic adaptiveness of trait self-enhancement: A mixed blessing? *Journal of Personality and Social Psychology, 74,* 1197–1208.

Raskin, R., & Hall, C. S. (1988). The narcissistic personality inventory. *Psychological Reports, 40,* 590.

Raskin, R., Novacek, J., & Hogan, R. (1991). Narcissism, self-esteem, and defensive self-enhancement. *Journal of Personality, 59,* 19–38.

Rosenberg, M. (1965). *Society and the adolescent self-image.* Princeton, NJ: Princeton University Press.

Rubin, M., & Hewstone, M. (1998). Social identity theory's self-esteem hypothesis: A review and some suggestions for clarification. *Personality and Social Psychology Review, 2,* 40–62.

Seligman, M. E. P. (1991). *Learned optimism.* New York: Knopf.

Spalding, L. R., & Hardin, C. D. (2000). Unconscious unease and self-handicapping: Behavioral consequences of individual differences in implicit and explicit self-esteem. *Psychological Science, 10,* 535–539.

Steele, C. M. (1988). The psychology of self-affirmation: Sustaining the integrity of the self. In L. Berkowitz (Ed.), *Advances in experimental social psychology* (Vol. 21, pp. 261–302). San Diego, CA: Academic Press.

Steele, C. M., Spencer, S. J., & Lynch, M. (1993). Self-image resilience and dissonance: The role of affirmational resources. *Journal of Personality and Social Psychology, 64,* 885–896.

Taforodi, R. W., & Swann, W. B., Jr. (1995). Self-liking and self-competence as dimensions of global self-esteem: Initial validation of a measure. *Journal of Personality Assessment, 65,* 322–342.

Tajfel, H. (1981). *Human groups and social categories.* Cambridge, England: Cambridge University Press.

Tajfel, H., Flament, C., Billig, M., & Bundy, R. (1971). Social categorization and intergroup behaviour. *European Journal of Social Psychology, 10,* 131–147.

Tajfel, H., & Turner, J. C. (1979). An integrative theory of intergroup conflict. In S. Worchel & W. G. Austin (Eds.), *The social psychology of intergroup relations* (pp. 33–47). Monterey, CA: Brooks/Cole.

Tice, D. (1991). Esteem protection or enhancement? Self-handicapping motives and attributions differ by trait self-esteem. *Journal of Personality and Social Psychology, 60,* 711–725.

Weinstein, N. D. (1980). Unrealistic optimism about future life events. *Journal of Personality and Social Psychology, 39,* 806–820.

Wilson, T. D., Hodges, S. D., & LaFleur, S. J. (1995). Effects of introspecting about reasons: Inferring attitudes from accessible thoughts. *Journal of Personality and Social Psychology, 69,* 16–28.

Wilson, T. D., Lindsey, S., & Schooler, T. Y. (2000). A model of dual attitudes. *Psychological Review, 107,* 101–126.

8

Approach–Avoidance Motivation and Self-Concept Evaluation

ANDREW J. ELLIOT AND RACHAEL R. MAPES

The distinction between approach and avoidance motivation has a long history in scientific psychology, as well as in intellectual thought more generally. The approach–avoidance distinction first appeared in the writings of the ancient Greek philosophers Democritus (460–370 B.C.E.) and Aristippus (435–356 B.C.E.), who advocated an ethical hedonism in which the pursuit of pleasure and the avoidance of pain were proscribed as the optimal guide for human behavior. Many years later the British philosopher Jeremy Bentham (1748–1832) articulated a psychological hedonism in which the pursuit of pleasure and the avoidance of pain were viewed descriptively (rather than prescriptively) as the way in which human beings actually behave. William James (1890/1950) identified pleasure and pain as "springs of action," describing them as strong reinforcers and inhibitors of behavior, respectively, and offered speculation regarding the neural mechanisms underlying approach and avoidance tendencies. Many of the most prominent contributors to psychological theory since the time of James have explicitly incorporated approach–avoidance concepts and principles into their work; this is true across theoretical and metatheoretical perspectives and across substantive domains of inquiry (see Elliot, 1999, for a review).

Widespread use of the approach–avoidance distinction in the theoretical arena has been emphatically validated in the empirical arena. Research across diverse literatures has repeatedly and consistently documented that approach and avoidance processes have distinct antecedents and consequences. These literatures include the following: animal learning (Gray, 1982; Overmier & Archer, 1989), attitudes (Cacioppo & Berntson, 1994; Tesser & Martin, 1996), cognitive appraisal (Lazarus, 1991; Tomaka & Blaskovich, 1994), coping (Moos & Schaeffer, 1993; Roth & Cohen, 1986), emotion (Higgins, Shah, & Friedman, 1997; Roseman, 1984), decision making (Kahneman & Tversky, 1979; Messick & McClintock, 1968), goals and self-regulation (Carver & Scheier, 1998; Elliot & Sheldon, 1998), health behavior (Rogers, 1975; Rothman & Salovey, 1997), memory (Forster & Strack, 1996; Kuiper & Derry, 1982), mental control (Newman, Wolff, & Hearst,

1980; Wegner, 1994), perception–attention (Derryberry, 1991; Dixon, 1981), psychobiology (Davidson, 1993; Depue & Iacono, 1989), psycholinguistics (Clark, 1974; Just & Carpenter, 1971), psychopathology (Fowles, 1988; Newman, 1987), and social interaction (Arkin, 1981; Tedeschi & Norman, 1985).

Given the long history and richly documented utility of the approach–avoidance distinction, it is surprising that in the contemporary scene this distinction is often ignored or overlooked in analyses of motivation, personality, and the self. Certainly this distinction has attracted increased attention in the past decade (see Cacioppo & Bernston, 1994; Carver & Scheier, 1998; Davidson, 1992; Elliot, 1997; Higgins, 1997; Lang, 1995), but theories, models, constructs, and hypotheses are still commonly espoused without consideration of approach–avoidance concepts or principles, despite their clear relevance. One possibility for this oversight is that many individuals equate approach–avoidance motivation with psychological hedonism, and they simply assent to this perspective at the assumptive level without considering the implications for theory and research. Another possibility is that many persons presume that approach and avoidance motivation are reciprocally related and, therefore, that conceptual statements offered in terms of approach implicitly implicate avoidance as well. It is also possible that researchers and theorists are not yet aware of the foundational nature of approach –avoidance processes and their applicability to a broad and diverse range of psychological phenomena.

We believe that explicit and intricate attention to the approach–avoidance distinction is critical to a deep understanding of motivation, personality, and the self. In this chapter, we focus primarily on the self, although, of course, discussions of the self invariably evoke issues pertaining to motivation and personality, and the approach–avoidance distinction itself is inextricably intertwined with motivation. In this chapter, we proceed as follows: First, we define approach and avoidance motivation and discuss terminological issues pertaining to the approach–avoidance distinction. Second, we use the approach–avoidance distinction as a lens through which to examine self-concept evaluation, with a primary focus on self-esteem conceptualization and measurement, and the motivation underlying evaluation of the self-concept. Third, and finally, we discuss issues pertaining to parsimony and offer pragmatic suggestions for how the considerations discussed herein may be implemented in the self literature.

APPROACH AND AVOIDANCE MOTIVATION

Definition

Approach motivation may be defined as the energization of behavior by or the direction of behavior toward positive stimuli (objects, events, or possibilities), whereas avoidance motivation may be defined as the energization of behavior by or the direction of behavior away from negative stimuli (objects, events, or possibilities). This definition of approach–avoidance motivation is most directly akin to Lewin's (1926, 1935) analysis of positive–negative valences and their accompanying forces. (Approach–avoidance terminology was first used in print by Hovland, 1937; Miller, 1937; and Sears, 1937, in the published proceedings of an American Psychological Association symposium on conflict. Although these scholars based their theoretical and empirical work on Lewin's, 1935, analysis of conflict situations, Lewin himself did not use approach–avoidance terminology per se to characterize the various types of conflict situations.)

The approach–avoidance distinction is rarely defined in explicit fashion as we have done herein, and several aspects of the definition that we have proffered are worth noting. First, being a motivational distinction, approach–avoidance encompasses both the energization of behavior—that is, the initial instigation or "spring to action" (James, 1890/1950, Vol. 2, p. 555) that orients the organism—and the direction of behavior—that is, the aim that guides the organism's behavior. Second, inherent in the approach–avoidance distinction is the concept of physical or psychological movement. Positively evaluated stimuli are inherently associated with an approach orientation to bring or keep the stimuli close to the organism (literally or figuratively), whereas negatively evaluated stimuli are inherently associated with an avoidance orientation to push or keep the stimuli away from the organism (literally or figuratively). Although positively and negatively evaluated stimuli produce (at a minimum) a physiological and somatic preparedness for physical movement toward and away from the stimuli, respectively (Arnold, 1960; Corwin, 1921), this preparedness may or may not be translated directly into overt behavior. Initial approach or avoidance inclinations may be overridden or channeled in various ways, some of which entail hierarchical combinations of approach and avoidance (e.g., an activated concern about failure that evokes attempts to succeed at all costs; see Elliot & Church, 1997). Third, positive–negative valence is conceptualized as the core evaluative dimension of approach–avoidance motivation. "Positive" and "negative" are presumed to take on somewhat different meanings in different contexts, including beneficial–harmful, liked–disliked, and desirable–undesirable. Research indicates that these dimensions are conceptually and empirically comparable to a high degree, although some empirical work suggests that they may be separable in certain instances (Berridge, 1999). At present, given their substantial comparability, we think it best to construe beneficial–harmful, liked–disliked, and desirable–undesirable as functionally equivalent dimensions that may be subsumed under the positive–negative rubric (i.e., in essence, the three dimensions are conceptualized as indicators of a positive–negative latent variable). Nevertheless, we are open to the possibility that subsequent research will establish a need to distinguish among these dimensions in defining the approach–avoidance distinction. Fourth, the term *stimuli* as used herein may represent concrete, observable objects–events–possibilities, or may represent abstract, internally generated representations of objects–events–possibilities.

Fifth, our definition of approach–avoidance motivation is applicable across all forms of animate life, from the single-cell amoeba to the human being (hence our use of the term *organism*). In order to survive, organisms must possess at least some rudimentary evaluative mechanism that impels them to move toward potentially positive stimuli and away from potentially negative stimuli (Schneirla, 1959; Tooby & Cosmides, 1990). In the amoeba, this mechanism is obviously extremely primitive and routinized, evoking rigid, constitutionally ingrained approach-and-withdrawal movements in response to stimuli (e.g., weak–intense light). The human being possesses many such evaluative mechanisms, and these mechanisms evoke approach and avoidance actions and action tendencies of diverse complexity and flexibility (Cacioppo, Gardiner, & Berntson, 1999). The sophistication of evaluative mechanisms varies tremendously across species, but it is important to reiterate that some type of evaluative mechanism must be posited to account for any systematic observation of approach–avoidance behavior (Schneirla, 1959). Sixth, our definition of approach–avoidance motivation is applicable across a wide array of levels and types of constructs used to account for functioning in human beings. Thus, affective, cognitive, and behavioral constructs may be conceptualized in approach–avoidance terms, and approach–avoidance processes are operative across levels of the neuraxis, from rudimentary reflexes to vaunted cortical processes (Berntson, Boyson, & Cacioppo, 1993; Elliot & Thrash, 2002).

Terminological Issues

Many different terms and labels have been used over the years to cover the basic conceptual space that we seek to cover with *approach–avoidance*. Each of the different designations tends to be associated with a somewhat different set of emphases. Three of the most common of these designations are considered here.

Hedonism (Pleasure–Pain)

Hedonism has been conceptualized in several different ways in the philosophical and psychological literatures. In philosophy, the Epicureans used the term quite broadly to refer to seeking the pleasures and avoiding the pains of both the mind and the body, whereas the British empiricists used the term more narrowly to refer to the pleasures and pains of bodily sensation (Boring, 1950; Cofer & Appley, 1964). In psychology, hedonism has typically been defined in the narrow sense in terms of bodily sensation and experienced affect (Franken, 1994; Young, 1961). Rozin (1999; see also Kahneman, Diener, & Schwarz, 1999) recently proposed a more inclusive view of hedonism, defining pleasure as "a positive experienced state that we seek and that we try to maintain or enhance" and pain as "a negative experienced state that we avoid and that we try to reduce or eliminate" (p. 112). This more inclusive view of hedonism is more akin to our conceptualization of approach–avoidance motivation than is the normative view of hedonism in the psychological literature. Rozin's definition remains narrower than our own, however, in that he uses the term *experience* to refer to conscious experience, whereas we include nonconscious and even reflexive processes under the approach–avoidance rubric as well.

Approach–Withdrawal

The *approach–withdrawal* distinction was introduced to the psychological literature by Schneirla (1959), a comparative psychologist, who argued that motivational analyses should be grounded in overt behavioral actions so that they are applicable to lower as well as higher organisms. Thus, he conceptualized approach and withdrawal motivation in terms of observable behavior toward stimuli and observable behavior away from stimuli, respectively. Davidson and colleagues (Davidson 1992; Sutton & Davidson, 1997; Tomarken, Davidson, Wheeler, & Doss, 1992; see also Harmon-Jones & Allen, 1997) currently utilize the approach–withdrawal distinction in broader fashion, to refer to action tendencies as well as overt action per se. Approach and withdrawal tendencies are presumed to be grounded in differential cortical activation: Approach tendencies are linked to activation of the left prefrontal cortex, whereas withdrawal tendencies are linked to activation of the right prefrontal cortex. These approach–withdrawal tendencies are posited to be the foundational dimensions of emotional experience. Our conceptualization of approach–avoidance is similar to Davidson and colleagues' conceptualization of approach–withdrawal, in that approach–avoidance refers to action tendencies as well as overt action per se. However, their approach–withdrawal distinction seems narrower than our approach–avoidance distinction, in that approach–withdrawal focuses on the issue of energization at the biological level, whereas approach–avoidance covers both energization and direction and is applicable to biologically based and psychologically based processes across the neuraxis.

Appetite–Aversion   The *appetite–aversion* distinction was first mentioned by Craig (1918), who conceptualized appetites and aversions in terms of internal states of agitation (i.e., energization) accompanied by a readiness to "consume" the "appeted" stimulus or "get rid of" the "disturbing" stimulus (pp. 93–94). Craig focused primarily on physiological instincts in his theorizing and considered basic reflexive mechanisms to be outside the purview of his appetite–aversion analysis (as did Tolman, 1932, who explicitly embraced Craig's distinction). In the contemporary literature, Lang and colleagues (Lang, 1995; Lang, Bradley, & Cuthbert, 1997) have utilized the appetite–aversion distinction in their analysis of emotion and reflexive behavior. Emotion is characterized as a motivationally tuned state of action readiness, and two basic brain systems are posited to underlie emotion: appetitive (consumatory) and aversive (defensive). Reflexive behaviors are also characterized in terms of the appetitive–aversive distinction. In both instances, *appetitive* is meant to connote consumatory and approach-oriented, whereas *aversive* is meant to connote defensive and avoidance-oriented. More complex, "tactical" behavior is also thought to be organized in terms of this appetitive–aversive distinction, but little detail is offered in this regard. (Interestingly, approach–avoidance terminology per se is utilized when "tactical" behavior is [briefly] discussed; see Lang, 1995, p. 373.) Our conceptualization of approach–avoidance is similar to Lang and colleagues' conceptualization of appetitive–aversive in that we view approach–avoidance as applicable to reflexive behavior. Indeed, given Lang and colleagues' incorporation of "tactical" behavior under the appetitive–aversive rubric, the two distinctions under consideration differ primarily in terms of emphasis (reflexive behavior is the central focus of the appetitive–aversive distinction to date, whereas it is simply one of many levels under consideration in the approach–avoidance distinction).

This discussion of terminological issues highlights the fact that there is a great deal of overlap in the way that the various designations have been utilized, both when they were originally articulated and as they are currently used in the literature. From our standpoint, the differences among the various terms are less important than their substantial conceptual convergence, and a move toward uniformity of terminology would be welcomed. In developing our definition of the approach–avoidance distinction, we have sought to be as precise, yet as inclusive, as possible. Precision is needed, because for the most part the various distinctions that have been utilized over the years have not been clearly defined, which has likely delayed attempts to integrate the various lines of inquiry. Inclusivity is needed so as to cover the full conceptual space under consideration across types of organisms, levels of analysis, and specific theoretical frameworks. We believe that the approach–avoidance distinction, as conceptualized herein, may be broadly applied to many different domains and that such application will yield many theoretical and empirical benefits. This distinction has received some attention in the self literature, but as we discuss in the following, it could be applied on a much broader basis.

APPROACH–AVOIDANCE MOTIVATION AND EVALUATION OF THE SELF-CONCEPT

Self-evaluation is a core area of inquiry in the self literature. There are several different ways in which the self is conceptualized and, accordingly, there are several different ways to examine self-evaluation. One critical distinction is between the self as an object of evaluation and the self as an executive or agent that does the evaluating and impels motivated behavior. The latter form of self-evaluation implicates constructs such as basic needs (Baumeister & Leary, 1995; Ryan, 1995; White, 1959), motive dispositions (Atkinson, 1957; McClelland, 1985; Murray, 1938), and goals (Dweck, 1986; Elliot & Thrash, 2001; Emmons, 1986). This form of self-evaluation is not the focus of the present discourse, because the approach–avoidance distinction has received significant attention in this arena (particularly regarding motive dispositions and goals; see Elliot, McGregor, & Thrash, 2002). Rather, we focus on the self as an object of evaluation—that is, the evaluation of the self-concept. We begin by discussing the nature and measurement of self-esteem and then move on to discuss the motivation commonly presumed to underlie evaluation of the self-concept.

Self-Esteem

Self-esteem is commonly construed as the positive or negative evaluation of the self-concept. In essence, the self-concept represents an object, and self-esteem represents an evaluation of or attitude toward that object (Rosenberg, 1965). Self-esteem is one of the most researched constructs in the literature of the self, yet there remains a lack of consensus in the field as to how self-esteem should be operationalized and conceptualized. One critical question that remains outstanding is whether global self-esteem represents a unidimensional or a multidimensional construct.

Rosenberg (1965) posited a unidimensional conceptualization of self-esteem and devised a 10-item measure based on this conceptualization that has long been the most popular self-esteem measure in the literature (Blascovich & Tomaka, 1991; Heatherton & Wyland, 2003). However, empirical work on the dimensionality of Rosenberg's measure has not consistently yielded evidence supportive of the unidimensional view. In fact, more often than not, exploratory factor analysis of this measure has revealed two factors, with the positively worded items (e.g., "I feel that I have a number of good qualities") loading on one factor and the negatively worded items (e.g., "Sometimes I think I am no good at all") loading on the second factor (Marsh, 1996; Owens, 1993; Tafarodi & Milne, 2002). The critical question is how these two factors should be interpreted.

One interpretation is that the two factors simply represent a methodological artifact. From this perspective, positively worded items load together and negatively worded items load together, because participants simply have a response set that causes them to answer all positive items in a uniform manner and all negative items in a uniform manner (Carmines & Zeller, 1974; Hensley & Roberts, 1976; Marsh, 1986). Another interpretation is that the two factors represent a substantive distinction worthy of theoretical attention. From this perspective, it is important to distinguish between a positive component of self-esteem (i.e., the degree to which the self-concept is evaluated positively) and a negative component of self-esteem (i.e., the degree to which the self-concept is evaluated negatively) and to acknowledge that these semi-independent constructs may have distinct antecedents and consequences (H. B. Kaplan & Pokorney, 1969; Owens, 1994; Shahani, Dipboye, & Phillips, 1990).

It is clear that in the contemporary literature, most researchers and theorists embrace a unidimensional conceptualization of self-esteem, thereby implicitly endorsing the methodological artifact interpretation of the factor-analytic data. Self-esteem is typically defined in unidimensional terms (along a bipolar positive–negative dimension), and sometimes simply in positive terms (e.g., "Self-esteem may be defined as the positivity of the person's evaluation of the self"; Baumeister, 1998; see also Coopersmith, 1967). Research on global self-esteem almost invariably utilizes a single variable to conceptualize the self-esteem construct. Rosenberg's (1965) 10-item measure continues to be the modal self-esteem measure used in empirical work; a self-esteem measure explicitly designed to assess separate positive and negative components has yet to be constructed (however, see Rose, 2002). We believe that the reason the unidimensional approach to self-esteem carries the day at present is that a clear theoretical rationale for separable positive and negative self-esteem components has not yet been articulated. This theoretical rationale may be derived directly from consideration of the approach–avoidance distinction.

Research on evaluative processes indicates that essentially any object (be it a concrete material entity or an abstract mental concept) that an individual encounters is automatically and instantaneously evaluated in terms of valence (Bargh, 1997; Osgood, Suci, & Tannenbaum, 1957; Zajonc, 1998). These automatic positive and negative evaluations have been shown to be directly associated with approach and avoidance behavioral predispositions, respectively (Chen & Bargh, 1999; Foerster, Higgins, & Idson, 1998; Solarz, 1960). Recent work by Cacioppo and colleagues (Cacioppo & Berntson, 1994; Cacioppo et al., 1997) has persuasively demonstrated that positive and negative evaluations emerge from separable evaluative channels and that the relationship between these channels can be reciprocal (producing unidimensional evaluations) or relatively independent (producing bidimensional evaluations). One characteristic that appears to determine when positive and negative evaluative mechanisms produce unidimensional versus bidimensional evaluative judgments is the complexity of the object under consideration. The more complex the object, the more likely it is to receive independent processing from positive and negative evaluative mechanisms, resulting in a bidimensional evaluative structure (see Ito, Cacioppo, & Lang, 1998).

Given the inherent richness and complexity of self-knowledge, we contend that for most individuals self-esteem is likely to be bidimensional. Specifically, self-esteem is posited to represent both a positive evaluative judgment of the self-concept that is based on aspects of the person that he or she is attracted to, and a negative evaluative judgment of the self-concept that is based on aspects of the person that he or she is repelled by. These self-concept evaluations at the global level likely emerge in large part from more specific self-evaluative processes that are themselves appetitive and aversive in nature. Individuals invest themselves in hoped for and feared possible selves (Markus & Nurius, 1986), approach and avoidance personal goals (Elliot & Sheldon, 1998), and promotion- and prevention-based self-guides (Higgins, 1998), and the evaluation of progress (or lack thereof) on these self-investments is undoubtedly an important determinant of positive and negative self-esteem judgments.

A bidimensional conceptualization of self-esteem is in accord with commonly expressed sentiments such as, "There is a part of myself that I like, and a part of myself that I don't like" or "I feel both good and bad about myself." At an intuitive level, people seem to resonate with the notion that they can simultaneously have positive and negative evaluations of the self, much as they may be ambivalent (literally, "of both valences") toward their parents (Maio, Fincham, & Lycett, 2000), their romantic partners (Fincham & Linfield, 1997), and many other highly valued objects. To be sure, individuals may possess enduring dispositions that shunt their self-evaluative processes toward unidimensionality; likely candidates are a high preference for consistency (Cialdini, Trost, & Newsom, 1995), a high personal need for simple structure (Neuberg & Newsom, 1993), and a low self-complexity (Linville, 1985). However, we suspect that overall, across persons, self-esteem judgments tend to conform to a bidimensional structure.

From this perspective, self-esteem measures such as that constructed by Rosenberg (1965) may be presumed to assess separable positive and negative components of self-esteem, despite the fact that they were designed to assess a unidimensional construct. In computing a composite self-esteem index by subtracting negative scores from positive scores, researchers simply eliminate the inherent bidimensionality of the data and treat it as if it were unidimensional. This procedure makes it impossible to interpret values that fall in the middle of the possible scale range. That is, individuals with high positive and high negative scores will appear identical to those with moderate positive and moderate negative scores, and those with low positive and low negative scores (see K. J. Kaplan, 1972, for a conceptual analogue in the literature on ambivalent attitudes, and Elliot, 1997, for a conceptual analogue in the achievement motivation literature).

In addition, this procedure overlooks the fact that the positive and negative dimensions of self-esteem likely have distinct antecedents and consequences. For example, in a longitudinal study of adolescents, Owens (1994) demonstrated that high school grades are a positive predictor of unidimensional self-esteem and that unidimensional self-esteem is a negative predictor of depression. However, he also showed that these results masked differential results for positive and negative self-esteem: Grades predicted positive self-esteem but had no impact at all on negative self-esteem, and negative self-esteem predicted depression, whereas positive self-esteem was unrelated to depression (see Shahani et al., 1990; Verkuyten, 2003, for related research). Clearly, much information is lost when a composite self-esteem index is computed and utilized alone in empirical research. By keeping positive and negative self-esteem separate, additional precision may be acquired regarding the nature of people's self-esteem, the antecedents of their self-esteem, and the implications of their self-esteem.[1] This added precision would likely be of applied, as well as conceptual, benefit. Pinpointing the component of self-esteem that is affected by various antecedents or that leads to various outcomes could help practitioners determine the specific target that should be the focus of their intervention efforts.

What about the response-bias interpretation of the factor-analytic data from the Rosenberg measure? Certainly response biases are operative when individuals complete the Rosenberg measure or any other self-esteem items, but two issues must be considered in this regard. First, it is important to note that such response biases can be of different types, with different influences on response output. For example, when individuals are presented with items of highly similar content that vary only in valence, they may tend to answer the positive and negative items in reciprocal fashion, glossing over more refined distinctions represented by the valence of the items. This is particularly likely to transpire when reciprocally valenced items are presented in close proximity (Thompson, Zanna, & Griffin, 1995) as they are on the Rosenberg measure. This type of response set would create an artifactual factor analytic solution, but one favoring a single factor rather than two factors. Second, even if response biases that artifactually favor a bidimensional solution are present, this does not preclude the possibility that a true, substantive bidimensionality is present as well. In light of the aforementioned literature on the separability of approach and avoidance evaluations, we think it is best to interpret the bidimensional factor solution commonly obtained in analyses of the Rosenberg measure as indicative of both substantive and biased processes as opposed to biased processes alone.

To this point, we have used the terms *unidimensional* and *bidimensional* in terms of valence, but it is important to note that other self-esteem dimensions and distinctions are discussed in the self-esteem literature as well. We believe that these other dimensions and distinctions may also benefit from consideration of the approach–avoidance distinction.

One such dimension is that between *explicit self-esteem*, the consciously accessible evaluation of the self-concept that may be accessed via self-report, and *implicit self-esteem*, the nonconscious evaluation of the self (i.e., "the automatic self"; Koole, Dijksterhuis, & van Knippenberg, 2001) that must be assessed through more intricate methodologies. Many of the methodologies used to assess implicit self-esteem focus on the association of self words to positive and negative words and phrases, most entail subtracting negative scores from positive scores, and all embrace a unidimensional as opposed to bidimensional evaluation framework (see Bosson, Swann, & Pennebaker, 2000, for a review).

If anything, the case for bidimensionality at the implicit level seems even stronger than the case for bidimensionality at the explicit level. At the explicit level, dissonance, control, or expectancy-based processes may all orient individuals toward crafting self-perceptions and evaluations that are more simple and consistent than is actually the case (Cacioppo et al., 1997). As such, even if the self-concept is automatically evaluated on separable positive and negative dimensions, this bidimensionality may be filtered out of the self-report data. At the implicit level, on the other hand, such revisionary processes presumably have less of an opportunity to operate, affording a more accurate assessment of self-concept evaluation (Greenwald & Banaji, 1995; Hetts, Sakuma, & Pelham, 1999). Thus, we would expect factor analyses of implicit self-esteem data to yield the most vivid documentation of the bidimensional nature of self-esteem, much as implicit self-esteem data have most vividly displayed self-enhancement biases (Koole et al., 2001).

Another important distinction that has been proffered by self theorists regarding self-esteem is that between the competence aspect of self-esteem and the social value aspect of self-esteem. Variants of these two self-esteem aspects have been distinguished by many different theorists over the years (see Diggory, 1966; Franks & Marolla, 1976; Harter, 1985; Silverberg, 1952; White, 1963). Perhaps the most elaborate articulation of this distinction has been offered recently by Taforodi and Swann (1995; see also Tafarodi & Milne, 2002; Tafarodi & Swann, 2001), who proposed that self-competence and self-liking be considered associated but conceptually and empirically distinguishable components of self-esteem. *Self-competence* refers to "the generalized sense of one's own efficacy or power," whereas *self-liking* refers to "the generalized sense of one's own worth as a social object, according to internalized values" (Tafarodi, 1998, p. 1181).

The approach–avoidance distinction is straightforwardly applicable to both the self-competence and self-liking dimensions. Valence is an inherent feature of the competence construct: Competence may be conceptualized in positive terms (i.e., competence) or in negative terms (i.e., incompetence; Elliot & McGregor, 2001). As such, one may experience and evaluate oneself in terms of how capable, effective, or able one is and may also experience and evaluate oneself in terms of how incapable, ineffective, or unable one is. These experiences–evaluative judgments are presumed to be separable (for analogues, see Atkinson, 1957; Elliot, 1997) for the reasons articulated above regarding the nature of evaluative processes. Likewise, valence is integral to the notion of social value. A person may experience or evaluate himself or herself as good, acceptable, or worthy, and a person may also experience or evaluate himself or herself as bad, unacceptable, or unworthy. These experiences–evaluative judgments are also presumed to be separable (for analogues, see Freud, 1923/1927; Sullivan, 1953) on the basis of the aforementioned consideration of evaluative processes. As such, it seems that models of self-esteem focused on the self-competence/self-liking distinction would do well to additionally consider the approach–avoidance distinction (see Aidman, 1998, for preliminary factor-analytic data on this issue).

Two other ways in which self-esteem is differentiated are *global* self-esteem versus *domain-specific* self-esteem or worth (e.g., academic, athletic, physical appearance; see Harter, 1999) and *trait* self-esteem versus *state* self-esteem (see Heatherton & Polivy, 1991). As may be inferred from our discourse thus far, we believe that the approach–avoidance distinction is applicable in these instances as well, and we would go so far as to suggest that the approach–avoidance distinction should be assumed to be relevant to any form of self-evaluative judgment unless it can be shown otherwise. Certainly there is variability in the degree to which such judgments are bidimensional. For example, it is likely that state self-esteem judgments are more likely to display tendencies toward unidimensionality than are trait self-esteem judgments, particularly in situations in which people encounter an important, unequivocally positive or negative event (for an analogue in the affect literature, see Diener & Emmons, 1984). Nevertheless, given our present understanding of evaluative processes, we think that it is wise to presume bidimensionality and to adjust from this assumption if and when the data indicate it is necessary.

Motivation Underlying Self-Concept Evaluation

An important component of the literature on self-concept evaluation has focused on the motivational impetus for self-evaluation processes. In the literature of the self, the term *motive* is used to refer to the reason why individuals engage in self-concept evaluation. However, *motive* is a specific term in the motivation literature that denotes a domain-general, affectively based disposition (Elliot, 1997; e.g., the fear of failure motive is conceptualized as the dispositional tendency to experience shame upon failure; see Atkinson, 1957; McGregor & Elliot, 2003). Given that this term has been used for more than half a century in the motivation literature (see McClelland, Atkinson, Clark, & Lowell, 1953) and that it is not what theorists of the self desire to convey in their discussions of self-evaluation, we recommend use of the more generic term *motivation* (and derivations thereof) when addressing the reasons underlying self-concept evaluation. We follow this recommendation herein.

Why do individuals engage in self-concept evaluation? Initially, theorists of the self posited three basic reasons why persons evaluate the self-concept, and this list has recently been expanded to include a fourth reason. Self-enhancement, self-verification, and self-assessment were the first reasons to be identified (Sedikides, 1993), and self-improvement is the reason that has recently been added (Wayment & Taylor, 1995; see Sedikides & Strube, 1997). Each of these motivations is typically labeled and conceptualized in approach terms. In the following, we examine the applicability of the approach–avoidance distinction to each of the four basic motivations for self-concept evaluation.

Self-Enhancement

Self-enhancement motivation is commonly defined as the desire for a positive self-concept (Brown, 1991; Greenwald, 1980). The evidence for this type of motivation is overwhelming, with researchers using a host of different paradigms and procedures to clearly document strivings and biases toward acquiring or maintaining a positive self-evaluation (see, e.g., research on illusions of control, unrealistic optimism, the above-average effect, recall bias, self-evaluation maintenance, self-affirmation; for reviews, see Dunning, 2001; Steele, 1988; Taylor & Brown, 1988; Tesser, 1988). Sedikides (1993; Sedikides & Strube, 1997) contended that self-enhancement is the primary and most basic motivation underlying self-concept evaluation, with the other motivations serving as means to self-enhancement.

Although most researchers have defined self-enhancement motivation in appetitive terms, some have made reference to aversive motivation in their definition. Sedikides (1993), for example, stated, "According to the self-enhancement view, individuals involved in self-evaluation desire to enhance the positivity of their self-conceptions or protect the self from negative information" (p. 318). Others have moved beyond definitional inclusion of avoidance motivation to elaborate on a difference between self-enhancement motivation and self-protection motivation. Arkin (1981) articulated a distinction between acquisitive motivation and protective motivation in his analysis of self-presentation (see also Wolfe, Lennox, & Cutler, 1986). Baumeister, Tice, and Hutton (1989) posited that individuals who score high on self-esteem measures are motivated by self-enhancement, whereas those who score low on self-esteem measures are motivated by self-protection (see also Dutton & Brown, 1997; Rhodewalt, Morf, Hazlett, & Fairfield, 1991; Wood, Giordano-Beech, Taylor, Michela, & Gaus, 1994). Research clearly supports the notion that individuals are motivated to avoid a negative self-conception, as well as being motivated to approach a positive self-conception (for reviews, see Birney, Burdick, & Teevan, 1969; Covington, 1992; Elliot, 1997; Higgins, 1997; Tice, 1993). Thus, in accordance with Arkin (1981), Baumeister et al. (1989), and others, we posit that self-enhancement motivation be conceptualized from both approach and avoidance perspectives in terms of self-aggrandizement and self-protection. Moreover, in accord with Cacioppo and colleagues' work on valenced evaluative processes (Cacioppo et al., 1997), we add that these two types of motivations may be construed as independent, such that both across and within situations persons may be motivated by self-aggrandizement alone, self-protection alone, both self-aggrandizement and self-protection, or neither self-aggrandizement nor self-protection.

Self-Verification

Self-verification motivation is typically defined as the desire for self-concept consistency (Festinger, 1957; Swann, 1983). That is, individuals are presumed to be motivated to maintain consistency between their existing self-conception and new self-relevant information. Self-concept consistency is viewed as desirable because it enables the individual to feel that the social environment is predictable and controllable. Much research attests to the fact that persons indeed seek out situations, interpret situations, and adopt behavioral strategies in situations that confirm their existing conception of the self (for reviews, see Aronson, Wilson, & Akert, 2002; Swann, 1990).

Although self-verification motivation is commonly construed as an exclusively appetitive desire, aversive motivation seems equally applicable to self-verification processes. Individuals may seek to maintain a consistent and stable self-concept in order to acquire predictability and control of the environment, or they may seek to avoid an inconsistent and unstable self-concept in order to evade a sense of unpredictability and a lack of control of the environment (see Swann, 1990, p. 415, for statements that could be interpreted as concordant with this proposal). We are not aware of any extant research that directly examines this approach–avoidance distinction in the self-verification literature, but some existing research may be interpreted from this perspective. For example, interaction experiments demonstrate that not only do persons choose to spend time with others who share their self-views but they also avoid spending time with others who do not share their self-views (see Swann, Wenzlaff, & Tafarodi, 1992). Likewise, in feedback studies, when individuals are presented with information that is self-refuting, they actively dismiss it, declare it nondiagnositic, seek to behaviorally disconfirm it, or try to undermine the credibility of the information source (see Brown & Smart, 1991; Frey & Stahlberg, 1986; Shrauger & Lund, 1975; Swann & Read, 1981). Furthermore, consistency processes in cognitive dissonance and balance theory research seem to be driven by the avoidance of self-based inconsistency (see Elliot & Devine, 1994). Thus, we posit that self-verification be considered from both approach and avoidance perspectives in terms of a desire to maintain or acquire self-concept consistency and a desire to avoid or eliminate self-concept inconsistency. These motivations may be considered independent and may be seen to vary as a function of the person or the situation.

Self-Assessment   Self-assessment motivation is often defined as the desire for an accurate or certain conception of the self (Festinger, 1954; Trope & Pomerantz, 1998). Individuals are presumed to seek out diagnostic information because knowing one's strengths and weaknesses allows one to pursue activities that one can successfully negotiate and to adopt goals that are within reach (Bandura, 1986). Research clearly attests to the viability of the self-assessment perspective; most empirical investigations have used a diagnosticity paradigm to demonstrate that persons seek accurate information about the self regardless of the valence of the information (for reviews, see Strube, Yost, & Bailey, 1992; Trope, 1986).

Although self-assessment is often conceptualized in approach terms, it is sometimes conceptualized in avoidance terms. That is, self-assessment is sometimes defined as the desire to reduce uncertainty about the self, and the assumption is that people strive for uncertainty reduction because of the costs involved in not being cognizant of one's strengths and weaknesses (Trope, 1986; Wheeler, Martin, & Suls, 1997). Approach-based and avoidance-based definitions or conceptualizations of self-assessment have not been considered in conjunction with each other;

they are merely differentially emphasized in different writings. To the best of our knowledge, no existing research has directly investigated the possibility of distinct approach and avoidance forms of self-assessment. It is interesting to note that a robust finding in the self-assessment literature is that self-assessment effects are strongest in experiments (or conditions of experiments) in which uncertainty is at a high level (see Roney & Sorrentino, 1995; Trope, 1979). This seems to indicate that self-assessment is not entirely appetitive but, at minimum, has an aversive component. Thus, we posit that self-assessment be considered from both approach and avoidance perspectives in terms of a desire to acquire certainty about the self-concept and a desire to avoid uncertainty about the self-concept. As with the other two motivations already overviewed, it seems reasonable to posit that the desire for certainty and the desire to avoid uncertainty are independent and vary as a function of person and situation.

Self-Improvement   Self-improvement motivation is defined as the desire to improve the self-concept (Taylor, Neter, & Wayment, 1995; Wood, 1989). In contrast to self-enhancement motivation, which is hedonic in nature, and self-verification and self-assessment motivation, which are both epistemic in nature (Tesser, 2003), self-improvement motivation is grounded in personal growth, making it organismic or humanistic in nature. Individuals are presumed to strive to better their attributes and abilities out of a desire for progress and maturation (Albert, 1977; Festinger, 1954; Wayment & Taylor, 1995). Although little research has been conducted to explicitly examine this type of motivation for self-evaluation, Taylor, Wayment, and colleagues (Taylor et al., 1995; Wayment & Taylor, 1995) suggested that the vast literature on goal striving and upward social comparison may be viewed as consistent with this perspective.

Self-improvement is conceptualized in purely approach terms, and some may have difficulty thinking of this type of motivational tendency in anything but appetitive terms. Nevertheless, upon careful consideration, it is clear that such motivation may also be cast in terms of avoidance. Change relative to one's idiographic baseline is the conceptual centerpiece of self-improvement motivation, and this change may be framed with regard to a positive possibility or a negative possibility (Elliot, 1999). That is, individuals may desire to get better in their attributes and abilities relative to their own personal baseline, or they may desire not to get worse in their attributes and abilities relative to their own personal baseline. Avoiding deterioration, stagnation, or even a slower rate of improvement than one deems personally acceptable all represent an avoidance aspect of self-improvement motivation. One interesting possibility is that people in the latter part of their careers or older adults may be particularly oriented to this type of avoidance motivation. For example, older individuals may be particularly prone to orient toward not losing their skills, abilities, or other valued attributes as they find their physical and cognitive capacities in decline and encounter difficulty in carrying out the activities of their youth. We are not aware of any existing research on self-evaluation motivation that focuses on the avoidance aspect of self-improvement per se, though work by Elliot and McGregor (2001) on mastery-avoidance achievement goals is certainly applicable to this issue. The fact that feelings of self-threat or inadequacy tend to instigate self-improvement motivation (Sedikides & Strube, 1997) seems to suggest an aversive component to this motivation in some instances. Thus, we posit that self-improvement be considered from both approach and avoidance perspectives in terms of the desire to improve self-attributes and abilities and the desire to avoid the deterioration of self-attributes and abilities. As with the other three motivations, it seems likely that the desire for improvement and the desire to avoid deterioration are independent, and vary as a function of person and situation.

Summary Table 8.1 summarizes our propositions regarding how the approach–avoidance distinction may be applied to the basic types of motivation underlying self-concept evaluation. Each type of motivation is posited to have a central focus that may be delineated in terms of both approach motivation and avoidance motivation. *Valence* is the central focus of self-enhancement motivation, and this type of motivation may be differentiated in terms of approaching a positive self-concept and avoiding a negative self-concept. *Consistency* is the central focus of self-verification motivation, and this type of motivation may be differentiated in terms of approaching a consistent self-concept and avoiding an inconsistent self-concept. *Certainty* is the central focus of self-assessment motivation, and this type of motivation may be differentiated in terms of approaching self-concept certainty and avoiding self-concept uncertainty. Finally, *change* is the central focus of self-improvement motivation, and this type of motivation may be differentiated in terms of approaching the development of self-aspects and avoiding the deterioration of self-aspects. It is likely that all individuals are motivated to some degree with regard to valence, consistency, certainty, and change of the self-concept. However, it is also likely that individuals differ systematically in the degree to which they focus on each in the evaluation process, and in the degree to which they are appetitively or aversively motivated within each type of motivation.

The different types of motivation underlying self-concept evaluation have proven somewhat difficult to differentiate in empirical work, because a behavior

TABLE 8.1. Applying the Approach–Avoidance Distinction to the Basic Motivations Underlying Self-Concept Evaluation

Type of motivation	Primary focus	Approach form	Avoidance form
Self-enhancement	Valence of the self-concept	Approach positive self-concept	Avoid negative self-concept
Self-verification	Consistency of the self-concept	Approach self-concept consistency	Avoid self-concept inconsistency
Self-assessment	Certainty of the self-concept	Approach self-concept certainty	Avoid self-concept uncertainty
Self-improvement	Change of self-concept	Approach development of self-aspects	Avoid deterioration of self-aspects

at the observable (phenotypic) level may represent many different types of (genotypic) motivation. This is not only the case across self-enhancement, self-verification, self-assessment, and self-improvement but would also be the case across approach and avoidance forms within each type of motivation. Researchers have gone to great lengths to carefully and, in many instances, creatively design empirical work that is able to separate the four types of motivation from each other. We contend that the time has come to design additional research that attends to the approach–avoidance distinction.

One final, broad-based comment with regard to self-concept evaluation is also in order. Although evaluation of the self-concept can certainly be adaptive (Sedikides & Skowronski, 2000), it is important to note that in contemporary Western culture, evaluation of the self-concept seems to have become something of an obsession (see Kernis, 2003; Ryan & Brown, 2003). That is, there is a tendency for individuals to become preoccupied with or absorbed in whether the self is positive (or not negative), consistent (or not inconsistent), known (or not unknown), and improving (or not declining), and this self-absorption seems less adaptive than neurotic and, ultimately, maladaptive. From this perspective, it is interesting to consider what determines the degree to which individuals evaluate the self-concept in the first place, which places the issue of self-concept evaluation in the broader context of personality and motivation. We suspect that a strong focus on evaluation of the self-concept (i.e., the self as object), in contrast to a more specific focus on evaluation of the ongoing actions of the self as agent, bespeaks avoidance motivation at this broader level (e.g., avoidance temperament, insecure attachment, fear of failure or rejection; see Elliot et al., 2002; Elliot & Reis, 2003; Elliot & Thrash, 2002).

CONCLUSIONS

In this chapter we have defined and clarified the conceptual nature of approach and avoidance motivation, applied the approach–avoidance distinction to the self-esteem construct, and made the case for implementing the approach–avoidance distinction into the literature on the motivation underlying self-concept evaluation. In so doing, we have highlighted the foundational nature of approach and avoidance motivational processes and have sought to communicate, both explicitly and implicitly, the utility of this basic motivational bifurcation. Indeed we would go so far as to state that in conceptualizing motivational constructs, it is best to presume that the approach–avoidance distinction is relevant and in need of attention, unless empirical or theoretical evidence suggests otherwise.

A possible objection to this broad application of the approach–avoidance distinction is that it makes the analysis of scientific phenomena more complicated, if not cumbersome. Indeed, in most instances, consideration of approach–avoidance motivation essentially doubles the number of constructs under scrutiny and more than doubles the complexity of the issues being investigated. It could be argued that one of the reasons for the widespread appeal and use of the self-esteem construct and the fourfold motivational conception of self-concept evaluation is that it is elegant in its simplicity. Accordingly, a fair question to ask is whether implementing the approach–avoidance distinction into the self-literature would actually dampen rather than facilitate interest in self-esteem and the motivation underlying self-concept evaluation.

Fundamental to this question is the issue of parsimony, which social scientists agree is a valued attribute of any theoretical conceptualization. *Parsimony* is often equated with *simplicity*, but it is important to note that this is not the correct meaning of the term. In the scientific context, *parsimony* denotes the simplest explanation that fully accounts for the conceptual space under consideration. Simple is not necessarily best; the simplest complete conceptualization is the best. Ignoring the approach–avoidance distinction may render the focal self issues more straightforward and appealing in the short run, but we contend that it also precludes a full understanding of their inherently (more) complex nature. In short, it is oversimplistic, and we believe that this oversimplicity would prove detrimental in the long run.

Although at a theoretical level we are arguing strongly for a full consideration of approach–avoidance motivation, at an empirical level we see the value of sometimes attending to the distinction and sometimes setting it aside. That is, we are not arguing that all research endeavors must fully separate approach and avoidance components of self-esteem or fully examine approach and avoidance components of self-concept evaluation. Pragmatically, there are many instances in which collapsing across the approach–avoidance distinction seems a viable alternative, much as in many empirical examinations of the Big Five trait dispositions, collapsing across facets of the traits seems a viable alternative (see Costa & McCrae, 1992). Certainly, the discussion herein points to the need for the development of self-esteem measures that incorporate separate approach and avoidance components and the need for innovative research paradigms that afford separation of approach and avoidance forms of each of the four motivations for self-concept evaluation. Once available, these measures and paradigms could be put to use when approach–avoidance considerations are central, and the more established measures and paradigms could be utilized when such concerns are peripheral. The important point is that researchers and theorists of the self acknowledge the theoretical centrality and utility of the approach–avoidance distinction, not that they feel obligated to make it the center of attention.

Never has the self been a more popular area of study than at the present time. Empirical and theoretical work on the self is thriving and, we think, many areas of the social sciences are benefiting as a result. The purpose of this chapter has been to highlight the relevance of the distinction between approach and avoidance motivation to one area of research on the self—that of self-concept evaluation. However, we believe that this fundamental motivational distinction is broadly applicable across the self literature, far beyond issues of self-concept evaluation. We urge other researchers and theorists to begin attending to approach–avoidance considerations in their work on the self. We suspect that over time, the self literature would become even more robust and influential as a result.

ACKNOWLEDGMENTS

Thanks are extended to Paul Rose, Romin Tafarodi, Abe Tesser, and Joanne Wood for their helpful comments on an earlier version of this chapter. Preparation of this chapter was supported in part by a Faculty Scholars grant from the W. T. Grant Foundation.

NOTE

1. It is interesting to note that in much of the extant research on self-esteem, items assessing the positive component of self-esteem display less variability than items assessing the negative component of self-esteem. Indeed, in many studies, there appears to be a restricted range in positive self-esteem scores, because most participants endorse the extreme positive response option on these items (see, e.g., Shanani et al., 1990). In such instances, observed results for unidimensional self-esteem are likely driven by the negative self-esteem items, though this is not acknowledged. Only separate consideration of positive and negative self-esteem variables will allow researchers to monitor this important (and over-looked) issue.

REFERENCES

Aidman, E. V. (1998). Analyzing global dimensions of self-esteem: Factorial structure and reliability of self-liking/self-competence scale. *Personality and Individual Differences, 24*, 735–737.

Albert, S. (1977). Temporal comparison theory. *Psychological Review, 84*, 485–503.

Arkin, R. M. (1981). Self-presentation styles. In J. T. Tedeschi (Ed.), *Impression management theory and social psychological research* (pp. 311–330). New York: Academic Press.

Arnold, M. B. (1960). *Emotion and personality* (Vols. 1 and 2). New York: Columbia University Press.

Aronson, E., Wilson, T. D., & Akert, R. M. (2002). *Social psychology* (4th ed.). Upper Saddle River, NJ: Prentice Hall.

Atkinson, J. (1957). Motivational determinants of risk-taking behavior. *Psychological Review, 64*, 359–372.

Bandura, A. (1986). *Social foundations of thought and action.* Englewood Cliffs, NJ: Prentice Hall.

Bargh, J. A. (1997). The automaticity of everyday life. In R. S. Wyer (Ed.), *The automaticity of everyday life: Advances in social cognition* (Vol. 10, pp. 1–61). Mahwah, NJ: Erlbaum.

Baumeister, R. F. (1998). The self. In D. T. Gilbert, S. T. Fiske, & G. Lindzey (Eds.), *The handbook of social psychology* (Vol. 2, 4th ed., pp. 680–740). New York: McGraw-Hill.

Baumeister, R. F., & Leary, M. R. (1995). The need to belong: Desire for interpersonal attachments as a fundamental human motivation. *Psychological Bulletin, 117*, 497–529.

Baumeister, R. F., Tice, D. M., & Hutton, D. G. (1989). Self-presentational motivations and personality differences in self-esteem. *Journal of Personality, 57*, 547–579.

Berntson, G. G., Boysen, S. T., & Cacioppo, J. T. (1993). Neurobehavioral organization and the cardinal principle of evaluative bivalence. *Annals of the New York Academy of Sciences, 702*, 75–102.

Berridge, K. C. (1999). Pleasure, pain, desire, and dread: Hidden core processes of emotion. In D. Kahneman, E. Diener, & N. Schwarz (Eds.), *Well-being: The foundations of hedonic psychology* (pp. 525–557). New York: Russell Sage Foundation.

Birney, R., Burdick, H., & Teevan, R. (1969). *Fear of failure.* New York: Van Nostrand Reinhold.

Blascovich, J., & Tomaka, J. (1991). Measures of self-esteem. In J. P. Robinson, P. R. Shaver, & L. S. Wrightsman (Eds.), *Measures of personality and social psychological attitudes* (Vol. 1, pp. 115–160). New York: Academic Press.

Boring, E. G. (1950). *A historical of experimental psychology.* New York: Appleton-Century-Crofts.

Bosson, J. K., Swann, W. B., Jr., & Pennebaker, J. W. (2000). Stalking the perfect measure of implicit self-esteem: The blind man and the elephant revisited? *Journal of Personality and Social Psychology, 79*, 631–643.

Brown, J. D. (1991). Accuracy and bias in self-knowledge. In C. R. Snyder & D. F. Forsyth (Eds.), *Handbook of social and clinical psychology: The health perspective* (pp. 158–178). New York: Pergamon Press.

Brown, J. D., & Smart, S. A. (1991). The self and social conduct: Linking self-representations to prosocial behavior. *Journal of Personality and Social Psychology, 60*, 368–375.

Cacioppo, J. T., & Berntson, G. G. (1994). Relationship between attitudes and evaluative space: A critical review, with emphasis on the separability of positive and negative substrates. *Psychological Bulletin, 115*, 401–423.

Cacioppo, J. T., Gardner, W. L., & Berntson, G. G. (1997). Beyond bipolar conceptualizations and measures: The case of attitudes and evaluative space. *Personality and Social Psychology Review, 1*, 3–25.

Carmines, E. G., & Zeller, R. A. (1974). On establishing the empirical dimensionality of theoretical terms: An analytical example. *Political Methodology, 1*, 75–96.

Carver, C., & Scheier, M. F. (1998). *On the self-regulation of behavior.* New York: Cambridge University Press.

Chen, M., & Bargh, J. A. (1999). Consequences of automatic evaluation: Immediate behavioral predispositions to approach or avoid the stimulus. *Personality and Social Psychology Bulletin, 25*, 215–224.

Cialdini, R. B., Trost, M. R., & Newsom, J. T. (1995). Preference for consistency: The development of a valid measure and the discovery of surprising behavioral implications. *Journal of Personality and Social Psychology, 69*, 318–328.

Clark, H. (1974). Semantics and comprehension. In T. Seebok (Ed.), *Current trends in linguistics* (Vol. 12, pp. 1291–1428). Lisse, The Netherlands: Mouton.

Cofer, C. N., & Appley, M. H. (1964). *Motivation: Theory and research.* New York: Wiley.

Coopersmith, S. (1967). *The antecedents of self-esteem.* San Francisco: Freeman.

Corwin, G. H. (1921). The involuntary response to pleasantness. *American Journal of Psychology, 32*, 363–370.

Costa, P. T., & McCrae, R. R. (1992). *NEO PI–R: Professional manual.* Odessa, FL: Psychological Assessment Resources.

Covington, M. (1992). *Making the grade: A self-worth perspective on motivation and school reform.* New York: Cambridge University Press.

Craig, W. (1918). Appetites and aversions as constituents of instincts. *Archives of disease in childhood, 3*, 91–107.

Davidson, R. J. (1992). Anterior cerebral asymmetry and the nature of emotion. *Brain and Cognition, 20,* 125–151.

Davidson, R. (1993). Parsing affective space: Perspectives from neuropsychology and psychophysiology. *Neuropsychology, 7,* 464–475.

Depue, R., & Iacono, W. (1989). Neurobehavioral aspects of affective disorders. *Annual Review of Psychology, 40,* 457–492.

Derryberry, D. (1991). The immediate effects of positive and negative feedback signals. *Journal of Personality and Social Psychology, 61,* 267–278.

Diener, E., & Emmons, R. A. (1984). The independence of positive and negative affect. *Journal of Personality and Social Psychology, 47,* 1105–1117.

Diggory, J. C. (1966). *Self-evaluation: Concepts and studies.* New York: Wiley.

Dixon, N. (1981). *Preconscious processing.* New York: Wiley.

Dunning, D. (2001). On the motives underlying social cognition. In A. Tesser & N. Schwarz (Eds.), *Blackwell handbook of social psychology: Intraindividual processes* (pp. 348–374). Oxford, England: Blackwell.

Dutton, K. A., & Brown, J. D. (1997). Global self-esteem and specific self-views as determinants of people's reactions to success and failure. *Journal of Personality and Social Psychology, 73,* 139–148.

Dweck, C. S. (1996). Motivational processes affecting learning. *American Psychologist, 41,* 1040–1048.

Elliot, A. J. (1997). Integrating "classic" and "contemporary" approaches to achievement motivation: A hierarchical model of approach and avoidance achievement motivation. In P. Pintrich & M. Maehr (Eds.), *Advances in motivation and achievement* (Vol. 10, pp. 143–179). Greenwich, CT: JAI.

Elliot, A. J. (1999). Approach and avoidance motivation and achievement goals. *Educational Psychologist, 34,* 149–169.

Elliot, A. J., & Church, M. A. (1997). A hierarchical model of approach and avoidance achievement motivation. *Journal of Personality and Social Psychology, 72,* 218–232.

Elliot, A. J., & Devine, P. G. (1994). On the motivational nature of cognitive dissonance: Dissonance as psychological discomfort. *Journal of Personality and Social Psychology, 67,* 382–394.

Elliot, A. J., & McGregor, H. A. (2001). A 2 × 2 achievement goal framework. *Journal of Personality and Social Psychology, 80,* 501–519.

Elliot, A. J., McGregor, H. A., & Thrash, T. M. (2002). The need for competence. In E. L. Deci & R. M. Ryan (Eds.), *Handbook of self-determination research* (pp. 361–387). Rochester, NY: University of Rochester Press.

Elliot, A. J., & Reis, H. T. (2003). Attachment and exploration in adulthood. *Journal of Personality and Social Psychology, 85,* 317–331.

Elliot, A. J., & Sheldon, K. M. (1998). Avoidance personal goals and the personality-illness relationship. *Journal of Personality and Social Psychology, 75,* 1282–1299.

Elliot, A. J., & Thrash, T. M. (2001). Achievement goals and the hierarchical model of achievement motivation. *Educational Psychologist, 13,* 139–156.

Elliot, A. J., & Thrash, T. M. (2002). Approach–avoidance motivation in personality: Approach and avoidance temperaments and goals. *Journal of Personality and Social Psychology, 82,* 804–818.

Emmons, R. A. (1986). Personal strivings: An approach to personality and subjective well-being. *Journal of Personality and Social Psychology, 51,* 1058–1068.

Festinger, L. (1954). A theory of social comparison processes. *Human Relations, 7,* 117–140.

Festinger, L. (1957). *A theory of cognitive dissonance.* Evanston, IL: Row, Peterson.

Fincham, F. D., & Linfield, K. J. (1997). A new look at marital quality: Can spouses feel positive and negative about their marriage? *Journal of Family Psychology, 11*, 489–502.

Foerster, J., Higgins, E. T., & Idson, L. C. (1998). Approach and avoidance strength during goal attainment: Regulatory focus and the "goal looms larger" effect. *Journal of Personality and Social Psychology, 75*, 1115–1131.

Forster, J., & Strack, F. (1996). Influence of overt head movements on memory for valenced words: A case of conceptual–motor compatibility. *Journal of Personality and Social Psychology, 71*, 421–430.

Fowles, D. (1988). Psychophysiology and psychopathology: A motivational approach. *Psychophysiology, 25*, 373–391.

Franken, R. E. (1994). *Human motivation* (5th ed.). Belmont, CA: Wadsworth.

Franks, D. D., & Marolla, J. (1976). Efficacious action and social approval as interacting dimensions of self-esteem: Tentative formulation through construct validation. *Sociometry, 39*, 324–341.

Freud, S. (1927). *The ego and the id* (J. R. Riviere, Trans.). London: Hogarth Press. (Original work published 1923)

Frey, D., & Stahlberg, D. (1986). Selection of information after receiving more or less reliable self-threatening information. *Personality and Social Psychology Bulletin, 12*, 434–441.

Gray, J. (1982). *The neuropsychology of anxiety: An inquiry into the functions of the septo-hippocampal system.* New York: Oxford University Press.

Greenwald, A. G. (1980). The totalitarian ego: Fabrication and revision of personal history. *American Psychologist, 35*, 603–618.

Greenwald, A. G., & Banaji, M. R. (1995). Implicit social cognition: Attitudes, self-esteem, and stereotypes. *Psychological Review, 102*, 4–27.

Harmon-Jones, E., & Allen, J. J. B. (1997). Behavioral activation sensitivity and resting frontal EEG asymmetry: Covariation of putative indicators related to risk for mood disorders. *Journal of Abnormal Psychology, 106*, 159–163.

Harter, S. (1985). Competence as a dimension of self-evaluation: Toward a comprehensive model of self-worth. In R. Leahy (Ed.), *The development of the self* (pp. 55–122). New York: Academic Press.

Harter, S. (1999). *The construction of the self: A developmental perspective.* New York: Guilford Press.

Heatherton, T. F., & Polivy, J. (1991). Development and validation of a scale for measuring state self-esteem. *Journal of Personality and Social Psychology, 60*, 895–910.

Heatherton, T. F., & Wyland, C. L. (2003). Assessing self-esteem. In S. J. Lopez & C. R. Snyder (Eds.), *Positive psychological assessment: A handbook of models and measures* (pp. 219–233). Washington DC: American Psychological Association.

Hensley, W. E., & Roberts, M. K. (1976). Dimensions of Rosenberg's self-esteem scale. *Psychological Reports, 38*, 583–584.

Hetts, J. J., Sakuma, M., & Pelham, B. W. (1999). Two roads to positive regard: Implicit and explicit self-evaluation and culture. *Journal of Experimental Social Psychology, 35*, 512–559.

Higgins, E. T. (1997). Beyond pleasure and pain. *American Psychologist, 52*, 1280–1300.

Higgins, E. T. (1998). Promotion and prevention: Regulatory focus as a motivational principle. *Advances in Experimental Social Psychology, 30*, 1–46.

Higgins, E. T., Shah, J., & Friedman, R. (1997). Emotional responses to goal attainment: Strength of regulatory focus as a moderator. *Journal of Personality and Social Psychology, 72*, 515–525.

Hovland, C. I. (1937). Differences in resolution of approach–approach and avoidance–avoidance conflicts. *Psychological Bulletin, 34,* 719.

Ito, T. A., Cacioppo, J. T., & Lang, P. J. (1998). Eliciting affect using the international affective picture system: Trajectories through evaluative space. *Personality and Social Psychology Bulletin, 24,* 855–879.

James, W. (1950). *The principles of psychology.* New York: Dover Press. (Original work published 1890)

Just, M., & Carpenter, P. (1971). Comprehension of negation with quantification. *Journal of Verbal Learning and Verbal Behavior, 12,* 21–31.

Kahneman, D., Diener, E., & Schwarz, N. (Eds.). (1999). Well-being: The foundations of hedonic psychology. New York: Russell Sage Foundation.

Kahneman, D., & Tversky, A. (1979). Prospect theory: An analysis of decision under risk. *Econometrica, 47,* 263–291.

Kaplan, H. B., & Pokorny, A. D. (1969). Self-derogation and psychosocial adjustment. *Journal of Nervous and Mental Disease, 149,* 421–434.

Kaplan, K. J. (1972). On the ambivalence–indifference problem in attitude theory and measurement: A suggested modification of the semantic differential technique. *Psychological Bulletin, 77,* 361–372.

Kernis, M. H. (2003). Toward a conceptualization of optimal self-esteem. *Psychological Inquiry, 14,* 83–89.

Koole, S. L., Dijksterhuis, A., & van Knippenberg, A. (2001). What's in a name: Implicit self-esteem and the automatic self. *Journal of Personality and Social Psychology, 80,* 669–685.

Kuiper, N., & Derry, P. (1982). Depressed and nondepressed content self-reference in mild depression. *Journal of Personality, 50,* 67–79.

Lang, P. J. (1995). The emotion probe: Studies of motivation and attention. *American Psychologist, 50,* 372–385.

Lang, P. J., Bradley, M. M. & Cuthbert, B. N. (1997). Motivated attention: Affect, motivation, and action. In P. J. Lang, R. F. Simons, & M. T. Balaban (Eds.), *Attention and orienting: Sensory and motivational processes* (pp. 97–135). Mahwah, NJ: Erlbaum.

Lazarus, R. (1991). *Emotion and adaption.* New York: Oxford University Press.

Lewin, K. (1926). Intention, will, and need. *Psychologische Forschung, 7,* 330–385.

Lewin, K. (1935). *A dynamic theory of personality.* New York: McGraw-Hill.

Linville, P. W. (1985). Self-complexity and affective extremity: Don't put all of your eggs in one cognitive basket. *Social Cognition, 3,* 94–120.

Maio, G. R., Fincham, F. D., & Lycett, E. J. (2000). Attitudinal ambivalence toward parents and attachment style. *Personality and Social Psychology Bulletin, 26,* 1451–1464.

Markus, H., & Nurius, P. (1986). Possible selves. *American Psychologist, 41,* 954–969.

Marsh, H. W. (1986). Global self-esteem: Its relation to specific facets of self-concept and their importance. *Journal of Personality and Social Psychology, 51,* 1224–1236.

Marsh, H. W. (1996). Positive and negative global self-esteem: A substantively meaningful distinction or artifactors? *Journal of Personality and Social Psychology, 70,* 810–819.

McClelland, D. C. (1985). How motives, skills, and values determine what people do. *American Psychologist, 40,* 812–825.

McClelland, D. C., Atkinson, J., Clark, R., & Lowell, E. (1953). *The achievement motive.* New York: Appleton-Century-Crofts.

McGregor, H. A., & Elliot, A. J. (in press). The shame of failure. *Personality and Social Psychology Bulletin.*

Messick, D., & McClintock, C. (1968). Motivational bases of choice in experimental games. *Journal of Experimental Social Psychology, 4,* 1–25.

Miller, N. E. (1937). Analysis of the form of conflict reactions. *Psychological Bulletin, 34,* 720.

Moos, R., & Schaefer, J. (1993). Coping resources and processes: Current concepts and measures. In L. Goldberger & S. Brenznitz (Eds.), *Handbook of stress: Theoretical and clinical aspects* (2nd ed., pp. 234–257). New York: Free Press.

Murray, H. A. (1938). *Explorations in personality.* New York: Oxford University Press.

Neuberg, S. L., & Newsom, J. T. (1993). Personal need for structure: Individual differences in the desire for simpler structure. *Journal of Personality and Social Psychology, 65,* 113–131.

Newman, J. (1987). Reaction to punishment in extraverts and psychopaths: Implications for the impulsive behavior of disinhibited individuals. *Journal of Research in Personality, 21,* 464–480.

Newman, J., Wolff, W., & Hearst, E. (1980). The feature-positive effect in adult human subjects. *Journal of Experimental Psychology: Human Learning and Memory, 6,* 630–650.

Osgood, C. E., Suci, G. J., & Tannenbaum, P. H. (1957). *The measurement of meaning.* Chicago: University of Illinois Press.

Overmier, J., & Archer, T. (1989). Historical perspectives on the study of aversively motivated behavior: History and new look. In T. Archer & L. Nilsson (Eds.), *Aversion, avoidance, and anxiety: Perspectives on aversively motivated behavior* (pp. 3–39). Hillsdale, NJ: Erlbaum.

Owens, T. J. (1993). Accentuate the positive—and the negative: Rethinking the use of self-esteem, self-deprecation, and self-confidence. *Social Psychology Quarterly, 56,* 288–299.

Owens, T. J. (1994). Two dimensions of self-esteem: Reciprocal effects of positive self-worth and self-deprecation on adolescent problems. *American Sociological Review, 59,* 391–407.

Rhodewalt, F., Morf, C., Hazlett, S., & Fairfield, M. (1991). Self-handicapping: The role of discounting and augmentation in the preservation of self-esteem. *Journal of Personality and Social Psychology, 61,* 122–131.

Rogers, R. (1975). A protection motivation theory of fear appeals and attitude change. *Journal of Psychology, 91,* 93–114.

Roney, C. J. R., & Sorrentino, R. M. (1995). Self-evaluation motives and uncertainty orientation: Asking the "who" question. *Personality and Social Psychology Bulletin, 21,* 1319–1329.

Rose, P. (2002). The happy and unhappy faces of narcissism. *Personality and Individual Differences, 33,* 379–392.

Roseman, I. (1984). Cognitive determinants of emotions: A structural theory. In P. Shaver (Ed.), *Review of personality and social psychology* (Vol. 5, pp. 11–36). Beverly Hills, CA: Sage.

Rosenberg, M. (1965). *Society and the adolescent child.* Princeton, NJ: Princeton University Press.

Roth, S., & Cohen, L. (1986). Approach, avoidance, and coping with stress. *American Psychologist, 7,* 813–819.

Rothman, A., & Salovey, P. (1997). Shaping perceptions to motivate healthy behavior: The role of message framing. *Psychological Bulletin, 121,* 3–19.

Rozin, P. (1999). Preadaptation and the puzzles and the properties of pleasure. In D. Kahneman, E. Diener, & N. Schwarz (Eds.), *Well-being: The foundations of hedonic psychology* (pp. 109–133). New York: Russell Sage Foundation.

Ryan, R. M. (1995). Psychological needs and the facilitation of integrative processes. *Journal of Personality, 63,* 397–427.

Ryan, R. M., & Brown, K. W. (2003). Why we don't need self-esteem: On fundamental needs, conditional love, and mindfulness. *Psychological Inquiry, 14,* 71–76.

Schneirla, T. C. (1959). An evolutionary and developmental theory of biphasic processes underlying approach and withdrawal. In M. R. Jones (Ed.), *Nebraska Symposium on Motivation* (pp. 1–42). Lincoln: University of Nebraska Press.

Sears, R. R. (1937). Resolution of conflicts between approach–avoidance responses. *Psychological Bulletin, 34,* 719–720.

Sedikides, C. (1993). Assessment, enhancement, and verification determinants of the self-evaluation process. *Journal of Personality and Social Psychology, 65,* 317–338.

Sedikides, C., & Skowronski, J. J. (2000). On the evolutionary functions of the symbolic self: The emergence of self-evaluation motives. In A. Tesser, R. E. Felson, & J. M. Suls (Eds.), *Psychological perspectives on self and identity* (pp. 91–117). Washington, DC: American Psychological Association.

Sedikides, C., & Strube, M. J. (1997). Self-evaluation: To thine own self be good, to thine own self be sure, to thine own self be true, and to thine own self be better. In M. P. Zanna (Ed.), *Advances in experimental social psychology* (Vol. 29, pp. 209–269). New York: Academic Press.

Shahani, C., Dipboye, R. L., & Phillips, A. P. (1990). Global self-esteem as a correlate of work-related attitudes: A question of dimensionality. *Journal of Personality Assessment, 54,* 276–288.

Shrauger, J. S., & Lund, A. K. (1975). Self-evaluation and reactions to evaluations from others. *Journal of Personality, 43,* 94–108.

Silverberg, W. V. (1952). *Childhood experience and personal destiny.* New York: Springer.

Solarz, A. K. (1960). Latency of instrumental responses as a function of compatibility with the meaning of eliciting verbal signs. *Journal of Experimental Psychology, 59,* 239–245.

Steele, C. M. (1988). The psychology of self-affirmation: Sustaining the integrity of the self. In L. Berkowitz (Ed.), *Advances in experimental social psychology* (Vol. 21, pp. 261–302). New York: Academic Press.

Strube, M. J., Yost, J. H., & Bailey, J. R. (1992). William James and contemporary research on the self: The influence of pragmatism, reality, and truth. In M. Donnelley (Ed.), *Representing the legacy of William James* (pp. 189–207). Washington, DC: American Psychological Association.

Sullivan, H. S. (1953). *The interpersonal theory of psychiatry.* New York: Norton.

Sutton, S. K., & Davidson, R. J. (1997). Prefrontal brain asymmetry: A biological substrate of the behavioral approach and inhibition systems. *Psychological Science, 8,* 204–210.

Swann, W. B., Jr. (1983). Self-verification: Bringing social reality into harmony with the self. In J. Suls & A. G. Greenwald (Eds.), *Psychological perspectives on the self* (Vol. 2, pp. 33–66). Hillsdale, NJ: Erlbaum.

Swann, W. B., Jr. (1990). To be adored or to be known? The interplay of self-enhancement and self-verification. In E. T. Higgins & R. M. Sorrentino (Eds.), *Handbook of motivation and cognition: Foundations of social behavior* (Vol. 2, pp. 408–448). New York: Guilford Press.

Swann, W. B., Jr., & Read, S. J. (1981). Acquiring self-knowledge: The search for feedback that fits. *Journal of Personality and Social Psychology, 41,* 1119–1128.

Swann, W. B., Jr., Wenzlaff, R. M., & Tafarodi, R. W. (1992). Depression and the search for negative evaluations: More evidence of the role of self-verification strivings. *Journal of Abnormal Psychology, 101,* 314–317.

Tafarodi, R. W. (1998). Paradoxical self-esteem and selectivity in the processing of social information. *Journal of Personality and Social Psychology, 74*, 1181–1196.

Tafarodi, R. W., & Milne, A. B. (2002). Decomposing global self-esteem. *Journal of Personality, 70*, 443–483.

Tafarodi, R. W., & Swann, W. B., Jr. (1995). Self-liking and self-competences as dimensions of global self-esteem: Initial validation of a measure. *Journal of Personality Assessment, 65*, 322–342.

Tafarodi, R. W., & Swann, W. B., Jr. (2001). Two-dimensional self-esteem: Theory and measurement. *Personality and Individual Differences, 31*, 653–673.

Taylor, S. E., & Brown, J. D. (1988). Illusion and well-being: A social psychological perspective on mental health. *Psychological Bulletin, 103*, 193–210.

Taylor, S. E., Neter, E., & Wayment, H. A. (1995). Self-evaluation processes. *Personality and Social Psychology Bulletin, 21*, 1278–1287.

Tedechsi, J., & Norman, N. (1985). Social power, self-presentation, and the self. In B. Schlenker (Ed.), *The self and social life* (pp. 293–322). New York: McGraw-Hill.

Tesser, A. (1988). Toward a self-evaluation maintenance model of social behavior. In L. Berkowitz (Ed.), *Advances in experimental social psychology* (Vol. 21, pp. 181–227). San Diego, CA: Academic Press.

Tesser, A. (2003). Self-evaluation. In M. R. Leary & J. P. Tangney (Eds.), *Handbook of self and identity* (pp. 275–290). New York: Guilford Press.

Tesser, A., & Martin, L. (1996). The psychology of evaluation. In E. T. Higgins & A. Kruglanski (Eds.), *Social psychology: Handbook of basic principles* (pp. 400–432). New York: Guilford Press.

Thompson, M. M., Zanna, M. P., & Griffin, D. W. (1995). Let's not be indifferent about (attitudinal) ambivalence. In R. E. Petty & J. A. Krosnick (Eds.), *Attitude strength: Antecedents and consequences* (pp. 361–386). Hillsdale, N. J.: Erlbaum.

Tice, D. M. (1993). The social motivations of people with low self-esteem. In R. F. Baumeister (Ed.), *Self-esteem: The puzzle of low self-regard* (pp. 37–53). New York: Plenum Press.

Tolman, E. C. (1932). *Purposive behavior in animals and men.* New York: Century.

Tomaka, J., & Blascovich, J. (1994). Effects of justice beliefs on cognitive appraisal of, and subjective, physiological, and behavioral responses to, potential stress. *Journal of Personality and Social Psychology, 67*, 732–740.

Tomarken, A. J., Davidson, R. J., Wheeler, R. E., & Doss, R. C. (1992). Individual differences in anterior brain asymmetry and fundamental dimensions of emotion. *Journal of Personality and Social Psychology, 62*, 676–687.

Tooby, J., & Cosmides, L. (1990). On the universality of human nature and the uniqueness of the individual: The role of genetics and adaptation. *Journal of Personality, 58*, 17–67.

Trope, Y. (1979). Uncertainty-reducing properties of achievement tasks. *Journal of Personality and Social Psychology, 37*, 1505–1518.

Trope, Y. (1986). Self-enhancement and self-assessment in achievement behavior. In R. Sorrentino & E. T. Higgins (Eds.), *Handbook of motivation and cognition* (Vol. 2, pp. 350–378). New York: Guilford Press.

Trope, Y., & Pomerantz, E. M. (1998). Resolving conflicts among self-evaluative motives: Positive experiences as a resource for overcoming defensiveness. *Motivation and Emotion, 22*, 53–72.

Verkuyten, M. (2003). Positive and negative self-esteem among ethnic minority early adolescents: Social and cultural sources and threats. *Journal of Youth and Adolescence, 32*, 267–277.

Wayment, H. A., & Taylor, S. E. (1995). Self-evaluation processes: Motives, information use, and self-esteem. *Journal of Personality, 63,* 729–757.

Wegner, D. (1994). Ironic process of mental control. *Psychological Review, 101,* 34–52.

Wheeler, L., Martin, R., & Suls, J. (1997). The proxy of social comparison for self-assessment of ability. *Personality and Social Psychology Review, 1,* 54–61.

White, R. W. (1959). Motivation reconsidered: The concept of competence. *Psychological Review, 66,* 297–333.

White, R. W. (1963). Ego and reality in psychoanalytic theory. *Psychological Issues, 3,* 1–210.

Wolfe, R. N., Lennox, R. D., & Cutler, B. L. (1986). Getting along and getting ahead: Empirical support for a theory of protective and acquisitive self-presentation. *Journal of Personality and Social Psychology, 50,* 356–361.

Wood, J. V. (1989). Theory and research concerning social comparisons of personal attributes. *Psychological Bulletin, 106,* 231–248.

Wood, J. V., Giordano-Beech, M., Taylor, K. L., Michela, J. L., & Gaus, V. (1994). Strategies of social comparison: Self-protection and self-enhancement. *Journal of Personality and Social Psychology, 67,* 713–731.

Young, R. K. (1961). *Motivation and emotion: A survey of the determinants of human and animal activity.* New York: Wiley.

Zajonc, R. B. (1998). Emotions. In D. T. Gilbert, S. T. Fiske, & G. Lindzey (Eds.), *The handbook of social psychology* (Vol. 2, 4th ed., pp. 591–632). New York: McGraw-Hill.

9

Self-Conscious Emotion and Self-Regulation

DACHER KELTNER AND JENNIFER S. BEER

What would life be like if the self-conscious emotions were absent from our daily experience, if there were no shame, embarrassment, guilt, or pride? At first blush one might think that such a life would be more pleasurable, free, and unconstrained by the regard of others. The self-conscious emotions, after all, are a frequent source of displeasure, constraint, and confusion in our social lives. In this chapter we arrive at the opposite conclusion: that the self-conscious emotions are vital to adaptive social living. In making this argument we first consider the elements of self-regulation. We rely on these notions to then organize what is known about the self-conscious emotions, focusing in particular upon embarrassment, shame, and guilt (less is known about the varieties of pride). In so doing we argue that the self-conscious emotions serve a regulatory function, repairing social relations in the face of transgressions. Finally, to lend additional credence to our analysis, we discuss our own studies of children with externalizing tendencies, children with autism who are high functioning, and adults with orbitofrontal damage, to show how the self-conscious emotions are compromised in relation to self-regulatory deficits.

THREE INGREDIENTS OF SELF-REGULATION

Humans lead complex social lives, coordinating their own interests with those of others in families, romantic bonds, work relationships, hierarchies, social groups, and numerous short-term encounters with relative strangers (Fiske, 1992). It is perhaps due to the complexity of our social relationships that we evolved a symbolic self, defined by a multiplicity of attributes and perspectives, all of which enable us to fulfill different expectations and roles in various ever-changing interactions (Sedikides & Skowronski, 1997).

The complexity of human social interaction imposes many demands upon the individual. We must abide by moral norms and social conventions, delay gratification, and subordinate self-interest vis-à-vis others' interests. All of these are complex and taxing tasks that are an essential foundation of human social life. All of these demands of social interaction presuppose a capacity for self-regulation.

Self-regulation refers to the process by which people exert control over their behavior to match their internal standards and expectations (e.g., Baumeister & Heatherton, 1996; Carver & Scheier, 1990). Different relationships are defined by different rules, standards, and expectations (e.g., Fiske, 1992). The capacity to modify social behavior according to relationship- and context-specific rules and expectations helps individuals meet the varying demands of different relationships.

What specific processes are involved when individuals self-regulate, that is, modify their behavior to match their standards? Three components consistently appear in the accounts of self-regulation (Baumeister & Heatherton, 1996; Carver & Scheier, 1990; Deci & Ryan, 1987; Gray & McNaughton, 2000; Higgins, 1987). These three components are most often conceived as forming a feedback loop. Therefore, the three components are not steps or stages, but rather points along a process that continually feeds back on itself (see Figure 9.1; adapted from Carver & Scheier, 1990).

Standards and Expectations   First, self-regulation involves internalized standards. Internalized standards are the expectations, ideals, goals, plans, or beliefs that people have for themselves, both from their own perspective and what they imagine to be the perspective of others. Depending on the particular theory, these standards may take different forms. For example, *self-discrepancy theory* (Higgins, 1987) proposes that the individual's behavior is guided by personal beliefs about how he or she would ideally like to be (ideal self) and should be (ought self). *Self-determination theory* (e.g., Deci & Ryan, 1987) proposes a continuum of standards; goals range from satisfying one's personal aspirations to goals arising from external pressures or demands. *Action identification theory* (e.g., Vallacher & Wegner, 1987) proposes that internalized standards may also range from concrete goals ("I won't comment on my friend's lopsided haircut") to more abstract goals ("I will become a pillar of justice for my community"). Additionally, in the social domain, standards may include what a person hopes to achieve as well as

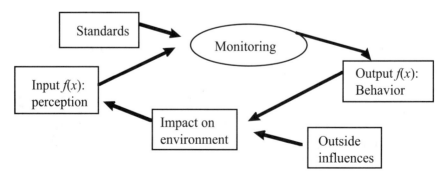

FIGURE 9.1.   Self-regulation feedback loop. Adapted with permission of Guilford Press.

strategies for achieving that goal (e.g., Carver & Scheier, 1990; Kihlstrom & Cantor, 2000).

Behavioral Monitoring and Self-Insight A second component of self-regulation is behavioral monitoring. Self-regulation requires that the individual monitor his or her current behavior online to determine whether it matches self-standards. Experimental techniques that make people more self-aware—for example, by placing a mirror in front of people or showing people a videotape of themselves (e.g., Carver & Scheier, 1990; Robins & John, 1997)—increase the likelihood that people will evaluate whether their behavior accords with how they would like to behave. This comparison of online behavior and self-standards may be fairly automatic and not specific to humans (e.g., Gray & McNaughton, 2000). The accuracy of these comparisons is also of theoretical interest. Whereas some researchers have argued that people generally tend to inflate their assessments of themselves and that such inflation is adaptive (e.g., Taylor & Brown, 1988), other researchers have claimed that successful self-regulation necessarily relies on accurate self-perceptions (Heatherton & Ambady, 1993).

Control Behavior to Match Standards Finally, the individual must exert control over his or her behavior to match self-standards. If the monitoring process reveals a discrepancy between an individual's actual behavior and internal standards, then that person must modify his or her behavior in accordance with self-standards. Various factors influence the ability to exert control over one's behavior. People may have a limited capacity to engage in behavioral control that is depleted by other goal-directed behavior or forms of constraint. Once self-regulatory capacity has been exhausted, changing behavior is increasingly difficult (e.g., Baumeister & Heatherton, 1996; Vohs & Heatherton, 2000). The capacity to control behavior has been shown to vary from person to person, and this variation in the capacity to self-regulate has important social and life outcomes (Block, 1996; Robins, John, Caspi, Moffitt, & Stouthamer-Loeber, 1996). People's beliefs about the capacity for changing behavior are important as well. Decades of research have shown that people's expectations about their competencies, their control, and their likelihood of success exert profound influences upon motivation and performance (e.g., Abramson, Seligman, & Teasdale, 1978; Bandura, 1977; Beer, 2002a; Dweck, Chiu, & Hong, 1995).

In sum, self-regulation theorists converge on three components that are essential to the processes by which people control their behavior. First, people have standards or expectations they are trying to maintain. Second, people must monitor their behavior online to assess whether it is in accordance with relevant standards. Finally, if behavior and standards are discrepant, then behavior must be changed to bring it in accordance with standards.

As we move toward a discussion of self-conscious emotion, it is interesting to note that many of the aforementioned elements of self-regulation also appear in appraisal theories of emotion. Appraisal theories highlight that emotion arises when people compare their own actions, or events in their external environment, with goals and expectations (e.g., Lazarus, 1991). These appraisals generate action tendencies, which guide the individual to act in ways that reduce the discrepancies among goals, expectations, and actions (e.g., Frijda, 1986). And, of course, the critical process that returns the individual to some more goal-congruent state is emotion. Our interest here is in the self-conscious emotions, which we argue are intimately intertwined with self-regulation.

SELF-CONSCIOUS EMOTION WITHIN SELF-REGULATION

As mentioned, the self-conscious emotions include states such as embarrassment, shame, guilt, and pride. Our own focus will be on embarrassment, shame, and guilt, which have been the subject of a spate of recent theory and empirical study (e.g., Baumeister, Stillwell, & Heatherton, 1994; Keltner & Buswell, 1997; Miller & Leary, 1992; Tangney & Fischer, 1995). This work suggests that these emotions involve the self-regulatory processes we outlined earlier. These emotions, as we see below, are closely related to important standards that govern social behavior. They involve self-awareness and the monitoring of one's actions, often by taking others' perspectives upon one's own actions. And they certainly have motivational properties that guide ensuing behavior, which is typically oriented toward a more goal-congruent state of affairs for the individual.

More specifically, we suggest that the self-conscious emotions—in particular shame, embarrassment, and guilt—serve two more specific functions that are required of self-regulation within interpersonal contexts. First, the experience of these self-conscious emotions provides information to the individual about which specific goal, expectation, or standard has been violated. The specific nature of the violation, empirical research shows, turns out to be quite different for the different self-conscious emotions. So too, it follows, are ensuing self-regulatory processes. Second, the outward displays of the different self-conscious emotions, documented in recent empirical research, serve slightly different appeasement functions. These displays serve as vital social signals, remediating social interactions that have gone awry. They provide information to observers that the individual is committed to social norms and morals and feels some remorse for the preceding transgression.

The Experience of Self-Conscious Emotions: Internal Signals of Specific Transgressions

The experience of emotion remains a scientific mystery. What the field of emotion has learned is that the experiential component of emotion provides rapid, compelling, attention focusing information to the individual about important events in the environment (Schwarz, 1990). Anger signals to the individual that injustice has occurred, sadness that loss has happened, fear that danger is imminent. This signal value of emotional experience also has the property of phenomenal absolutism: That is, it feels absolutely true, whether the evidence justifies such a belief

(Frijda, 1986). In this way, the experience of an emotion often arises in seconds or milliseconds and, due to appraisal processes beyond conscious awareness, presents to the individual a state of affairs that cannot be reasoned away and must be acted upon.

The experience of self-conscious emotions—particularly in Western European cultures—is poignantly unpleasant but at the same time richly informative of important events and necessary courses of action. Specifically, the experience of embarrassment, shame, and guilt signal that the individual has transgressed important social standards. This claim summarizes dozens of studies of the antecedents and appraisal processes associated with different self-conscious emotions (for reviews, see Keltner & Buswell, 1997; Miller, 1992; Tangney & Fischer, 1995).

In studies of the antecedents of self-conscious emotions, researchers have employed several methodologies. In some, participants described several situations that produced self-conscious emotions, and researchers then classified these according to specific taxonomies (e.g., Miller, 1992). In others, participants were asked to describe in great detail one situation that produced a self-conscious emotion (e.g., Parrott & Smith, 1991). In still others, participants rated the phenomenological and contextual properties of events that produce self-conscious emotions (Miller & Tangney, 1994; Tangney, Miller, Flicker, & Barlow, 1996). These kinds of studies suggest the following.

The antecedents of embarrassment most typically involve violations of social conventions, which refer to the consensually agreed-upon rules that typically govern public social interactions (e.g., rules related to greeting, dress, or manners of eating). Thus, people commonly report experiencing embarrassment following their own physical pratfalls (e.g., tripping), cognitive shortcomings (e.g., forgetting the name of a new acquaintance), loss of body control (e.g., belching or uncontrolled flatulence), failure to maintain privacy (e.g., having one's feelings disclosed), or awkward social interactions, or when they have been teased by others or been the object of undesirable social attention (Edelmann, 1987; Keltner & Buswell, 1996; Miller, 1992; Miller & Tangney, 1994; Sattler, 1966).

Shame and guilt follow different transgressions than those of embarrassment. Shame follows the failure to live up to expectations, either one's own or those of significant others, that define the "core self," "ego ideal," or character (Babcock & Sabini, 1990; Lazarus, 1991; Tangney, 1992; Tangney, Marschall, Rosenberg, Barlow, & Wagner, 1992; Tangney et al., 1996). Thus, commonly reported antecedents of shame include failing at an achievement-related task, hurting another's feelings, and failing to act in accordance with personal ideals—for example, as a caring, industrious, or intelligent person. Shame in this way is highly personal and idiosyncratic; it has to do with how the individual is faring when compared to that person's ideal self (Higgins, 1987).

Guilt, on the other hand, follows transgressions of moral rules that govern behavior toward others (Tangney, 1992). By *moral* it is meant that the rules are assumed to be applicable across people, contexts, and cultures; associated with punishment (or reward, when positively instantiated); and obligatory. Consistent with this assertion, empirical studies reveal that the common antecedents of guilt include lying, cheating, stealing, infidelity, and neglecting personal duties (Keltner

& Buswell, 1996; Tangney, 1992; Tangney et al., 1996). Participants in one study rated the antecedents of shame and guilt to be twice as moral in their connotations as those of embarrassment (Tangney et al., 1996), consistent with previous speculations (e.g., Goffman, 1956, 1967; Harré, 1990).

Taken together, the studies we have just reviewed suggest that the experiences of embarrassment, shame, and guilt signal that the individual has violated a social standard. In the case of embarrassment, the individual is likely to infer that he or she violated a social convention. In the case of shame, the individual is likely to infer that he or she has failed to live up to expectations that define the core self. In the case of guilt, the individual will feel that he or she has violated a moral rule that governs behavior toward others (e.g., through lying, cheating, stealing, or infidelity).

Before turning to a second broad regulatory function of the self-conscious emotions, we take a moment to speculate about the implications of the findings we have just reviewed. First, we would expect the experience of embarrassment, shame, and guilt to serve as vital guides to socially appropriate behavior. Experiences of these emotions are likely to motivate individuals to avoid those specific transgressions in the future, and even engage in actions that make the transgressions less likely. A guilt-ridden parent, for example, might take special care not to harm a child's feelings in the particular way that originally generated the guilt. An embarrassed teen, having worn the wrong clothes to a party, would take special care in the future to know the appropriate attire for the occasion and dress accordingly. Through generalization processes, experiences of self-conscious emotion associated with one particular event and domain would generalize to related actions within a domain. A shame-inducing comment about sexual prowess (or lack thereof), for example, might become associated with other beliefs about the body and sexuality. An embarrassing public speech might color all future experiences of public performance. Early experiences of self-conscious emotion, then, might signal which classes of action to avoid.

The experience of self-conscious emotions, then, guides our participation in the social moral world. In-the-moment experiences of self-conscious emotion signals what we have done wrong right now. The anticipation of self-conscious emotions provides clues as to what future actions to avoid. This discussion highlights the importance of having reliable access to the experience of such emotions, a theme to which we return in our discussion of self-regulatory deficits.

The Display of Self-Conscious Emotions: External Signals of Social-Moral Commitment

Violations of social standards threaten the very basis of cooperative social interactions and communities. They suggest that the culprit is not willing or capable of abiding by the conventions, morals, and ideals that serve as the basis of cooperative alliances and smooth-flowing interactions. The acts that trigger self-conscious emotion, from minor pratfalls to moral misconduct, raise the unsettling possibility that the individual is unable to adhere to, or uninterested in adhering to, standards of public behavior, thereby subjecting the individual to harsh judgment and ostracism. What is needed is a mechanism that allows the individual to correct the mistake, to repair the momentarily disturbed relationship. The nonverbal displays of the self-conscious emotions, recent evidence shows, serve this repair function, restoring relations when they have gone awry.

A first wave of research on the nonverbal displays of self-conscious emotions asked whether these emotions are expressed in distinct, and perhaps universal, displays. This research was guided by two criteria that have shaped the study of emotional expression more generally (e.g., Ekman, 1993). First, the experience of the self-conscious emotions had to be induced in the laboratory. Second, unique expressive behaviors had to be shown to occur during one self-conscious emotion but not the others; that is, careful analysis of the behaviors associated with the self-conscious emotions had to document distinct signals for each. The answer from this line of research is partially affirmative: Shame and embarrassment have distinct signals, but guilt does not appear to have one.

In the relevant studies, the experiences of embarrassment and shame were shown to correlate with distinct nonverbal displays (e.g., Keltner, 1995). Shame is associated with coordinated gaze and downward head movement. The embarrassment display reliably unfolded in the following sequence during a 5-s period: gaze aversion, a smile control (which inhibits the smile), a non-Duchenne smile (which only involves the *zygomatic major* muscle action that pulls the corners of the lips upward), a second smile control, downward head movement, and then face touching, which occurred about 25% of the time. Researchers have documented a similar display in embarrassed young children, starting at about 18 months of age (Lewis, Sullivan, Stanger, & Weiss, 1989) and in people in different cultures in their naturalistic interactions (Eibl-Eibesfeldt, 1989).

Are these displays of shame and embarrassment universal? Indeed, a recent study (Haidt & Keltner, 1999) suggests that this may be so. Participants in the United States and rural India were presented with photos of the previously described shame and embarrassment displays as well as with photos of other widely studied emotions (e.g., anger, fear, disgust, sadness, surprise). Participants were asked to describe the display in their own words, because experimental prompts potentially bias research results. Participants from these two dramatically different cultures reliably identified the displays of embarrassment and shame and provided similar descriptions of situations that would produce the displays. Again, the embarrassment display prompted participants in both cultures to come up with stories about minor transgressions; the shame display led participants to tell stories about more serious violations. This study also documented that the tongue bite, an appeasement gesture used throughout Southeast Asia, was judged as embarrassment in India but not in the United States.

A first clue to the regulatory function of these displays came from a review of studies of appeasement behaviors in nonhuman species (Keltner & Buswell, 1997). These behaviors were identified when one organism signaled to a likely aggressor in a fashion that produced reduced aggression and increased reconciliation (for definitions, see de Waal, 1986). The appeasement displays of several different species were considered, ranging from nonhuman primates, such as chimpanzees and apes, to dogs and rabbits. Nonhuman appeasement displays consistently

involved many of the actions seen in the nonverbal displays of human embarrassment and shame. These include gaze aversion; smiling behavior; downward head
movements that display the neck; reduced physical size, which is the outcome of
the shoulder shrugging and downward head movement seen in human embarrassment; self-touching or grooming; and, in some nonhuman primates, the reddening
of the skin.

In these studies of nonhuman appeasement, these behaviors were observed
when one conspecific signaled behaviors that reduced the aggression of another
conspecific, typically a dominant organism in the context of likely conflict. In many
of these studies, appeasement displays produced reconciliation behavior such as
grooming, embracing, sexual play, or close contact (de Waal, 1986, 1988; de Waal
& van Roosmalen, 1979). How much evidence is there to suggest that displays of
embarrassment and shame similarly promote social reconciliation, restoring
social relations that have momentarily gone awry? As it turns out, the evidence is
quite robust.

Relevant research suggests that the display of self-conscious emotion leads to
emotions and behaviors in others that help remedy social transgressions (see
Keltner & Buswell, 1997, for relevant citations). The studies have exposed participants to displays of self-conscious emotions in different ways: Participants have
watched an individual knock over a supermarket display, informed a confederate
of bad news, judged a hypothetical defendant convicted of selling drugs, or judged
political candidates. Across these different methods, participants were more likely
to forgive, like, and approach the individual who displayed self-conscious emotion
more than the comparison individual who displayed other nonverbal behavior or
no emotion. Parents punish children less if they display embarrassment and related
behavior following transgressions; similarly, individuals will volunteer for additional hours to help an embarrassed confederate more than a poised confederate.

Embarrassment and shame appear to bring about different kinds of social
reconciliation, which is not surprising in light of the different transgressions that
produce these emotions in the first place (see Keltner et al., 1997). Embarrassment, as we have seen, follows transgressions of social conventions and appeases
others by eliciting lighthearted emotions in observers, such as amusement. As a
result, empirical evidence indicates that observers of embarrassing acts are most
likely to discount the importance of the transgression (Cupach & Metts, 1990,
1992; Cupach, Metts, & Hazleton, 1986; Keltner, Young, & Buswell, 1997; Semin
& Manstead, 1982; Sharkey, 1991; Sharkey & Stafford, 1990; Tangney et al., 1996).

Shame follows more serious transgressions of standards related to the core
self (Tangney et al., 1996), as we have seen, and displays of shame appease
observers by eliciting sympathy, concern, and compassion (Keltner et al., 1997).
Sympathy is more likely to prompt observers to offer forgiveness and help
(Eisenberg et al., 1989). In empirical studies, observers of shame displays are
more likely to express an interest in comforting the ashamed individual (Keltner
et al., 1997).

Our discussion of the reconciliation processes that shame and embarrassment
displays evoke helps shed light on one of the mysteries of self-conscious emotions:
that they are so powerfully, and at times perplexingly, contagious. For example,

studies find that people are quite prone to feel embarrassment themselves when watching a stranger engage in embarrassing acts (Miller, 1987). People even show the physiological signs of blushing (elevated cheek temperature and cheek coloration) when they watch a friend engage in an embarrassing performance of the Star-Spangled Banner (Shearn, Bergman, Hill, Abel, & Hinds, 1992). Why are the self-conscious emotions so contagious? Because that contagious response prompts observers to help remedy the situation. Interestingly, in nonhuman primates, third-party "mediators," upon observing others in conflict, encourage reconciliation with affiliative gestures of their own (de Waal, 1979, 1989). In humans, contagious embarrassment and shame lead others to act in ways, such as diverting attention (Leary & Meadows, 1991) or offering support (Cupach & Metts, 1990), that minimize the damage to the embarrassed individual's social identity.

A Summary Many emotions are involved in regulation—that is, in guiding individuals toward more stable and rule-bound social relations (e.g., Shiota, Campos, Keltner, & Hertenstein, 2004). Certain positive emotions such as love and gratitude motivate commitments to specific relationships. Other focused, negative emotions, including anger and disgust, help regulate the behavior of other individuals, signaling when they have acted inappropriately and motivating punitive action that brings those individuals' actions more in line with social rules. And the self-conscious emotions of embarrassment, shame, and guilt help regulate the self within social interactions, signaling when the individual has acted inappropriately and communicating to others the awareness of the deviant act, thereby restoring social relations.

We now turn our attention to when self-conscious emotions are disruptive. Although we have emphasized the social benefits that the self-conscious emotions bring about, it is clear that this is with respect to specific situations—namely, when individuals have committed mistakes and seek reconciliation. In many other contexts the self-conscious emotions actually prove to be problematic. Excesses—the frequent and intense experience—of self-conscious emotions have been linked to extreme shyness, tension, the pervasive fear of negative evaluation, and even dysphoria and depression (e.g., Miller, 1995, 1996). Here, one might argue that the frequent experience of self-conscious emotion leads to the overregulated self, to excessive inhibition and self-awareness. In the remainder of the chapter we are interested in the other end of the continuum, in cases where deficits in self-conscious emotion relate systematically to deficits in self-regulation, to problems in control and increased antisocial behavior. We now turn to studies that have explored this thesis.

EMPIRICAL STUDIES OF DISRUPTIONS IN SELF-CONSCIOUS EMOTION

It is widely claimed that individuals who are less inclined toward self-conscious emotions are more prone to difficulties with self-regulation and increased antisocial behavior. These claims follow from our preceding analysis. Self-conscious emotions do many things that promote adaptive social relationships. The experiencing of self-conscious emotions signals inappropriate behavior. Their well-timed display signals to others one's awareness of the social transgression and prompts remedial inferences and behaviors. Individuals who experience and display little in the form of self-conscious emotions, by implication, should be more inclined to violate social norms and less likely to restore social relations following norm violations (e.g., in interpersonal conflict). Variants of this hypothesis were advanced long ago by Darwin (1872) and Goffman (1956, 1957) and are embedded in cultural conceptions of the "shameless" individual.

How then can we address these claims about the regulatory function of self-conscious emotions? In our own efforts we have related systematic variation in such emotions to variation in the regulation of social behavior. Unfortunately, variation in the kind of social behavior that these emotions inhibit—the everyday faux pas, inappropriate disclosures, violations of character, immoral acts—are unlikely to occur in the laboratory and are fairly difficult to capture with observational methods. Individuals are socialized from a very early age to regulate their behavior. Just as walking and talking begin as effortful processes and eventually become automatic, behavioral regulation becomes a well-learned process that is difficult to override in experimental or naturalistic studies. Therefore, special populations may be helpful in creating variance in the presence of self-conscious emotions as well as variance in behavioral regulation.

More generally, this is consistent with a long-standing approach to the study of emotion-specific functions: the study of groups with specific disorders (e.g., Keltner & Gross, 1999; Keltner & Kring, 1998). To the extent that an emotion or class of emotions serves a specific function (self-regulation, in the case of the self-conscious emotion), then disruptions in that emotion should correlate with fairly specific and predictable problems in social behavior. Based on this reasoning, three of our recent studies suggest that these early intuitions about the self-regulatory function of self-conscious emotion were well founded.

Embarrassment and Externalizing Disorder

Most generally, we have argued that the self-conscious emotions help regulate the self in a fashion that leads to socially and morally appropriate behavior. If true, then a relative deficit in the experience or display of self-conscious emotions should be associated with the tendency to violate social mores, norms, and morals.

In a first test of this hypothesis about the regulatory function of self-conscious emotions, we assessed the relationship between spontaneous displays of one such emotion—in this case, embarrassment—and externalizing disorder (Keltner, Moffitt, & Stouthamer-Loeber, 1995). Externalizing disorder is defined by several antisocial tendencies that are related to failures at self-regulation. These include aggression, indexed in reports of fighting and hostility, as well as delinquent actions, as evident in reports of such acts as stealing and vandalism. In light of our foregoing analysis, one would expect externalizing children to show relatively little embarrassment in spontaneous interactions.

As a test of this hypothesis, young boys were observed while they were taking an interactive IQ test. In this test the 10-year-old boys were individually given a series of questions that they were to answer that sampled knowledge that one might find in an encyclopedia: "What is a barometer?" "What is iambic pentameter?" "Who was Charles Darwin?" This test, by its design, gave all boys the opportunity to fail in front of an authority figure—a clear elicitor of embarrassment similar to other failures of knowledge shown to evoke embarrassment. These boys' facial expressions of emotion were coded using a modified version of Ekman and Friesen's Facial Action Coding System (Ekman & Friesen, 1976), which identifies the facial actions associated with several different emotions (in addition, face touches were coded, given their involvement in embarrassment). The measures of facial expression were related to teacher ratings of the boys' levels of externalizing disorder.

The IQ test produced frequent embarrassment, anger, and fear, as the boys made intellectual mistakes in front of an authority figure (one wonders what the effects of those emotions were on the children's performances). Consistent with the notion that self-conscious emotion serves a regulatory function, young boys who were most prone to antisocial aggression and delinquent behavior, the externalizers, displayed the least embarrassment. Of course, embarrassment was sampled in one context, an academic one, and one must resist the temptation to conclude that these antisocial boys lack any self-conscious emotion. The experience of emotion was not assessed, and more important, self-conscious emotion was assessed in one context. These antisocial boys might show ample embarrassment in other nonacademic contexts. Nevertheless, this proved to be some of the first evidence linking self-regulatory deficits to deficits in embarrassment. Subsequent studies would reveal this pattern of results to generalize across different disorders and different ways of assaying self-conscious emotion.

Autism and Deficits in the Knowledge of Self-Conscious Emotions

Autism is defined by a host of social difficulties, including problems with nonliteral communication, understanding others' social intentions, and linking speech and actions to social context (Flavell, 1999). More generally, theorists have observed that children with autism, even those with typical language abilities, known as children with high functioning autism (HFA), have difficulties with many of the elements of self-regulation that we outlined earlier. Thus, a central deficit of autism is difficulty with theory of mind (Capps & Sigman, 1996), which refers to the ability to understand others' mental states, and it ranges in complexity from the relatively simple understanding that others may have different desires than oneself to the more complicated ability to theorize about others' beliefs, thoughts, and intentions (Flavell, 1999). Theory of mind is clearly involved in monitoring one's own behavior, which depends critically on taking others' perspectives. Autism also involves difficulties in appreciating social standards.

In light of these social difficulties experienced by children with autism, researchers have been interested in emotional correlates of autism. For children with autism who are not high functioning, emotion-related deficits appear to be broad and pervasive, involving deficits in both understanding and recognition (Hobson, 1991; Ozonoff, Pennington, & Rogers, 1991). For individuals with HFA, emotion-related deficits appear to be more specific. When prompted, children with HFA demonstrate relatively intact emotion concepts and recognition ability for happiness, sadness, fear, and anger (Capps et al., 1992; Ozonoff et al., 1990). These children had difficulty, however, in recounting experiences of self-conscious emotions. Namely, children with HFA conveyed factual, rather than personal, knowledge of the self-conscious emotions, whereas they did relate personalized accounts of non-self-conscious emotions. They also required more experimental prompts to recall experiences of embarrassment.

In our own research, we presented photographs of self-conscious emotions (shame and embarrassment) and other widely studied emotions (anger, disgust, fear, happiness, sadness, and surprise) to children with HFA and to typically developing children matched on a variety of measures (e.g., IQ, age). The children were asked to choose a term from many different terms to describe the emotion in each photo.

As expected, the children with HFA performed equally well in judging the photos of the widely studied facial expressions of anger, disgust, fear, happiness, sadness, and surprise. They appeared, in spite of their many social deficits, to perceive these emotions in the face much as typically developing children do. Where they differed was in their inferences about self-conscious emotions. These children were approximately half as accurate as the typically developing control children in correctly labeling photographs of embarrassment and shame displays. Further, the differences in the HFA and typically developing groups in the recognition of self-conscious emotions disappeared when differences in theory of mind were controlled for. This evidence suggests that the ability to take others' perspectives, so central to self-regulation, in part accounts for the difficulties children with autism experience in understanding self-conscious emotion.

Orbitofrontal Brain Damage: A Model for Studying Poor Regulation of Social Behavior

The brain's frontal lobes have been characterized as centers of regulation or executive control. The orbitofrontal region of the frontal lobes, which rests behind and above the eye orbits (i.e., in Brodmann's Areas 11, 12, 14, 47), is particularly involved in the regulation of social behavior. The orbitofrontal cortex is richly connected to areas associated with emotional and social processing, including the amygdala, anterior cingulate, and Somatosensory Areas I and II (e.g., Adolphs, 1999; Brothers, 1996). Damage to the orbitofrontal region of the frontal lobes does not impair language, memory, or sensory processing, but it does disrupt social regulation.

Both clinical characterizations and anecdotal evidence suggest that orbitofrontal damage impairs the ability to regulate social behavior. Perhaps the most famous case study of orbitofrontal damage is that of Phineas Gage (e.g., Harlow, 1848). Harlow's description of Gage following his injury is filled with references to poor regulation of social behavior. For example, Harlow noted that Gage's "equilibrium … between his intellectual capacities and animal propensities seems to have been destroyed. He is … impatient of restraint or advice when it conflicts with his desires" (pp. 389). Contemporary descriptions of orbitofrontal damage are consistent with difficulties in regulating behavior, particularly in discriminating which social behaviors are appropriate for interactions with strangers in comparison with those appropriate for well-known others. For example, orbitofrontal patients have been observed to greet strangers by kissing them on the cheek and hugging them (Rolls, Hornak, Wade, & McGrath, 1994), engage in uncontrolled and tasteless social behavior such as inappropriate joking (Stuss & Benson, 1984), and disclose in an overly intimate fashion that which might be more appropriate for a close friend or family member (Beer, 2002b). It is important to note that these regulatory deficits in the social domain are not associated with damage to other areas of the brain associated with regulatory function. In comparison to other brain areas, damage to the orbitofrontal cortex selectively impairs the regulation of social behavior and therefore provides a model for understanding the mechanisms underlying this process.

A series of studies suggest that orbitofrontal patients' poor self-regulation is associated with dysfunctional self-conscious emotions. In this line of studies, we asked whether orbitofrontal patients show little evidence of self-conscious emotion, or whether these emotions fail to serve a self-regulatory function. The evidence we have generated favors the latter interpretation. Orbitofrontal patients tend to experience self-conscious emotions in a manner that reinforces their inappropriate behavior rather than correcting it (Beer, Heerey, Keltner, Scabini, & Knight, 2003). In one study, orbitofrontal patients and healthy controls participated in two social interaction tasks. Participants had to tease experimenters and generate a title for a boring paragraph. In comparison to control participants, the orbitofrontal patients were not embarrassed by and actually felt more proud of their teasing behavior, even though it was objectively more inappropriate than that of control participants. Similarly, orbitofrontal patients did not realize that they did not deserve praise for their title and tried to modestly acknowledge the compliments by showing embarrassment. In contrast, control participants were mostly amused by the outlandish praise and did not feel the need to counteract any violations of modesty with an appeasing embarrassment display. In another study, orbitofrontal patients, healthy controls, and dorsolateral prefrontal patients participated in a self-disclosure task with an experimenter they had just met (Beer, 2002b). Even though the orbitofrontal patients disclosed overly personal information that was inappropriate for the context (e.g., about their sexual preferences), they were less embarrassed than healthy and patient controls who disclosed appropriately. Together, these findings suggest that orbitofrontal patients are unable to benefit from their experiences with self-conscious emotions, as they are never generated in relation to their mistakes, only their successes.

On a related note, there is also evidence that orbitofrontal patients have difficulty recognizing self-conscious emotions in others. For example, orbitofrontal patients had more difficulty than controls in recognizing facial expressions of embarrassment and shame (Beer et al., 2003). Additionally, a case study of an orbitofrontal patient found that he had trouble identifying when characters in vignettes felt embarrassed (Blair & Cipolotti, 2000).

CONCLUDING REMARKS

We have argued that embarrassment, shame, and guilt promote self-regulation, that they are a voice of the conscience. These emotions signal when the individual has violated social norms, moral codes, and character ideals. When communicated, these emotions restore the individual's standing within ongoing social relations. Both of these functions are vital to the more general process by which the individual regulates the self to meet social standards and rules.

The evidence we have reviewed is consistent with this general analysis of embarrassment, shame, and guilt. Individuals with deficits in self-regulation—namely, children with externalizing disorder, children with HFA, and adults with frontal lobe damage—all showed deficits in self-conscious emotion. This research is just a beginning, and it raises as many questions as it answers. For example, the studies of the elicitors and displays of the self-conscious emotions reveal that embarrassment, shame, and guilt are tailored to very specific social contexts. Embarrassment repairs violations of social conventions, shame the violations of character ideals, and guilt the harm done to others. Our studies of specific patients almost exclusively focused on embarrassment, neglecting shame and guilt. This raises the question of whether patients with deficits in self-regulation, like those we have studied, show deficits in specific self-conscious emotions or deficits across the self-conscious emotions. It would be quite remarkable to find groups with deficits in specific self-conscious emotions. Such evidence would allow researchers to begin to marshal evidence about specific central nervous system processes that are specific to the different self-conscious emotions.

Excesses in the self-conscious emotions are just as interesting a field of study. We earlier noted that excesses in embarrassment are associated with shyness, and excessive shame and guilt with depression. Chronic proneness to embarrassment, shame, or guilt (e.g., Edelmann & McCusker, 1986; Gilbert & Trower, 1990; Miller, 1995) should correlate with hyperactive self-regulatory processes (e.g., the hyperawareness of social standards or the excessive monitoring of social behavior) and disrupted social interactions of a different variety than those that we have studied. We would expect these individuals to overinterpret social interactions in terms of their own mistakes and shortcomings; we likewise would expect them to be too oriented to repairing relations that have not gone awry. It is in the deficits and excesses of human emotion where we often discern the functions of emotion, even those like embarrassment, shame, and guilt.

REFERENCES

Abramson, L. Y., Seligman, M. E., & Teasdale, J. D. (1978). Learned helplessness in humans: Critique and reformulation. *Journal of Abnormal Psychology, 87*, 49–74.

Adolphs, R. (1999). Social cognition and the human brain. *Trends in Cognitive Sciences, 3*, 469–479.

Babcock, M. K., & Sabini, J. (1990). On differentiating embarrassment from shame. *European Journal of Social Psychology, 20*, 151–169.

Bandura, A. (1977). Self-efficacy: Toward a unifying theory of behavioral change. *Psychological Review, 84*, 191–215.

Baumeister, R. F., & Heatherton, T. A. (1996). Self-regulation failure: An overview. *Psychological Inquiry, 7*, 1–15.

Baumeister, R. F., Stillwell, A. M., & Heatherton, T. F. (1994). Guilt: An interpersonal approach. *Psychological Bulletin, 115*, 243–267.

Beer, J. S. (2002a). Implicit self-theories and shyness. *Journal of Personality and Social Psychology, 83*, 1009–1024.

Beer, J. S. (2002b). *Self-regulation of social behavior.* Unpublished doctoral dissertation, University of California, Berkeley.

Beer, J. S., Heerey, E. A., Keltner, D., Scabini, D., & Knight, R. T. (2003). The self-regulatory function of self-conscious emotion: Insights from patients with orbitofrontal damage. *Journal of Personality and Social Psychology, 85*, 594–604.

Blair, J., & Cipolotti, L. (2000). Impaired social response reversal: A case of "acquired sociopathy." *Brain, 123*, 1122–1141.

Block, J. (1996). Some jangly remarks on Baumeister and Heatherton. *Psychological Inquiry, 7*, 28–32.

Brothers, L. (1996). Brain mechanisms of social cognition. *Journal of Psychopharmacology, 10*, 2–8.

Capps, L., & Sigman, M. (1996). Autistic aloneness. In R. D. Kavanaugh, B. Zimmerberg, & S. Fein (Eds.), *Emotion: Interdisciplinary perspectives* (pp. 273–296). Hillsdale, NJ: Erlbaum.

Capps, L., Yirmiya, N., & Sigman, M. (1992). Understanding of simple and complex emotions in non-retarded children with autism. *Journal of Child Psychology and Psychiatry, 33*, 1169–1182.

Carver, C. S., & Scheier, M. (1990). Principles of self-regulation: Action and emotion. In E. T. Higgins & R. M. Sorrentino (Eds.), *Handbook of motivation and cognition: Foundations of social behavior* (pp. 3–52). New York: Guilford Press.

Cupach, W. R., & Metts, S. (1990). Remedial processes in embarrassing predicaments. In J. Anderson (Ed.), *Communication yearbook* (Vol. 13, pp. 323–352). Newbury Park, CA: Sage.

Cupach, W. R., & Metts, S. (1992). The effects of type of predicament and embarrassability on remedial responses to embarrassing situations. *Communication Quarterly, 40*, 149–161.

Cupach, W. R., Metts, S., & Hazleton, V., Jr. (1986). Coping with embarrassing predicaments: Remedial strategies and their perceived utility. *Journal of Language and Social Psychology, 5*, 181–200.

Darwin, C. (1872). *The expression of emotions in man and animals.* New York: Philosophical Library.

Deci, E. L., & Ryan, R. M. (1987). The support of autonomy and the control of behavior. *Journal of Personality and Social Psychology, 53*, 1024–1037.

de Waal, F. B. M. (1986). The integration of dominance and social bonding in primates. *Quarterly Review of Biology, 61,* 459–479.

de Waal, F. B. M. (1988). The reconciled hierarchy. In M. R. A. Chance (Ed.), *Social fabrics of the mind* (pp. 105–136). Hillsdale, NJ: Erlbaum.

de Waal, F. B. M. (1989). Behavioral contrasts between bonobo and chimpanzee. In P. G. Heltue & L. A. Marquant (Eds.), *Understanding chimpanzees* (pp. 154–175). Cambridge, MA: Harvard University Press.

de Waal, F. B. M., & Ren, R. (1988). Comparison of the reconciliation behavior of stumptail and rhesus macaques. *Ethology, 78,* 129–142.

de Waal, F. B. M., & van Roosmalen, A. (1979). Reconciliation and consolation among chimpanzees. *Behavioral Ecology and Sociobiology, 5,* 55–66.

Dweck, C. S., Chiu, C., & Hong, Y. (1995). Implicit theories and their role in judgments and reactions: A world from two perspectives. *Psychological Inquiry, 6,* 267–285.

Edelmann, R. J. (1987). *The psychology of embarrassment.* Chichester, England: Wiley.

Edelmann, R. J., & McCusker, G. (1986). Introversion, neuroticism, empathy, and embarrassability. *Personality and Individual Differences, 7,* 133–140.

Eibl-Eibesfeldt, I. (1989). *Human ethology.* New York: Aldine de Gruyter.

Eisenberg, N., Fabes, R. A., Miller, P. A., Fultz, J., Shell, R., Mathy, R. M., & Reno, R. R. (1989). Relation of sympathy and distress to prosocial behavior: A multimethod study. *Journal of Personality and Social Psychology, 57,* 55–66.

Ekman, P. (1993). Facial expression and emotion. *American Psychologist, 48,* 384–392.

Ekman, P., & Friesen, W. V. (1976). Measuring facial movement. *Journal of Environmental Psychology and Nonverbal Behavior, 1,* 56–75.

Fiske, A. P. (1992). Four elementary forms of sociality: Framework for a unified theory of social relations. *Psychological Review, 99,* 689–723.

Flavell, J. H. (1999). Cognitive development: Children's knowledge about the mind. *Annual Review of Psychology, 50,* 21–45.

Frijda, N. (1986). *The emotions.* Cambridge, England: Cambridge University Press.

Gilbert, P., & Trower, P. (1990). The evolution and manifestation of social anxiety. In W. R. Crozier (Ed.), *Shyness and embarrassment: Perspectives from social psychology* (pp. 144–180). Cambridge, England: Cambridge University Press.

Goffman, E. (1956). Embarrassment and social organization. *American Journal of Sociology, 62,* 264–271.

Goffman, E. (1967). *Interaction ritual: Essays on face-to-face behavior.* Garden City, NY: Anchor.

Gray, J. A., & McNaughton, N. (2000). Neural anxiety systems: Relevant fault-lines to track and treat disorders. *European Journal of Neuroscience, 12,* 311.

Haidt, J., & Keltner, D. (1999). Culture and facial expression: Open-ended methods find more expressions and a gradient of recognition. *Cognition and Emotion, 13,* 225–266.

Harlow, J. M. (1848). Passage of an iron rod through the head. *Boston Medical and Surgical Journal, 39,* 389–393.

Harré, R. (1990). Embarrassment: A conceptual analysis. In W. R. Crozier (Ed.), *Shyness and embarrassment: Perspectives from social psychology* (pp. 87–118). Cambridge, England: Cambridge University Press.

Heatherton, T. F., & Ambady, N. (1993). Self-esteem, self-prediction, and living up to commitments. In R. F. Baumeister (Ed.), *Self-esteem: The puzzle of low self-regard* (pp. 131–145). New York: Plenum Press.

Heckhausen, H. (1984). Emergent achievement behavior: Some early developments. In J. Nicholls (Ed.), *Advances in motivation and achievement: Vol. 3. The development of achievement motivation* (pp. 1–32). Greenwich, CT: JAI.

Higgins, E. T. (1987). Self-discrepancy theory: A theory relating to self and affect. *Psychological Review, 94*, 319–340.

Hobson, J. A. (Ed.). (1989). *Abnormal states of brain and mind.* Cambridge, MA: Birkhaeuser.

Hobson, R. P. (1991). What is autism? *Psychiatric Clinics of North America, 14*, 1–17.

Hornak, J., Rolls, E. T., & Wade, D. (1996). Face and voice expression identification in patients the emotional and behavioural changes following ventral frontal lobe damage. *Neuropsychologia, 34*, 247–261.

Keltner, D. (1995). The signs of appeasement: Evidence for the distinct displays of embarrassment, amusement, and shame. *Journal of Personality and Social Psychology, 68*, 441–454.

Keltner, D., & Buswell, B. (1996). Evidence for the distinctness of embarrassment, shame, and guilt: A study of recalled antecedents and facial expressions of emotion. *Cognition and Emotion, 10*, 155–172.

Keltner, D., & Buswell, B. N. (1997). Embarrassment: Its distinct form and appeasement functions. *Psychological Bulletin, 122*, 250–270.

Keltner, D., & Gross, J. J. (1999). Functional accounts of emotion. *Cognition and Emotion, 13*, 467–480.

Keltner, D., & Harker, L. A. (1998). The forms and functions of the nonverbal display of shame. In P. Gilbert & B. Andrews (Eds.), *Interpersonal approaches to shame* (pp. 78–98). Oxford, England: Oxford University Press.

Keltner, D., & Kring, A. M. (1998). Emotion, social function, and psychopathology. *Review of General Psychology, 2*, 320–342.

Keltner, D., Moffitt, T., & Stouthamer-Loeber, M. (1995). Facial expressions of emotion and psychopathology in adolescent boys. *Journal of Abnormal Psychology, 104*, 644–652.

Keltner, D., Young, R., & Buswell, B. N. (1997). Appeasement in human emotion, personality, and social practice. *Aggressive Behavior, 23*, 359–374.

Kihlstrom, J. F., & Cantor, N. (2000). Social intelligence. In R. J. Sternberg (Ed.), *Handbook of intelligence* (pp. 359–379). New York: Cambridge University Press.

Lazarus, R. S. (1991). *Emotion and adaptation.* New York: Oxford University Press.

Leary, M. R., & Meadows, S. (1991). Predictors, elicitors, and concomitants of social blushing. *Journal of Personality and Social Psychology, 60*, 254–262.

Lewis, M., Sullivan, M. W., Stanger, C., & Weiss, M. (1989). Self development and self-conscious emotions. *Child Development, 60*, 146–156.

Metts, S., & Cupach, W. R. (1989). Situational influence on the use of remedial strategies in embarrassing predicaments. *Communication Monographs, 56*, 151–162.

Miller, R. S. (1987). Empathic embarrassment: Situational and personal determinants of reactions to the embarrassment of another. *Journal of Personality and Social Psychology, 53*, 1061–1069.

Miller, R. S. (1992). The nature and severity of self-reported embarrassing circumstances. *Personality and Social Psychology Bulletin, 18*, 190–198.

Miller, R. S. (1995). On the nature of embarrassability: Shyness, social-evaluation, and social skill. *Journal of Personality, 63*, 315–339.

Miller, R. S. (1996). Embarrassment: *Poise and peril in everyday life.* New York: Guilford Press.

Miller, R. S., & Leary, M. R. (1992). Social sources and interactive functions of embarrassment. In M. Clark (Ed.), *Emotion and social behavior* (pp. 202–221). New York: Sage.

Miller, R. S., & Tangney, J. P. (1994). Differentiating embarrassment from shame. *Journal of Social and Clinical Psychology, 13*, 273–287.

Ozonoff, S., Rogers, S. J., & Pennington, B. F. (1991). Asperger's syndrome: Evidence of an empirical distinction from high-functioning autism. *Journal of Child Psychology & Psychiatry & Allied Disciplines, 32*, 1107–1122.

Parrott, W. G., & Smith, S. F. (1991). Embarrassment: Actual vs. typical cases and classical vs. prototypical representations. *Cognition and Emotion, 5*, 467–488.

Robins, R. W., & John, O. P. (1997). Self-perception, visual perspective, and narcissism: Is seeing believing? *Psychological Science, 7*.

Robins, R. W., John, O. P., Caspi, A., Moffitt, T. E., & Stouthamer-Loeber, M. (1996). Resilient, overcontrolled, and undercontrolled boys: Three replicable personality types. *Journal of Personality and Social Psychology, 70*, 157–171.

Rolls, E. T., Hornak, J., Wade, D., & McGrath, J. (1994). Emotion-related learning in patients with social and emotional changes associated with frontal lobe damage. *Journal of Neurology, Neurosurgery, and Psychiatry, 57*, 1518–1524.

Sattler, J. M. (1966). Embarrassment and blushing: A theoretical review. *Journal of Social Psychology, 69*, 117–133.

Schwarz, N. (1990). Feelings as information: Informational and motivational functions of affective states. In E. T. Higgins & R. M. Sorrentino (Eds.), *Handbook of motivation and cognition* (Vol. 2, pp. 527–561). New York: Guilford Press.

Sedikides, C., & Skowronski, J. J. (1997). The symbolic self in evolutionary context. *Personality and Social Psychology Review, 1*, 80–102.

Semin, G. R., & Manstead, A. S. R. (1982). The social implications of embarrassment displays and restitution behavior. *European Journal of Social Psychology, 12*, 367–377.

Sharkey, W. F. (1991). Intentional embarrassment: Goals, tactics, and consequences. In W. Cupach & S. Metts (Eds.), *Advances in interpersonal communication research* (pp. 105–128). Normal: Illinois State University.

Sharkey, W. F., & Stafford, L. (1990). Responses to embarrassment. *Human Communication Research, 17*, 315–342.

Shearn, D., Bergman, E., Hill, K., Abel, A., & Hinds L. (1990). Facial coloration and temperature responses in blushing. *Psychophysiology, 27*, 687–693.

Shearn, D., Bergman, E., Hill, K., Abel, A., & Hinds, L. (1992). Blushing as a function of audience size. *Psychophysiology, 29*, 431–436.

Shiota, M., Keltner, D., Campos, B., & Hertenstein, M. (in press). Positive emotion and the regulation of interpersonal relationships. In P. Phillipot and R. Feldman (Eds.), *Emotion regulation*. Hillsdale, NJ: Erlbaum.

Stone, V. E., Baron-Cohen, S., & Knight, R. T. (1998). Frontal lobe contributions to theory of mind. *Journal of Cognitive Neuroscience, 10*, 640–656.

Stuss, D. T., & Benson, D. F. (1984). Neuropsychological studies of the frontal lobes. *Psychological Bulletin, 95*, 3–28.

Tangney, J. P. (1990). Assessing individual differences in proneness to shame and guilt: Development of the self-conscious affect and attribution inventory. *Journal of Personality and Social Psychology, 59*, 102–111.

Tangney, J. P. (1991). Moral affect: The good, the bad, and the ugly. *Journal of Personality and Social Psychology, 61*, 598–607.

Tangney, J. P. (1992). Situational determinants of shame and guilt in young adulthood. *Personality and Social Psychology Bulletin, 18*, 199–206.

Tangney, J. P., & Fischer, K. W. (1995). *Self-conscious emotions: The psychology of shame, guilt, embarrassment, and pride*. New York: Guilford Press.

Tangney, J. P., Marschall, D., Rosenberg, K., Barlow, D. H., & Wagner, P. (1992). *Children's and adult's autobiographical accounts of shame, guilt, and pride experiences: A qualitative analysis of situational determinants and interpersonal concerns.* Manuscript submitted for publication.

Tangney, J. P., Miller, R. S., Flicker, L., & Barlow, D. H. (1996). Are shame, guilt, and embarrassment distinct emotions? *Journal of Personality and Social Psychology, 70,* 1256–1264.

Taylor, S. E., & Brown, J. D. (1988). Illusion and well-being: A social psychological perspective on mental health. *Psychological Bulletin, 103,* 193–210.

Vallacher, R. R., & Wegner, D. M. (1987). What do people think they're doing? Action identification and human behavior. *Psychological Review, 94,* 3–15.

Vohs, K. D., & Heatherton, T. F. (2000). Self-regulatory failure: A resource-depletion approach. *Psychological Science, 11,* 249–254.

10

On the Hidden Benefits of State Orientation: Can People Prosper Without Efficient Affect-Regulation Skills?

SANDER L. KOOLE, JULIUS KUHL,
NILS B. JOSTMANN, AND KATHLEEN D. VOHS

Personal mastery over one's emotional life is a highly valued psychological commodity. Hollywood films glorify men and women who manage to heroically overcome their worst fears and frustrations. Religious doctrines proclaim the importance of achieving inner peace amid worldly turmoil. On top of all this, an army of self-help books, TV shows, and Web sites advertise such virtues as positive thinking, self-efficacy, and emotional intelligence. Although popular claims about the benefits of affect regulation are probably exaggerated, empirical research has confirmed that efficient affect regulation is vital to several key aspects of human functioning (Gross, 2002; Kuhl & Koole, 2004). For instance, successful affect regulation has been found to foster emotional well-being (Baumann, Kaschel, & Kuhl, 2003a), positive interpersonal relations (Butler et al., 2003), and goal achievement (Kuhl, 1981). Based on these and similar findings, some authors have argued that affect-regulation skills may be even more important than IQ in terms of promoting beneficial outcomes for the individual and society at large (Goleman, 1995).

Despite the well-known benefits of efficient affect regulation, people are not always successful at keeping their feelings in check. Virtually everyone occasionally experiences feelings that are very difficult to control, such as a raging bout of anger, an immobilizing episode of depression, or overwhelming anxiety. However, some people are especially prone to become flooded by uncontrollable feelings (Kuhl, 1981; Kuhl & Beckmann, 1994a; Pyszczynski & Greenberg, 1987). The latter group may become virtually immobilized by their feelings of depression, anxiety, self-doubt, or other aversive emotions. Because own affective states seem to dominate the functioning of these individuals, we refer to them as *state-oriented* individuals (Kuhl, 1981). On the basis of people's self-reports, up to 50% of the "normal," nonnclinical population in Western countries may be predisposed toward state orientation (Koole, 2003; Kuhl, 1994). State orientation thus appears to be a very common psychological condition. The widespread prevalence of state orientation challenges prevailing notions about the importance of efficient affect regulation. Why do so many people regularly allow their feelings to go out of control? Does state orientation always signify maladaptive coping? Or is it conceivable that state orientation has some psychological advantages?

In the present chapter, we propose that state orientation, defined as the inability to exert volitional control over one's feelings,[1] has both psychological costs and benefits. Because of modern society's emphasis on personal efficacy and control, the benefits of state orientation are easily overlooked. Accordingly, our goal in this chapter is to present a theoretical analysis that identifies some of the trade-offs that are involved in state-oriented coping. In the next paragraphs, we begin by taking a closer look at the theory and research on state orientation. After that, we review some arguments for believing that state orientation can sometimes be adaptive and discuss potential ways in which state orientation may lead to favorable outcomes. Finally, we consider some of the broader implications of the hidden benefits of state orientation for the theoretical understanding of affect regulation and volitional action control.

THEORY OF ACTION VERSUS STATE ORIENTATION

The notion of state orientation was first introduced during the early 1980s in a series of studies that sought to integrate the literatures on achievement motivation and learned helplessness. In learned helplessness research, participants are first subjected to a series of uncontrollable failures on a training task after which their performance on a test task is measured. The usual finding is that uncontrollable failure during training leads to performance drops during the test task (e.g., Hiroto & Seligman, 1975; Maier & Seligman, 1976). Initially, these findings were taken to mean that causal attributions of uncontrollability induce low generalized expectations of success. On the basis of expectancy-value theories of motivation (Atkinson, 1957), generalized low expectations of success should lead to generalized motivation losses and, hence, low performance on the test task.

However, subsequent research challenged the viability of classic learned helplessness theory. In particular, research showed that uncontrollable failure reliably leads to reduced perceptions of controllability on the training task, but not on the test task (Kuhl, 1981). Despite the absence of learned helplessness effects on people's expectancies, uncontrollable failure readily induced performance drops on the test task. As such, behavioral learned helplessness effects occurred even when people's motivation to perform well had remained fully intact. According to Kuhl's action control theory (1981, 1984), this seemingly paradoxical phenomenon is due to people's tendency to ruminate about their own states after failure, a condition that was labeled as *state orientation*. The notion of state orientation was contrasted with *action orientation*, which was defined as a focus on task relevant cognitions. Because state-oriented ruminations deprive people of cognitive resources, state orientation may undermine performance during subsequent tasks. Consistent with this, state-oriented individuals were found to be disproportionately vulnerable to the performance-undermining effects of uncontrollable failure (Brunstein & Olbrich, 1985; Kuhl, 1981). By contrast, action-oriented individuals displayed hardly any evidence of learned helplessness effects.

Later research identified volitional affect regulation as the main underlying mechanism with respect to which action-oriented individuals differ from state-oriented individuals (Beckmann & Kuhl, 1984; Kuhl, 2000; Koole & Jostmann, in press). Action-oriented individuals are capable of self-regulating aversive affect in a highly efficient manner, which enables them to pursue their goals in a self-determined, unhesitating manner. By contrast, state-oriented individuals are unable to exert volitional control over aversive affect. *Personality systems interactions* (PSI) theory (Kuhl, 2000; Kuhl & Koole, 2004) spells out in more detail how affect regulation influences volitional action control. PSI theory assumes that volitional action depends on the well-coordinated interplay between self-regulatory functions. The coordination of these personality systems interactions is achieved through affective changes. That is, changes in positive or negative affect are assumed to channel the person's self-regulatory resources toward particular psychological systems. Affect regulation thus plays a vital role in the volitional regulation of action. The presumed connection between affect regulation and action control fits with everyday observations that strong-willed individuals are able to tolerate many frustrations and overcome many threats in order to achieve their goals.

PSI theory further distinguishes between coping with negative affect and coping with inhibited positive affect. Inhibited positive affect occurs when people are unable to obtain desired positive outcomes. For instance, an office worker might be forced to cancel a date with a romantic interest because his employer requires him to work overtime. PSI theory refers to inhibited positive affect as *frustration*. When positive affect becomes frustrated, people will become more inclined to engage in analytic problem-solving efforts and to formulate explicit plans in order to restore the flow of positive outcomes. For instance, the office worker from our example might resolve to buy concert tickets for his dating partner, in order to make things up to her. The psychological system that supports such planning is referred to as *intention memory*, which is defined as a system that maintains explicit intentions activated in working memory. PSI theory further assumes that intention memory operates in close collaboration with analytic thinking process.

Once intention memory has formulated an appropriate intention, the next issue becomes how to translate the intention into action. PSI theory assumes that the implementation of an intention is greatly facilitated by *intuitive behavior programs*, low-level action schemas that specify which concrete action steps are required to execute the intention. For instance, our well-intentioned office worker may need to remind himself to take enough cash with him the next day, to make an extra stop on the way to work to buy the tickets, to call up his date, and so on.

In order to access such intuitive behavior programs, PSI theory assumes that people need to restore the positive affect that became inhibited with the activation of intention memory (Kuhl & Kazén, 1999). Positive affect may be either restored externally (e.g., through pep talks or encouragement from others) or internally (e.g., by reminding oneself of the positive outcomes that can be obtained by taking action). On some occasions, however, there might be a lack of pep talks or encouragement, and people may be unable to self-generate positive affect. PSI theory postulates that positive affect serves to energize intuitive behavior programs. Thus, when positive affect is chronically low, individuals will have trouble engaging the behavior programs that are required to execute their intentions. Paradoxically, this lack of behavioral initiative may occur even when the individual's intention is highly accessible on a cognitive level. This first form of state orientation is hence called *hesitation*.

Increases in negative affect arise when individuals are exposed to threatening or unexpected events. For instance, the hardworking office worker in our example is likely to experience negative affect if his boss threatens to fire him if he refuses to work overtime. PSI theory argues that people find it increasingly difficult to follow their own emotional preferences and intuitions when negative affect is raised. This is because high levels of negative affect lead to inhibition of *extension memory*. Extension memory is a central executive system that operates according to parallel processing principles (Nowak, Vallacher, Tesser, & Borkowski, 2000). Because extension memory is a parallel processing system, it is capable of integrating many self-representations, emotional preferences, and autobiographical knowledge into a coherent course of action (Baumann & Kuhl, 2002). The functional basis for extension memory is provided by prefrontal networks in the brain's right hemisphere. The organization of the right hemisphere is much like a global network that integrates information from a vast variety of input systems; as such, it is ideally suited for integrative information processing (Beeman et al., 1994). The cognitive structures of extension memory are too extended to be completely accessible to conscious experience. Nevertheless, extension memory activation has some experiential correlates, which include feelings of freedom (Yalom, 1980), mastery (Dweck, 1986), and self-determination (Deci & Ryan, 2000).

As long as individuals maintain access to extension memory, they have an intuitive sense of what they want, what is most meaningful to them, and why they do the things they do. For instance, our troubled office worker might sense intuitively that his date is more important to him than his low-paying job and therefore tell his boss that he refuses to work overtime on this particular evening. Conversely, individuals who lose access to extension memory will be inclined to experience feelings of alienation, internal conflict, and disorientation. In this case, our office worker might feel compelled to comply with his boss and work overtime, ruminating all the while on the conflict this will create with his dating partner. According to PSI theory, individuals who cannot down-regulate negative affect are likely to experience inhibited access to extension memory. This second form of state orientation is called *preoccupation*, because it is typically accompanied by negative ruminations and inner conflict. When people cannot intuitively sense what they want, they are incapable of the timely detection and prevention of unwanted thoughts and experiences.

INDIVIDUAL DIFFERENCES IN ACTION VERSUS STATE ORIENTATION

People's action versus state orientation may vary from situation to situation or as a function of more stable individual differences. Under extreme stress, almost everyone is bound to become state oriented. This is because extreme amounts of stress may exceed even the affect-regulation capacity of chronically action-oriented individuals. Under more moderate conditions, however, individual differences in action versus state orientation are likely to emerge. Because chronic state orientation provides the greatest puzzle to affect-regulation theories, the present chapter focuses mainly on individual differences in state orientation. Kuhl (1981, 1994) and colleagues have developed a self-report instrument to measure individual differences in action versus state orientation, the Action Control Scale (ACS90). Illustrative items of the ACS90 are presented in Table 10.1.

In line with PSI theory, the ACS90 distinguishes between *preoccupation*, which relates to coping with high negative affect, and *hesitation*, which relates to coping with inhibited positive affect. Each item of the ACS90 presents individuals

TABLE 10.1. Illustrative Items of the Action Control Scale–90 (Kuhl, 1994)

Preoccupation (Threat-Related Action Orientation)
When I have lost something that is very valuable to me and I can't find it anywhere:
    A. I have a hard time concentrating on anything else.
    B. I put it out of my mind after a little while.[a]
If I've worked for weeks on a project and then everything goes completely wrong with the project:
    A. It takes me a long time to adjust myself to it.
    B. It bothers me for a while, but then I don't think about it anymore.[a]
When I am being told that my work is completely unsatisfactory:
    A. I don't let it bother me for too long.[a]
    B. I feel paralyzed.
Hesitation (Demand-Related Action Orientation)
When I know I must finish something soon:
    A. I have to push myself to get started.
    B. I find it easy to get it over and done with.[a]
When I am getting ready to tackle a difficult problem:
    A. It feels like I am facing a big mountain I don't think I can climb.
    B. I look for a way to approach the problem in a suitable manner.[a]
When I have a boring assignment:
    A. I usually don't have a problem getting through it.[a]
    B. I sometimes just can't get moving on it.

[a]Action-oriented responses.

with a description of a stressful situation and two different ways of responding to the situation, an action- or a state-oriented response. Individuals are asked to choose which response is most characteristic of them. The number of times that an individual chooses a state-oriented response is taken as an indicator of the individual's level of state orientation (alternatively, responses on the ACS90 are often coded in the action-oriented direction). Notably, the ACS90 does not ask participants to provide introspective judgments of their affect-regulation skills but asks participants to report on the consequences that these skills (or the lack thereof) have for their behavior. Accordingly, the ACS90 may also tap into affect-regulation mechanisms that are inaccessible to introspection but whose impact can nonetheless be observed in one's overt behavior.

Individual differences in action versus state orientation are fairly stable over time. For instance, a recent study among 56 Dutch undergraduates found a test–rest reliability of .78 for hesitation and .68 for preoccupation (both $ps < .001$) over a 6-month period (Jostmann, 2003). Research among German participants has found similar stabilities across periods from 3 to 12 months (Kuhl & Beckmann, 1994a). Moreover, state orientation appears to be a commonly occurring coping response. In a study of 1,357 Dutch university students, Koole (2003) found that 57.9% scored above the conceptual midpoint of the preoccupation scale, whereas 49.7% scored above the conceptual midpoint of the hesitation scale. Around half of this nonclinical sample could thus be characterized as predominantly state-oriented. Considering that action orientation is probably more socially desirable than state orientation in an independent culture such as the Netherlands, these self-reports might well underestimate the true prevalence of state orientation.

In line with PSI theory, preoccupation and hesitation have emerged as separate factors in factor-analytic studies (Diefendorff, Hall, Lord, & Strean, 2000; Kuhl, 1994) and have differential effects that are elicited by different manipulations (e.g., Koole, 2004). Unique effects of preoccupation have emerged in response to self-threatening conditions, such as repeated failure (Kuhl, 1981), physical pain (Kuhl, 1983), and mortality salience (Baumann & Kazén, 2003; Koole & Van den Berg, 2004). Unique effects of hesitation have emerged in response to demanding conditions, such as performance-contingent rewards (Koole, in press), time pressure (Stiensmeier-Pelster, 1994), and uncompleted intentions (Goschke & Kuhl, 1993). However, preoccupation and hesitation are often positively correlated and sometimes yield similar effects under similar circumstances. The empirical convergence between preoccupation and hesitation probably reflects the natural confounding between high negative and low positive affect, which are often triggered by identical conditions. Moreover, when socialization conditions involve high negative affect and low positive affect, a conditioned connection between preoccupation and hesitation may develop (e.g., when parents habitually respond to a child's anxiety with demands or to a child's frustration with fear-arousing communication). Because of this natural confounding and because preoccupation and hesitation both refer to affect-regulation skills, it is often meaningful to talk about state- and action-oriented individuals in general, irrespective of the more fine-grained distinction between preoccupation and hesitation.

To date, more than 40 published studies have found theoretically predicted effects of action versus state orientation (for reviews, see Diefendorff et al., 2000; Kuhl, in press; Kuhl & Beckmann, 1994a). Effects of action orientation have been obtained across a wide range of different measures and domains, including intention memory, physiological arousal, medicine intake, therapeutic outcomes, athletic performance, and work psychology. Moreover, the effects of action orientation are not due to achievement motivation (H. Heckhausen & Strang, 1988), self-esteem (Koole & Jostmann, in press), or emotional suppression and reappraisal strategies (Koole, 2004) and occur over and above the effects of the "Big Five" personality dimensions (Baumann & Kuhl, 2002; Diefendorff et al., 2000; Palfai, 2002).

Theoretically, the effects of action versus state orientation can be grouped into five categories. First, stress leads state-oriented individuals to experience perseverating negative affect and/or decreases in positive affect (Brunstein & Olbrich, 1985; Rholes, Michas, & Shroff, 1989). Second, stress interferes with the execution of complex tasks among state-oriented individuals (Kuhl, 1981; H. Heckhausen & Strang, 1988), even though state-oriented individuals (particularly those high on hesitation) are capable of maintaining complex intentions in working memory (Goschke & Kuhl, 1993). Third, stress disrupts complex forms of intuition (e.g., judging the coherence of complex stimuli) among state-oriented individuals, particularly those high in preoccupation (Baumann & Kuhl, 2002). Fourth, stress inhibits cognitive access to emotional preferences and implicit self-representations among state-oriented individuals (Baumann & Kuhl, 2003; Koole, 2004). Fifth, state-oriented individuals have an increased risk of developing psychological symptoms (Baumann, Kaschel, & Kuhl, 2003; Kuhl & Helle, 1986) and personality disorders (Baumann, Kaschel, & Kuhl, 2003b).

Across all the aforementioned domains, the disruptive effects of stress have been largely absent among action-oriented individuals. Indeed, action-oriented individuals frequently show enhanced functioning under stress (Jostmann & Koole, 2003; Koole & Jostmann, in press). Taken together, research indicates that state-oriented individuals are indeed less skilled affect regulators than are action-oriented individuals and that, as a result, state-oriented individuals experience various self-regulatory problems under stress.

IS STATE ORIENTATION SELF-DESTRUCTIVE?

So far our discussion has come up with little to suggest that state orientation can ever be adaptive. Even many state-oriented individuals themselves seem to question the merits of their habitual coping style, judging by the popularity of self-help books and therapies that aim to boost the efficiency of people's affect-regulation skills. Does it make sense, then, to be looking for possible benefits of state orientation? Isn't state orientation a purely self-destructive coping strategy?

In addressing these issues, it is noteworthy that state orientation appears to be malleable by personal experience. In particular, Kästele (1988) examined individual differences in extraversion, neuroticism, and state orientation among mono- and dizygotic twins. Replicating previous studies (Jang, Liveley, & Vernon, 1996), Kästele found that extraversion and neuroticism were more similar among monozygotic twins than among dizygotic twins. State orientation, however, was no more similar among monozygotic than among dizygotic twins. The genetic component in state orientation thus appears to be relatively modest. This conclusion fits with PSI theory, which argues that the development of state orientation is strongly influenced by socialization experiences (Kuhl, 2000, 2001). Specifically, PSI theory posits that responsiveness to an infant's emotional expressions will foster action orientation, whereas neglecting or even punishing these expressions will promote state orientation (Kuhl, 2000). Developmental research supports this line of reasoning (Keller & Gauda, 1987; Volling, McElwain, Notaro, & Herrera, 2002). Notably, the person's action versus state orientation may also change later in life, for instance, through therapy (Kaschel & Kuhl, 2004; Schulte, Hartung, & Wilke, 1997).

The malleability of state orientation provides a first indication that it may evolve as a psychological adaptation to the environment. A further indication is the common prevalence of state orientation. As already noted, around 50% of a sample of 1,357 Dutch university students had state orientation scores above the conceptual midpoint of the ACS90 (Koole, 2003). Moreover, merely 4.6% of the sample reported not a single state-oriented response on the hesitation subscale, and a mere 2.8% reported not a single state-oriented response on the preoccupation subscale. Thus, many individuals who are relatively action oriented still display state-oriented coping responses now and then. If state orientation is a purely self-defeating coping style, then this self-defeating tendency is remarkably widespread. Some years ago, Baumeister and Scher (1988) concluded that "normally functioning" individuals rarely engage in purely self-defeating behaviors. Indeed, most seemingly self-defeating behaviors were either not experienced as such by the individuals themselves, based on erroneous beliefs about the consequences of these behaviors, or involved some kind of trade-off between costs and benefits. It seems worthwhile to see to what degree these three explanations are applicable to state orientation.

First, state-oriented individuals might interpret their coping behavior much differently than do outside observers. An analogy may be drawn here with masochism. Masochistic individuals engage in a variety of painful and self-degrading actions. These actions, however, apparently provide a sense of deep satisfaction to the masochists themselves (Baumeister, 1991). To the masochist, therefore, masochism is anything but self-defeating. Is state orientation like masochism, painful to behold but gratifying from within? The evidence suggests something else. As already noted, state-oriented individuals typically report lower levels of positive affect and higher levels of negative affect than action-oriented individuals. This affective contrast becomes even further enhanced under stressful circumstances (Rholes et al., 1989). Importantly, these self-reports are backed by evidence from implicit measures (Koole & Jostmann, in press) and physiological responses (H. Heckhausen & Strang, 1988; Rosahl, Tennigkeit, Kuhl, & Haschke, 1993). Overall, it seems fair to say that state-oriented individuals are as much bothered by their affect-regulation difficulties as an outside observer might suspect.

Misinformation is another common cause of self-defeating behavior (Baumeister & Scher, 1988). Thus, state-oriented individuals might engage in maladaptive coping practices because they espouse erroneous beliefs about the coping process. One possibility is that state-oriented individuals have somehow remained oblivious to the benefits of efficient affect regulation. This seems rather unlikely, however, as the advantages of affect regulation are widely acclaimed and publicized throughout society. Alternatively, state-oriented individuals might mistakenly believe that they are unable to control their feelings and, consequently, give up prematurely on regulating their feelings. However, this account is contradicted by evidence that state-oriented individuals often frantically try to control their feelings when they are besieged by negative affect (Brunstein & Olbrich, 1985; Kuhl, 1981). Moreover, state orientation is moderately positively correlated with chronic tendencies toward emotion suppression (Koole, in press). Although emotion suppression tends to be an ineffective strategy (Gross & John, 2003), this finding suggests that many state-oriented individuals are actively trying to control their feelings. The available evidence therefore indicates that state-oriented individuals are not simply misinformed about the inefficiency of their affect-regulation practices. Rather, it appears that state-oriented individuals are lacking in some of the basic skills that are necessary to get a grip on their feelings.

If the trouble with state orientation does not arise from state-oriented individuals' perverted tastes or misinformed beliefs, then perhaps state orientation involves some kind of trade-off. The costs of having inefficient affect-regulation skills have by now become fairly obvious. But what about the benefits of inefficient affect-regulation skills? From the present perspective, we can distinguish at least three ways in which state orientation may be beneficial. First, the functional deficits of state orientation emerge primarily under acute stress. When external conditions are pleasant and supportive, then state-oriented individuals may be able to function quite well and even outperform their action-oriented counterparts. Second, the lack of self-regulation that the state oriented display under stress might have certain functional benefits. In particular, the tendency toward hesitation may prevent state-oriented individuals from engaging in premature action, whereas preoccupation with negative ruminations might sensitize state-oriented individuals to potential threats. Finally, even when state orientation does not directly benefit the individual, it might have some important benefits to the social environment. In the following sections, we explore these three potential benefits of state orientation—benefits through external support, benefits from not regulating the self, and social benefits—in more detail.

BENEFITS THROUGH EXTERNAL SUPPORT

As the Beatles observed some time ago, a little help from one's friends can make it much easier to get by in life. Partners, friends, and other sympathetic individuals can help us in a variety of ways, which range from simply keeping us company to listening to our grievances or giving a big hug. Research indicates that social support is remarkably effective in alleviating acute stress, both at psychological and physiological levels (Mikulincer & Florian, 2002; Uchino, Cacioppo, & Kiecolt-Glaser, 1996). Accordingly, affective support from close others may help state-oriented individuals to do well even without the ability to self-regulate their own affective states.

Because state-oriented individuals have much to gain from external support, they may be especially open to relationships with supportive others. Indeed, a recent study found that state-oriented individuals have a greater preference for *symbiotic* relationships—ones in which one partner helps and supports the other partner in overcoming his or her personal problems and frustrations—than do action-oriented individuals (Gunsch, 1996). Symbiotic relationships offer major advantages to state-oriented individuals, because such relationships may function as "niches" (Tesser, 2001) in which state-oriented individuals can obtain the emotional comfort that they are unable to attain by themselves. Thus, it seems particularly adaptive for state-oriented individuals to be on the lookout for symbiotic relationships.

Action-oriented individuals can probably do without symbiotic relationships, because they can rely on their own affect-regulation resources. Nevertheless, state-oriented individuals may benefit action-oriented partners in certain ways. For example, state-oriented individuals' sensitivity to potential risks may counteract the action-oriented partners' tendency toward excessive optimism. State-oriented individuals' sensitivity to their own and others' feelings may help to remedy the emotional insensitivity that sometimes characterizes very active people. Finally, state-oriented individuals' willingness to give in may form a good basis for relationships with rather self-assertive partners. Symbiotic relationships are by definition desired for instrumental reasons—for instance, the way one is always cheered up by the other's sunny disposition. Reasons that are more intrinsic to the relationship (i.e., another's unique personality) are typically less important to a symbiotic relationship.

As a consequence, symbiotic relationships might not always have the same quality as more authentic relationships (Schülein, 1989). However, more optimistic scenarios are also feasible. For instance, a symbiotic relationship might deepen when the person feels secure enough to engage in a more personal interchange.

In independent cultures that emphasize self-reliance, symbiotic relationships may be typecast as being overly dependent or exploitative. By contrast, interdependent cultures that emphasize mutual dependence may be more open to the positive sides of affective dependency (Markus & Kitayama, 1998). In interdependent cultures, emotional autonomy may be regarded as an egocentric attempt to separate oneself from the rest of the social community, whereas emotional dependency may be regarded as a sign of being connected with the social network. Moreover, an action-oriented individual's inability to accept and express states of helplessness or weakness can be disadvantageous even in independent cultures: A compulsive inclination to pretend to be strong, cool, and independent can hinder a person from receiving support from others when in need. In addition, open expression of helplessness and weakness may be a necessary condition for motivating social partners to provide the responsiveness that fosters the development of affect-regulatory skills in the long run (Kuhl, 2000).[2] Empirical findings confirm this expectation: Mothers who tried to cope with the their infants' death showed fewer depressive symptoms 18 months later when they went through a period of state-oriented rumination, provided they lived in unconstrained social relationships (Lepore, Silver, Wortman, & Wayment, 1996). Presumably, expressing one's sad state of mind signals to others that emotional support is needed and keeps them from expecting too much performance too early in the coping process (Herrmann & Wortman, 1985).

Beyond the long-term maintenance of social relations, state-oriented individuals may also seize more readily on affective support on a moment-to-moment basis. This mechanism was recently tested by Koole and Jostmann (in press, Study 1). In this study, action-and state-oriented participants were exposed to performance-contingent or noncontingent rewards. Based on previous research, noncontingent rewards were expected to create a tension-free atmosphere whereas contingent rewards were expected to create a tense atmosphere (Ryan, Mims, & Koestner, 1983). Before and after the visualization, participants reported on their moods. To the extent that state-oriented individuals are eager to "seize" on the cognitive accessibility of a supportive environment, they should display considerable mood improvements in a tension-free context, perhaps even more than action-oriented individuals.

The predicted pattern was indeed obtained by Koole and Jostmann (in press). Upon receiving noncontingent rewards, state-oriented participants displayed reliable decreases in tension, which endured at least 10 min after the visualization. By contrast, action-oriented participants displayed no mood improvements after visualizing an accepting relationship. A very different pattern emerged when participants received performance-contingent rewards: Here, action-oriented participants displayed strong decreases in tension, whereas state-oriented participants displayed nonsignificant increase in tension.

In sum, state-oriented individuals seem more prepared to "seize" on positive affect that is generated by a supportive context than action-oriented individuals, who mainly seem to regualte their moods in a demanding context.

Affective support may also facilitate performance among state-oriented individuals in other self-regulation domains unrelated to mood. For instance, Baumann and Kuhl (2003) found that a positive mood manipulation caused state-oriented individuals to have fewer confusions between tasks that were assigned versus self-chosen. Accordingly, affective support may help state-oriented individuals to maintain cognitive access to their authentic self.

Another recent study examined the effects of action versus state orientation on implicit self-evaluation (Koole, 2004). In this study, action-and state-oriented participants were asked to visualize either a relationship partner who was highly accepting of them or a partner who was very critical and demanding of them. Based on previous research, this manipulation was expected to trigger habitual relationship patterns among the participants (Baldwin & Sinclair, 1996). To assess implicit self-evaluation, the study used a validated reaction time measure (Hetts, Sakuma, & Pelham, 1999). As can be seen in Figure 10.1, state-oriented individuals

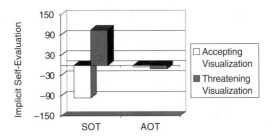

FIGURE 10.1. Implicit self-evaluations related to loss of autonomy as a function of visualization and threat-related action orientation (Koole, 2004). During the experimental task, participants evaluated positive and negative target words that were preceded by self-related primes (the word *I*) or neutral primes (*xx*). Implicit self-evaluations were computed by subtracting evaluation latencies to self-primed targets from evaluation latencies to neutral-primed targets. Latencies were coded such that higher numbers indicate greater activation of implicit evaluations of the self as weak and dependent. SOT = threat-related state orientation; AOT = threat-related action orientation.

activated implicit evaluations of the self as weak and dependent after a threat-related visualization, an effect that was not observed among action-oriented individuals. By contrast, state-oriented individuals inhibited implicit evaluations of the self as weak and dependent after an accepting visualization, an effect that was not displayed by action-oriented individuals. Thus, affective support enabled state-oriented individuals to ward off implicit feelings of self-doubt to a greater degree than action-oriented individuals.

According to PSI theory, affective support facilitates self-regulation because it permits individuals to access self-regulatory systems that otherwise become inhibited by aversive affect. Based on this logic, it may also be possible for the environment to activate relevant self-regulatory systems directly, without the mediation of the affective systems. For instance, preoccupation is characterized by inhibition of extension memory (i.e., high-level intuitions) and its associated implicit self-representations due to persistent negative affect. This inhibition may be overcome either by removing negative affect or by directly priming extension memory. In line with this notion, Kuhl and Beckmann (1994b) found that the alienating effects of a monotonous task disappeared among state-oriented individuals when these individuals were provided with a meaningful interpretation of a rather monotonous task (monitoring a visual display that was explained to be important for controllers in a nuclear power plant). Presumably, experiencing a task as meaningful prevented alienation because it encouraged state-oriented individuals to activate their self-system (i.e., extension memory). Access to extension memory may even be secured through nonconscious means. Koole and Coenen (2003) found that state-oriented individuals who were subliminally primed with self-related words remained creative after performing a boring task, whereas state-oriented individuals who were subliminally primed with a neutral word became less creative after performing a boring task (action-oriented individuals were creative regardless of experimental condition). Taken together, the environment may facilitate state-oriented individuals either through affective support or by directly priming self-regulatory systems that have become inaccessible to state-oriented individuals.

BENEFITS FROM NOT REGULATING THE SELF

External support can help state-oriented individuals to resolve many of their self-regulatory problems. However, external support is not always available to everyone who needs it. Consequently, it seems inevitable that state-oriented individuals will at some point encounter stress without the backup of an external support system. Thus vulnerable and exposed, state-oriented individuals are bound to undergo the various phenomena that have been identified by previous research: persistent negative affect, uncontrollable ruminations, decreased performance at complex tasks, alienation, internal conflict, incoherent experience, reduced creativity, loss of autonomy, and so on. This side of state orientation at first glance seems anything but adaptive. However, before jumping to conclusions, let's consider why state orientation has these kinds of effects.

Under stress, state-oriented individuals go through a very diverse list of symptoms. It seems quite challenging to relate this whole list to a single underlying mechanism. Still, we argue that state-oriented coping mechanisms hang together for a reason. When state-oriented individuals are besieged by acute stress, central executive processes appear to become dissociated from lower level processes. Consequently, high-level goals and intentions can no longer guide the person's movements, leading to hesitation-related phenomena such as performance decreases and failure to enact one's goals. In a similar vein, high-level cognitive networks concerning self-knowledge and emotional preferences can no longer become integrated with new experiences, leading to preoccupation-related phenomena such as rumination and alienation.

Stress thus causes state-oriented individuals to switch from a *top–down* mode of action control, in which high-level systems guide and direct the low-level processes that mediate the person's behavior, toward a *bottom–up* mode of action control, in which low-level processes determine behavior with little supervision of high-level systems.[3] This movement from top–down toward bottom–up action control can be understood as a psychological *regression* (Kuhl, 2001), during which more primitive or elementary behavior control systems take precedence over more sophisticated forms of action control. Because top–down action control is involved in the coordination of the complete range of a person's self-regulatory mechanisms, movement toward lower levels of action control can be expected to have diverse effects across many different subsystems. Regression may thus be the underlying theoretical mechanism that connects the remarkably diverse effects of action versus state orientation.

One of the first psychologists to recognize the importance of regression as a coping mechanism was Freud (1938/1989), who observed that some of his clients seemed to fall back on infantile behavior patterns. Freud found that, consistent with the link between regression and (failed) affect regulation, regressive behaviors occurred especially when his clients were undergoing painful experiences. He linked regression to his developmental model (of oral, anal, and genital stages, etc.) and considered regression as essentially a maladaptive form of coping.

Our perspective on regression departs from the Freudian conception in several important aspects. First, we hold that regression may include any movement from higher, more sophisticated levels toward lower, more elementary levels of action control. For instance, regression might cause a person to switch from intentional action control toward well-practiced behavioral routines that were learned during adulthood rather than childhood. This view is more consistent with Janet's (1903) original concept of *psychasthenia* than with Freud's developmental interpretation of regression. Janet defined psychasthenia as a loss of high-level processing—that is, as an impairment of "mental synthesis," a concept that anticipated modern concepts of coherence-producing functions (Bolte, Goschke, & Kuhl, 2003; Kasser & Sheldon, 1995).

Another distinctive feature of our concept of regression is that the reduction of top–down control need not always be maladaptive. First, compared with high-level action control, low-level action control entails lesser demands on energy resources (Vohs & Baumeister, 2004) and requires less attention (Gilbert, Pelham, & Krull, 1988) and less coordination among different subsystems (Kuhl, 2001). Low-level action control can thus be maintained under extremely challenging conditions, long after high-level action control systems have already collapsed. Moreover, low-level action control can usually be implemented more quickly than can high-level action control. Even the most efficient forms of high-level action control may take at least a few seconds to become translated into behavior (Koole & Jostmann, in press; Rosahl et al., 1993). By contrast, low-level action control may permit people to act within a fraction of a second (Libet, 1985). A classic example of the differential efficiency of high- and low-level action control can be found in the attribution literature (Gilbert et al., 1998). People can make person attributions very rapidly and automatically, whereas taking the situations into account involves more effortful and time-consuming cognitive processing. Under acutely threatening circumstances, making only automatic person attributions could save precious time and resources and thus be vital to survival.

Second, regression can be advantageous in environments that are completely unpredictable and erratic (Kuhl & Beckmann, 1994a). High-level forms of action control are typically based on complex rules or regularities that are extracted from the environment. Whenever such regularities do not exist or are no longer valid, high-level action control will be unable to produce any benefits over low-level action control. When goals or desires turn out to be unrealistic, for example, state orientation may be necessary in order to disengage from those goals and incentives (J. Heckhausen & Schulz, 1995; Klinger, 1975).

Finally, prolonged phases of regression may be the motor for personal development and deeper forms of learning (Kuhl, 2001; McClelland, McNaughton, & O'Reilly, 1995) because profound self-development requires self-revision ("accommodation") rather than chronic self-assertiveness in terms of applying existing self-knowledge ("assimilation"). To be able to revise self-schemas, one has to be able to inhibit existing ones, which is tantamount to our definition of regression. This notion is consistent with classic psychodynamic ideas (Jung, 1936) and empirical findings suggesting that personality styles or types associated with an increased tolerance for negative affect (e.g., introversion, neuroticism, and state orientation) are characterized by a strong desire for promoting self-development, a striving for personal truthfulness, and a search for deeper meaning in life (Biebrich & Kuhl, 2002). Drawing from Christian and Eastern religions, Schopenhauer (1818/1995) described the *negation of will* as a prerequisite for overcoming cognitive bias, the cause of distorted perception of the world and of oneself. According to Schopenhauer's philosophy of will, mature individuals always have a touch of resignation and depression. Empirical research confirms the claim inherent in this fundamental criticism of human volition. Willful action requires biased processing such as attentional neglect of goal-irrelevant information (Beckmann & Kuhl, 1984; Harmon-Jones & Harmon-Jones, 2002). As a result, overreliance on top–down volitional control may undermine the development of an unbiased perception of oneself and of the world.

Hesitation and preoccupation, the two most studied forms of state orientation, can be seen as two specific forms of regression. Hesitation effectively prevents high-level intentions from influencing the person's behavior, so that behavior control is only possible through lower level systems such as habits or routines. As a form of regression, hesitation may be adaptive when planful action is unlikely to produce positive outcomes. For instance, when the environment is very complex or unpredictable, it may be better to "sit still" and wait before one engages in a risky course of action. Research has indeed shown that, relative to action-oriented individuals, state-oriented individuals (especially of the hesitation type) take more time to deliberate on decision problems (Niederberger, Engemann, & Radtke, 1987; Stiensmeier-Pelster, 1994).

Notably, this difference in decision time emerges especially when the decision problems are relatively inconsequential. For more consequential decisions, action-oriented individuals increase their decision times to the level of state-oriented individuals. State-oriented individuals are thus inclined to devote much attention to their decisions, regardless of the consequences that are attached to these decisions. This pattern could be adaptive in dangerous environments where even decisions that seem relatively minor could turn out to have detrimental consequences later on. Their willingness to keep an open mind about things (and themselves) can make state-oriented individuals more objective information processors than action-oriented individuals. Indeed, research has shown that state-oriented individuals—unlike their action-oriented counterparts—do not become more inclined to devalue rejected alternatives (Beckmann & Kuhl, 1984) and remain less certain about a decision (Stiensmeier-Pelster, 1994), even after they have made the decision.

State-oriented individuals of the preoccupation-type are unable to inhibit intrusive thoughts and negative ruminations. In terms of our regression account, preoccupation appears to prevent high-level cognitive representations (i.e., extension memory) from controlling the person's experience, such that experience comes under the control of low-level cognitive systems that are highly sensitive to incongruencies and negative affect. Research has indeed shown that the ruminations of state-oriented individuals (particularly those of the preoccupation type) typically involve either low-level features of an uncompleted task (Baumann & Kuhl, 2003) or negative self-reflective thoughts (Brunstein & Olbrich, 1985). A study by Beckmann (1989) found further that state-oriented individuals who had been deprived of an expected reward (a condition that presumably induces stress) subsequently displayed better performance on a simple perceptual task (i.e., recognizing tachistoscopically presented words). Preoccupation thus goes hand in hand with facilitation of low-level perception, consistent with our regression account.

As a form of regression, preoccupation may be adaptive when high-level representations of one's past experiences cannot be used to deal with new events. For instance, when one encounters a very dangerous situation that has not been encountered before, one is probably well-advised to screen the situation for new information without assigning too much priority to the high-level overview of one's inner needs, motives, and other high-level concerns. The facilitation of low-level perceptual processing displayed by state-oriented individuals should be highly adaptive under this kind of circumstance because it facilitates selective attention to the most relevant information.

SOCIAL BENEFITS

We have now identified some potential benefits of state orientation from the perspective of the state-oriented person him- or herself. Yet state-oriented individuals do not operate in a vacuum. As we saw earlier, social relationships appear to play an important role in shaping individuals' predisposition toward state orientation (Kuhl, 2000). In addition, the self-regulatory benefits that state-oriented individuals may derive through symbiotic relationships point to the relevance of state orientation to interpersonal interaction. Any complete understanding of the costs and benefits of state orientation must therefore consider how a person's state orientation interacts with the interests of the social environment.

Because of our culture's emphasis on self-reliance and personal autonomy, society may often react negatively to state-oriented individuals. Indeed, a recent study showed that managers in the workplace give lower evaluations of state-oriented workers of the hesitation type (Diefendorff et al., 2000). Conceivably, managers may react negatively to the volitional inefficiency and indecisiveness that accompany hesitation. This interpretation is bolstered by findings that state orientation (in interaction with other personality styles) was associated with lower sales performance among the managers of a large insurance company (Kuhl & Kazén, 2003). In a related vein, people may become exasperated by the ceaseless ruminations and anxieties that characterize the preoccupation type of state orientation. Consistent with this, research indicates that students with chronic depression (who are likely to be high in preoccupation; Kuhl & Helle, 1986) receive more negative evaluations from their roommates (Swann, Wenzlaff, Krull, & Pelham, 1992).

Even though state-oriented individuals may not be particularly popular, society may still have something to gain from them. One striking quality of state-oriented individuals is their ability to follow external directives, even when this is at the expense of their own personal needs (Kuhl & Kazén, 1994). This remarkable talent for self-denial is presumably based on the inhibition of high-level self-representations (i.e., extension memory) that characterizes state-oriented individuals (especially under acute stress). High-level self-representations contain information about one's own emotional preferences and autobiographical experiences. Consequently, inhibition of the self renders state-oriented individuals extremely sensitive to social demands and expectations. Indeed, research has shown that state-oriented individuals are more prone toward conformity in the classic Asch paradigm relative to action-oriented individuals (Beckmann, 1997). Moreover, state-oriented individuals identify with others' demands to such a degree that they become prone to mistake external directives for self-chosen goals (Baumann & Kuhl, 2003; Kuhl & Kazén, 1994). Ironically, this "self-infiltration effect" becomes especially strong when the externally suggested goals run counter to state-oriented individuals' own emotional preferences (Kazén, Baumann, & Kuhl, 2003). This is presumably because disliked goals are more prone to trigger negative affect, which further undermines the ability of state-oriented individuals to access their true emotional preferences.

State-oriented individuals' inclination to conform with social pressures leads these individuals to embark on activities that bring them no genuine emotional satisfaction (Kazén et al., 2003), at least in the short run. Nevertheless, the social environment is likely to benefit from the conformity of state-oriented individuals. For instance, a manager might get his or her state-oriented office workers to work long hours of overtime, even when this means that these workers will neglect their social lives. As long as the behavior in question does not require sophisticated self-regulation skills, the self-inhibition that accompanies self-infiltration should not lead to decreases in performance. Indeed, strong identification with unpleasant activities may motivate state-oriented individuals to invest more effort in the activities than would action-oriented individuals. This prediction was recently tested by Koole and Jostmann (in press). In this study, participants were first required to perform some basic arithmetic sums, a task that pretests had revealed to be simple but rather boring. One half of the participants could earn a few Euros extra by performing better on a second set of similar arithmetic sums. Presumably, this manipulation created some pressure toward self-infiltration of the arithmetic task. The remaining participants received an extra few Euros, allegedly because they had performed exceptionally well compared with other participants during the first set of sums. The latter manipulation simply affirmed participants' ability to do well on the task.

After the reward-contingency manipulation, all participants were asked to perform a second set of arithmetic sums. Participants' performance on these sums is displayed in Figure 10.2. In the noncontingent reward condition, state-oriented participants were outperformed by action-oriented participants. Conceivably, the noncontingent reward manipulation led to an increase in achievement motivation among action-oriented individuals, because this manipulation emphasized

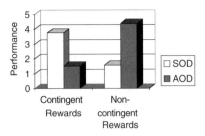

FIGURE 10.2. Arithmetic performance as a function of performance contingency and demand-related action orientation (Koole & Jostmann, in press). As a means of controlling for individual differences in arithmetic ability, arithmetic performance during a pretest was subtracted from the test performance. SOD = demand-related state orientation; AOD = demand-related action orientation.

participants' ability to do well in the task and contained no explicit pressure to perform well. By contrast, in the performance-contingent reward condition, state-oriented participants outperformed action-oriented individuals. This positive side of state orientation may be regarded as a specific form of *frustration tolerance*: State-oriented individuals seem to be good at unattractive tasks that are externally assigned to them and require a lot of self-discipline. They can thus be persistent and successful at tasks or activities that cannot be made "attractive," even by the most creative self-motivational efforts. Indeed, state-oriented individuals' ability to stick with unattractive tasks can even become undermined by rewarding procedures (Fuhrmann & Kuhl, 1998). At any rate, the Koole and Jostmann (in press) findings indicate that performance pressures may sometimes induce state-oriented individuals to outperform action-oriented individuals. Theoretically, this effect should occur under the same conditions as the self-infiltration effect (Kuhl & Kazén, 1994)—that is, for unattractive activities and under stress. An additional requirement is probably that the performance should be relatively simple, so that it does not call on high-level self-regulation.

State-oriented individuals' conformity with social pressures may constitute an important building block of modern society, which frequently requires its members to engage in monotonous and intrinsically unattractive activities (Martin, 1999). However, state orientation may have further social benefits. More specifically, important benefits may arise from the complementarity between action- and state-oriented members of social groups. As we have seen throughout this chapter, action- and state-oriented individuals possess very different strengths and weaknesses. Accordingly, the two types may jointly accomplish more than each would accomplish on their own. For instance, action-oriented individuals may provide emotional support to state-oriented individuals when state-oriented individuals are under acute stress and unable to calm themselves down. In turn, state-oriented individuals may contribute their sensitivity for potential risks (as a remedy against excessive optimism), their sensitivity for their own and others' feelings (as a remedy against the emotional insensitivity that sometimes characterizes very active people), or their willingness to give in to their more self-assertive group members.

Initial support for the complementary nature of action and state orientation has been obtained among airline crews consisting of an action-oriented pilot and a state-oriented copilot, which were found to be more effective than fully action-oriented or state-oriented crews (Haschke & Kuhl, 1995). Similar mutually beneficial exchanges may be an important vehicle for social and cultural advancement (Baumeister, 2005).

SUMMARY AND CONCLUSIONS

Contemporary society and psychological research have jointly emphasized the vital importance of possessing efficient affect-regulation skills (Goleman, 1995; Gross, 2002; Kuhl & Koole, 2004). Even so, many individuals continue to have a hard time in controlling their own affective states (Kuhl & Beckmann, 1994a; Martin & Tesser, 1996). These "state-oriented" individuals are at increased risk for developing functional deficits under stress, including drops in complex cognitive performance, alienation from the self and their own emotional preferences, impaired ability to execute intended actions, and even psychological disorders. At the same time, state orientation is highly prevalent, as around half of the individuals within nonclinical populations profess to have a state-oriented coping style. In view of the widespread prevalence of state orientation, we raised some important questions about the adaptive significance of state orientation. Is state orientation always maladaptive? Or might there exist some hidden benefits of state orientation?

Our analysis suggests at least three ways in which state orientation can be adaptive. First, external support may help state-oriented individuals to remain free from stress and thus to avoid the self-regulatory problems that state-oriented individuals tend to experience under acute stress. Indeed, state-oriented individuals may outperform action-oriented individuals under supportive conditions, even at complex tasks (Menec, 1995). Second, state orientation can have certain advatantages under acute stress. In very dangerous and unpredictable environments, high-level action control systems may not be useful, because high-level systems are predicated on the existence of (complex) regularities in the environment. Under conditions of low controllability, state orientation may be adaptive because it leads to the channeling of energy resources toward lower level control systems (i.e., through self-regulatory regression). More specifically, preoccupation-type state orientation may help to keep an individual's attention focused on a potential threat rather than downplaying actual threats and risks to maintain an inappropriate form of action control. Hesitation-type state orientation may prevent the individual from engaging in premature action. Third, state orientation can have important benefits within the broader context of interpersonal relationships. State orientation may foster conformity and even identification with social demands that run counter to the state-oriented person's own emotional preferences. Moreover, state-oriented individuals may complement action-oriented individuals in important ways, so that groups or dyadic relationships can function better when they incorporate both kinds of individuals.

Although the present chapter has emphasized the potential benefits of state orientation, we certainly do not mean to argue that state orientation is always superior to action orientation. Rather, we believe that the choice between a state- versus action-oriented way of coping involves a trade-off among various costs and benefits. We thus do not dispute that state orientation frequently has important disadvantages (Kuhl & Beckmann, 1994a; Kuhl & Koole, 2004). However, we also find that state orientation is not purely self-destructive, given that the functional costs of state orientation can be offset by potential benefits. State orientation thus seems similar to other apparently self-destructive behaviors that upon closer inspection involve a trade-off between psychological costs and benefits (Baumeister & Scher, 1988). Notably, our notion of trade-off does not imply a conscious decision on the part of the individual to be either state- or action-oriented. Rather, we assume that the predisposition toward state- or action-orientation becomes established across multiple coping experiences, beginning during infancy (Kuhl, 2000). The "decision" to cope with life events in a state- or action-oriented manner may thus develop unconsciously and over an extended period of time. At the same time, personal predispositions may maintain some level of flexibility, as action versus state orientation can be changed in adults through directed therapy (Kaschel & Kuhl, 2004; Schulte et al., 1997).

The notion that state orientation involves a trade-off between costs and benefits is important for both theoretical and practical reasons. Theoretically, our understanding of affect-regulation processes remains incomplete as long as our understanding of why individuals fail to develop efficient affect-regulation skills remains obscure. Simply assuming that inefficient affect regulation is always maladaptive may thus stand in the way of a true understanding of the psychology of affect regulation. An analogy may be drawn here with the study of self-esteem, which was initially hailed by psychologists as an antidote to virtually all imaginable personal and societal problems. This overly optimistic view was corrected only after the sobering results of some 20,000 subsequent studies became known (Baumeister, Campbell, Krueger, & Vohs, 2003). Given that affect regulation is nowadays advertised as the hallmark of emotional intelligence (Goleman, 1995), affect-regulation researchers might similarly become tempted to simply take the merits of their favorite psychological construct at face value. We therefore encourage affect-regulation researchers to take an open-minded approach to the question of whether strong affect-regulation skills are always beneficial.

Keeping an open mind to the possible benefits of state orientation seems equally important for practical purposes. The (implicit or explicit) goal of many therapies is to increase the efficiency of affect-regulation skills and, thus, to make people more action-oriented (Schulte et al., 1997). Because of this orientation, it may be easy for therapists to overlook the benefits that people may obtain from being state oriented and to overlook the fact that not every state-oriented person develops psychological symptoms. The social functions of state orientation seem equally relevant to the therapeutic process. For instance, the social environment may often gain from keeping individuals state oriented so that these individuals will comply more easily with unpleasant social demands. An intervention that attempts to transform a state-oriented client into an action-oriented one without taking the potential trade-offs into account may cause serious harm in the client's network of interpersonal relationships.

In this chapter, we observed how both society and psychologists alike have placed a premium on efficient affect-regulation skills. From this perspective, state-oriented individuals are suffering a miserable lot, as they are unable to take charge of their emotional lives. Taking a contrarian point of view, we have argued that there exists another side to state orientation. State orientation may have important benefits through social support, through regression from self-regulatory resources that are not always useful, and through substantial altruistic contributions within a broader social context. It thus seems unwise to write state orientation off as a purely self-destructive coping style.

NOTES

1. Personality systems interactions theory (Kuhl, 2001) also distinguishes nonvolitional forms of affect regulation, which are mediated by more automatic systems that operate independently of central executive processes. Examples of nonvolitional forms of affect regulation are the perceptual blocking of undesirable information (Bruner & Postman, 1948) or repression (Weinberger, Schwarz, & Davidson, 1979). These more automatic forms of affect regulation are typically less flexible than volitional forms, because automatic affect regulation is not attuned to the person's action goals. Theoretically, the construct of action versus state orientation refers only to volitional, top–down forms of affect regulation. Because the present chapter is only concerned with volitional affect regulation, we will use the term *affect regulation* in the present context to refer to volitional affect regulation. This more narrow use of the term corresponds to the typical understanding of it as a volitional process.

2. Given the aforementioned evidence that state orientation is positively correlated with emotional suppression tendencies (Koole, 2004), it appears that state-oriented individuals often refrain from expressing their negative affect to others. Conceivably, suppressors are more likely to develop a state orientation, because their emotional inhibition prevents them from developing volitional affect-regulation skills. If this reasoning holds, state-oriented individuals high on emotion suppression might be in an especially difficult predicament, because their emotion regulation styles keep these individuals from obtaining the very affective support that could help them resolve their self-regulatory problems. However, it is also possible that state-oriented individuals often feel reluctant to burden others with their negative affect. According to the latter interpretation, the correlation between state orientation and emotion suppression is a socially adaptive pattern. More research is needed to explore these various possibilities.

3. Strictly speaking, lower levels of self-regulation still represent internal forms of regulation, so that regressive functioning might be said to be "bottom" and not "bottom–up." However, the lower the level of self-regulation, the more the person's behavior is controlled by rigid mechanisms which have an almost one-to-one relation with the external stimuli that are encountered by the person. More specifically, high-level behavior control has access to a host of possible values, motives, and behavioral alternatives that are weighted in a complex manner to determine behavior. To quote the well-known Paul Simon song, a person who relies on high-level

behavior control might see at least "fifty ways to leave a lover" before deciding how to end his or her relationship. By contrast, low-level behavior control consists of rather rigid stimulus–response (S-R) links, in which the encountering of one critical stimulus is sufficient to trigger the corresponding behavior with almost 100% certainty. To stick with our song example, the person who relies on low-level behavior control might see only one way to leave his or her lover (e.g., running away) or may even fail to see any way at all and may thus remain stuck within the confines of a stifling relationship. In this sense, regression could be said to induce more bottom–up control by the environment.

REFERENCES

Adler, A. (1922). *Über den nervösen Charakter* [On nervous character] (3rd ed.). Munich, Germany: Bergmann.

Atkinson, J. W. (1957). Motivational determinants of risk-taking behavior. *Psychological Review, 64,* 359–372.

Baldwin, M. W., & Sinclair, L. (1996). Self-esteem and "if ... then" contingencies of interpersonal acceptance. *Journal of Personality and Social Psychology, 71,* 1130–1141.

Baumann, N., Kaschel, R., & Kuhl, J. (2003a). *Affect regulation and motive-incongruent achievement orientation: Antecedents of subjective well-being and symptom formation.* Manuscript submitted for publication, University of Osnabrück, Germany.

Baumann, N., Kaschel, R., & Kuhl, J. (2003b). *From personality styles to symptom formation: The moderating role of self-regulation.* Manuscript submitted for publication, University of Osnabrück, Germany.

Baumann, N., & Kazén, M. (2003). *Mortality salience and self-complexity: Does a differentiated self moderate the effects of reminders of death?* Paper presented at the University of Osnabrück, Germany.

Baumann, N., & Kuhl, J. (2002). Intuition, affect, and personality: Unconscious coherence judgments and self-regulation of negative affect. *Journal of Personality and Social Psychology, 83,* 1213–1223.

Baumann, N., & Kuhl, J. (2003). Self-infiltration: Confusing assigned tasks and self-selected in memory. *Personality and Social Psychology Bulletin, 29,* 487–498.

Baumeister, R. F. (1991). *Escaping the self: Alcoholism, spirituality, masochism, and other flights from the burden of selfhood.* New York: Basic Books.

Baumeister, R. F. (2005). *The cultural animal: Human nature, meaning, and social life.* New York: Oxford University Press.

Baumeister, R. F., Campbell, J. D., Krueger, J. I., & Vohs, K. D. (2003). Does high self-esteem cause better performance, interpersonal success, happiness, or healthier lifestyles? *Psychological Science in the Public Interest, 4,* 1–44.

Baumeister, R. F., & Sher, S. J. (1988). Self-defeating behavior patterns among normal individuals: Review and analysis of common self-destructive tendencies. *Psychological Bulletin, 104,* 3–22.

Beckmann, J. (1989). Erhöhte Leistung bei unzureichender Motivationskontrolle [Heightened performance during insufficient motivation control]. *Zeitschrift für experimentelle und angewandte Psychologie, 36,* 1–15.

Beckmann, J. (1997). *Alienation and conformity.* Unpublished manuscript, Max Planck Institute for Psychological Research, Munich, Germany.

Beckmann, J., & Kuhl, J. (1984). Altering information to gain action control: Functional aspects of human information processing in decision-making. *Journal of Research in Personality, 18,* 223–279.

Beeman, M., Friedman, R. B., Grafman, J., Prez, E., Diamond, S., & Lindsay, M. B. (1994). Summation priming and coarse encoding in the right hemisphere. *Journal of Cognitive Neuroscience, 6*, 26–45.

Biebrich, R., & Kuhl, J. (2002). Selbststeuerung und affektive Sensibilität: Persönlichkeitsspezifische Antezedenten der Depressivität [Self-regulation and emotional sensitivity: Personality-related antecedents of depression]. *Zeitschrift für Psychologie, 219*, 74–86.

Bolte, A., Goschke, T., & Kuhl, J. (2003). Emotion and intuition: Effects of positive and negative mood on implicit judgments of semantic coherence. *Psychological Science, 14*, 416–421.

Bruner, J. S., & Postman, L. (1948). Symbolic value as an organizing factor in perception. *Journal of Social Psychology, 27*, 203–208.

Brunstein, J. C., & Olbrich, E. (1985). Personal helplessness and action control: Analysis of achievement-related cognitions, self-assessments, and performance. *Journal of Personality and Social Psychology, 48*, 1540–1551.

Butler, E. A., Egloff, B., Wilhelm, F. H., Smith, N. C., Erickson, E. A., & Gross, J. J. (2003). The social consequences of expressive suppression. *Emotion, 3*, 48–67.

Carter, C. S., Lederhendler, I. I., & Kirkpatrick, B. (1997). *The integrative neurobiology of affiliation.* New York: New York Academy of Sciences.

Deci, E. L., & Ryan, R. M. (2000). The "what" and "why" of goal pursuits: Human needs and the self-determination perspective. *Psychological Inquiry, 11*, 227–268.

Diefendorff, J. M., Hall, R. J., Lord, R. G., & Strean, M. L. (2000). Action-state orientation: Construct validity of a revised measure and its relationship to work-related variables. *Journal of Applied Psychology, 85*, 250–263.

Freud, S. (1989). *Abriss der Psychoanalyse* [Outline of psychoanalysis]. Frankfurt, Germany: Fischer. (Original work published 1938)

Fuhrmann, A., & Kuhl, J. (1998). Maintaining a healthy diet: Effects of personality and self-reward versus self-punishment on commitment to and enactment of self-chosen and assigned goals. *Psychology and Health, 13*, 651–686.

Gilbert, D. T., Pelham, B. W., & Krull, D. S. (1988). On cognitive busyness: When person perceivers meet persons perceived. *Journal of Personality and Social Psychology, 54*, 733–740.

Goleman, D. (1995). *Emotional intelligence: Why it can matter more than IQ.* London: Bloomsbury.

Goschke, T., & Kuhl, J. (1993). Representation of intentions: Persisting activation in memory. *Journal of Experimental Psychology: Learning, Memory, and Cognition, 19*, 1211–1226.

Gross, J. J. (2002). Emotion regulation: Affective, cognitive, and social consequences. *American Psychologist, 39*, 281–291.

Gross, J. J., & John, O. P. (2003). Individual differences in two emotion regulation processes: Implications for affect, relationships, and well-being. *Journal of Personality and Social Psychology, 85*, 348–362.

Gunsch, D. (1996). *Self-determination and personality styles in intimate relationships.* Unpublished master's thesis, University of Osnabrück, Germany.

Harmon-Jones, E., & Harmon-Jones, C. (2002). Testing the action-based model of cognitive dissonance: The effect of action orientation on postdecisional attitudes. *Personality and Social Psychology Bulletin, 28*, 711–723.

Haschke, R., & Kuhl, J. (1995). Frust und Fliegen [Frustration and flying]. *Aeromed Info, 6*, 1–2.

Heckhausen, H., & Strang, H. (1988). Efficiency under record performance demands: Exertion control—An individual difference variable? *Journal of Personality and Social Psychology, 55,* 489–498.

Heckhausen, J., & Schulz, R. (1995). A life-span theory of control. *Psychological Review, 102,* 284–304.

Herrmann, C., & Wortman, C. B. (1985). Action control and the coping process. In J. Kuhl & J. Beckmann (Eds.), *Action control: From cognition to behavior* (pp. 151–180). New York: Springer.

Hetts, J. J., Sakuma, M., & Pelham, B. W. (1999). Two roads to positive regard: Implicit and explicit self-evaluation and culture. *Journal of Experimental Social Psychology, 35,* 512–559.

Hiroto, D. S., & Seligman, M. E. P. (1975). Generality of learned helplessness in man. *Journal of Personality and Social Psychology, 31,* 311–327.

Janet, P. (1903). *Les obsessions et al psychasthénie* [**XXXX**]. Paris: Félix Alcan.

Jang, K. L., Livesley, W. J., & Vernon, P. A. (1996). Heritability of the Big Five personality dimensions and their facets: A twin study. *Journal of Personality, 64,* 577–591.

Jostmann, N. B. (2003). [Stability of action versus state orientation]. Unpublished raw data, Free University Amsterdam.

Jostmann, N. B., & Koole, S. L. (2003). *Executive functioning under stress: The moderating role of action orientation.* Manuscript in preparation, Free University Amsterdam.

Jung, C. G. (1990). *Typologie.* Munich, Germany: dTV. (Original work published 1936)

Kaschel, R., & Kuhl, J. (2004). Motivational counseling in an extended functional context: Personality systems interaction theory and assessment. In W. M. Cox & E. Klinger (Eds.), *Handbook of motivational counseling: Motivating people for change* (pp. 99–119). Sussex, England: Wiley.

Kästele, G. (1988). Anlage- und umweltbedingte Determinanten der Handlungs- und Lageorientierung nach Misserfolg in Vergleich zu anderen Persönlichkeitseigenschaften [Genetic and environmental determinants of failure-related action- and state orientation in comparison with other personality traits]. Unpublished doctoral dissertation, University of Osnabrück, Germany.

Kazén, M., Baumann, N., & Kuhl, J. (2003). Self-infiltration versus self-compatibility checking in dealing with unattractive tasks: The moderating influence of state versus action orientation. *Motivation and Emotion, 27,* 157–197.

Keller, H., & Gauda, G. (1987). Eye contact in the first months of life and its developmental consequences. In R. Rauh et al. (Eds.), *Advances in psychology: Psychobiology and early development* (Vol. 46, pp. 129–142). Amsterdam: North-Holland.

Klinger, E. (1975). Consequences of commitment to and disengagement from incentives. *Psychological Review, 82,* 1–25.

Koole, S. L. (2003). [Action versus state orientation among 1,357 Dutch university students]. Unpublished raw data, Free University Amsterdam.

Koole, S. L. (2004). Volitional shielding of the self: Effects of action orientation and external demands on implicit self-evaluation. *Social Cognition, 22,* 117–146.

Koole, S. L., & Coenen, L. (2003). *Being creative under difficult circumstances: The moderating role of action orientation.* Manuscript in preparation, Free University Amsterdam.

Koole, S. L., & Jostmann, N. (2003). *Getting a grip on your feelings: Effects of action orientation and social demand on intuitive affect regulation.* Unpublished manuscript, Free University Amsterdam.

Koole, S. L., & Van den Berg, A. E. (2004). Paradise lost and reclaimed: A motivational analysis of human-nature relations. In J. Greenberg, S. L. Koole, & T. Pyszczynski (Eds.), *Handbook of experimental existential psychology* (pp. 86–103). New York: Guilford Press.

Kuhl, J. (1981). Motivational and functional helplessness: The moderating effect of state versus action orientation. *Journal of Personality and Social Psychology, 40*, 155–170.

Kuhl, J. (1983). Motivationstheoretische Aspekte der Depressionsgenese: Der Einfluss von Lageorientierung auf Schmerzempfinden, Medikamentenkonsum und Handlung-skontrolle [Motivation-theoretical aspects of the development of depression: The influence of state orientation on the experience of pain, drug consumption, and action control]. In M. Wolfersdorf, R. Staub, & G. Hole (Eds.), *De depressiv Kranke in der psychiatrischen Klinik: Theorie und Praxis der Diagnostik und Therapie*. Weinheim, Germany: Beltz Verlag.

Kuhl, J. (1984). Volitional aspects of achievement motivation and learned helplessness: Toward a comprehensive theory of action-control. In B. A. Maher (Ed.), *Progress in experimental personality research* (Vol. 13, pp. 99–171). New York: Academic Press.

Kuhl, J. (1994). Action versus state orientation: Psychometric properties of the Action Control Scale (ACS–90). In J. Kuhl & J. Beckmann (Eds.), *Volition and personality* (pp. 47–59). Göttingen, Germany: Hogrefe & Huber.

Kuhl, J. (2000). A functional-design approach to motivation and self-regulation: The dynamics of personality systems interactions. In M. Boekaerts, P. R. Pintrich, & M. Zeidner (Eds.), *Handbook of self-regulation* (pp. 111–169). San Diego, CA: Academic Press.

Kuhl, J. (2001). *Motivation und Persönlichkeit: Interaktionen psychischer Systeme* [Motivation and personality: Interactions between psychic systems]. Göttingen, Germany: Hogrefe.

Kuhl, J. (in press). Individual differences in self-regulation. In J. Heckhausen (Ed)., *Motivation and action*. Cambridge, England: Cambridge University Press.

Kuhl, J., & Beckmann, J. (1994a). *Volition and personality: State versus action orientation*. Göttingen, Germany: Hogrefe & Huber.

Kuhl, J., & Beckmann, J. (1994b). Alienation: ignoring one's preferences. In J. Kuhl & J. Beckmann (Eds.), *Volition and personality: Action versus state orientation* (pp. 375–390). Göttingen, Germany: Hogrefe & Huber.

Kuhl, J., & Fuhrmann, A. (1998). Decomposing self-regulation and self-control: The volitional components checklist. In J. Heckhausen & C. Dweck (Eds.), *Life span perspectives on motivation and control* (pp. 15–49). Mahwah, NJ: Erlbaum.

Kuhl, J., & Helle, P. (1986). Motivational and volitional determinants of depression: The degenerated-intention hypothesis. *Journal of Abnormal Psychology, 95*, 247–251.

Kuhl, J., & Kaschel, R. (2004). Entfremdung als Krankheitsursache: Selbstregulation von Affekten und integrative Kompetenz [Alienation as a determinat of symptom formation: Self-regulation of affect and integrative competence]. *Psychologische Rundschau, 55*, 61–71.

Kuhl, J., & Kazén, M. (1994). Self-discrimination and memory: State orientation and false self-ascription of assigned activities. *Journal of Personality and Social Psychology, 66*, 1103–1115.

Kuhl, J., & Kazén, M. (2003). *Impress them or convince them? Sales performance, social needs, and psychological well-being as a function of histrionic vs. action-oriented personality*. Manuscript submitted for publication.

Kuhl, J., & Koole, S. L. (2004). Workings of the will: A functional approach. In J. Greenberg, S. L. Koole, & T. Pyszczynski (Eds.), *Handbook of experimental existential psychology* (pp. 411–430). New York: Guilford Press.

Lepore, S. J., Silver, R. C., Wortman, C. B., & Wayment, H. A. (1996). Social constraints, intrusive thoughts, and depressive symptoms among bereaved mothers. *Journal of Personality and Social Psychology, 70,* 271–282.

Libet, B. (1985). Unconscious cerebral initiative and the role of conscious will in voluntary action. *Behavioral and Brain Sciences, 2,* 529–566.

Maier, S. F., & Seligman, M. E. P. (1976). Learned helplessness: Theory and evidence. *Journal of Experimental Psychology: General, 105,* 3–46.

Markus, H. R., & Kitayama, S. (1998). The cultural psychology of personality. *Journal of Cross-Cultural Psychology, 29,* 63–87.

Martin, L. L. (1999). I-D compensation theory: Some implications of trying to satisfy immediate-return needs in a delayed culture. *Psychological Inquiry, 10,* 195–208.

Martin, L. L., & Tesser, A. (1996). Some ruminative thoughts. In R. S. Wyer (Ed.), *Advances in social cognition* (Vol. 9, pp. 1–47). Mahwah, NJ: Erlbaum.

McClelland, J. L., McNaughton, B. L., & O'Reilly, R. C. (1995). Why there are complementary learning systems in the hippocampus and neocortex: Insights from the successes and failures of connectionist models of learning and memory. *Psychological Review, 102,* 419–457.

Menec, V. H. (1995). *Volition and motivation: The effect of distracting learning conditions on students differing in action control and perceived control.* Unpublished doctoral dissertation, University of Manitoba, Winnipeg, Manitoba, Canada.

Metcalfe, J., & Mischel, W. (1999). A hot/cool analysis of delay of gratification: Dynamics of willpower. *Psychological Review, 106,* 3–19.

Mikulincer, M., & Florian, V. (2002). The existential function of close relationships: Introducing death to the science of love. *Personality and Social Psychology Review, 7,* 20–40.

Niederberger, U., Engemann, A., & Radtke, M. (1987). Umfang der Informationsverarbeitung bei Entscheidungen: Der Einfluβ von Gedächtnisbelastung und Handlungsorientierung [Extent of information processing in decision making: The impact of memory load and action orientation]. *Zeitschrift für experimentelle und angewandte Psychologie, 34,* 80–100.

Palfai, T. P. (2002). Action-state orientation and the self-regulation of eating behavior. *Eating Behaviors, 3,* 249–259.

Pyszczynski, T., & Greenberg, J. (1987). Self-regulatory perseveration and the depressive self-focusing style: A self-awareness theory of reactive depression. *Psychological Bulletin, 102,* 122–138.

Ritz-Schulte, G. (2004). Problembearbeitung und Beziehungsgestaltung bei Persönlichkeitsstörungen [Problem analysis and relational therapy in personality disorders]. Göttingen, Germany: Hogrefe.

Rholes, W. S., Michas, L., & Shroff, J. (1989). Action control as a vulnerability factor in dysphoria. *Cognitive Therapy and Research, 13,* 263–274.

Rosahl, S. K., Tennigkeit, M., Kuhl, J., & Haschke, R. (1993). Handlungskontrolle und langsame Hirnpotentiale: Untersuchungen zum Einfluss subjectiv kritischer Wörter (Erste Ergebnisse) [Action control and slow brain potentials: Investigations on the influence of subjectively critical words. Preliminary findings]. *Zeitschrift für Medizinische Psychologie, 2,* 1–8.

Ryan, R., Mims, V., & Koestner, R. (1983). Relation of reward contigency and interpersonal context to intrinsic motivation: A review and test using cognitive evaluation theory. *Journal of Personality and Social Psychology, 45*, 736–750.

Schülein, J. A. (1989). Symbiotische Beziehungen und gesellschaftliche Entwicklung [Symbiotic relations and societal development]. In *Psyche, 11*.

Schopenhauer, A. (1995). *The world as will and idea*. London: Everymans. (Original work published 1818).

Schulte, D., Hartung, J., & Wilke, F. (1997). Handlungskontrolle der Angstbewältigung: Was macht Reizkonfrontationsverfahren so effektiv? [Action control in coping with anxiety: What makes exposure paradigms so effective?] *Zeitschrift für Klinische Psychologie, 26*, 118–128.

Sheldon, K. M., & Kasser, T. (1995). Coherence and congruence: Two aspects of personality integration. *Journal of Personality and Social Psychology, 68*, 531–543.

Stiensmeijer-Pelster, J. (1994). Choice of decision-making strategies and action versus state orientation. In J. Kuhl & J. Beckmann (Eds.), *Volition and personality: Action versus state orientation* (pp. 329–340). Göttingen, Germany: Hogrefe & Huber.

Swann, W. B., Jr., Wenzlaff, R. M., Krull, D. S., & Pelham, B. W. (1992). Allure of negative feedback: Self-verification strivings among depressed persons. *Journal of Abnormal Psychology, 101*, 293–306.

Tesser, A. (2002). Constructing a niche for the self: A bio-social, PDP approach to understanding lives. *Self and Identity, 1*, 185–191.

Uchino, B. N., Cacioppo, J. T., & Kiecolt-Glaser, J. K. (1996). The relationship between social support and physiological processes: A review with an emphasis on underlying mechanisms and implications for health. *Psychological Bulletin, 119*, 488–531.

Vohs, K. D., & Baumeister, R. F. (2004). Ego depletion, self-control, and choice. In J. Greenberg, S. L. Koole, & T. Pyszczynski (Eds.), *Handbook of experimental existential psychology* (pp. 398–410). New York: Guilford Press.

Volling, B. L., McElwain, N. L., Notaro, P. C., & Herrera, C. U. (2002). Parents' emotional availability and infant emotional competence: Predictors of parent–infant attachment and emerging self-regulation. *Journal of Family Psychology, 16*, 447–465.

11

The Roles of the Self
in Priming-to-Behavior Effects

S. CHRISTIAN WHEELER,
KENNETH G. DEMARREE,
AND RICHARD E. PETTY

Research has shown that the activation of stereotypes and traits can influence subsequent behavior. For example, activation of the African American stereotype can lead both African Americans (Steele & Aronson, 1995) and non–African Americans (Wheeler, Jarvis, & Petty, 2001) to perform poorly on a standardized test. Similarly, activation of the eldery person stereotype can lead both older individuals (Hausdorff, Levy, & Wei, 1999) and college students (Bargh, Chen, & Burrows, 1996) to walk more slowly. Although the effects of stereotype activation on behavior have been robustly demonstrated by many researchers in several domains, the underlying mechanisms for the effects have proven difficult to determine conclusively (Wheeler & Petty, 2001).

In this chapter, we briefly review some of the different accounts that have been proposed for prime-to-behavior effects and then describe a new account that involves the active self-concept. Evidence consistent with this active-self account is reviewed, and the effects of the self on the magnitude and direction of prime-to-behavior effects are described. We conclude by considering the active-self account in the context of the other alternative formulations.

PROPOSED MECHANISMS FOR PRIME-TO-BEHAVIOR EFFECTS

A number of different prime-to-behavior mechanisms have been proposed. In this section, we first review two popular accounts—automatic behavior (ideomotor theory) and goal activation (auto-motive theory)—and then present our active-self framework.

Ideomotor Theory

The basic premise of ideomotor theory is that ideation is a sufficient factor for initiating action (Carpenter, 1893; James, 1890/1950). Ideomotor theory suggests that thought does not require will as a sidekick to initiate action; thought alone is sufficient, at least in the absence of inhibitory factors. According to James (1890/1950), the willing is in the thought itself: "To attend to [an action] is the volitional act, and the only inward volitional act which we ever perform" (p. 819). A wide array of evidence consistent with the ideomotor notion is found in the accounts of individuals who engage in actions without the perception of willing them. For example, many occult phenomena popular as party tricks and other informal diversions in the late 19th century (see Wegner, 2002, for a review) involved actions for which the actors felt no conscious intentions. Many of these phenomena involved communication with spirits through means of facilitating devices such as Ouija boards, pendulums, or tables. In the latter example, individuals would place their hands beneath the table, summon the dead, and ask them questions. The dead would presumably answer these questions by various means, including the tapping of table legs and the turning of the table itself. Perhaps not surprisingly, research subsequently exposed these and other phenomena to be the result of the participating individuals and not of the occult. Equally interesting, however, are the sincere protestations among the participants, who insisted that they played no causal role in the actions. Although these participants were thinking about and anticipating certain actions (e.g., that the table leg would tap twice to indicate "no"), they believed that they had nothing to do with the action's execution. Hence, the thought itself was sufficient to initiate the action in the absence of experience of will.

The ideomotor account for stereotype prime-to-behavior effects is similar to that of James and Carpenter, but just a few steps removed. The stereotype affects behavior, according to this account, by activating related behavioral representations (Bargh, Chen, & Burrows, 1996). Stereotypes include traits and other information relevant to a category of people. Most relevant for our concerns is the notion that individuals have knowledge of the behaviors that typify the traits included in the stereotype. Hence, this account holds that activation of the stereotype leads to activation of traits, which leads to the activation of related behavioral representations. On it goes through the concatenated activation of associated constructs until the behavior is initiated. For example, exposure to terms that would invoke an older individual stereotype (e.g., *bingo, Florida*) could make other aspects of the stereotype (e.g., *slow*) accessible in memory (e.g., Devine, 1989). Associated with these traits are trait-related behavioral representations. For example, a behavioral instantiation of the slow older individual stereotype is walking slowly. If this behavioral representation were to be sufficiently activated, the action would then result.

Various features of the ideomotor account have received support. For example, imagining an action activates the same areas of the brain as actually engaging in the action, and perception of an action can increase the likelihood of its execution in oneself (see Dijksterhuis & Bargh, 2001, for a review). Hence, support for the perception–behavior link has been obtained both at the neurophysiological and behavioral level.

Auto-Motive Theory

Auto-motive theory (Bargh, 1990; Bargh & Gollwitzer, 1994; Chartrand & Bargh, 1996) is similar to ideomotor theory in that it suggests that behavior can be directed by the unconscious activation of mental representations. However, whereas ideo-motor theory describes the automatic and direct activation of behavioral representations, the auto-motive model describes how behavior can be indirectly affected via the automatic activation of goals and motivations (Bargh, 1997). The theory suggests that goals can be automatically activated by environments in which that goal has been consciously activated repeatedly. Over time, the activation of the goal becomes more automatic until conscious activation of the goal becomes unnecessary. More recently it has been suggested (Bargh, Gollwitzer, Lee-Chai, Barndollar, & Troetschel, 2001) that goals could be activated by stereotypes or stereotyped targets as well. For example, activation of the professor stereotype could activate the goal to solve intellectual problems or to achieve. Experimentally, goal states have been primed by presenting participants with goal-related words (e.g., *impression*, to activate an impression-formation goal; Chartrand & Bargh, 1996) or by priming them with individuals that might be associated with different goals in memory (e.g., a friend vs. a coworker; Fitzsimons & Bargh, 2003).

Bargh and colleagues (Bargh et al. 2001) suggested that many effects previously explained by ideomotor processes could in fact be explained by automatically activated motivations, as proposed by auto-motive theory. Auto-motive theory could demystify the influence of primes on complex behaviors requiring complex behavioral chains, they argued, because activated goals can flexibly operate over time and interact with the environment to reach a desired end state—unlike automatically activated behaviors, which are presumably more static and temporally restricted. Individuals are likely to have flexible behavioral routines capable of helping them approach desired end states.

As a replacement for ideomotor theory, auto-motive theory has some ambiguities. First, in the context of stereotype activation, it is not clear that individuals have developed complex goal-directed behavioral routines for the goals of others. Second, many behaviors shown to be influenced by primes seem unlikely to be goal directed, either because they are undesirable (e.g., acting stupidly) or unintentional (e.g., older people probably do not have the goal of walking slowly). Third, as described below and elsewhere (Wheeler & Petty, 2001), the precise goal activated by exemplars or stereotypes is not always clear a priori. For example, it is possible that presentation of the African American stereotype would activate the goals of African Americans, but it is also possible that one's goals toward African Americans would be activated (see Chen, 2000). Similarly, activation of significant-other exemplars (e.g., one's mother) could potentially activate the goals of that exemplar, that exemplar's goals for oneself (Shah, 2003), or one's goals toward that exemplar (Fitzsimons & Bargh, 2003). Despite these ambiguities in predicting trait and stereotype goal-related behaviors, the notion that goals can be automatically activated and pursued continues to receive support.

Because primes can have many different associations, distinguishing between the ideomotor and auto-motive accounts can be challenging. Researchers in this area have typically supported the goal activation account by showing that prime-induced behavior can mimic behavior resulting from consciously activated goals. For example, primes can create behavior that increases in intensity over time, occurs in the face of obstacles, and is resumed after interruption (Bargh et al. 2001).

An Active Self-Concept Account

We refer to the third possible account for prime-to-behavior effects as the *active self-concept account*. According to this account, primes can sometimes work to temporarily influence conceptions in the activated or working self-concept and these modified self-conceptions can then determine the actions that occur. In traditional priming impression-formation studies (e.g., Higgins, Rholes, & Jones, 1977), temporarily accessible information from a previous context is (mis)attributed to a perceptual target, presumably because the source of activation is confused (e.g., Higgins, 1998; Mussweiler & Neumann, 2000). In a similar fashion, accessible information could sometimes bias representations of the self.

The self is a complex and multifaceted cognitive representation that can include myriad types of information including one's personality traits and characteristics, important relationships, group memberships, behavioral tendencies, and goals. The representation of self-knowledge has been described in various ways, including schematic (e.g., Markus, 1977), hierarchical (e.g., T. B. Rogers, 1981), and as a multidimensional space (e.g., Breckler & Greenwald, 1982, cited in Greenwald & Pratkanis, 1984), among others (for reviews, see Greenwald & Pratkanis, 1984; Kihlstrom & Cantor, 1984; Markus & Wurf, 1987).

Despite organizational differences across the models, most analyses assume that the representation of self-information in memory shares features with other types of representations, such as one's attitudes or beliefs about the world. Much like other types of represented information, self-information can influence encoding, interpretation, and retrieval of related information (e.g., Kihlstrom et al., 1988). Additionally, self-information can vary with respect to its complexity (e.g., Linville, 1985), clarity (e.g., Campbell, 1990), and accessibility (e.g., Markus, 1977).

Theorists have proposed that the self is an important determinant of behavior (e.g., Cross & Markus, 1990). Linking an idea or action to the self, they have argued, makes it self-relevant and therefore increases the likelihood of action (Cross & Markus, 1990; Hull, Slone, Meteyer, & Matthews, 2002), and research indicates that the content of the active or working self-concept can affect behavioral responses (e.g., Ruvolo & Markus, 1992). Hence, the extent to which activated information is included in the self-concept could have implications for the direction and magnitude of subsequent behavior.

Traditionally, most models of self-representation have shared the characteristic that the self-knowledge represented in these different structures has been assumed to be explicit. That is, these different types of information are known to the person and can be retrieved and explicitly reported (e.g., C. R. Rogers, 1951). Much as primes can bias individuals' explicit judgments about others' personality characteristics (e.g., Higgins et al. 1977), they could also bias one's explicit judgments about oneself (e.g., Stapel & Koomen, 2000).

Other recent research has suggested that individuals may sometimes have implicit self-information that is inaccessible to conscious awareness (e.g., Greenwald et al., 2002; Greenwald & Farnham, 2000; Hetts, Sakuma, & Pelham, 1999). That is, information can be represented in memory and linked to the self, but the individual can be unaware of it. This information can include the same types of dimensions reflected in explicit self-representations, including evaluations (Hetts et al., 1999), group memberships (Greenwald et al., 2002), traits (Greenwald & Farnham, 2000), and motivations (McClelland, Koestner, & Weinberger, 1989). These implicit self-representations might also be subject to influence by primed content.

Considerably more research has been conducted on the explicit rather than the implicit self-concept, though they could share some of the same features. Research on the explicit self-concept has emphasized the simultaneous stability and malleability of self-representations (e.g., Markus & Kunda, 1986). Although some individuals may be resistant to influences on the self in some domains (e.g., Markus, 1977), individuals' working self-concepts have been shown to be, on average, relatively malleable. For example, individuals believe themselves to be more helpful after complying with a request (e.g., DeJong, 1979), heavier when surrounded by less heavy people (e.g., McGuire & Padawer-Singer, 1976), and more extraverted after describing ways in which they are outgoing (e.g., Fazio, Effrein, & Falender, 1981). Little is known about the malleability of the implicit self-concept. However, research on implicit attitudes suggests that implicit constructs can be significantly influenced by situational factors (e.g., Dasgupta & Greenwald, 2001; Lowery, Hardin, & Sinclair, 2001), and it seems plausible that implicit self-conceptions could also be susceptible to contextual influences.

Once altered, both implicit and explicit self-concept representations have the potential to alter behavior. For example, some research shows that the implicit self-concept is more likely to guide spontaneous behaviors, whereas explicit self-representations are more likely to guide more deliberate behaviors (Asendorpf, Banse, & Muecke, 2002). To simplify presentation throughout the remainder of the chapter, we refer to the active self-concept as the *self-concept* (implicit or explicit) that guides behavior in the measured domain, though we acknowledge that implicit and explicit self-representations may have influences on different types or aspects of behaviors and could potentially be influenced by different contextual factors.

Some of the variability in the active self could be due to the voluminous quantities of information individuals have about themselves. Individuals have been shown to have complex and multifaceted identities, and only a small subset of identity-relevant material can be accessed at any given time (e.g., Linville &

Carlston, 1994; Niedenthal & Beike, 1997). As a result, the active self of individuals could differ depending on the subset of identity-relevant material that happens to be salient and accessible in that context (Markus & Wurf, 1987).

The limits of malleability of the self-concept and their relationship to chronic self-knowledge have not been fully tested. As a result, different models regarding the way in which primes could bias accessible self-information are plausible. It is possible that the effects of the prime on the self and behavior are dependent on the types of self-content available in memory. Alternately, it is possible that effects of the prime could be relatively independent of stored self-linkages.

Biased Activation Model One possible model by which the self could play a role in prime to behavior effects, the *biased activation model*, involves the selective activation of a biased subset of individuals' identities (see Figure 11.1). Primes could be one sort of contextual influence that could bias the subset of self-information that is accessible, but the extent of the bias could depend on the type and amount of information available for activation. For example, the magnitude of the effect of an "extraversion" prime on behavior could depend both on one's chronic level of extraversion and the amount of extraversion-relevant material in the self-concept available for activation. According to this model, if two individuals chronically report equal levels of extraversion but have different amounts of extraversion self-concept material available for activation, larger extraversion priming effects should be observed in the individual for whom there is more extraversion self-material in memory.

Figure 11.1 provides a visual depiction of this model. This hypothetical individual has social, artistic, and calm as chronically accessible aspects of her self-concept, but also has the traits of lazy, aggressive, and athletic included in her self-concept. After being primed with the African American stereotype, the stereotype-consistent self-concept traits lazy, aggressive, and athletic are made accessible and thus bias her self-concept to be more stereotype-consistent than it is in the absence of the prime. Again, as noted above, the activated traits could be in awareness such that the conscious working self-concept is modified, or the activated traits might be below the level of conscious awareness, thereby producing a change in the implicit self concept.

Expansion Model Another possible model, the *expansion model*, suggests that the boundary between self and nonself is permeable. As a result, information not typically associated with the self could, under some circumstances, cross the boundary and be considered self-descriptive. Hence, according to this model, the chronic self-concept would not necessarily place a limitation on the effects of primes on behavior. Some potential support for this mechanism comes from the literature on source monitoring (Johnson, Hashtroudi, & Lindsay, 1993). Although this literature has generally focused on memory-related phenomena (e.g., Dodhia & Metcalfe, 1999; Mather, Johnson, & De Leonardis, 1999), recent research has also examined the effects of source monitoring on judgment. For example, Mussweiler and Neumann (2000) found that judgmental assimilation occurs when the source of accessibility can be (mis)attributed to the self, and contrast occurs when accessibility is attributed to an outside source. Although the effects of accessibility on judgments about others may not always be the same as the effects on self-judgments and behavior (e.g., Smeesters, Warlop, Van Avermaet, Corneille, & Yzerbyt, 2003), some research suggests that similar results occur across the three domains. For example, a "distinct" (Stapel & Koomen, 2001) exemplar prime is likely to produce contrast in judgment about others (Stapel, Koomen, & van der Plight, 1997), in perceptions of the self (Dijksterhuis et al., 1998), and in behavior (Dijksterhuis, et al. 1998). Thus, misattribution of the source of construct accessibility could potentially allow primed content to cross the barrier into the active self-concept in the absence of such information's being chronically stored prior to the prime.

Figure 11.1 provides a visual depiction of this model. This hypothetical individual initially does not have any stereotype-consistent traits included in her chronic self-concept. After being primed with the African American stereotype, some stereotype consistent traits become associated with the self, despite their lack of inclusion in the self-concept prior to the prime.

Although proposed as alternative accounts, it is possible that the expansion of self to include primed nonself material would depend on its coherence with the other elements of the self-concept. For example, a woman who considers herself to be a frank, rugged sports fan might report higher aggression after an African American prime than would a woman who considers herself to be a quiet, bookish cat lover, even if each woman believes herself to be equally nonaggressive prior to the prime. This is because the trait of aggressiveness is plausibly more consistent with the self-concept of the former woman than the latter woman. Additionally, it is possible that the amount of bias could depend on the extent of overlap between the stereotype and the self-concept. For example, a woman primed with the African American stereotype who has some stereotype-consistent traits (e.g., lazy and religious) in her self-concept could have greater bias from other stereotype-consistent, but semantically unrelated, traits (e.g., aggressive) than would someone who had no stereotype-consistent self-concept traits. In this instance, the former woman would still show expansion of the self-concept to include new material (i.e., aggressive), consistent with the expansion model, but this extent of bias would depend on the extent of overlap between semantically unrelated self-stereotype content. Hence, self-conceptions could sometimes extend to nonself traits, but the likelihood of such inclusion could depend on the traits that are part of the self-concept prior to the prime.

EVIDENCE FOR THE ROLE OF THE SELF IN PRIME TO BEHAVIOR EFFECTS

A growing body of research is consistent with the active-self model of prime-to-behavior effects. Although primes can have many different types of effects on behavior, these effects can be coherently understood by considering the influence

A

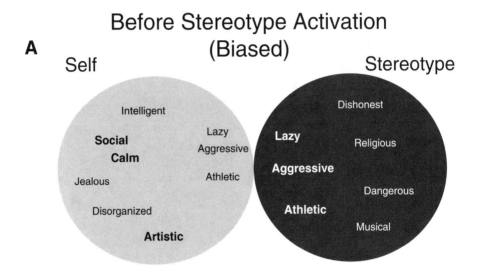

Before Stereotype Activation (Biased)

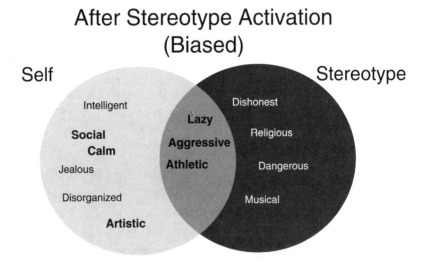

After Stereotype Activation (Biased)

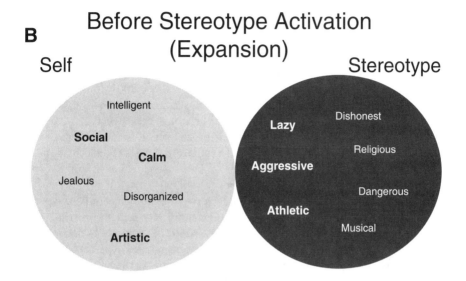

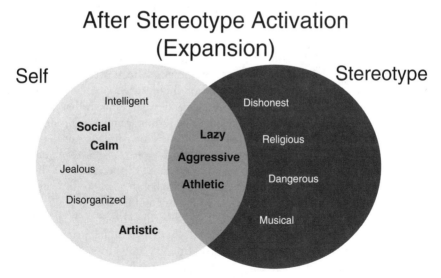

FIGURE 11.1. Visual depiction of biased activation model (A) and expansion model (B). Items in bold indicate constructs that are the most accessible following activation of the categories. (Within the self-concept, these items would constitute the working self-concept.)

of the prime on the active self-concept. We review different kinds of effects and discuss the possible role of the self in each effect.

Assimilation Effects

The first type of effect that a prime can have on judgments and behaviors is assimilation, and this is the most frequently demonstrated behavioral consequence of trait, stereotype, and goal primes (see Wheeler & Petty, 2001, for a review). In this type of effect, individuals primed with a trait, stereotype, or goal subsequently behave congruently with the implications of the primed construct. For example, individuals primed with the African American stereotype act more aggressively (Bargh et al. 1996) and perform worse on standardized tests (Steele & Aronson, 1995; Wheeler et al., 2001). Both of these behaviors are consistent with the behaviors implied by the African American stereotype.

Although the effects of non-self-relevant stereotypes on behavior have typically been explained by an ideomotor account, they could also sometimes result from the biased activation of prime-consistent material in the active self-concept.[1] For example, individuals primed with the African American stereotype could perceive themselves to be more aggressive or less good at math. If the self is involved in determining assimilation to primed constructs, the effects of the prime might not be equivalent for everyone. Instead, the extent of the effect of the prime on behavior could depend on the extent to which the self is easy to influence and is actively linked to the primed constructs. Additionally, prime effects could depend on idiographic self-concept ties to the primed construct and on the extent to which the self is used to determine action.

Accessibility of a Stable Self-Concept
If primes can affect behavior by temporarily modifying self-representations, then the effects of a prime on behavior should be reduced when individuals have highly accessible and stable self-representations. In support, some research studies have shown that activation of the self can diminish prime-to-behavior effects. For example, Dijksterhuis and van Knippenberg (2000) showed that the presence of a mirror can decrease the effects of primes on behavior. They argued that the mirror can activate alternative goals and behavioral cues to action that interfere with the action of the prime. Making one's actual goals and behavioral cues salient can therefore presumably diminish the effectiveness of the prime in modifying them.

Similarly, other research has shown that when the chronic self is activated or made salient just prior to reception of a prime, the effects of that prime on behavior are diminished. For example, in one experiment (Smeesters, Warlop, Yzerbyt, Corneille, & Van Avermaet, 2003), participants' social value orientations were determined on the basis of their decisions on the Ring Measure of Social Values (Liebrand, 1984). In this task, participants chose between pairs of money allocations for themselves and another person. Based upon their choices and the consistency with which they make them, they can be defined as high- or low-consistency prosocial or proself individuals. These individuals then engaged in a task designed to increase their self-focus or not. Following the self-focus task, they were primed with businessperson, religious person, or neutral stereotype content. Finally, participants played a dictator game in which they freely allocated chips to themselves and a partner.

Results indicated that social value orientation had a significant effect such that prosocial individuals allocated more chips to their partner than did the proself individuals. Additionally, there was a significant effect of prime, such that the religious primes led to higher allocations to the other than did the neutral primes, which in turn led to higher allocations to the other than did the business primes. These effects were moderated by self-focus, however. First, self-focus increased the extent to which low-consistency individuals acted in accordance with their dispositional social value orientation. Second, self-focus decreased the effect of the priming manipulation on behavior. Hence, self-focus elicited prior to the prime increased the effect of dispositional self-conceptions on behavior and decreased the effect of primed stereotype content on behavior.

These types of effects are consistent with the active-self perspective. More precisely, activation of one's chronic individual self-concept prior to reception of the prime should lead to a reduction in the biasing effects of the prime. If primes operate, at least in some cases, by the activation of biased contents that are perceived as part of the self, then activation of one's longstanding self-concept prior to reception of the prime should interfere with this biasing effect. To the extent that the chronic, personal self-content is highly accessible prior to the prime, assimilation to situationally activated material should be minimized.

Integration of the Prime With the Self   In contrast to the research just reviewed, other research indicates that activation of the self can increase the magnitude of priming effects. In these studies, however, the self is activated concurrently with the primed content and serves to foster the formation of linkages between the primed content and the self. These studies show that self-prime linkages can increase the magnitude of priming effects.

For example, research by Fenigstein and Levine (1984) showed that the effect of a prime on individuals' interpretations of fictional scenarios can depend on the extent to which the prime is coactivated with the self. In one experiment, participants wrote stories containing either causal words or neutral words. Additionally, the stories were either to contain pronouns related to the self (e.g., *me*) or not. Participants then read a series of fictional scenarios in which they were to imagine themselves as actors. Results indicated that participants attributed a greater causal role to themselves in the scenarios when primed with the causal words, but only when the causal words were coactivated with the self. The researchers argued that self-attention facilitates access to self-related knowledge and that this can increase the processing of information in self-relevant terms.

Wheeler, Jarvis, and Petty (2001) showed that self-linkage can also increase the magnitude of the effects of primes on behavior. In these experiments, non–African American participants were randomly assigned to write an essay about a day in the life of a college student. Half of the participants were randomly assigned to write about a day in the life of Erik Walker, whom most participants assumed was White. The other half of the participants was randomly assigned to write about a day in the life of Tyrone Walker, whom most participants assumed was African American. They were subsequently given a difficult mathematical test. Results indicated that participants performed more poorly on the test when they had previously written about Tyrone versus having written about Erik. The lowered test results of individuals who wrote about Tyrone were not observed equally among all participants, however. Test performance decrements were observed only among those individuals who spontaneously wrote about Tyrone from the first-person perspective. That is, those participants who linked the negative out-group performance stereotype to the self exhibited the performance decrements.

Using an individual-differences approach, Hull et al. (2002) demonstrated that individuals who are high in private self-consciousness tend to exhibit larger prime-to-behavior effects than do those low in private self-consciousness. They argued that these results occurred because individuals high in private self-con-sciousness are those who are most likely to spontaneously process information in self-relevant ways. Because high private self-consciousness individuals may, under some circumstances, spontaneously form more or stronger prime–self linkages, they can exhibit larger behavioral changes after primes than low private self-consciousness individuals.

Thus, a number of studies are consistent with the notion that nonconsciously instigated behavior depends on the extent to which the primed content is associated with the self-concept. Individuals whose self-concept is more likely to include or encompass the activated constructs as part of the self exhibit larger effects.

In the above examples, a link between the self and the primed content is an antecedent to the assimilative effects of a prime. It may also be useful to think of such an integration of self and prime as a consequence of the stereotype activation, which may of course be moderated by the initial linkages between self and prime. In one study examining this, we (DeMarree, Wheeler, & Petty, 2004) relied on a paradigm used in research on interpersonal relationships (Aron, Aron, Tudor, & Nelson, 1991) and social identity (Smith & Henry, 1996). Specifically, Aron et al. (1991) postulated that our mental representations of significant others are incor-porated to some extent into our own self-schemas. Using a modified *me/not me* reaction time task based on Markus's (1977) schematicity measure, they found that people were quicker to respond to traits that matched both the self and the relationship partner compared to those traits that differed between the self and relationship partner. This pattern of responding was taken as evidence of overlap in the representation of the self and the relationship partner. Parallel findings have indicated that our social groups can also be incorporated into our self-concept (Aaker & Lee, 2001; Coats, Smith, Claypool, & Banner, 2000; Smith & Henry, 1996). If primed stereotypes are incorporated into the active self-concept, we should expect to find a similar pattern of results. Participants who incorporate an activated stereotype into the self-concept would respond more quickly to self-descriptive (i.e., *me*), stereotype-relevant words and slower to nonself descriptive (*not me*), stereotype-relevant words, compared to control-prime participants.

The task DeMarree et al. (2003) used was similar to those used previously (e.g., Aron et al. 1991), except that it was preceded by an African American prime (either a scrambled sentence task [see Srull & Wyer, 1979] or the Tyrone vs. Eric essay prime described earlier). For the reaction time task, participants had to indicate whether a word flashed on the screen was self-descriptive or not by pressing either the "me" or the "not me" key. Some of these words were related to the African American stereotype as indicated by previous research (e.g., Devine, 1989). A pattern indicative of the "inclusion of the stereotype in the self" would be faster responding when endorsing stereotype-relevant words (*me* responses), and slower responses when rejecting these words (*not me* responses) when primed with the African American stereotype than when not primed. Correcting for response times to stereotype-irrelevant traits, we found a significant Prime × Self-Descriptiveness (*me/not me*) interaction in the predicted pattern (see Figure 11.2). Interestingly, the effect was in equal part due to the slowing of the *not me* responses and the speeding of *me* responses among primed participants compared to control-prime participants (DeMarree et al., 2004). This is critical, because the slowing of *not me* responses reduces the plausibility of simple accessibility-based alternatives, which would predict faster responding—regardless of the self-descriptiveness of the words—because of the ease with which these words are processed.

Assimilation to Situational Selves   Many priming stimuli have idiographic associations for individuals. For example, being primed with your own mother's name could activate self-information in you that would differ from the type of information activated in someone else who was not acquainted with your mother. Research in this domain suggests that significant-other exemplars can activate the behaviors, goals, and self-concept information that are associated with the individual (Baldwin, 1992).

For example, the activation of significant-other exemplars can result in the activation of goals one has toward that person (Fitzsimons & Bargh, 2003). A prime of one's spouse could activate the goals of intimacy and helpfulness if these are one's goals toward one's spouse. Additionally, significant-other exemplars can activate that exemplar's goals for oneself (Shah, 2003). For example, if Hank's

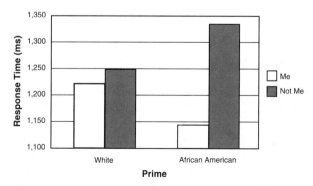

FIGURE 11.2. Response latencies for endorsed and nonendorsed traits following a stereotype prime. Data from DeMarree et al. (2004).

mother always insisted that he be a high achiever, achievement-related goals may be salient to Hank after being primed with his mother's name.

Additional types of information could also possibly be activated. For example, a significant-other exemplar could activate that exemplar's own goals (e.g., "She wants to be more empathetic"), one's idiosyncratic associations with that exemplar (e.g., "I proposed to her after that great concert"), or one's behavioral tendencies when with that person (e.g., "She always makes me stutter").

Although these different activated elements could frequently be congruent, they could sometimes be in competition (e.g., when one person desires intimacy that the other does not). Given the wide array of possible behavior-relevant information that could be activated, the potential for conflict is likely to be nontrivial. It is possible that one would be most likely to act congruently with the most accessible or most applicable associations with that exemplar (see Higgins, 1996). In some situations, though, competing behavioral tendencies could be both highly accessible and applicable. For example, after being primed with a competitive friend with whom one would like to be cooperative, the concepts of competition and cooperation might be both highly accessible and applicable to the same behavioral situation.

It is possible that behavior in such situations would be driven by the portions of the self-concept that are associated with the exemplar (see, e.g., Baldwin, 1992). Significant-other exemplars are likely to be linked to the self-representation in memory along with the behavioral patterns and scripts that are associated with interactions with that person (see Andersen & Chen, 2002). Hence, when one's mother becomes salient, so too could one's self when with mother (e.g., Ogilvie & Ashmore, 1991).

Consistent with this idea, evidence suggests that the behavioral effect that occurs following a significant-other exemplar prime depends on the precise relationship one has with the exemplar. For example, activation of an exemplar's goals for oneself occurs only when one is close to the exemplar (Shah, 2003). One could be more likely to behave or wish to behave congruently with the goals of an individual to the extent that one is close to that individual. Alternately, individuals could be close to each other to the extent that their behavior and goals are compatible.

Interestingly, research on transference has shown that these effects can also emerge when an exemplar is not a significant other but merely resembles a significant-other exemplar. The similar features of an unknown person can activate the representation of the known person, which can in turn affect the goals and perceptions of the perceiver. For example, Andersen and colleagues have shown that transference can affect perceptions of a person who resembles a significant-other exemplar (e.g., Andersen & Baum, 1994), as well as affecting one's goals and self-representations. Motivations to be close to or distant from a new person can be predicted on the basis of the person's resemblance to a personally relevant individual that one has such motivations toward (Hinkley & Andersen, 1996). When a novel person resembles a significant other to whom one wishes to be close, the motivation to be close to the novel individual is engaged. When a novel person resembles a significant other from whom one wishes to be distant, the motivation to be distant from the novel individual is engaged (see Andersen & Chen, 2002, for a review of these types of findings).

Changes in the active self-concept have also been shown in a transference paradigm. Hinkley and Andersen (1996) assessed individuals' descriptions of themselves when with significant others and also the descriptions of the characteristics of those significant others. At a subsequent session, participants were exposed to novel individuals who resembled one of the significant others assessed in the initial session. Participants then completed a measure of their current self-concept. Results indicated that participants' self-reported characteristics resembled their reported selves when with the significant others to a greater degree when the novel individuals resembled the significant others.

These findings suggest that many priming effects may have strong idiographic components. Being primed with an individual's name or personal characteristics can lead to differing effects depending on the individuals one knows that have that name or have similar characteristics. Individuals may also have idiosyncratic patterns of activation following exposure to exemplars with whom one has no personal relationship. For example, an individual who has only seen John Travolta's earlier movies may have different associations with his name than an individual who has only seen his more recent work, even if neither individual knows Travolta personally.

Parallel effects could follow from stereotype activation. Although many stereotypes are consensually shared among members of a population, the specific features of the stereotype that are salient upon exposure to a stereotype prime could differ across individuals. For example, individuals who have had positive experiences with African Americans may respond differently to an African American prime than those who have had negative experiences with African Americans.

Hence, although research on significant-other exemplars appears at first to differ in important ways from research on other priming effects, it may in fact share many similarities. Although mental representations of significant-other exemplars could differ in their complexity and accessibility from representations of stereotypes or non-significant-other exemplars, all types of constructs are potentially capable of activating behavioral representations and goals that differ idiographically. Additionally, both could work by affecting the active self.

Individual-Differences Evidence for the Active-Self

View   Work from our own laboratories has begun to examine an additional self-based prediction, namely that the effects of primes on judgment and behavior should be strongest among those whose selves are most likely to be influenced by subtly primed material and who consistently rely on their self-conceptions in guiding behavior. There is one individual-differences variable that plausibly relates to both the tendency to have one's implicit or explicit self-representations shaped by subtly primed constructs, and using one's self-representation to direct behavior.

This individual difference is referred to as *self-monitoring* (Snyder, 1974). Self-monitoring concerns the extent to which individuals deliberately modify their behavior to meet explicit social demands. High self-monitors are social chameleons who are not troubled by inconsistency between their attitudes, traits, and behaviors. Low self-monitors, on the other hand, look inward and rely heavily on their attitudes, traits, and beliefs to guide their actions. They display high levels of congruence between their attitudes and behaviors (Snyder & Swann, 1976; Snyder & Tanke, 1976), inner states and self-presentation (Ickes, Layden, & Barnes, 1978) and between their personality characteristics and behaviors (Lippa, 1978). As Snyder and Campbell (1982) put it, "To live one's life according to the principled theory of self ... would require low-self-monitoring individuals to pay serious attention to their own internal states, dispositions, and personal characteristics in order to guide their social behavior" (p. 191).

Additionally, some evidence suggests that low self-monitors are more likely to change their behavior and self-perceptions in response to information perceived to be dispositionally diagnostic. For example, low self-monitors exhibit more attitude change after a freely chosen counterattitudinal behavior than do high self-monitors (Snyder & Tanke, 1976), and they evince greater behavioral change in response to false feedback regarding their dispositional characteristics (Fiske & von Hendy, 1992). Accessible mental contents could provide an additional piece of information that could be perceived as relevant and diagnostic with respect to the self. Because of their consistency between inner states and behavior and because low self-monitors' self-conceptions are more responsive to ostensibly diagnostic self-information, they could show larger changes in the self-concept following a prime than would high self-monitors.

Hence, low self-monitors are more likely to adjust their self-conceptions based on dispositionally diagnostic information, attend to their inner states, and use their self-conceptions as guides to their behavior. Therefore, primes are plausibly more likely to influence the active self-conceptions (either implicit or explicit) of low self-monitors, and furthermore, these biased self-conceptions should have greater effect on the actions taken by low self-monitors, who use such representations to guide their social behavior. In contrast, high self-monitors are less likely to look internally, less likely to confuse subtly activated mental contents with the self, and less likely to rely on internal cues to guide their actions.

In an initial test of this hypothesis (DeMarree, Wheeler, & Petty, 2004), participants wrote essays about a day in the life of Tyrone (vs. Erik) Walker to prime the African American stereotype (or not; see Wheeler et al., 2001). Following the essay task, participants completed an implicit aggression measurement task that ostensibly concerned subliminal language perception. Participants were told that a word would be flashed on the screen so quickly that they would not be able to see it. After the presentation of the word, they were then given a list of four words and were to select the word that matched the word that was flashed. They were told to select "a word that feels similar in meaning to the feeling you experience while the word is being flashed." None of the subliminally presented stimuli were actually words. Instead, we presented letter strings (e.g., *aggrimely*) that resembled all four of the response options in appearance but had one or more letters different from all of the response options (e.g., *aggressive*, *aggregate*, *agriculture*, *agreement*). Half of the trials were target trials, in which one of the four response options was an aggression-relevant word (e.g., *aggressive*, *beat*, *angry*).

Following this task, we included several questions targeted to tap aspects of participants' identity that might be consistent with the African American stereotype. These items were created based on existing literature and included items such as the number of hours they study on an average week, their high school grade point average, and the time they wake up each morning. Based on a maximum-likelihood factor analysis, these measures were standardized and recoded, where necessary, and were averaged to create a single index of African American identity. Because aggression is an element of the African American stereotype (Chen & Bargh, 1997; Devine, 1989), we expected low self-monitors would feel more aggressive and be more likely to perceive these aggressive feelings and thus would select more aggression-relevant stimuli following the Tyrone prime than following the Erik prime. High self-monitors, on the other hand, should be less likely to perceive any differences in their feelings of aggressiveness and thus should be less likely to show this assimilation pattern. A similar pattern of findings on the identity items would also indicate that low self-monitors feel more like a stereotypical member of the primed category.

We submitted these two indices to a Prime × Self-Monitoring multivariate analysis of variance, treating self-monitoring as a continuous variable that was allowed to interact with prime. The predicted Prime × Self-Monitoring interaction emerged, such that low self-monitors displayed greater African American identity following the Tyrone prime than following the Erik prime, and no such effect was observed among high self-monitors. Looking at these indices separately, there was a significant interaction on the aggression measure such that there was an assimilative effect of prime among low, but not among high, self-monitors (see Figure 11.3). Analysis of the identity index indicated a marginally significant interaction, such that low self-monitors who wrote about Tyrone reported more stereotype-consistent self-characteristics than did those who wrote about Erik; the opposite was the case for high self-monitors (DeMarree et al., 2003). Hence, participants' explicitly reported self-characteristics became more similar to the characteristics suggested by the prime, but only when they were low in self-monitoring.

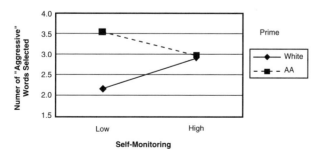

FIGURE 11.3. Aggression scores by prime and self-monitoring (±1 *SD* of self-monitoring). AA = African American. Data from DeMarree et al. (2004).

To extend these findings, we examined whether moderational effects for self-monitoring could be obtained using a self-schema matching persuasion paradigm in which elaboration is itself an indirect indicator of the self-concept (Petty, Wheeler, & Bizer, 2000; Wheeler, 2002). In this paradigm, advertisements are framed to match or mismatch a specific trait or self-characteristic of the recipient (see Petty et al., 2000). Manipulated orthogonally to the message frame is the quality of the arguments in the message body. Research using this type of paradigm has shown that individuals elaborate more on messages that match aspects of their self-conceptions than messages that mismatch their identities (e.g., Petty et al., 2000; Wheeler, Petty, and Bizer, in press). We sought to replicate these effects, but using primed identity characteristics rather than chronic identity characteristics. If primed identity characteristics bias self-perceptions, then individuals should engage in greater elaboration of messages matching the primed identities, rather than messages matching their chronic identities. These effects should be particularly likely to occur among low self-monitors, who are most likely to have their self-conceptions influenced by primes and to act consistently with their identities.

In this experiment (Wheeler, DeMarree, & Petty, 2004), White participants were primed by means of a scrambled sentence task. Embedded within the scrambled sentences were words relevant (or not) to the African American stereotype. Following the priming task, participants viewed an ad framed to match either an African American or White identity by including names of rap and rhythm-and-blues artists or rock artists, respectively, in the background image of an advertisement for a CD player. Argument quality was manipulated orthogonally to the message frame.

If primes temporarily bias self-perceptions, participants could perceive the African American ad to be more self-relevant following activation of the African American stereotype and exhibit greater information processing as a result. This pattern was observed among low self-monitors (see Figure 11.4).[2] They distinguished more between the strong and weak arguments in the matched ads than in the mismatched ads, regardless of whether there was a "real" match (White control-primed participants viewing White ads) or primed match (White African American-stereotype-primed participants viewing the African American ads). High self-monitors did not exhibit a matching effect. This study is consistent with the notion that the primes were incorporated into participants' identities and that the ads framed to match the activated stereotype were seen as self-relevant. Additionally, it provides further support that the effect of primes is dependent on the extent to which individuals rely on internally accessible information to guide behavior. In this case, the primed identities led to increased processing of primed-matched messages, but only among low self-monitors, who are likely to act consistently with their internal states.

Contrast Effects on Behavior

In the prior section, we demonstrated that these assimilation effects—both on self-perceptions and on behaviors such as information processing—were more evident for individuals who linked the prime content to the self and for low self-

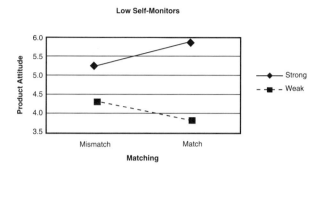

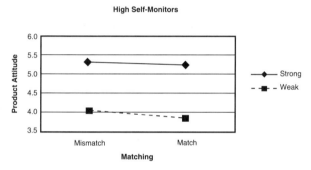

FIGURE 11.4. Attitude reports as a function of matching condition, argument quality, and self-monitoring (±1 *SD* of self-monitoring). Data from Wheeler et al. (2004).

monitoring individuals. This suggests that the priming-to-behavior assimilation effects involve some influence on the active self-concept. It is also important to note, however, that contrast effects have been demonstrated in this literature under some circumstances.

One relevant stream of research was reported by Dijksterhuis et al. (1998). In a series of studies, they showed that although the activation of stereotypes (e.g., *supermodel*) can lead to assimilative behaviors (acting less intelligently), the activation of stereotype exemplars (e.g., Claudia Schiffer) can lead to contrastive behaviors (acting more intelligently). How is it that such effects occur? The authors argued that contrast resulted because the extreme exemplars provided highly discrepant and concrete comparison targets. When presented with Claudia Schiffer, one may think, "I'm a rocket scientist compared to her!" Because stereotypes are more diffuse, the authors argued, they are less likely to act as a comparison point and, hence, less likely to elicit contrast. This is the same logic applied to assimilation versus contrast effects in social judgment (e.g., see Stapel & Koomen, 2001b; Stapel, Koomen, & van der Plight, 1997).

Notably, the contrast account can also involve the self. In this case, highly discrepant exemplars may lead to social comparison and subsequent perceptions of the self that contrast from the exemplar's characteristics. Note that, according to this account, even though the exemplar still activates its category membership associations (e.g., Claudia Schiffer activates *stupid*), these associations alone do not drive behavior. Rather, the prime-induced changes in self-perception (e.g., "I am smart") account for the observed behavioral effects (e.g., improved performance on trivia questions).

In Experiment 3, Dijksterhuis et al. (1998) provided intriguing evidence consistent with the notion that self-change could be responsible for the corresponding effects on behavior. In this experiment, participants were primed with a smart stereotype (*professor*) or a smart exemplar (Albert Einstein). Following the priming procedure, participants completed a lexical decision task in which they judged letter strings as either words or nonwords. The words used in this task were neutral or related either to intelligence or to stupidity. Immediately preceding each target to be judged, participants were subliminally primed with one of two sets of words: self-related words (e.g., *I* or *me*) or neutral words (e.g., *it*). Results indicated that the professor stereotype prime facilitated responses to intelligence-related words. A rather different pattern was shown for exemplar primes. Responses to intelligence-related words were facilitated following activation of Einstein, but so too were responses to stupidity-related words when preceded by a self-relevant prime.

Two features of this experiment are particularly noteworthy. First, the exemplar prime of Einstein subsequently activated intelligence and stupidity, but the resulting behavior reflects that of the feature uniquely tied to the self (i.e., stupidity, because people would feel less intelligent than Einstein).[3] Hence, these activation patterns suggest a bias in the self-concept resulting from the prime, and they are consistent with the self as an executive initiator of action. That is, information activation would have guided behavior, but the direction of the behavior would have presumably been driven by the information tied uniquely to the self. Second, this research suggests that patterns of self-activation need not always be assimilative. Under some situations, such as those promoting comparison to a highly discrepant exemplar, contrastive self-related information can be activated.

As reviewed in the previous section, research using significant-other exemplars has often shown assimilation effects, rather than contrast effects. However, significant-other and non-significant-other exemplars need not always show assimilation and contrast effects, respectively. For example, assimilation to non-significant-other exemplars can lead to assimilative self-perceptions when the characteristics of the exemplar seem achievable (Lockwood & Kunda, 1997, 1999) or when social self-construals are activated (Stapel & Koomen, 2001a). Similarly, contrast from the characteristics of the individual is possible for each type of exemplar. For example, individuals could perform poorly on a test following any very smart exemplar prime, whether it is one's Nobel Prize–winning brother or Einstein. When the characteristics of a significant-other exemplar are sufficiently salient and extreme, they could exert the same influence on behavior as the characteristics of other extreme exemplars. Whether assimilation or contrast to an exemplar occurs depends on a wide variety of factors (for reviews, see Markman & McMullen, 2003; Mussweiler, 2003; Stapel & Koomen, 2000), but both significant-other and non-significant-other exemplars could vary along these factors.

However, as already discussed, significant-other and non-significant-other exemplars can sometimes differ in the types of content that they activate in memory. In the significant-other exemplar assimilation effects reviewed previously, the assimilation was to the goals of the exemplar for oneself or the goals of one toward that exemplar, not to the characteristics of the exemplar himself or herself. However, contrast from these types of goals could also occur. For example, if one has habitually rejected another's goals for oneself (e.g., a punk teenager's rejection of his mother's desire for him to be a preppie), contrast from the mother's goals for him could result. To the extent that a non-significant-other's goals are salient and highly discrepant from one's own, contrast from these goals could also possibly result. For example, a Ku Klux Klansman primed with Martin Luther King Jr. might act more racist, therefore contrasting King's goals of racial equality.

Although these predictions are necessarily speculative due to lack of data, there is no reason why primes of significant-other and non-significant-other exemplars would necessarily always lead to different effects. Although these two types of exemplars could naturally vary both in their typical extremity and in the nature of the associations they activate, to the extent that these are controlled, the effects could be comparable.

CONCLUSIONS

In summary, the active-self perspective provides a flexible means for predicting and understanding how the activation of stereotypes, traits, and exemplars will affect behavior in multifaceted ways. Although the automatic behavior accounts initially appeared to imply that assimilation would always occur in response to activated constructs, the working-self perspective presented here does not. Assimilative, contrastive, or relational components of the self could be activated after exposure to primes. Self-representations may play a role in directing behavior by determining the types of emotions, perceptions, goals, and behavioral representations that are activated and executed and, in this sense, could provide some insight into the selection, direction, and magnitude of behavioral change that results from construct activation.

Although the behavioral effects we reviewed here were all presumably congruent with the changed self-conception, they need not always be. We believe that behavioral priming effects can result from multiple mechanisms and that behavior does not invariably follow directly from accessible behavioral representations, motivational representations, or self-representations (Wheeler & Petty, 2001). Myriad automatic and controlled processes can intervene to modify or override the behavioral propensities set in motion by the prime. These intervening processes have the potential to amplify or reverse the tendencies induced by the prime (Markman & McMullen, 2003).

For example, as discussed elsewhere (Wheeler & Petty, 2001), individuals may attempt to counteract undesired behaviors (e.g., acting stupidly), at least when they are aware of the biasing agent or its effects on behavior. The ease with which the behaviors can be modified is likely to depend on the nature of the behavioral domain. For example, stereotype-induced performance decrements are often exacerbated in the face of attempts to avoid them (Steele & Aronson, 1995).

The active self formulation has unique potential to integrate these diverse mechanisms conceptually. Understanding the types of activated self-representations and individuals among whom they are influential lends insight into which behavioral representations and goals will be activated subsequently and also perhaps into how individuals will perceive others or their surroundings. This account is not intended to be a substitute for the ideomotor or auto-motive formulations; presumably all behavior is preceded by the activation of behavioral or motivational representations. Instead, the working self formulation provides a basis for predicting which types of motivational and behavioral representations will be activated after exposure to social targets. This perspective allows prediction of a broader array of effects than previous main-effect formulations and permits prediction of behavioral reactions in response to rich and multifaceted social primes.

NOTES

1. The assimilative influence of self-relevant stereotypes on behavior has often been explained using another mechanism, stereotype threat (e.g., Steele & Aronson, 1995), though these effects, too, could be explained by ideomotor or the active-self account (see Wheeler & Petty, 2001).

2. The graph depicts the pattern observed using the 25-item Self-Monitoring Scale (Snyder, 1974). Although these means are in the predicted pattern, the three-way interaction achieved conventional significance levels only on the other-directedness subscale. The other-directedness subscale is the most similar to the theoretical construct of self-monitoring (Briggs & Cheek, 1988), and it reflects the degree to which individuals look to others for behavioral guidance, conform to social situations, mask their true feelings, and seek to please others.

3. No behavioral measures were included in this experiment measuring activation patterns. The other experiments in the paper suggest that behavioral contrast (here, acting stupidly) would have been the resulting behavior. Because the measures were not included in the same study, however, it is possible that these activation patterns did not play a mediational role in the direction of behavior.

REFERENCES

Aaker, J. L., & Lee, A. Y. (2001). "I" seek pleasures and "we" avoid pains: The role of self-regulatory goals in information processing and persuasion. *Journal of Consumer Research, 28*, 33–49.

Andersen, S. M., & Baum, A. (1994). Transference in interpersonal relations: Inferences and affect based on significant-other representations. *Journal of Personality, 62*, 459–497.

Andersen, S. M., & Chen, S. (2002). The relational self: An interpersonal social-cognitive theory. *Psychological Review, 109*, 619–645.

Aron, A., Aron, E. N., Tudor, M., & Nelson, G. (1991). Close relationships as including other in the self. *Journal of Personality and Social Psychology, 60*, 241–253.

Asendorpf, J. B., Banse, R., & Muecke, D. (2002). Double dissociation between implicit and explicit personality self-concept: The case of shy behavior. *Journal of Personality and Social Psychology, 83*, 380–393.

Baldwin, M. W. (1992). Relational schemas and the processing of social information. *Psychological Bulletin, 112*, 461–484.

Bargh, J. A. (1990). Auto-motives: Preconscious determinants of social interaction. In E. T. Higgins & R. M. Sorrentino (Eds.), *Handbook of motivation and cognition: Foundations of social behavior* (Vol. 2, pp. 93–130). New York: Guilford Press.

Bargh, J. A. (1997). The automaticity of everyday life. In R. S. Wyer, Jr. (Ed.), *Advances in social cognition* (Vol. 10, pp. 1–61). Mahwah, NJ: Erlbaum.

Bargh, J. A., Chen, M., & Burrows, L. (1996). Automaticity of social behavior: Direct effects of trait construct and stereotype activation on action. *Journal of Personality and Social Psychology, 71*, 230–244.

Bargh, J. A., & Gollwitzer, P. M. (1994). Environmental control of goal-directed action: Automatic and strategic contingencies between situations and behavior. In W. D. Spaulding (Ed.), *Integrative views of motivation, cognition, and emotion* (pp. 71–124). Lincoln: University of Nebraska Press.

Bargh, J. A., Gollwitzer, P. M., Lee-Chai, A., Barndollar, K., & Troetschel, R. (2001). The automated will: Nonconscious activation and pursuit of behavioral goals. *Journal of Personality and Social Psychology, 81*, 1014–1027.

Briggs, S. R., & Cheek, J. M. (1988). On the nature of self-monitoring: Problems with assessment, problems with validity. *Journal of Personality and Social Psychology, 54*, 663–678.

Campbell, J. D. (1990). Self-esteem and clarity of the self-concept. *Journal of Personality and Social Psychology, 59*, 538–549.

Carpenter, W. B. (1893). *Principles of mental physiology, with their applications to the training and dicipline of the mind, and the study of its morbid conditions.* New York: Appleton.

Chartrand, T. L., & Bargh, J. A. (1996). Automatic activation of impression formation and memorization goals: Nonconscious goal priming reproduces effects of explicit task instructions. *Journal of Personality and Social Psychology, 71*, 464–478.

Chen, M. (2000). *Racial category activation as a precursor to nonconscious interpersonal motivation: A reconceptualization of stereotype priming effects.* Unpublished doctoral dissertation, New York University, New York.

Chen, M., & Bargh, J. A. (1997). Nonconscious behavioral confirmation processes: The self-fulfilling consequences of automatic stereotype activation. *Journal of Experimental Social Psychology, 33*, 541–560.

Coats, S., Smith, E. R., Claypool, H. M., & Banner, M. J. (2000). Overlapping mental representations of self and in-group: Reaction time evidence and its relationship with explicit measures of group indentification. *Journal of Experimental Social Psychology, 36*, 304–315.

Cross, S. E., & Markus, H. R. (1990). The willful self. *Personality and Social Psychology Bulletin, 16*, 726–742.

Dasgupta, N., & Greenwald, A. G. (2001). On the malleability of automatic attitudes: Combating automatic prejudice with images of admired and disliked individuals. *Journal of Personality and Social Psychology, 81*, 800–814.

DeJong, W. (1979). An examination of self-perception mediation of the foot-in-the-door effect. *Journal of Personality and Social Psychology, 37*, 2221–2239.

DeMarree, K. G., Wheeler, S. C., & Petty, R. E. (2004). *The shifting self: Effects of primes and self-monitoring on the self-concept and persuasion.* Unpublished manuscript.

Devine, P. G. (1989). Stereotypes and prejudice: Their automatic and controlled components. *Journal of Personality and Social Psychology, 56,* 5–18.

Dijksterhuis, A., & Bargh, J. A. (2001). The perception–behavior expressway: Automatic effects of social perception on social behavior. In M. P. Zanna (Ed.), *Advances in experimental social psychology* (Vol. 33, pp. 1–40). San Diego, CA: Academic Press.

Dijksterhuis, A., & Knippenberg, A. V. (2000). Behavioral indecision: Effects of self-focus on automatic behavior. *Social Cognition, 18,* 55–74.

Dijksterhuis, A., Spears, R., Postmes, T., Stapel, D., Koomen, W., van Knippenberg, A., et al. (1998). Seeing one thing and doing another: Contrast effects in automatic behavior. *Journal of Personality and Social Psychology, 75,* 862–871.

Dodhia, R. M., & Metcalfe, J. (1999). False memories and source monitoring. *Cognitive Neuropsychology, 16,* 489–508.

Fazio, R. H., Effrein, E. A., & Falender, V. J. (1981). Self-perceptions following social interaction. *Journal of Personality and Social Psychology, 41,* 232–242.

Fenigstein, A., & Levine, M. P. (1984). Self-attention, concept activation, and the causal self. *Journal of Experimental Social Psychology, 20,* 231–245.

Fiske, S. T., & von Hendy, H. M. (1992). Personality feedback and situational norms can control stereotyping processes. *Journal of Personality and Social Psychology, 62,* 577–596.

Fitzsimons, G. M., & Bargh, J. A. (2003). Thinking of you: Nonconscious pursuit of interpersonal goals associated with relationship partners. *Journal of Personality and Social Psychology, 84,* 148–163.

Greenwald, A. G., Banaji, M. R., Rudman, L. A., Farnham, S. D., Nosek, B. A., & Mellott, D. S. (2002). A unified theory of implicit attitudes, stereotypes, self-esteem, and self-concept. *Psychological Review, 109,* 3–25.

Greenwald, A. G., & Farnham, S. D. (2000). Using the Implicit Association Test to measure self-esteem and self-concept. *Journal of Personality and Social Psychology, 79,* 1022–1038.

Greenwald, A. G., & Pratkanis, A. R. (1984). The self. In R. S. Wyer & T. K. Srull (Eds.), *Handbook of social cognition* (Vol. 3, pp. 129–178). Hillsdale, NJ: Erlbaum.

Hausdorff, J. M., Levy, B. R., & Wei, J. Y. (1999). The power of ageism on physical function of older persons: Reversibility of age-related gait changes. *Journal of the American Geriatrics Society, 47,* 1346–1349.

Hetts, J. J., Sakuma, M., & Pelham, B. W. (1999). Two roads to positive regard: Implicit and explicit self-evaluation and culture. *Journal of Experimental Social Psychology, 35,* 512–559.

Higgins, E. T. (1996). Knowledge activation: Accessibility, applicability, and salience. In E. T. Higgins & A. W. Kruglanski (Eds.), *Social psychology: Handbook of basic principles* (pp. 133–168). New York: Guilford Press.

Higgins, E. T. (1998). The aboutness principle: A pervasive influence on human inference. *Social Cognition, 16,* 173–198.

Higgins, E. T., Rholes, W. S., & Jones, C. R. (1977). Category accessibility and impression formation. *Journal of Experimental Social Psychology, 13,* 141–154.

Hinkley, K., & Andersen, S. M. (1996). The working self-concept in transference: Significant-other activation and self change. *Journal of Personality and Social Psychology, 71,* 1279–1295.

Hull, J. G., Slone, L. B., Meteyer, K. B., & Matthews, A. R. (2002). The nonconsciousness of self-consciousness. *Journal of Personality and Social Psychology, 83,* 406–424.

Ickes, W., Layden, M. A., & Barnes, R. D. (1978). Objective self-awareness and individuation: An empirical link. *Journal of Personality, 46,* 146–161.

James, W. (1950). *The principles of psychology.* Oxford, England: Dover. (Original work published 1890)

Johnson, M. K., Hashtroudi, S., & Lindsay, D. S. (1993). Source monitoring. *Psychological Bulletin, 114,* 3–28.

Kihlstrom, J. F., & Cantor, N. (1984). Mental representations of the self. In L. Berkowitz (Ed.), *Advances in experimental social psychology* (Vol. 17, pp. 1–47). New York: Academic Press.

Kihlstrom, J. F., Cantor, N., Albright, J. S., Chew, B. R., Klein, S. B., & Niedenthal, P. M. (1988). Information processing and the study of the self. In L. Berkowitz (Ed.), *Advances in experimental social psychology* (Vol. 21, pp. 145–178). New York: Academic Press.

Liebrand, W. B. (1984). The effect of social motives, communication and group size on behaviour in an *N*-person multi-stage mixed-motive game. *European Journal of Social Psychology, 14,* 239–264.

Linville, P. W. (1985). Self-complexity and affective extremity: Don't put all of your eggs in one cognitive basket. *Social Cognition, 3,* 94–120.

Linville, P. W., & Carlston, D. E. (1994). Social cognition of the self. In P. G. Devine & D. L. Hamilton (Eds.), *Social cognition: Impact on social psychology* (pp. 143–193). San Diego, CA: Academic Press.

Lippa, R. (1978). Expressive control, expressive consistency, and the correspondence between expressive behavior and personality. *Journal of Personality, 46,* 438–461.

Lockwood, P., & Kunda, Z. (1997). Superstars and me: Predicting the impact of role models on the self. *Journal of Personality and Social Psychology, 73,* 91–103.

Lockwood, P., & Kunda, Z. (1999). Increasing the salience of one's best selves can undermine inspiration by outstanding role models. *Journal of Personality and Social Psychology, 76,* 214–228.

Lowery, B. S., Hardin, C. D., & Sinclair, S. (2001). Social influence effects on automatic racial prejudice. *Journal of Personality and Social Psychology, 81,* 842–855.

Markman, K. D., & McMullen, M. N. (2003). A reflection and evaluation model of comparative thinking. *Personality and Social Psychology Review, 7,* 244–267.

Markus, H. (1977). Self-schemata and processing information about the self. *Journal of Personality and Social Psychology, 35,* 63–78.

Markus, H., & Kunda, Z. (1986). Stability and malleability of the self-concept. *Journal of Personality and Social Psychology, 51,* 858–866.

Markus, H., & Wurf, E. (1987). The dynamic self-concept: A social psychological perspective. *Annual Review of Psychology, 38,* 299–337.

Mather, M., Johnson, M. K., & De Leonardis, D. M. (1999). Stereotype reliance in source monitoring: Age differences and neuropsychological test correlates. *Cognitive Neuropsychology, 16,* 437–458.

McClelland, D. C., Koestner, R., & Weinberger, J. (1989). How do self-attributed and implicit motives differ? *Psychological Review, 96,* 49–72.

McGuire, W. J., & Padawer-Singer, A. (1976). Trait salience in the spontaneous self-concept. *Journal of Personality and Social Psychology, 33,* 743–754.

Mussweiler, T. (2003). Comparison processes in social judgment: Mechanisms and consequences. *Psychological Review, 110,* 472–489.

Mussweiler, T., & Neumann, R. (2000). Sources of mental contamination: Comparing the effects of self-generated versus externally provided primes. *Journal of Experimental Social Psychology, 36,* 194–206.

Niedenthal, P. M., & Beike, D. R. (1997). Interrelated and isolated self-concepts. *Personality and Social Psychology Review, 1,* 106–128.

Ogilvie, D. M., & Ashmore, R. D. (1991). Self-with-other representation as a unit of analysis in self-concept research. In R. C. Curtis (Ed.), *The relational self: Theoretical convergences in psychoanalysis and social psychology* (pp. 282–314). New York: Guilford Press.

Petty, R. E., Wheeler, S. C., & Bizer, G. Y. (2000). Attitude functions and persuasion: An elaboration likelihood approach to matched versus mismatched messages. In J. M. Olson (Ed.), *Why we evaluate: Functions of attitudes* (pp. 133–162) Hillsdale, NJ: Erlbaum.

Rogers, C. R. (1951). *Client-centered therapy.* New York: Houghton-Mifflin.

Rogers, T. B. (1981). A model of the self as an aspect of the human information processing system. In N. Cantor & J. F. Kihlstrom (Eds.), *Personality, cognition, and social interaction* (pp. 193–214). Hillsdale, NJ: Erlbaum.

Ruvolo, A. P., & Markus, H. R. (1992). Possible selves and performance: The power of self-relevant imagery. *Social Cognition, 10*(1), 95–124.

Shah, J. (2003). Automatic for the people: How representations of significant others implicitly affect goal pursuit. *Journal of Personality and Social Psychology, 84,* 661–681.

Smeesters, D., Warlop, L., Van Avermaet, E., Corneille, O., & Yzerbyt, V. (2003). Do not prime hawks with doves: The interplay of construct activation and consistency of social value orientation on cooperative behavior. *Journal of Personality and Social Psychology, 84,* 972–987.

Smeesters, D., Warlop, L., Yzerbyt, V., Corneille, O., & Van Avermaet, E. (2003). *About prisoners and dictators: The role of other-self focus, social value orientation, and stereotype primes in shaping cooperative behavior.* Unpublished manuscript.

Smith, E. R., & Henry, S. (1996). An in-group becomes part of the self: Response time evidence. *Personality & Social Psychology Bulletin, 22,* 635–642.

Snyder, M. (1974). Self-monitoring of expressive behavior. *Journal of Personality and Social Psychology, 30,* 526–537.

Snyder, M., & Campbell, B. H. (1982). Self-monitoring: The self in action. In J. Suls (Ed.), *Psychological perspectives on the self* (Vol. 1, pp. 185–207). Hillsdale, NJ: Erlbaum.

Snyder, M., & Swann, W. B. (1976). When actions reflect attitudes: The politics of impression management. *Journal of Personality and Social Psychology, 34,* 1034–1042.

Snyder, M., & Tanke, E. D. (1976). Behavior and attitude: Some people are more consistent than others. *Journal of Personality, 44,* 501–517.

Srull, T. K., & Wyer, R. S. (1979). The role of category accessibility in the interpretation of information about persons: Some determinants and implications. *Journal of Personality and Social Psychology, 37,* 1660–1672.

Stapel, D. A., & Koomen, W. (2000). Distinctiveness of others, mutability of selves: Their impact on self-evaluations. *Journal of Personality and Social Psychology, 79,* 1068–1087.

Stapel, D. A., & Koomen, W. (2001a). I, we, and the effects of others on me: How self-construal level moderates social comparison effects. *Journal of Personality and Social Psychology, 80,* 766–781.

Stapel, D. A., & Koomen, W. (2001b). Let's not forget the past when we go to the future: On our knowledge of knowledge accessibility. In G. B. Moskowitz (Ed.), *Cognitive social psychology: The Princeton Symposium on the Legacy and Future of Social Cognition* (pp. 229–246). Mahwah, NJ: Erlbaum.

Stapel, D. A., Koomen, W., & van der Plight, J. (1997). Categories of category accessibility: The impact of trait concept versus exemplar priming on person judgments. *Journal of Experimental Social Psychology, 33,* 47–76.

Steele, C. M., & Aronson, J. (1995). Stereotype threat and the intellectual test performance of African Americans. *Journal of Personality and Social Psychology, 69,* 797–811.

Wegner, D. M. (2002). *The illusion of conscious will.* Cambridge, MA: MIT Press.

Wheeler, S. C. (2002). *Personality schemata and attitude change: Self-schema matching can increase elaboration of persuasive messages.* Unpublished doctoral dissertation, Ohio State University, Columbus.

Wheeler, S. C., DeMarree, K. G., & Petty, R. E. (2003). *A match made in the laboratory: Persuasion and matches to primed self-schemata.* Unpublished manuscript.

Wheeler, S. C., Jarvis, W. B. G., & Petty, R. E. (2001). Think unto others: The self-destructive impact of negative racial stereotypes. *Journal of Experimental Social Psychology, 37,* 173–180.

Wheeler, S. C., & Petty, R. E. (2001). The effects of stereotype activation on behavior: A review of possible mechanisms. *Psychological Bulletin, 127,* 797–826.

Wheeler, S. C., Petty, R. E., & Bizer, G. Y. (in press). Self-schema matching and attitude change: Situational and dispositional determinants of message elaboration. *Journal of Consumer Research.*

Author Index

T

Subject Index

A

"Above average effect," 119
ACC (Anterior cingulate cortex)
  neuroimaging studies, 86–87
  reactivity and self-awareness, 86–87
  and self-awareness, 86
Action identification theory, 198
Action misperception, 108, 118–119; see also
  Agency
  and cognitive dissonance, 119–120
  ideal agency goals, 119
  self-esteem, 119
  studies of, 120–121
  willing the action, 120–121
Action orientation, 219; see also State orientation
  affect regulation skills, 223
  individuals differ from state-oriented, 219
  vs. state orientation, 223
  twin studies, 224
Adaptation, 3
Adaptive defense mechanisms, 33
Affectivity correlation with other traits, 39
Affirmation
  as continuum, 5–6
  partner, 2
Agency; see also Action misperception; Apparent
  mental causation; Intention confabulation
  action misperception, 108, 109
  apparent mental causation, 108, 109,
    115–118
    illusion of control, 117–118
  authorship processing, 107–108
  defined, 104
  deities as agents, 105
  features of, 105
  human failings, 105, 106–107
  ideal
    action misperception, 119
    components missing, 107
    defined, 105
    deities as, 105
    motivated inferences, 107–108
    perceptions distorted, 121–122
    perfect agent, 105
  idealization processes, 106–109
  intention confabulation, 108, 109
    by children, 110
    and cognitive dissonance, 110–112
    left-brain interpreter, 113–114

and post-hypnotic suggestion, 112–113
  in split-brain patients, 113–114
and post-hypnotic suggestion, 112–113
snap decisions, 104
supernatural, 104
as survival mechanism, 104
AI (Artificial intelligence) agent, 105
AI (Authenticity Inventory), see Authenticity
  Inventory (AI)
Amygdala in X-system, 92
Anger, see Self-conscious emotions
Anosognosia, 88–89
Anterior cingulate cortex (ACC), see ACC
  (Anterior cingulate cortex)
Anxiety and self-focus, 87
Apparent mental causation, 108, 115–118, 174;
  see also Agency
  priciples of, 115
Appeasement displays, 203–204
Appetite-aversion, 175–176
Approach–avoidance distinction, see
  Approach–avoidance motivation
Approach–avoidance motivation, 171ff
  appetite-aversion, 175–176
  bidimensional self-esteem, 178
  certainty, 185
  change, 185
  consistency, 185
  defined, 172–174
  ethical hedonism, 171
  hedonism, 174
  motivation terminology, 181
  self-assessment motivation, 183–184
  self-competence, 180
  self-enhancement motivation, 182–183
  self-esteem concepts, 177
  self-improvement motivation, 184–185
  self-liking, 180
  self-verification motivation, 182–183
  valence, 180, 185
Approach motivation, see Approach–avoidance
  motivation
Approach–withdrawal, 174–175
Attachement styles, 39–40
Authentic functioning, 31–32
  costs and benefits, 42
Authenticity, xii–xiii, 39
  Authenticity Inventory (AI), 36; see also
    Authenticity Inventory (AI)
  awareness, 32–33